T0300960

"Questions about digital platforms are paramount in today's economy. Belleflamme and Peitz have written a book for people who want to understand many of the drivers of success that have been hypothesized by economists. This is a very useful book to read for people who are interested in policy or firm strategy. It is particularly valuable because unlike many textbooks it focuses on the cutting edge of economics research."

Catherine Tucker, Massachusetts Institute of Technology

"Paul Belleflamme and Martin Peitz put their many years of research and policy work into this comprehensive book that covers the key economic and policy aspects of platforms, which have been playing an increasingly important role in our lives. The authors successfully walk the tightrope between rigor and accessibility for a broader audience, making it an ideal book for those seeking an introduction to platform economics. Key aspects of network effects, direct and indirect externalities, pricing, and platform design strategies are covered in depth, balancing theoretical concepts with empirical facts and case studies. *The Economics of Platforms: Concepts and Strategy* will surely provide an excellent resource and reference for policy makers, business practitioners, researchers, and students of both undergraduate- and graduate-level programs."

Steve Tadelis, University of California, Berkeley

"A comprehensive and rigorous exposition of the economic analysis of platforms. The book covers in an accessible way a wide range of topics such as design, information management, pricing, or start-up. The presentation is clear, including material at the forefront of the economic literature. Written by two leading scholars in the domain, the book caters to a wide range of readers, from students and professors to businesspeople and policy makers, with minimum economic background. A must-read for anyone interested in the economics of platforms."

Bruno Jullien, Toulouse School of Economics

"Numerous books have been written about platforms but none of them cover the economics behind platforms in any depth. This path-breaking book fills the gap, covering the key concepts and applications of platform strategy in an accessible but thorough way. As well as being a must-read for practitioners and academic scholars who want to understand platform strategy, it is an ideal textbook for business school or economics courses on the digital economy or platforms. Extensive real-world cases from around the world bring to life the economic analysis and numerical examples."

Julian Wright, National University of Singapore

The Economics of Platforms

Digital platforms controlled by Alibaba, Alphabet, Amazon, Facebook, Netflix, Tencent and Uber have transformed not only the ways we do business but also the very nature of people's everyday lives. It is of vital importance that we understand the economic principles governing how these platforms operate. This book explains the driving forces behind any platform business with a focus on network effects. The authors use short case studies and real-world applications to explain key concepts such as how platforms manage network effects and which price and non-price strategies they choose. This self-contained text is the first to offer a systematic and formalized account of what platforms are and how they operate, concisely incorporating path-breaking insights in economics over the last twenty years.

Paul Belleflamme is Professor of Economics at UCLouvain.

Martin Peitz is Professor of Economics at the University of Mannheim.

The Economics of Platforms

Concepts and Strategy

PAUL BELLEFLAMME
Université catholique de Louvain, Belgium

MARTIN PEITZ
University of Mannheim, Germany

CAMBRIDGE
UNIVERSITY PRESS

University Printing House, Cambridge CB2 8BS, United Kingdom

One Liberty Plaza, 20th Floor, New York, NY 10006, USA

477 Williamstown Road, Port Melbourne, VIC 3207, Australia

314-321, 3rd Floor, Plot 3, Splendor Forum, Jasola District Centre, New Delhi - 110025, India

103 Penang Road, #05-06/07, Visioncrest Commercial, Singapore 238467

Cambridge University Press is part of the University of Cambridge.

It furthers the University's mission by disseminating knowledge in the pursuit of
education, learning and research at the highest international levels of excellence.

www.cambridge.org
Information on this title: www.cambridge.org/9781108482578
DOI: 10.1017/9781108696913

First published 2021

A catalogue record for this publication is available from the British Library

Library of Congress Cataloging in Publication data
Names: Belleflamme, Paul, author. | Peitz, Martin, author.
Title: The economics of platforms : concepts and strategy / Paul Belleflamme, Martin Peitz.
Description: Cambridge, UK ; New York : Cambridge University Press, [2021]
  | Includes bibliographical references.
Identifiers: LCCN 2021008512 (print) | LCCN 2021008513 (ebook) | ISBN
  9781108482578 (hardback) | ISBN 9781108696913 (ebook)
Subjects: LCSH: Multi-sided platform businesses. | BISAC: BUSINESS &
  ECONOMICS / Economics | BUSINESS & ECONOMICS / Microeconomics
Classification: LCC HD9999.M782 B45 2021 (print) | LCC HD9999.M782
  (ebook) | DDC 338.7–dc23
LC record available at https://lccn.loc.gov/2021008512
LC ebook record available at https://lccn.loc.gov/2021008513

ISBN 978-1-108-48257-8 Hardback
ISBN 978-1-108-71074-9 Paperback

Additional resources for this publication at www.cambridge.org/belleflamme-peitz

Contents

Figures

Tables

Cases

Preface

A few years ago, we started our project on a book with a broad coverage of the economics of platforms. We remember the times when new platforms were mushrooming,[1] strategy pundits were talking of a "platform revolution,"[2] allegedly anticompetitive practices were rare, and mergers involving platforms were hardly scrutinized by competition authorities.

Over the last few years, many of the newly created platforms have shut down, while a handful of others have gained a foothold in their respective market segments, to the point of raising competition issues that have attracted media attention. Also, as the ever increasing publication of academic and policy work on platforms has become impossible to digest, we have barely caught up with new developments on the policy and the research front. Thus, instead of getting closer to finishing our book project, we felt that the gap was widening between our partial draft and what we should write.

Confronted with this dilemma, we decided to take a shortcut by splitting our grand project into two shorter books. This first book focuses on *concepts and strategy*; we aim to shed light on conceptual issues regarding platforms and on the strategic decisions of a monopoly platform. We largely keep away from strategic interaction between platforms and from regulatory policy questions about platforms. This is reserved for our follow-up book (which we are currently working on) that centers on *competition and policy*.

In the process of completing this book, our and many others' attention has been absorbed by the COVID-19 pandemic. On the one hand, this is just one further reminder that our topic is not the most pressing issue in this world. On the other hand, the pandemic has shown us that digital services – many of them delivered by digital platforms – are essential for the working of our society and economy. Large digital platforms have been affected differentially by the pandemic: On the one hand, digital platforms active in the mobility and hospitality sectors have taken a bad hit because of lockdown, stay-at-home, and social distancing policies. On the other hand, the same policies have also boosted home delivery, digital communication, and

---

[1] "There's an Uber for Everything Now" was a headline you could read in the *Wall Street Journal* in 2015. See www.wsj.com/articles/theres-an-uber-for-everything-now-1430845789.
[2] See Parker, Van Alstyne, and Choudary (2016).

the consumption of some digital products, to the benefit of the digital platforms that cater to these needs; also, "prosocial" platforms emerged in many countries, demonstrating that platform businesses are able to quickly address the pressing needs of the most vulnerable among us.

The pandemic should add to the public awareness that externalities – and "network effects" as their specific incarnation – are essential to understand the workings of society and the economy. Individual behavior affects the spread of the virus; in particular, individual decisions regarding social distancing and mask wearing affect the likelihood by which the virus spreads. The adoption and usage of corona contact-tracing apps affect the individual and societal benefit from such apps. The more users install and use the tracing app, the more capable the app is of informing an individual user about the risks they have been exposed to. This allows for more effective testing and a better adjustment of individual behavior (for instance, self-isolation in case of high-risk contact). These are all clear examples of positive direct network effects: The wider the adoption of a given behavior or application, the larger the benefits that this behavior or application confers to all (adopters and also, to a lesser extent, nonadopters).

In case there was any doubt, the COVID-19 pandemic demonstrates how much we rely on digital platforms for our daily life. So, we had better try to understand how they work. This book is the modest effort by two economists to look at the fundamental role that platforms play in making and managing markets. This is a first step in this direction, which we hope to complement in our follow-up book.

This book benefited from many comments we received from colleagues, students, and practitioners over the years when teaching about the economics of platforms. We are grateful for specific comments we received from Chiara Fumagalli, Andrei Hagiu, Doh-Shin Jeon, Eric Toulemonde, and Julian Wright on parts of the book. We are grateful to our partners, Catherine and Diana, for coping with the adjustments in our work-life balance when writing this book.

The topic of platforms and, in particular, digital platforms has raised a lot of policy interest recently. Are we hired guns? Here are our disclosure statements. Paul is a member of DERN, the Digital Economics Research Network.[3] Paul also regularly serves as an independent academic expert on matters related to the economics of platforms for regulatory bodies – such as the European Commission, the UK Parliament or the Belgian Competition Authority – and economic think tanks – such as the Centre on Regulation in Europe (CERRE), the Center for European Policy Studies (CEPS), or BRUEGEL. Paul does not have any financial stakes in any platform. Over the years, Martin has authored or coauthored a number of policy reports related to the economics of platforms for the European Commission, the German Federal Ministry of Economic Affairs, CERRE, and GSMA, all of them written in academic

---

[3] Created in 2020, the network aims at bringing together academia and private companies: Scholars pursue theory and evidence-based research with full academic freedom and autonomy, while partner firms contribute to the scientific activity by sharing data and institutional knowledge; at the time of this writing, the network gathers scholars from seven universities and is funded by Google; more partner firms, research institutions, and scholars are expected to join the network in the near future.

independence; he also worked as an economic expert on platform-related issues and cases for a number of competition authorities. Martin did not work for any platform over the last ten years and does not have any financial stakes in any platform. In any case, Paul and Martin do use a lot of services offered by digital platforms, large and small.

Getting Started

Motivation

This book analyzes firms that manage the interaction between their users. More specifically, the book considers markets in which users enjoy benefits that depend on the decisions of other users (meaning that users are subject to network effects) and a firm, operating the "platform," takes decisions that partly determine how large those benefits are and who will obtain which benefit.

Such platforms pervade our everyday lives and contribute to an increasing share of economic activity; they also raise important societal issues through their innovative activities and practices. Of particular interest are "two-sided platforms" in which a firm caters to heterogeneous users with different needs or interests (think, for instance, of an intermediary that runs an e-commerce platform on which buyers and sellers interact). Intermediaries operating a two-sided platform determine which products to show to which consumers and which product information to release; they also guide information gathering of consumers and often control or regulate information release by sellers; they may further determine the terms and conditions under which a transaction is to be carried out by fixing the price sellers can charge to buyers or by fixing nonprice elements of the contract between buyer and seller (e.g., cancellation terms, dispute settlement on the platform).

The operations of platforms put into question the way many academic economists have thought about the functioning of markets. First, the way markets operate (and which allocation will result) depends on the incentives and means of a platform operator that monitors and controls the interaction between its users. A for-profit platform provides services and taxes trade and interaction (by charging a price to at least some of its users or by bundling its service with other services that generate revenues elsewhere); in many ways, the platform plays the role that the state or some nonprofit actors could play.[1] Second, processes like the exchange of information and even, possibly, the formation of prices are no longer decentralized but controlled by the platform. An example of a platform with centralized price-setting is Uber, which sets the prices at which drivers and travelers can interact. This stands in sharp

---

[1] For instance, Booking and Airbnb offer services to hotels and landlords on one side and guests on the other side for short-term stays in a hotel or apartment, and charge for their services. Similarly, some nonprofit local tourist boards offer services to local landlords, which include a portal for hotel and apartment bookings, and charge a fee for its services.

contrast with standard microeconomic teaching, which imagines markets operated by some "invisible hand" that brings supply and demand together. Instead, what we describe here are situations in which trade is carried out under the *visible* hand of the intermediary managing the platform.[2]

Intermediaries operating platforms have created possibilities for interactions between users where nonorganized marketplaces often have failed to properly solve coordination problems and asymmetric information problems. In particular, intermediaries can provide a safe trading environment, attract key participants with special offers, and make infrastructure investments that facilitate trade or interaction. They may thus fully or partially replace other forms of markets or institutions; they may also create markets that previously did not exist. Many of those intermediaries are driven by profit motives (at least from some stage of their existence), but there remain other intermediaries that keep on operating on a nonprofit basis (e.g., Wikipedia). In the past, many such central places for trade or interaction were (and still are) subject to specific rules set (or directly controlled) by the government.[3]

A Little Bit of History

Marketplaces as meeting points of traders and consumers have existed for thousands of years. For example, traders and consumers in ancient Greece could find a meeting place in the *agora*, while in the Roman Empire, the *forum* and the *macellum* served as, respectively, open-air and indoor marketplaces.[4] These marketplaces operated under local rules and were not privately run. Meeting places (such as the Roman forum) also served for the exchange of news, which again features network effects because, with more participation, more diverse and more credible news could be obtained.

Starting with the late Middle Ages, exchanges allowing trade in obligations and government securities were first set up in France, in some city states of Northern Italy and later in what is now Belgium. In the seventeenth century, with the emergence of publicly traded companies, the trading of stocks started to flourish on the Amsterdam bourse; the Dutch East India Company and the Dutch West India Company were the two major companies whose stocks were traded. Also in the seventeenth century, auction houses for arts and valuables appeared in London. These platforms benefited from network effects by providing liquidity.[5] A seller was confident

---

[2] We are not claiming that it is a novel approach of the literature on two-sided platforms to have a party implementing a pricing system that balances demand and supply. The literature on market intermediation has analyzed a variety of settings in which intermediaries run marketplaces that are preferred by at least some users and thus replaces decentralized trade because they fix prices on both sides of the market; for an overview, see Spulber (1999). Furthermore, double auctions are used to find market-clearing prices (see Wilson, 1985; Satterthwaite and Williams, 1989; McAfee, 1992); such allocation mechanisms have been applied in a number of markets, e.g., wholesale electricity markets.

[3] Languages and currencies also allow for interactions to take place, feature coordination problems, and were often, at least partly, government-controlled.

[4] In the macellum, vendors sold food products. They were constrained in their pricing and their produce was subject to some quality control by a public authority (see de Ruyt, 1983, pp. 356–358).

[5] For a discussion of network effects on stock exchanges, see Pagano and Padilla (2005). In particular, risk-averse participants benefit from a more liquid market; see Pagano (1989).

about finding interested buyers, and a buyer was confident about finding appropriate supplies.

Jumping straight into the twenty-first century, we observe the important role of digital platforms in creating economic value, the breathtaking rise of stock market valuations of some of them, and the growing policy concern about the economic and political power of GAFAM (Google, Amazon, Facebook, Apple, and Microsoft) in the US-dominated part of the world. The policy reports that were released recently in several places around the world are evidence of this growing concern.[6] We also see the power of other non-US-based platforms in the China-dominated part of the world (the acronym there is BATX, which stands for Baidu, Alibaba, Tencent, Xiaomi), with important overlaps in some countries and homegrown behemoths in others.

Preliminaries

Network effects and scale economies lie at the core of the success of platforms. When we say that a platform *enjoys* network effects or scale economies, this is often misleading, as it often takes ingenuity and effort to make network effects (and scale economies) happen. Sometimes luck replaces ingenuity (e.g., a good platform design may have been picked by accident), and often effort involves a lot of experimentation (e.g., by testing out modifications on a small group of users).

Network effects can be considered as scale economies on the demand side. In a way, they are the mirror image of scale economies of production: In the case of network effects, an expansion of the firm's customer base increases the benefit that goes to each consumer while, in the case of scale economies, this expansion reduces the average cost of production and thus generates a benefit that goes to the firm (for a given price). Given the proximity – but also the differences – between the two concepts, it is useful to take a closer look at them.

For simplicity, consider a population of identical users with unit demand. A user's net utility is computed as the difference between their gross utility, U, and the price they must pay to access the platform, A. With network effects, we have $U(N) - A$, where U is increasing in the number of users N under positive network effects. With constant marginal costs of production, c, and price equal to marginal cost ($A = c$), the net utility is $U(N) - c$. With scale economies in production, the marginal cost depends on N and is decreasing in N. With price equal to marginal cost, the price is $c(N)$ and the net utility of a user is $U - c(N)$.[7]

---

[6] In particular, we think of the reports from the EC (Crémer et al., 2019), the UK (Furman et al., 2019), and the USA (Scott Morton et al., 2019). For a comparison of the policy recommendations made in these three reports, see Ennis and Fletcher (2020). Australia, Benelux, BRICS, France, Germany, Italy, Japan, the Netherlands, Portugal, and UNCTAD also released their own reports in 2019.

[7] In the real world, network effects and scale economies may be present at the same time. For instance, when Amazon (as a retailer) ships more products, it gains from scale economies of the logistics network (therefore $c(N)$ is decreasing) and, at the same time, consumers may benefit from it through quicker delivery (as demand becomes more predictable, Amazon's stocking decisions better reflect consumer tastes). Thus, if Amazon were to price at marginal cost, users' net benefit would be $U(N) - c(N)$.

In both cases – network effects and scale economies – the net utility is increasing in the number of users N. What is the socially optimal size of the user base? The optimality condition is that the marginal social benefit is equal to the marginal cost. With network effects, the total gross benefit is $N \times U(N)$ and, thus, the marginal benefit is $U(N) + N \times U'(N)$. Hence, the optimal N satisfies $U(N) + N \times U'(N) = c$. Here, marginal-cost pricing does not implement the socially optimal outcome but is feasible for a private firm in the sense that a platform forced to set price equal to marginal cost does not make a loss and, thus, does not exit (since we assume that there are constant marginal cost and no fixed cost). Nonoptimality follows from the fact that participation will increase as long as $U(N) - A \geq 0$. To obtain socially optimal participation levels, we would need $A = c - N \times U'(N) < c$. That is, the firm would need to implement below marginal-cost pricing. In the presence of scale economies, the total cost is $C(N)$ with $C''(N) = c'(N) < 0$. The socially optimal N satisfies $U = c'(N)$. Marginal-cost pricing implements the socially optimal outcome but is not feasible in the sense that a private firm would make losses under marginal-cost pricing, $N \times c(N) < C(N)$.

The relationship between network effects and scale economies is less straightforward if a platform caters to two different user groups that are possibly connected through cross-group network effects or that feature decreasing unit costs.[8] Suppose that there are two groups, X and Y, that group X exerts a positive cross-group effect on group Y, and that marginal costs are constant and equal to c; that is, a user of group Y obtains a gross benefit of $U_Y(N_X) - c$ with $U_Y(N_X)$ increasing in N_X (and with N_K, $K \in \{X, Y\}$, denoting the number of users of group K that are present on the platform). Alternatively, there may be scale economies in the provision to group Y from more participation of group X; that is, $c(N_X)$ is a decreasing function of N_X. Let us compare the net surplus for group Y users under marginal-cost pricing in the two cases. With network effects, we have $U_Y(N_X) - c$ and with scale economies, we have $U - c(N_X)$. In both cases, the net surplus is increasing in N_X. While this shows that the similarity between network effects and scale economies extends to two-sided platforms, the property that the unit costs of serving a user from group Y decreases with the participation of group-X users appears to be less relevant in practice.[9] Moreover, a platform may be restricted in its ability to set prices that take into account the opportunity cost of losing a user of one group. For instance, the platform may face pricing restrictions such that users of one group cannot receive negative prices.[10]

[8] Cross-group network effects exist when users in one group care about the participation of users of another group; we define them formally in Chapter 1.

[9] One case in point could be the following. If users of group Y are distributed in space and a platform compensates them for travel time, then an increase in N_X reduces the expected cost to reach a user of group X since average travel time goes down. Takeout meals from restaurants whose ordering and delivery is facilitated by platforms are a possible application: Suppose that the number of restaurants on a platform is given; group Y consists of available riders to deliver meals, while group X contains the consumers ordering meals.

[10] We address the pricing strategy of a platform subject to network effects and such pricing constraints in Chapter 5.

In the formal analysis of the book, we focus on network effects and mostly assume that there are no scale economies of production. We explain the mechanisms by which different types of network effects arise and how a platform's strategy affects the strength of those network effects. We acknowledge that it may depend on the exact types of contract between one group of users and the platform as to whether scale economies are better classified as being on the supply side (because they reduce the platform's unit costs) or on the demand side (because they increase the user's willingness to pay, leading then to network effects). To see this, take the example of a food-delivery platform. If the platform pays riders per hour they are available, then a better prediction of demand (because of increased volume) reduces in expectation the number of riders (relative to the number of expected deliveries) that have to be hired in any given hour to make sure that a certain delivery time is typically met; as a result, the platform experiences decreasing unit costs – an instance of supply-side economies of scale. By contrast, if riders are paid per drop, improved demand predictions make the platform more attractive to riders because they obtain more reliable information as to whether they may actually be needed; this is then an instance of demand-side economies of scale.[11]

Approach

In this book, we mostly follow the theoretical literature on multi-sided platforms that emerged in the early 2000s.[12] This literature first focused on card payment systems such as Visa and Mastercard, which Rochet and Tirole (2002) analyzed as two-sided platforms with merchants on one side and consumers on the other side.[13] This

[11] Both types of contract can be observed in the industry. For example, in the UK Just Eat (part of Just Eat Takeaway) pays per hour including waiting time (according to its website for riders, www.takeaway.com/drivers/uk/, last accessed November 24, 2020). Another food-delivery platform is Deliveroo. According to the UK tabloid *Daily Mirror*, "there are two pay structures with Deliveroo. With the original model, riders are paid an hourly wage that is then topped up with a small additional payment for each delivery. There is now a second model where riders are exclusively paid based on deliveries, but with a larger fee." (John Fitzsimons, "Deliveroo: How to become a rider and what you can earn," *Daily Mirror*, July 12, 2018, updated May 28, 2020).

[12] An early literature studied markets with direct and indirect network effects that were started with communication networks in the 1970s (Artle and Averous, 1973; Rohlfs, 1974) and continued in the 1980s with a particular focus on compatibility (Farrell and Saloner, 1985, 1986; Katz and Shapiro, 1985, 1986) – we will have a closer look at this issue in Chapter 3. There is also an abundant literature on platforms in management science; for recent and comprehensive books grounded in this literature, see, e.g., Parker, Van Alstyne, and Choudary (2016) and Cusumano, Gawer, and Yoffie (2019).

[13] The peculiar feature of Visa and Mastercard (in contrast, e.g., to American Express) is that they do not contract with consumers and merchants directly but let banks do so: On the one hand, banks are issuers of cards to consumers and, on the other, they provide transaction processing services to merchants and play the role of "acquirer." Typically the issuing bank is different from the acquiring bank. When the merchant pays a fee to the acquiring bank, whereas consumers are not charged by the issuing bank (or even receive a subsidy), the acquiring bank has to make a payment to the issuing bank – this is the "interchange fee." Gans and King (2003) show that the interchange fee is neutral and, thus, does not affect the equilibrium outcome when there is payment separation between cash and credit transactions. Payment separation is violated if the no-surcharge rule applies to sellers, which prevents them from charging different prices depending on the type of transaction.

concept of two- or multi-sided platforms was then applied more generally – see the seminal research articles by Caillaud and Jullien (2003), Rochet and Tirole (2003, 2006), Anderson and Coate (2005), Parker and van Alstyne (2005), and Armstrong (2006). Since then, an impressive body of research has developed and examined an ever-increasing range of issues relating to markets with multi-sided platforms.

Economic theory helps us to build rigorous arguments, pointing to the implications of particular assumptions about the market environment faced by a platform and the strategic choices available to it. Throughout the book, we try to keep theoretical models as simple as possible; when suitable, models are exposed in a general way; otherwise, they are formulated as numerical examples or just explained in words. Important takeaways from our investigation are formulated as "lessons." At many points, we provide real-world facts and insights formulated as "cases," which complement our theory-based exposition. We also point to empirical work that provides further guidance.

Our theoretical analyses are hopefully accessible to readers without advanced training in calculus and, therefore, serve the purpose of making arguments precise without creating barriers to understanding because of the mathematics that are needed. Somewhat more complicated arguments are summarized in words, which allows for a quicker reading by skipping the associated formal exposition.

We provide relevant references in this book, but do not claim to provide an exhaustive literature guide. Our aim is to provide some basic insights based on platforms being seen as managers or organizers of the interaction between users. The key feature on which we base our exposition is the presence of network effects. We rely on advances in the literature on (two-sided) platforms that have been made over the last twenty years. Our focus is on economic insights that can be shown in simple, stylized settings.

Outline

This book is organized in six chapters. In **Chapter 1**, we distinguish different types of network effects and define platforms as facilitators of interaction and trade and, more specifically, as managers of network effects. For-profit platforms face two issues: (i) how to create value for participants and (ii) how to manage interaction or trade on the platform. Many digital platforms initially focus on the first issue and do not necessarily have a concrete monetization model in mind. We provide a classification of different types of platforms, which we illustrate with a number of real-world examples.

In **Chapter 2**, we take a closer look at multiple sources of network effects and how platform design choices and user behavior relate to those network effects. In particular, we elaborate on rating and recommender systems. The former aggregate user

Rochet and Tirole (2002) and Wright (2004) compare private to social incentives of setting the interchange fee and its impact on the prices on the two sides. Wright (2004) provides conditions under which private and social incentives coincide and under which they do not.

experiences and, thus, address asymmetric information problems. We show under which conditions rating systems lead to positive network effects. Also, recommender systems rely on information about user behavior and possibly enable users to make better informed decisions or reduce the cost of decision-making (in particular, users have to search less to find good matches). Again, we show under which conditions recommender systems lead to network effects. In addition, we discuss their effects on the distribution of sales between "mass-market" and "niche" products. Both rating and recommender systems rely on the processing of choice data. More generally, platforms may collect or have access to data about user choices and other variables that are relevant to predict these choices. They may use this information not only to inform and steer some group of users but also for monetization purposes on other sides of the market. In particular, this information may affect, in a buyer-seller relationship, which gains from trade are realized and how these gains are shared. This raises the question about whether and how the collection and processing of more data relate to network effects. Here, we establish conditions under which more and better data lead to network effects and discuss the types of network effects that may arise.

In **Chapter 3**, we consider platforms catering to one group of users who are connected through network effects. We first formalize the impact of network effects on user demand. Users have to form expectations about the participation decision of fellow users who have not yet chosen whether to adopt a network good. As we will see, there are some economic environments in which, for some set of prices, different allocations can be rationalized through self-fulfilling expectations. In other environments, this issue does not arise and only a single allocation can be supported with self-fulfilling expectations. We then consider platform pricing for this network good and uncover to what extent a platform internalizes network effects in its pricing decisions. Furthermore, we investigate how network effects shape a platform's compatibility choice when there are two network goods. In particular, we formalize the compatibility decision of a platform introducing a new network good that can either use the same standard as a preexisting network good or be incompatible with it.

In **Chapter 4**, we ask whether and how a firm wants to establish a platform and how it can grow. We explore a firm's economic trade-offs between choosing a (two-sided) platform model and alternative modes of organization. Within the two-sided platform model, we expose the difficulties that a firm will inevitably encounter when trying to bring two groups of agents together. Potential users need to be convinced that they will find other users on the platform with whom they can interact. The key question is thus how to convince them. In this context, we formalize the "chicken-and-egg-problem" and discuss firm strategies that may solve it. We also discuss the strategies that platforms can implement to increase the level of trust among users, thereby securing their participation and, possibly, intensifying the network effects. Finally, we discuss how a platform can use its strong position for some intermediation service to succeed when offering other intermediation services.

In **Chapter 5**, we take a closer look at pricing decisions by a two-sided platform. The presence of various user groups opens the possibility for differential pricing. As we will see, differential pricing is desirable to tackle the interdependence between the users' decisions. In the presence of heterogeneous users, the profit-maximizing price structure will be jointly determined by the price elasticities and the network effects. We describe the different types of prices that a platform might choose. We will see that the profit-maximizing pricing structures often have the feature that different groups of users face different price-cost margins; we also address the question of whether a profit-maximizing platform charges users only for access or also for the transactions they conduct on the platform. A platform may be restricted in the available price instruments; also participation may be sequential or some users may not be able to observe all prices. We analyze how a platform responds in its choice of strategy in such circumstances.

In **Chapter 6**, we consider economic environments that are richer in the ways the two user groups interact and in the ways a platform can manage this interaction. First, we extend the analysis to two-sided e-commerce platforms on which sellers compete with each other and discuss in which way a platform manages competition on its platform. In particular, if a platform can only charge sellers, it makes profits from participating in the sellers' gross profits and may therefore be inclined to safeguard high industry profits. However, since high industry profits stem from high prices, this discourages user participation. We address how this trade-off affects platform pricing and product variety. Second, we consider a platform that allows buyers to obtain information about more products as is the case with price comparison engines. We show how the platform's price strategies affect the market outcome and, in particular, the degree of price dispersion that arises naturally with differential information among users (some knowing only their local sellers and others obtaining information by accessing the platform). Third, we revisit the issue of product variety, which a platform can also manage through its design of rating, reviews and recommender systems; we assess the extent to which the incentives of a profit-maximizing platform when designing these systems are aligned with those of the users. We also examine the extent to which an intermediary wants to increase price transparency on the platform. Fourth, we consider platform design regarding the information and price instruments that are made available to sellers on the platform. For instance, the platform may provide sellers with buyers' personal data and, thus, facilitate differential pricing.

We close the book with an Epilogue in which we point towards a number of issues that we leave for our next book.

How to Use the Book

We hope to have written a book that turns out to be useful for students of economics and business, researchers, practitioners, and policy makers. We aimed at making technical material accessible so that it can be digested by advanced undergraduate and master students in economics. For those readers who are less inclined to follow mathematical expressions, we also endeavor to guide them smoothly through the book.

The book aims to introduce key concepts and, even if it does not claim to be all-encompassing, it will hopefully serve as a reference for economists in academia and be of relevance to competition economists working at agencies and consultancies. Introductory notions of industrial organization, microeconomics, and game theory will certainly facilitate the reading, but they are not necessary. Our intention is indeed to present all the main concepts in a simple and clear way, to illustrate them with short case studies, to develop simple models that establish formally several insights, and to summarize the main lessons that can be drawn from more complex developments. As a result, most of the contents of the book should also be accessible to students, practitioners, and professionals with an interest in the topic, who have been exposed to some economics thinking (even if economics is not their main background); we think, in particular, of lawyers, managers, and IT professionals.

The book can be used, in economics and business programs, for an elective course on network effects and platforms. Until our second book on competition and regulation is published, to complement this book, teachers may want to add some basic models of competing platforms; to this end, they may rely on the exposition in surveys such as Belleflamme and Peitz (2018a) or our textbook treatment in Belleflamme and Peitz (2015, chapter 22); they may also use the theory guide to competition policy contributions with respect to platforms that is provided by Jullien and Sand-Zantman (2021).

More broadly, our book can be used as a source for a course on the digital economy or on peer-to-peer networks; it can further serve as supplementary material for a course on industrial organization that takes a particular interest in platforms. Finally, we also hope that our book will prove useful to competition practitioners when considering some of the conceptual issues regarding platforms that arise when changing the law, when formulating guidelines, and in competition cases.

1 Platforms: Definitions and Typology

According to historians, European trade took off at the end of the twelfth century in what is now the North of France, in the county of Champagne.[1] It is in this period that this county started to host regular trade fairs, which lasted for six weeks and rotated among six cities. Merchants came from all over Europe because they were confident that they would meet each other at these fairs. This confidence was instilled by the count of Champagne through his authoritative and clever running of the fairs. Everything was done to provide merchants with a safe and efficient business environment. The count of Champagne actively selected the participants, especially by keeping away dubious businessmen. Once admitted, all participants were on a level playing field, as the count carefully avoided granting any privilege to anyone. The fair locations were fortified, and impartial institutions were put in place to enforce contracts and resolve disputes. The count also guaranteed loans and the replacement of cash by notary bills to settle transactions. In exchange for all these services, the count took a small share of each transaction and quickly amassed a fortune.

What the count of Champagne started around 1180 is known today as a "platform." A platform can be roughly seen as *an entity that enables interactions between users so as to generate value from these interactions* (we provide a more precise definition in Section 1.3). Implicit behind this description is the observation that although users benefit from interacting, they have a hard time organizing the interaction by their own means. This is because the interaction generates external effects: One user's decisions as to whether and how much to interact affect the well-being of other users. In general, the more users there are, the more valuable the interaction becomes for each user. External effects of this specific sort are called (positive) "network effects" (for reasons that will be clarified in this chapter). The problem is that network effects make the interaction hard to organize, as users fail to take them into account when making their decisions: As long as users are not compensated for the benefits they bring to others, they are insufficiently keen to start the interaction on their own.

As a result, a valuable interaction may fail to occur, unless some third-party intermediary finds ways to "internalize" the network effects. In troubled medieval Europe,

---

[1] See Fisman and Sullivan (2016).

traders were not able to make transactions safe by themselves, until the count of Champagne started to act as a trusted market-maker. Because the Champagne fairs played a decisive role in getting the interaction among traders started and in keeping it running, they can certainly be called a platform. And so can their modern-day, digital, versions, such as Airbnb, Amazon, Alibaba, Facebook, Kickstarter, Uber, and the like. The reason why platforms are so prevalent nowadays is that the Internet and digital technologies have dramatically reduced a number of transaction costs, thereby facilitating a wide array of interactions.

As the previous discussion suggests, the key to understanding platforms and classifying them is to characterize the various network effects that they manage. In this chapter, we analyze various forms of network effects. As a network effect is an external effect, it is important to identify the economic agent who generates it (the "originator") and the one who is affected (the "receiver"). If originator and receiver are seen to belong to a common group of agents, one talks of a "within-group" network effect; otherwise, if they are seen to belong to different groups, one talks of a "cross-group" network effect. In both cases, it is also crucial to determine whether network effects are positive or negative. Crossing the two dimensions (within- vs. cross-group and positive vs. negative), we obtain a number of typical situations, which we describe in Sections 1.1 and 1.2. We then confront these typical situations with reality and, on this basis, we propose a definition of platforms and ways to categorize them in Section 1.3.

1.1   Within-Group Network Effects

We focus in this section on network effects that arise within a particular group of users. We start by defining within-group network effects and identifying their sources (1.1.1). We then explain that when these network effects are positive, they generate a self-reinforcing process called an "attraction loop" (1.1.2). Finally, we discuss how attraction loops shape the way users choose among platforms (1.1.3).

1.1.1   Definition and Sources

In many market environments, consumers or other market participants derive a utility not only, and sometimes not even primarily, from a product or service but from the interaction with other consumers or other market participants. Users (as we generically call them) are forming a network that connects them with one another. As the network changes, so does the value that each user attaches to the interaction. That is, when an additional user joins the network, they affect the well-being of the other users. This external effect is called a *network effect*. When the additional user and the other users are consumers of the same product or service, or when they play the same role in some interaction, they are seen to belong to a common "group." The network effects that exist among them are then called *within-group network effects*. They are also called *direct* network effects, as the action of one user (e.g., consuming some product) directly affects the well-being of the other users.[2]

DEFINITION 1   *A **network effect** describes the impact that an additional user of a product or service, or an additional participant to some interaction, has on the value that other users or participants attach to this product, service, or interaction. When users belong to the same group, one talks of **within-group** or **direct network effects**.*

For instance, social norms, languages, and communication devices generate *positive* within-group (direct) network effects: The more they are adopted, the larger the utility they confer to their adopters. In the presence of positive within-group (direct) network effects, the member of a group finds a higher activity level of the group attractive. There also exist circumstances leading to *negative* direct network effects.[3] Road congestion and traffic jams are the prototypical examples of negative network effects: The more drivers choose a particular road at a particular moment, the slower the traffic on that road at that moment and, thereby, the lower the utility for every driver.

The size of a network is generally taken as the source of the network effects: As the network grows larger, its value for its users increases (positive network effects) or decreases (negative network effects). This describes well what happens, for instance, with social norms. In contrast, for communication means (e.g., a particular language or an instant messaging application), a user is primarily concerned with the decision of the subset of users with whom they have regular interactions; hence, the identity of the users of the network matters as well. However, the difference between the two situations disappears if a potential adopter is initially not informed about who is a user but only has a belief about how many there are. In this case, the expected number of users is the best estimate about the expected benefit from adoption and a higher expected number makes it more attractive to adopt.

It may also depend on the identity of the member of the group whether the network effect is positive or negative. Think of fashion fads. They generate positive network effects for those individuals whose utility increases when they conform with the choices of others. Yet the exact opposite applies for snobs, who value the idea of having different tastes than the "mass": For them, having someone choosing like them generates a negative network effect.[4]

---

[2] Here, we stress participation. In some instances, also the level of engagement matters. For instance, on a social network, it is not just the number of users that contributes to the network effect but also the frequency and intensity with which users participate to the network.

[3] There is no consensus in the use of the term network effect. Some authors use this term only if there is a positive effect of more participation on utility. We prefer to use the term in a generic way and indicate the sign of the effect.

[4] See, e.g., Grilo, Shy, and Thisse (2001).

1.1.2   Attraction Loops

An important consequence of network effects is that they make users' decisions inter-dependent: The value of taking some action depends on how many (and possibly which) users take the same action.[5] In the presence of positive direct network effects, this means that as users benefit more strongly from other users in their group taking a particular action, they have a stronger incentive to take this action themselves. This generates a self-reinforcing process that we call an *attraction loop*: The more users take a particular action, the more attractive this action becomes and the more users will follow. A group of friends may be subject to an attraction loop. An activity proposed by a small subset may be seen with skepticism by the rest of the group; however, the more group members agree on joining the activity, the more attractive it becomes for the remaining members to join as well.

DEFINITION 2   *The presence of positive direct network effects gives rise to an* **attraction loop***: The higher the activity level of the group, the more attractive it becomes for each group member to increase their activity level, feeding back into the group's overall activity level.*

There are a number of examples of platforms characterized by attraction loops. Empirical evidence on the strength of the attraction loop requires a quantification that may be difficult to obtain (for a discussion, see, e.g., Rysman, 2019), but their presence is obvious in many situations. As just discussed, communication networks are characterized by attraction loops. Indeed, if a communication platform only offers communication services, it does not provide a stand-alone utility and users can only be enticed to adopt it if others are expected to do so.[6]

To formalize network effects arising on a communication platform, we consider the classic example of a communication system in a local telephone exchange (as represented by the star network of Figure 1.1).[7] When a user joins the network,

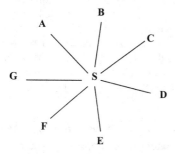

Figure 1.1 A simple star network

---

[5] We analyze the demand for a product featuring within-group network effects in detail in Chapter 3.

[6] As we discuss in Section 1.3, the picture may be more complex if users are heterogeneous with respect to their usage decisions.

[7] This paragraph is borrowed from Belleflamme and Peitz (2015, pp. 584–585).

they exert a positive externality on all users of the network because of the additional communication possibility. Thus, there is non-rivalry in consumption among the existing users (abstracting from the possibility of congestion). More specifically, user A accesses the network by purchasing a link from their location A to the local switch S (link AS). If user B has subscribed to a similar link (link BS), A and B are able to call each other. The links AS and BS can be seen as two complementary goods which, when combined, create a valuable system. If the network is comprised of n subscribers, there are $n(n-1)/2$ systems of this sort. Hence, an extra subscriber joining the network creates n new systems, which benefits all existing subscribers and is the source of the network effects.

Examples of communication systems are the telegraph system; fixed-line and mobile-phone telephony; communication apps such as Skype; messaging apps such as WhatsApp and Snapchat. Attraction loops are also a characteristic of dedicated tracing apps such as COVID-19 tracing apps; photo-sharing apps such as Instagram; social networks such as LinkedIn, Xing, Facebook, Myspace; and search engines such as AltaVista and Google Search providing purely organic search results (abstracting from sponsored search). Another example is the app Waze, as Case 1.1 illustrates.

CASE 1.1 DIRECT NETWORK EFFECTS ON WAZE[8]

Waze is an application for smartphones with GPS support; it enables its users to obtain real-time travel times, route details, traffic updates, and location-dependent information. The application was developed by the Israeli start-up Waze Mobile, founded in 2008. Waze became a big hit in its home country and was then acquired by Google in 2013 (at close to US$1 billion). As of 2018, Waze claims to be used by 100 million drivers; and the application is available in forty languages.

Waze differs from traditional GPS navigation software in its "community" or "social" nature as it relies on its users providing complementary map data and other traffic information. To have real utility, the app requires a critical mass of users in a particular country or region (otherwise, little real-time traffic information is available). Users are indeed encouraged (through a system of points and badges) to report accidents, traffic jams, speed and police traps, as well as to update roads, landmarks, house numbers, and so forth. There is thus a source of direct network effects: The more users contribute by feeding in information, the more useful is the "social mapping" service that Waze offers. Direct network effects also come from "passive" users, that is, those who do not actively share information: Like other GPS software, Waze collects anonymous information about its users' speed and location, and processes this data to improve the service as a whole. In a nutshell, the larger the network of users, the better the service.

Noteworthy is the fact that nonadopters may also benefit from an increased adoption of a given platform, yet to a lesser extent than adopters. In the case of Waze, nonadopters may enjoy smoother traffic flow on the congested roads they continue to use thanks to the adjustments made by Waze users. A similar phenomenon applies to COVID-19 tracing apps: If such an app works as intended, the more the app is adopted, the lower the contagion rate, which also benefits nonadopters; yet,

---

[8] This case is taken almost verbatim from Belleflamme and Peitz (2015, p. 578).

adopters get the extra benefit of being informed about the risk they are exposed to. This shows, more generally, that network effects are not necessarily "network specific": There often exist "spillovers" to nonadopters or to adopters of other platforms (when platforms are partially compatible). We will return to these issues in the next chapters.

Attraction loops may also be present for products with a stand-alone utility such as text-processing systems (e.g., Microsoft Word) and video games. In the former case, users may choose a text-processing system also because texts can be sent back and forth within a group if all users have chosen the same system. Similarly, video games provide a stand-alone utility when they can be played solitarily, along with an additional utility that is increasing with the number of adopters (the larger the network, the larger the probability of finding somebody to play with at a given moment in time).

An attraction loop may arise through two different channels. First, it arises if a user benefits from more interaction when the number of users is larger; most of the examples presented here share this feature. Second, users may benefit primarily from the quality of the service, but this quality may itself depend on the number of users; this applies to search engines such as Google Search or AltaVista and the traffic app Waze. In these examples, a user only cares indirectly about the number of users, as the results of a search query or the suggested route are better the more users are active on the respective system.[9]

In some cases, both channels are present. On systems with user-generated content (e.g., YouTube in its origins), a larger number of users increases the variety of available content and, therefore, often the consumer experience;[10] in addition, users may benefit from "shared experience" with friends or the public at large – another benefit that increases with the number of users on the system.

1.1.3   Impacts on Platform Choices

In many of the examples we have looked at so far, users can choose among several platforms to achieve the benefits of interaction: languages, communication channels, video game consoles, search engines, and so forth. Attraction loops make this choice quite peculiar insofar as they often induce users to coordinate on joining a single platform, at the expense of all the other platforms. A so-called "winner-takes-all" outcome may then emerge, with the following two interesting properties. First, even though the platforms to choose from appear to be ex ante symmetric, the market

---

[9] The quality of the search engine depends not only on engagement but also on the way it is constructed. Google started out with several innovations leading to higher quality search even absent a large user base: In particular, it made use of the link structure of the Web to calculate a quality ranking, the so-called PageRank; see Brin and Page (1998).

[10] We can talk of within-group effects if each user is equally likely to contribute content that is equally liked by everybody. If, by contrast, the set of users who upload content is disjoint from the set of users who view content, there are two separate groups and thus there are no within-group network effects. In reality, we are likely to be between these extremes: Some users focus on uploading, others on viewing and yet others are quite active in both ways. We return to this issue in Section 1.2.4.

is likely to end up in an asymmetric situation. Second, the benefit of coordinating on a single platform may lead some users to adopt actions that do not give them the highest stand-alone utility; that is, some users may decide to go against their personal tastes.[11]

To see this, let us develop a very simple model with two platforms, named X and Y, and two types of users, named X-lovers and Y-lovers.[12] Users arrive randomly on the market and have to choose between the two platforms. In a world without network effects, users would only compare the stand-alone utilities that the two platforms offer. If we assume that K-lovers perceive the stand-alone utility of platform K as larger ($K \in \{X, Y\}$), and if the two types of users are equally represented in the population, then the two platforms should have an equal market share in the long run. At each period, there is an equal chance that any platform will be chosen. It is like repeatedly tossing a fair coin: The law of large numbers predicts an equal number of tails and heads in the long run.

Things change dramatically in the presence of positive direct network effects that are platform-specific (i.e., they are limited to users who adopt the same platform). If users are myopic and care not only about stand-alone utilities but also about the possibility of interacting with other users, their choice is affected by the current market shares of the two platforms when their turn comes to make a choice. The natural tendency to choose the platform of one's taste (i.e., platform X for an X-lover or platform Y for a Y-lover) may then be overturned. To give some structure to the model, suppose that users place a value of 10 on having their preferred stand-alone utility and a value of 1 on interacting with any other user. Then, when a Y-lover arrives on the market, they will decide to join platform X if they observe that platform X counts at least 10 more users than platform Y: The advantage of platform X in terms of network effects outweighs the disadvantage it faces for Y-lovers in terms of stand-alone utilities. From then on, all users will join platform X irrespective of their type: Platform X will see an increase of its market share and platform Y will never catch up. It is as if the coin we flip repeatedly became increasingly unfair: The more, say, heads are drawn, the more the weight distribution of the coin becomes asymmetric so that the probability of heads increases. This kind of process leads eventually to a state in which only one result obtains. In our example, this means that a single platform will eventually take the whole market.

Even if this extreme prediction partly follows from the simplicity of the setting, it shows that positive direct network effects, and the attraction loops that they generate, have consequential impacts on the long-run market outcome. We return more fully to this issue in Chapter 3, where we will extend the previous model in several directions.

---

[11] This applies to environments in which users are forward-looking and thus try to predict not yet observed decisions by fellow users. It also applies to environments in which users are myopic and base their decision exclusively on observed behavior. We address user expectations at a later point. Here, we consider myopic users.

[12] This model is adapted from Arthur (1989).

1.2   Cross-Group Network Effects

In the previous examples, users could not be easily told apart: They were all consumers of the same product or service, or they all had the potential to interact with one another in the same capacity. There are, however, many environments in which users appear to belong to separate groups and the interaction mostly takes place among users of different groups. Trading platforms are a case in point as they allow buyers and sellers to interact. One talks here of *cross-group network effects*, insofar as an additional user to the platform affects the well-being of users *in another group*. On a trading platform, buyers are, everything else being equal, typically better off the more sellers are present, and vice versa: Both groups exert a positive cross-group network effect on the other group. Content platforms that carry advertising provide another example. Here, vertically integrated content is offered to entice consumers to join the platform. Consumers then may pay directly for participation or indirectly with their attention to advertising, which is bundled with content. If consumers' utility is decreasing in the volume of advertising, advertisers exert a negative cross-group network effect on consumers, while consumers exert a positive cross-group network effect on advertisers.

DEFINITION 3   *A **cross-group network effect** is a network effect that an additional user in some group exerts on users belonging to another group.*

Consider platforms linking two groups of agents. As illustrated by the two previous examples, cross-group network effects can be positive, negative, or nonexistent. We ignore situations in which the cross-group effect is negative in both directions. We acknowledge that such situations may happen in the real world. For instance, tensions between ethnic groups may be characterized by mutual negative cross-group network effects. However, since we focus in this book on platforms that facilitate the interaction between groups (or within groups), a situation of mutually negative cross-group network effects is of little interest because the immediate implication is that the ties between the two groups should be severed.[13]

That leaves us with three typical situations. The first situation, called the *attraction spiral*, is symmetric insofar as each group exerts positive network effects on the other group; trading platforms linking buyers and sellers belong to this category. The second situation, which we call the *attraction/repulsion pendulum*, is asymmetric: Cross-group network effects are positive in one direction but negative in the other; ad-financed content platforms fit this description when consumers dislike advertising. Finally, another asymmetric situation, called the *attraction spillover,* occurs when one group positively affects, but is unaffected by, the other group. We describe the three situations in turn. We identify the two groups as A and B, and we note by n_A and n_B their respective activity level (which can be approximated by their numbers of users).

---

[13] A platform that provides positive stand-alone utilities to users in both groups may nevertheless survive even in the presence of mutual negative cross-group effects.

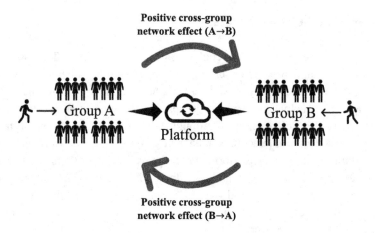

Figure 1.2 Attraction spiral

1.2.1   Attraction Spiral

In this situation, each group exerts a positive network effect on the other. That is, a higher activity level in one group attracts members of the other group on the platform. As a result, the activity level in each group is an increasing function of the activity level in the other group: n_A increases with n_B and vice versa. We depict this situation in Figure 1.2, where the arrival of an extra user in a group is used to symbolize a higher activity level in this group.

Because the attraction is mutual, the interaction between the two groups generates two interesting properties. First, the mutual attraction creates a positive feedback loop across the two groups, which we call an *attraction spiral*. To see this, suppose that the activity level in group A goes up for some reason. As n_B is an increasing function of n_A, this causes an increase of group B's activity level. And as n_A is also an increasing function of n_B, more members of group A are attracted to the platform, which attracts in turn more members in group B and so on and so forth. Activity levels therefore spiral upward, leading to actual increases that are larger than the initial ones.

DEFINITION 4   *If a higher activity level in one group makes it more attractive for the other group's members to increase their activity level and vice versa, such cross-group effects give rise to an **attraction spiral**.*

If we measure the strength of the network effect exerted by members of group B on members of group A by β_A and this strength is independent of the activity level, the attractiveness for a member of group A positively depends on $\beta_A n_B$. Vice versa, the attractiveness for a member of group B positively depends on $\beta_B n_A$. Suppose, for the sake of the example, that the dependence is one to one: One extra user in group A attracts β_B additional users in group B and one extra user in group B attracts β_A additional users in group A. Then if the initial increase is one more user in group A, we have successively β_B additional users in group B, $\beta_A \beta_B$ additional users in group

A, $\beta_A\beta_B^2$ additional users in group B, and so on and so forth. Adding up, we finally have $1 + \beta_A\beta_B + \beta_A^2\beta_B^2 + \beta_A^3\beta_B^3 + \cdots = 1/(1 - \beta_A\beta_B)$ additional users in group A and $\beta_B + \beta_A\beta_B^2 + \beta_A^2\beta_B^3 + \beta_A^3\beta_B^4 + \cdots = \beta_B/(1 - \beta_A\beta_B)$ additional users in group B. For instance, if $\beta_A = 1/3$ and $\beta_B = 1/2$ (i.e., it takes two users in group A to have one more user in group B and three users in group B to have one more user in group A), an initial increase of ten users in group A translates into an actual increase of twelve users in group A and six users in group B.

Examples of attraction spirals abound. In this book, we will often return to a buyer-seller environment in which sellers and buyers value marketplaces with many of their counterparties. Cases in point are electronic marketplaces such as eBay and platforms of the sharing economy such as Airbnb. In both instances, buyers and sellers are attracted by a large number of participants on the other side, as this increases the probability of a successful match.

The second noteworthy property of the mutual attraction across two groups is that it generates positive *indirect network effects* among the members of each group. As just explained, an initial increase in activity level in one group leads to a final increase that is more than proportional. As a consequence, more participation in group A ends up benefiting all members in group A, not directly through some within-group network effects but indirectly through the combination of two positive cross-group network effects. Indirect network effects have been studied in the context of "system goods," which typically combine some hardware with a variety of software. Those system goods do not generate direct network effects per se, as their primary function is not to facilitate the interaction among their users. Yet, they generate indirect network effects as more adoption encourages the supply of a larger quantity or variety of software, which contributes to make the whole system more valuable for users.

Empirical evidence of positive indirect network effects can be provided by studying the hardware-software choice.[14] As the analyses of Ohashi (2003) and Park (2004) indicate, indirect network effects played an important role in the VCR format competition between VHS and Betamax in the 1970s and 1980s. According to their estimates, the value of the network effect grew from US$ 5.6 million in 1978 to US$ 343 million in 1986 in the USA using constant 1978 US$. VHS gained a network advantage that explains at least 70–86 percent of (the logarithm of) relative sales of VHS to Betamax players. Gandal, Kende, and Rob (2000) found a positive cross-elasticity between CD player adoption and the variety of CD titles. This is consistent with mutual positive cross-group external effects between listeners on one side and music labels and musicians on the other side. Similarly, complementarities are also found between DVD player adoption and the amount of content available on DVDs (see Dranove and Gandal, 2003, and Karaca-Mandic, 2011). In particular, in the year 2001, a 1 percent increase in new DVD releases raised DVD player sales by 0.5 percent, and a 1 percent increase in DVD player installed base increased the

---

[14] Imposing a particular substitution pattern one can apply the nested logit approach to this choice problem such that the choice of the nest corresponds to a hardware choice and the choice of a compatible software as the choice within the nest.

number of new DVD releases by 0.19 percent. Finally, in the early days of personal digital assistants (PDA) in which Palm had a particularly strong position, indirect network effects explained around 22 percent of the log-odds ratios of the sales of all Palm O/S-compatible PDAs to Microsoft O/S-compatible PDAs – the remaining 78 percent are explained by differences in prices and model features (see Nair et al., 2004). The next case looks at cross-group network effects on an advertising-funded platform.

CASE 1.2 INDIRECT NETWORK EFFECTS IN THE MARKET FOR YELLOW PAGES

While today users often obtain information on businesses through the Internet, yellow pages have been the main source of information for a long period. For instance, if somebody needed a plumber, yellow pages were a source of information about whom to contact. Yellow pages are directories that provide information on businesses (in particular phone number and address) and are ordered according to categories. Businesses pay for detailed listings, while consumers typically receive the directory for free. Paid listings can be seen as informative advertising, as they provide information to consumers.

Yellow pages used to be a very profitable business. As reported by Rysman (2004) based on industry sources, an average book generated revenues of around US$ 3.8 million at a production cost of US$ 1 million. The market was big: Overall revenues were reported to be US$ 11.5 billion in 1997 (according to Elliott, 1998, cited in Rysman, 2004).

Rysman presents a model in which listed businesses – these are the advertisers in the model – decide on how much to advertise in each of the competing directories and users decide which, if any, directory to use. Directories maximize their profit with respect to the overall advertising level. The simple monopoly trade-off is that a higher ad level depresses the ad price. However, ad levels affect user demand and this generates an interdependence between directory choices.

Profit maximization leads to the first-order condition that gives advertising price (in log) as a linear function of advertising level in log, usage in log (with parameter β_A), and other explanatory variables. On the user side, demand is assumed to stem from a discrete choice problem that users face – the utility that a user attaches to a directory depends linearly on the ad level in log.[15] The market share of a directory relative to the one of the outside option then linearly depends on the ad level with parameter β_B (market shares and ad levels in logs).

In his structural model, Rysman finds that β_A and β_B are positive and statistically significant.[16] This means that users exert a positive cross-group network effect on advertisers and vice versa, leading to an attraction spiral. In other words, a directory is particularly valuable to a consumer if it provides detailed listings by many businesses, while it is valuable to businesses if it is consulted by many consumers.

As discussed by Rysman (2019), if cross-group, but not within-group, external effects are present, the empirical identification problem is simplified. The participation and usage decisions on each side may be modeled with simultaneous

---

[15] The demand model is specified as a nested logit model, with all yellow pages in one nest and the outside option in the other nest.

[16] To identify the parameters in his model, Rysman (2004) uses a number of instruments. In particular, the number of people who recently moved into the area covered by a directory is used as an instrument for usage, as new arrivals to an area are likely to use yellow pages more often than long-time residents. The platform's decision on how much advertising to take depends on its marginal cost in acquiring additional advertisers, which is proxied by the local wage, as sales staff is likely to be based within or at least close to the geographic area covered by the directory.

equations where the interdependence of the equations arises due to cross-group network effects.

Another example of positive indirect network effects can be found in the choice of geographical locations by firms. Following the seminal work of Marshall (1890), the economic geography literature explains why firms can benefit from locating close to one another; one explanation is that when more firms locate in the same region, more workers (or, more generally, input suppliers) are drawn to this region, which in turn makes the region more attractive for firms.[17] We see in this last example that network effects do not arise directly from the firms making the same choice but indirectly through the induced decisions of another group of agents (i.e., workers and/or input suppliers).

As we have seen, mutual positive cross-group network effects lead to an attraction spiral such that an increase of participation or usage on one side leads to more participation or usage on the other side, which in turn makes participation or usage more attractive on the first side. Therefore, if one group is exposed to a positive demand shock (e.g., the platform offers a larger stand-alone utility to this group of users), this leads to more participation by users from the other group, which in turn leads to more participation of the former; thus, the demand shock starts an attraction spiral with increasing participation of both groups.

A different mechanism applies if participation on one side changes but the impact of the other side is such that users adjust their behavior while keeping participation constant. Examples are e-commerce or entertainment platforms with a fixed number of sellers or content providers who decide about their services or content quality. More participation on the buyer side here may induce sellers/content providers to invest more in quality, which in turn attracts additional users to the platform. The platform that uses its price instruments to extract profits must be aware of the fact that higher prices charged by the platform weaken the attraction spiral. In the following formal exposition, we explicitly introduce a profit-maximizing platform that brings together buyers and content providers. There is a fixed number of content providers; each provider offers different content to buyers at some price; in addition, sellers choose the quality of their product. Sellers incur a fixed cost in quality that increases in quality at an increasing rate. The larger the number of buyers on the platform, the higher will be the chosen content quality. Thus, an attraction spiral is at work according to which more participation on one side leads to a larger network benefit enjoyed by the other side, as this side improves the quality of interaction. The following model formalizes this mechanism – less mathematically oriented readers may prefer to skip it.

We consider an entertainment platform that intermediates between content providers and end users; both groups are assumed to be of mass 1. A user spends their income y on an outside good x_0 and on consuming x_i units of content by

---

[17] For a comprehensive textbook on this topic, see Fujita and Thisse (2013).

provider i. The marginal utility is decreasing in the number of units of content that are consumed. In particular, users consuming x units of content derive a marginal utility of $r - x$, where r measures the content quality (which is assumed to be the same across content providers). If the platform charges a fixed fee of A on the user side and content providers charge p per unit, then users maximize their net utility $(r - x)x - px + y - A$ subject to x. Thus, the utility-maximizing consumption level is $x = (r - p)/2$ and the associated value of consumers (gross of any opportunity cost from signing up with the platform) is $(r - p)^2/2 - A$, relative to consuming only the outside option. If consumers have heterogeneous opportunity costs, we can express the user demand for participation as a function of p and A.

Each individual content provider takes the number of users n_B as given, since each content provider is infinitesimally small. A content provider's profit is $n_B x(p - a) - C(r)$, where a is the per-unit fee charged by the platform, C is the cost of quality r, and $x = (r - p)/2$. Each content provider chooses price and quality. The profit-maximizing price is $p = (r + a)/2$. Inserting this price in the profit function, we have $n_B(r - a)^2/8 - C(r)$. Suppose that $C(r) = r^3/3$. Then, the first order condition of profit maximization gives $n_B(r - a)/4 - r^2 = 0$. The profit-maximizing solution is $r = \frac{1}{8}n_B + \frac{1}{8}\sqrt{n_B^2 - 16an_B}$ (as long as $a < n_B/16$). This means that quality is a function $r(n_B; a)$ which is increasing in n_B. Assuming that the outside option is uniformly distributed (and there is mass 1 of users per interval of length 1), user demand, $n_B(r; a, A) = (r - a)^2/8 - A$, is a function that is increasing in r. Solving this system gives $r^*(a, A)$ and $n_B^*(a, A)$. The platform then maximizes $n_B ax + An_B = n_B^*(a, A)a(r^*(a, A) - a)/4 + An_B^*(a, A)$ with respect to a and A.

In most of the book attraction spirals are with respect to participation or usage decisions; other adjustments may well happen on top, but we do not look into these. However, it is useful to keep in mind that an attraction spiral may also take place via other changes of behavior, such as quality adjustments by sellers on one side of the platform.

1.2.2   Attraction/Repulsion Pendulum

Attraction is not always mutual. While one group may be attracted by the other, this other group may react with indifference (as discussed in the next subsection) or even repulsion. In the latter case, the activity level of group $i \in \{A, B\}$ is an increasing function of the activity level of the other group j ($j \neq i$), while the activity level of the other group j is a decreasing function of the activity level of group i. Thus, if for some reason the activity level in group A goes up, this causes an increase of group B's activity level, which repels members in group A and, in turn, makes the pendulum swing back by decreasing group A's activity level. As a result of a lower activity level by group A, group B is less active, which, in turn, increases group A's activity level and so forth. We call this environment an *attraction/repulsion pendulum* and we

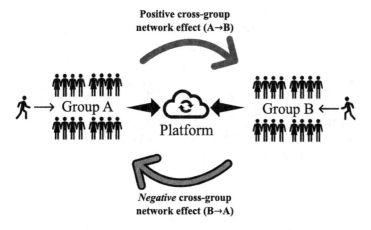

Figure 1.3 Attraction/repulsion pendulum

represent it in Figure 1.3. Since n_A is an increasing function of n_B but n_B a decreasing function of n_A, the fact that a higher activity level of one group increases the activity level of the other group which, in turn, makes it less attractive for members of group A to increase their activity means that there is a *negative indirect network effect* experienced by members of group A (and, correspondingly, also by members of group B).

Let us adapt our previous linear formalization to the present context. We posited that the attractiveness for a member of group A depends on $\beta_A n_B$, and the attractiveness for a member of group B depends on $\beta_B n_A$. Here, we assume that β_A is positive while β_B is negative. Taking $\beta_A = 1/2$ and $\beta_B = -1/2$, we have that if ten more members initially join group A, the attraction/repulsion pendulum would eventually lead two of them to leave, while driving away four members in group B.[18]

DEFINITION 5   *If a higher activity level in one group makes it more attractive for the other group's members to increase their activity level and if, by contrast, members in the other group tend to be repelled by a higher activity level of the first group, such cross-group effects give rise to an* **attraction/repulsion pendulum**.

For example, as a web browser is adopted by more users, it becomes more attractive for hackers. Thus, there is a positive cross-group network effect from users to hackers. However, attraction is not mutual: The more hackers there are, the less inclined are potential users to adopt the web browser as hacking activities repel them. Another example is locations (e.g., neighborhoods, restaurants, or bars) that attract tourists because of their local culture ("meet the locals"). While these tourists are attracted by the presence of locals, this feeling is not returned by locals; instead, they feel repelled.

---

[18]   The actual number of participants in groups A and B are computed respectively as
$10 \times 1/(1 + 1/4) = 8$, and $10 \times (-1/2) \times 1/(1 + 1/4) = -4$.

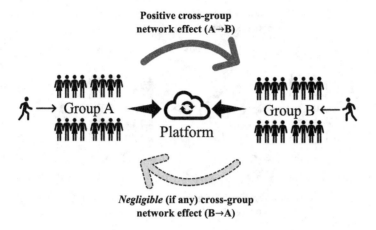

Figure 1.4 Attraction spillover

1.2.3   Attraction Spillover

Finally, the positive attraction that one group feels for the other may be met with indifference, as depicted in Figure 1.4. One group, say group A, exerts a positive network effect on group B but group B exerts no network effect, neither positive nor negative, on group A. As a result, the activity level of group B, n_B, is an increasing function of n_A, while the activity level of group A is not affected by the activity level of group B. We are then in a situation that we call an *attraction spillover*.

DEFINITION 6   *If a higher activity level in one group makes it more attractive for the members of other group to increase their activity level, but the attractiveness is not affected in the opposite direction, such cross-group effects give rise to an* **attraction spillover**.

   An example of such a situation may be the interaction between groups of "professionals" and "amateurs," in which amateurs obtain a benefit from the higher activity level of the experts (e.g., because they can obtain valuable information from them and the more expert activity there is the more likely is such an information spillover), whereas experts do not benefit from the presence of anybody (e.g., because they are already perfectly informed). Then, amateurs are attracted to places in which experts congregate. The spillover is not necessarily about information. Amateurs may enjoy being seen with or seeing experts, whereas the opposite may not hold true.

   The two groups of participants may be the same type of agents but active on the platform at different points in time. Consider a situation with early and late users. The more early users buy on a platform in the first period, the better the upgraded version that can be sold in the second period. Everything else being equal, users in the second period find participation more attractive the larger the number of purchases in the first period. Thus, first-period users exert a positive network effect on second-period users (but the latter do not affect the well-being of the former).

1.2.4   Within- or Cross-Group Network Effects?

Before closing this section, let us stress that there might sometimes be a thin line between within- and cross-group network effects. It may indeed be tricky to determine whether the users of a platform belong to the same group or whether they should be split into separate groups.

Telecommunication networks provide a nice illustration of the difficulty in drawing a clear line between within- and cross-group network effects. Most of the economic literature on telecommunication networks assumes, for simplicity, uniform calling patterns – that is, an equal likelihood for each subscriber to call and be called by any other subscriber;[19] this assumption of fully symmetric participants implies a single group exhibiting within-group network effects. Another simplifying assumption would be to consider that some people only make calls, while others only receive calls (e.g., restaurants and customers who want to order for delivery or make a reservation); in that case, there would be two distinct groups, with only cross-group network effects. The reality is naturally somewhere between these two extremes: Subscribers are heterogeneous in their propensity both to make calls and to receive calls. Moreover, calling patterns are largely reported to be nonuniform: Most subscribers have a "calling circle," that is, a subset of subscribers with whom they interact more frequently than with others.[20] Seen from an individual subscriber's perspective, network effects are then mostly within-group (i.e., inside the calling circle), cross-group network effects (i.e., outside the calling circle) being relatively limited. If these calling circles are not overlapping, we may distinguish many separate groups characterized by strong within-group network effects and weak cross-group network effects.[21]

Online games provide another environment for a platform with, at first sight, a single user group – in this case, the players – that is subject to network effects;

---

[19] See, for instance, Armstrong (1998), Laffont, Rey, and Tirole (1998a,b), and de Bijl and Peitz (2002).

[20] See, e.g., Hoernig, Inderst, and Valletti (2014). Hence, on top of the number of subscribers in the network, one also needs to consider the set of connections existing among the subscribers (who is connected to whom) and, potentially, the direction and intensity of these connections (to what extent are subscribers calling – or being called – by other subscribers). That is, it is important to understand the network *structure* and how this structure was formed. Such questions are central to the "social networks approach" to network economics, which uses a variety of methods (graph theory, game theory, probability theory, matrix algebra) to study which networks will eventually form when individuals have the discretion to choose their connections. (For a comprehensive textbook on this topic, see Jackson (2008); for a shorter survey applied to the digital economy, see Goyal (2012).) In this book, we follow the "industrial organization approach" to network economics, which focuses on goods that exhibit network effects and on the strategic interaction between the providers and users of these goods.

[21] With such a network structure, a platform with a small user base may be viable, as the overall network size does not make an important contribution to the attractiveness of a platform.

yet, after a closer look, one observes a richer structure, featuring within-group and cross-group network effects, as illustrated in Case 1.3.

CASE 1.3 SURVEY EVIDENCE OF CROSS-GROUP NETWORK EFFECTS IN ONLINE POKER

Wimmer et al. (2018) ran a survey among players of online poker in which they asked them to evaluate the presence of other players on the attractiveness of a poker site. Clearly, the more players are active on a site, the shorter the waiting time to play. This suggests that there are positive within-group network effects. However, a closer look reveals that players are heterogeneous in their abilities. Poker, as with all zero-sum games in which success depends on players' abilities, has the property that winning probabilities increase with the ability of a player and decrease with the ability of other players. If we distinguish between low-skilled and high-skilled players, then every player finds a site more attractive if there are more low-skilled players. If the reduced waiting time from a larger pool is dominated by the reduced probability of winning, then every player finds a site less attractive if there are more high-skilled players. Thus, evaluated in a mixed pool, we would expect that there are positive within-group and cross-group network effects generated by low-skilled players and negative within-group and cross-group network effects generated by high-skilled players. In line with this hypothesis, the authors find that more participation by low-skilled players makes the poker site more attractive, while participation by high-skilled players does the opposite.

Since people can write and read on Wikipedia and no other users are involved, one may suspect that there is a single user group. However, some users are almost exclusively readers, whereas others may frequently update and add content. Thus, in this case also we can distinguish different groups, contributors, and noncontributors. To shed light on the nature of network effects, natural experiments are an interesting way to gain insights into the presence and type of within-group and cross-group network effects. A natural experiment takes place if, for instance, a system consisting of two or more groups that are linked through network effects is exposed to a shock that directly affects the user base of one or more groups. The following case on Wikipedia illustrates that mutual positive cross-group network effects may be present in the context of the private provision of public goods.

CASE 1.4 NETWORK EFFECTS ON WIKIPEDIA

Wikipedia is an example of successful private provision of a public good. While one may expect that Wikipedia suffers from the free-rider problem – that is, people are less willing to contribute the larger the number of users – Zhang and Zhu (2011) find the opposite using data on Chinese Wikipedia in 2005. The shutdown of Wikipedia in mainland China in October 2005 allows them to analyze the response by contributors from other places (e.g., Taiwan, Hong Kong, Singapore) to this shock in readership and number of contributors. Since the number of potential contributors has dropped, the free-rider problem suggests that nonblocked users are more likely to contribute. By contrast, Zhang and Zhu find that contribution levels of nonblocked users dropped by more than 40 percent with the shutdown. As they argue, "contributors receive social benefits from their contributions, and the shrinking group size reduces these social benefits" (p. 1601). Distinguishing between contributors and noncontributors, this suggests that there are positive cross-group network effects from noncontributors to contributors. Clearly, we also expect positive cross-group network effects from contributors to noncontributors to be present, as the latter benefit from improved content on Wikipedia.

The previous examples show that many platforms that may be thought to cater to a single group of users are better described, upon closer examination, as serving multiple groups because of heterogeneous network effects.

Furthermore, one should also note that if a platform facilitates the interaction between two (clearly distinct) groups of users, within-group and cross-group network effects are present and may be difficult to disentangle. Take the example of peer-to-peer marketplaces like Uber or Airbnb, which enable the interaction between providers and consumers of services; clearly, each group exerts positive cross-group network effects on the other group. Yet, the quality of the matching between peers from the two groups increases with the volume and reliability of data that the platforms collect from providers and consumers alike. Hence, also a form of within-group network effects appears: The larger the participation on one side, the more data is generated (about feedbacks, reputation, reviews, geo-localization, etc.), which enhances the quality of the platform's service and, thereby, the utility of *all* users on the same side.[22]

In a nutshell, disentangling within- and cross-group network effects may be hard in some environments. This may not be a problem for a number of issues. For instance, if we are concerned with the success of a platform in increasing its user base over time, we understand that positive network effects – whether within or mutual across groups – generate positive feedback loops; that is, whether there is an attraction *loop* or an attraction *spiral* is not key for that purpose. Yet, determining the exact nature of the network effects may prove much more crucial when it comes to designing specific platform strategies. In the poker example, for instance, a platform that considers that network effects are of the within-group kind would deploy strategies to attract any player, irrespective of their skills; yet, such strategy may lead to an excess of high-skilled players, which may eventually reduce the attractiveness of the platform.

To conclude this section, let us stress that the analysis of a platform starts with the identification of the user groups and the relevant network effects. If users cannot be separated in different groups, then a social planner would want to leverage positive within-group network effects (while mitigating potential negative effects). If sorting users into separate groups makes sense, then network effects within each group and across any pair of groups need to be evaluated. For each type of network effects, one should ask whether these effects are positive, negative, or negligible. Collecting the answers to these questions should give useful insights regarding the strategies that the platform may want to deploy. Figure 1.5 depicts a simple tool that can be used to give a systematic (and graphical) account of the network effects that can exist on a platform that facilitates the interaction between two groups or audiences (*A* and *B*). When there are more than two groups (e.g., three groups), it may be more convenient to use a matrix such as the one in Table 1.1 to perform the same exercise.

---

[22] We return to the interplay between data and network effects in the next chapter.

Table 1.1 Network effects matrix for a three-sided platform

	Group A	Group B	Group C
Group A	$(A \to A) +? -? \emptyset?$	$(A \to B) +? -? \emptyset?$	$(A \to C) +? -? \emptyset?$
Group B	$(B \to A) +? -? \emptyset?$	$(B \to B) +? -? \emptyset?$	$(B \to C) +? -? \emptyset?$
Group C	$(C \to A) +? -? \emptyset?$	$(C \to B) +? -? \emptyset?$	$(C \to C) +? -? \emptyset?$

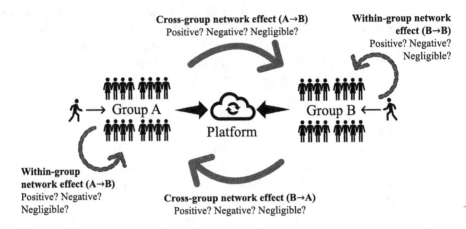

Figure 1.5 Mapping the network effects on a platform

1.3 Platform Definition and Typology

Now that we have introduced the different types of network effects – within-group vs. cross-group, positive vs. negative – and how their combination leads to a number of typical situations, we are in position to clarify the concept of platform. We first make explicit our definition of platforms (1.3.1). We then confront this definition with a number of real-life cases; we will see that being a platform is a matter of degree (1.3.2). Finally, on the basis of the previous discussions, we propose different ways to classify platforms (1.3.3).

1.3.1 A Definition of Platforms

In our view, an entity must meet two key requirements to be considered a platform. First, the entity must facilitate the interaction between users who are linked by some form of network effects. Second, the entity must manage these network effects in an active way. We thus define platforms as follows.[23]

---

[23] The management literature also emphasizes the presence of network effects as a key characteristic of platforms. As noted by Evans and Gawer (2016) in their survey (p. 6): "A fundamental feature of platforms is the presence of network effects: platforms become more valuable as more users use them."

DEFINITION 7   *A **platform** is an entity that brings together economic agents and actively manages network effects between them.*

Even though platform-like intermediaries have existed for a long time, the rapid development of digital technologies has vastly expanded the possibilities of meeting the requirements that make an entity a platform. Digital technologies allow intermediaries to decrease considerably the transaction costs that users must bear to interact (costs related to, e.g., search, matching, screening, contracting, trust, reputation, dispute resolution, booking management, etc.). At the same time, intermediaries can rely on digital technologies to manage network effects more actively, and to add or redistribute value through price and nonprice instruments.

Our definition may seem too narrow for those who do not see the presence of network effects as an essential feature of platforms. We admit that there are interesting issues of intermediation that are not linked to network effects. Also, as discussed in the introductory chapter, it may be economies of scale and scope, rather than network effects, that contribute more importantly to the success of an intermediary or a firm aggregating the demand of one group of users.[24]

Conversely, our definition may seem too broad for those who see multisidedness as the main characteristics of platforms. One can indeed often read in the business press, policy documents, or the academic literature that platforms are defined as entities that actively manage (cross-group) network effects between *two or multiple groups of* economic agents. We believe that this focus on multisidedness is ill-suited for our purpose. We see three reasons for that, which are illustrated by the brief history we give in Case 1.5 of three current "giant" digital platforms (Facebook, Google Search, and Amazon):

(1) These platforms started by (and are still to a large extent) managing within-group network effects.
(2) These platforms have gradually included the management of cross-group network effects into their business model and monetization strategy.
(3) Some of the competition challenges (e.g., that some markets with platforms have a tendency to tip towards one platform) are present irrespective of multisidedness: All that is needed is that an attraction loop or attraction spiral is present and sufficiently strong.

In other words, when it comes to assessing the source of market power for platforms, all types of network effects play an important role; moreover, including additional sides on a platform is an endogenous decision (which we will discuss in Chapter 4). Adopting a narrower definition of platforms would lead us to analyzing these issues too selectively. However, we acknowledge that some issues are specific

---

[24] Scale economies vs. network effects may depend on the particular choice made by an intermediary, as mentioned in the introduction to this book. A particular instance is certifying intermediaries. If the intermediary carries out inspection itself, it benefits from the scale of its operations. By contrast, if it aggregates experiences by users, it manages network effects between users. See Chapter 2, for more details on the latter.

to two- or multi-sided platforms, which will lead us to dedicate large parts of this book (and of the second one) to this subset of entities.

CASE 1.5 A VERY SHORT HISTORY OF AMAZON, FACEBOOK, AND GOOGLE SEARCH

Since politicians, the public, and competition authorities are taking a closer look at a very few large platforms,[25] we find it useful at this point to take a quick look at three of them: Amazon, Facebook, and Google Search.

Amazon originally operated as an electronic retailer selling books and, in some countries, determined the retail price itself, whereas the publisher was setting the wholesale price.[26] In contrast with traditional retailers, the consumer experience on Amazon depends positively on the number of users if these users provide valuable product reviews and ratings. In addition, Amazon observed the click and purchase behavior of individual users, on the basis of which it could provide recommendations. Recommendations tend to become more useful the more users are active on Amazon. Both features give rise to positive within-group network effects (as we argue more formally in the next chapter). However, at least at the start, there did not exist cross-group effects from buyers to sellers, and Amazon did not operate as a two-sided platform; it only operated an online sales channel for books. It is only at a later stage that Amazon, by establishing its Marketplace, added another group, namely independent sellers; the addition of this group generated positive cross-group network effects between buyers and sellers. However, Amazon's main strength vis-à-vis rivals continued to come, arguably, from the positive within-group network effects on the buyer side.

Facebook built its monetization model on providing advertisers with the possibility of (targeted) display advertising. To the extent that private users rather dislike advertising, Facebook is exploiting the user base it maintains because of the social networking benefits (which are within-group network effects) to provide benefits to advertisers. It then charges advertisers for this service. Here, users exert a positive cross-group network effect on advertisers, while advertisers exert a presumably negative cross-group network effect on users. Clearly, advertising here serves as a monetization device (which benefits from a large, interconnected user base, as it allows for better targeting). However, the strength of Facebook in the marketplace is arguably due to within-group network effects arising from social networking among users. An alternative strategy by Facebook could have been to charge users for participation or usage.[27] Using the narrower definition proposed elsewhere, Facebook would not be classified as a platform, even though the interaction between users would continue to be present.

Google Search also built its monetization model on providing advertisers with the possibility of (targeted) advertising through a sponsored search entry. Such sponsored search entries may

---

[25] The first detailed proposal by an agency of how to deal with Google and Facebook is the report by the Australian Competition and Consumer Commission (ACCC); see ACCC (2019). For disclosure purposes, we report that Martin Peitz served as economic expert to ACCC in the investigation that led to the report.

[26] In those countries in which resale-price maintenance (RPM) for books is legal, the publisher determines both wholesale and retail price. If this is the case, an intermediary has no price instruments available to affect its revenues apart from, possibly, charging fixed fees and adding a handling fee. Thus, publishers set a price floor on the consumer side.

[27] For a long time, the possibility of charging users was clearly ruled out, as Facebook claimed on its homepage "Free and always will be." Yet, on August 7, 2019, this slogan was quietly replaced by "Quiet and easy," which made observers speculate about a potential change in Facebook's monetization strategy. See www.businessinsider.com/facebook-changes-free-and-always-will-be-slogan-on-homepage-2019-8.

well be appreciated by users. Still, to the extent that the quality of organic search is decisive for the search engine's attractiveness in the eyes of users, Google Search is monetizing the user base by charging advertisers for becoming visible to users. The strength of Google Search in the marketplace is arguably due to within-group network effects arising from the high quality of its search results based on the wealth of search data it has available and the quality of its algorithm. To the extent that users appreciate well-targeted sponsored ads, positive cross-group network effects may come into play. However, we would need more information to evaluate whether users are really better off with better-targeted sponsored ads (as advertisers may adjust the price they charge to consumers if they know consumer characteristics). Instead of opening the platform to sponsored search entries, an alternative strategy by Google could have been to charge users for participation or usage. In this case, advertisers would not be present.

In sum, abstracting from heterogeneity among users, within-group external effects on the user side are a prominent force that has made these three platforms popular. Even today, it can be argued that the attractiveness for people using Amazon, Google Search, and Facebook stems to a large extent from the strength of positive within-group network effects and less so on cross-group network effects (if at all).

1.3.2   What Is (and What Is Not) a Platform?

Platforms have multiple instruments available to manage network effects. While prices charged to different participants are the most obvious, there is a long list of other instruments that may be available to the platform; we will amply study these instruments in the following chapters. What matters for now is to use our definition to analyze a large array of entities from a platform perspective. We do so for a number of real-world examples. For each entity, we discuss the extent to which it can be considered to be a platform. Let us start with four cases in which network effects are clearly present; the issue then is whether these network effects are actively managed or not.

The original Facebook
Facebook started as a social networking site that allowed students to interact. An attraction loop can be seen as part of the DNA of a social networking site, as it lives from the possibility it gives to its users to interact and engage with others. By designing how people can interact and be informed about activities by Facebook friends, Facebook clearly manages these network effects. Thus, according to our definition, Facebook is a clear case of platform (even when abstracting from the advertising possibilities it offers to businesses).

Wikipedia
The online encyclopedia Wikipedia relies on content provided by users. If all readers are potential contributors, the more users there are, the more likely it is that somebody encounters an error or has additional knowledge. Correcting or adding content increases the quality available. If users undertake such actions systematically – for example, with a fixed probability – more active users improve the experience of each individual user and, thus, positive within-group network effects are present on Wikipedia. Alternatively, we can view the group of contributors to be a strict

subset of the group of all users. In this case, noncontributing users benefit from the cross-group network effect from more contributors being active; and contributing users benefit from the positive within-group network effect. The ease with which changes to the entries can be made, the degree of encouragement to contribute to content generation, and the mechanism of quality control are all determined by the design of Wikipedia. Thus, even though Wikipedia is not a profit-maximizing entity, it is not a passive intermediary: It manages the degree of network effects. So, Wikipedia fulfills the two requirements of our definition and can thus be seen as a platform. As just argued, Wikipedia can be considered to be a two-sided platform, as some users are consumers of content whereas others are active in providing content. To the extent that contributors are motivated by a large readership, there are mutual positive cross-group network effects (see Case 1.4) generating an attraction spiral.

Uber

The ride-hailing app Uber matches drivers and passengers. Different from other peer-to-peer platforms in the sharing economy (e.g., Airbnb), Uber has centralized the pricing decision; that is, it is not individual drivers who announce prices or passengers who submit quotes, but it is Uber that operates a pricing algorithm setting the price for a particular ride. A driver experiences positive cross-group network effects for at least two reasons. More passengers reduce expected idle times and reduce the expected distance between the location of the driver and the pick-up point. A passenger experiences positive cross-group network effects because it reduces the expected waiting time (a free driver is more likely to be available and the expected distance between the location of an available car and the location of the passenger decreases). Through its algorithm and price incentives Uber can try to manage driver and passenger usage.

Esperanto

Esperanto is a spoken language that was constructed at the end of the nineteenth century. The objective of its creator, L. L. Zamenhof, was to create a flexible language that would be easy to learn; people around the globe would use it as a second language, which would facilitate international understanding and, thereby, foster world peace. Like any other language, Esperanto generates positive within-group network effects: The more people speak the language, the more interesting it is for other people to learn it. Yet, in spite of the existence of the World Esperanto Congress (which holds annual conferences) and the official support of the United Nations (since 1954), no entity seems sufficiently able (or willing) to manage actively these network effects. This contributes to explaining why Esperanto has never reached a critical mass of users; it faces the problem that it lacks an installed base of native speakers. It is estimated that Esperanto has about 2 million speakers; this is a rather small community in view of its universal purpose (Esperanto is, nevertheless, the most widely spoken constructed language in the world).

Let us move on to some more disputable cases. We start with supermarket chains and contrast the case of Aldi with the case of Tesco; we argue that the first should not be seen as a platform, while the second could be. We proceed in a similar way for blogs, arguing that a personal blog is not, per se, a platform but may become one once additional authors are invited to join and/or when advertising is used as a monetization strategy.

Aldi

Aldi is a discounter with a selection of groceries offered regularly and a temporary selection of food and nonfood products. Initially, it only offered private labels; it now also offers some manufacturer brands. Arguably, network effects are not present or at least not very prominent among the shoppers (abstracting from congestion effects). In summary, Aldi is not considered a platform because the first condition in our definition is not met.

Tesco

Tesco is a supermarket chain that offers a selection of branded manufacturers' and private label products. At a first glance, we would not view Tesco as a platform, since it is a retailer that buys products and then sells them under its own terms (similar to Aldi but with a larger share of manufacturer brands and more product variety). However, if Tesco focuses its business model into renting out shelf space to sellers, it operates to a platform and manages network effects; it can do so, for instance, by deciding on how to determine the terms for different categories of products, in a similar manner to a shopping mall operator that manages cross-group network effects among shops and buyers. As is frequently observed, supermarket chains such as Tesco ask for slotting allowances for products to be carried, obtain preferential shelf space, or be advertised.[28] The more consumers visit a retailer, the more attractive it is for a brand manufacturer to participate. Conversely, the more attractive brands are carried or made visible to consumers, the more consumers will participate. Thus, even in the case of high-street retailing, mutual positive cross-group network effects may be present, giving rise to an attraction spiral. Tesco manages these network effects through the use of price and nonprice instruments (e.g., by offering free parking or by guiding consumers to products that are a good match or to some that are a somewhat worse match but give higher returns to Tesco).

Blogs

A blog is a web site that is regularly updated with new content, usually written in an informal style. Many blogs are launched by a single writer who wants to share their views on a given subject. Such individual blogs cannot be seen as platforms, as they do not meet any of the two requirements of our definition. Other blogs are run by a group of individuals, who may act as an editorial board. The blog would then

---

[28] See, for instance, *The Economist*, "Buying up the shelves," business section, June 18, 2015. As Cairns (1962, p. 34) observes, "The business of the retailer may also be regarded as selling to suppliers the space at his disposal. Such space is valuable to suppliers because in most cases it provides their only opportunity to establish contact with ultimate consumers."

become a platform, insofar as the editorial board takes actions to attract both writers and readers. An example is the blog www.IPdigIT.eu, which Paul Belleflamme runs together with Alain Strowel, his colleague from the Law Faculty at UCLouvain. Although both authors first used the blog as a medium to disseminate their own work, they quickly realized that the only way to attract more readers was to expand the group of authors. They thus invited a number of colleagues (among them, Martin Peitz) to write for the blog, arguing that this would give them access to a larger audience. In other words, the cofounders started to exploit positive cross-group network effects between two groups: writers and readers. Doing so, they turned IPdigIT into a platform with the aim of initiating an attraction spiral. Another way for an individual blog to become a platform (in the sense of our definition) is to use advertising as a (unique or complementary) source of revenues. The blog then links advertisers to readers; as long as readers dislike seeing ads alongside the content that the author posts, the blog exhibits an attraction/repulsion pendulum.

In light of this list of examples, the reader may be led to believe that any entity that enables trade should normally be considered a platform. To dispel this erroneous feeling, we develop two more examples to help understand when such an enabler of trade is not called a platform.

Independent petrol stations

An independent petrol station enables trade between an oil company and retail customers for gasoline, but there are no network effects involved. The petrol station contracts a certain quantity with the oil company (and possibly several companies). Then, the oil company does not care how many customers frequent the petrol station. Customers only care about the price and availability of petrol and do not care about the number of oil companies competing with each other. However, one could construct a hypothetical case that customers benefit from positive cross-group network effects. This would be the case if, first, the petrol station rented out pumps to different oil companies; second, it informed customers how many pumps operated by oil companies it has; third, based on this information, customers make the decision whether to drive to the place; and fourth, oil companies set their petrol prices. Clearly, this is not how petrol stations operate.

Notaries

A notary is an example of an entity that enables trade between buyers and sellers and charges a regulated commission. Such an entity does not satisfy our definition since it is hard to see what are the network effects (unless the presence of other economic agents has an effect on the information held by an economic agent) and, in case there are, the entity may not have instruments at its disposal to manage them.

Table 1.2 summarizes our analysis of the different examples. As these examples illustrate, it is hardly possible to draw a sharp dividing line between which entity satisfies our definition of a platform and which one does not: It is often a question of degree and focus. What we aim to develop in this book is an understanding about

Table 1.2 Platform or not?

	Network effects are ...		
	... present?	... managed?	Platform?
Original Facebook	Yes (same-group)	Yes	**Yes**
Wikipedia	Yes (same-group)	Yes	**Yes**
Uber	Yes (cross-group)	Yes	**Yes**
Esperanto	Yes (same-group)	No	**No**
Aldi	No	No	**No**
Tesco	Yes (cross-group)?	Yes?	**Yes?**
Individual blog	No	No	**No**
Group or ad-financed blog	Yes (cross-group)	Yes	**Yes**
Petrol stations	No	No	**No**
Notaries	No	No	**No**

how to analyze economic environments in which some entities can be considered platforms. It may then turn out (i) that network effects appear not to be prominent, or (ii) that, while prominent, the platform cannot actively manage those network effects, or (iii) that the platform aspect is secondary to the issue (e.g., that a particular firm enjoys a monopoly position). Clearly, in the first and third situations (and possibly in the second situation as well), economic analysis abstracting from network effects is appropriate. To the contrary, in other situations, the platform aspect is central for an understanding of a business and the market in which it operates. In this book, we explore such platform businesses.

1.3.3 Different Types of Platforms

Typologies of platforms abound. Different typologies focus on different dimensions of platforms and, thereby, serve different purposes. As far as this book is concerned, our objective is twofold: On the one hand, we want to identify the underlying economic forces behind platforms' strategies; on the other hand, we want to understand how platforms perform. To this end, we propose a typology of platforms that is in line with our definition (see Definition 7) and that focuses on how platforms create and capture economic value. We present this typology first and then we move to other typologies that have been put forward.

Value Creation and Capture

Two questions are key to determining how platforms design their strategies and how they perform. First, how does the platform *create* economic value? In particular, which network effects does the platform actively manage? Second, how does the platform *capture* economic value? In other words, which monetization strategy does the platform use?

As far as *value creation* is concerned, we distinguish between three options. The first two options consist in leveraging mutual positive cross-group network effects (attraction spiral) or positive within-group network effects (attraction loop). In the former case, separate groups of users can be clearly distinguished and their two-sided interaction lies at the core of value creation. In the latter case, the value comes more from facilitating the interaction among the users of a single group; yet, the platform may consider adding another group of users at some point as an additional device to capture value and possibly to create additional value. The third option consists in creating value mainly through stand-alone products or services. Here, network effects are not central for value creation, but they may nevertheless be instrumental for value capture, as we now discuss.

Regarding *value capture* (monetization), we identify two major options. Platforms can charge users enjoying positive network effects or offer a bundle including a "bad." The first option is often implemented through a "freemium strategy," which amounts to propose two versions of the service: a "free" version with limited features (or lower quality) along with a premium version that offers more features (or higher quality) for a price. In the presence of positive network effects, the free version is a powerful instrument to attract a critical mass of users and, thereby, increase the willingness-to-pay of some users for the premium version; the key, of course, is to "convert" a sufficient number of free users into paying premium customers. The idea behind the second option is to bundle the service with advertising and/or the transfer of personal or anonymized data (providing such data is not necessarily a bad). In general, users face no monetary payment, but they often incur a shadow cost of being exposed to ad nuisance or having their privacy invaded (whether and to what extent these are "bads" is an empirical question).[29] Importantly, an entity that creates value mainly through stand-alone services fits our platform definition if it captures this value by bundling the services with a "bad" that is subject to cross-group network effects.

Crossing the two dimensions and their respective options, we can classify platforms into five different categories. For the sake of illustrating how to use the typology, we relate some well-known platforms to the different categories. As depicted in Figure 1.6, we use our typology in a dynamic way to show how entities may, through time, move across categories (as they adapt their business model) or end up being listed in different categories (as they diversify their offering).

Consider first the upper line, where platforms capture value by charging the users of their services. Starting with the left-hand cell, we find three platforms. There is Netflix, which offers online streaming of movies and series; through its recommender system, Netflix generates positive within-group network effects for its subscribers.[30] Amazon also appears in this cell for its retailing activities; positive within-group network effects follow from the rating and review systems that Amazon has put in place (see Chapter 2 for more). Finally, we place the "original" LinkedIn in this cell: At

---

[29] In Chapter 5, we formally analyze the freemium strategy in which the "free" version contains advertising.

[30] As Netflix buys the rights to diffuse the content produced by others or produces its own content, we do not consider it a two-sided platform.

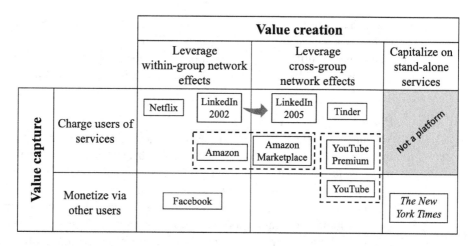

Figure 1.6 A typology of platforms based on value creation and capture

its creation in 2002, LinkedIn was purely a social network connecting professionals. Moving to the middle cell, we find Amazon and LinkedIn again: Amazon for its marketplace activity and LinkedIn for its current version (which started in 2005). As explained in Case 1.5, Amazon started to exploit positive cross-group network effects once it opened its platform to third-party sellers. As for LinkedIn, it launched its jobs and subscriptions paid options in 2005, thereby adding the group of businesses to the platform and leveraging positive cross-group network effects between employers posting jobs and job seekers posting their curriculum. We also place Tinder, a dating platform, in this cell. Finally, we do not list any entity in the right-hand cell, as they cannot be considered as platforms: Network effects are not instrumental in creating or capturing value.

Consider now the bottom row in Figure 1.6. Here, platforms do not or do not only charge the users of their main services (which can involve within- or cross-group network effects, or no network effects at all) but add another group of users – typically advertisers – for monetization purposes. Facebook appears in the left-hand cell, as it exploits direct network effects (see the discussion above). We list YouTube in the middle cell, as its main purpose is to link two groups of users: those who mainly view content and those who mainly post content. We note, however, that YouTube recently introduced an advertising-free subscription-based service, which justifies that we also list it in the upper-middle cell of the table. Finally, a newspaper like the *New York Times* appears in the right-hand cell: It serves a unique group of users, within which network effects are negligible, but it is a platform insofar as it "sells" its readers' attention to advertisers. Note that when readers dislike advertising, an attraction/repulsion pendulum is at work, meaning that the value that the platform creates for advertisers by taking them on board comes partly at the expense of the value that it destroys for readers (we will return to this trade-off in the following chapters).

As already discussed, this typology serves quite well the objective that we pursue in this book – namely, to understand how platforms design their strategies. However, platforms may differ along a number of other dimensions that may also be relevant for our analysis. We therefore describe other potential typologies of platforms.

Platform Objectives

Maximizing profits is by no means the only objective that platforms may pursue; for instance, Wikipedia is a non-profit organization. In this book, we mainly focus on *for-profit platforms*. What is important to note is that the distinction between for-profit and nonprofit platforms may be harder to make than one might think at first glance. It is indeed observed that many digital platforms started without a clear monetization model in mind; they simply hoped that, after growing a sufficiently large user base, a successful monetization strategy would emerge (including the possibility of being taken over by some other firm). In this case, from a dynamic perspective, it would be misleading to label such a digital platform as "nonprofit." However, abstracting from dynamic issues, such a firm may well initially be analyzed as if it were a nonprofit platform maximizing the size of its user base under some budget constraint.

Platform Instruments

An orthogonal classification of platforms that has been made is between transaction and nontransaction platforms.[31] While the former are characterized by trade taking place on the platform, the latter facilitates information exchange. On transaction platforms, the platform can charge buyers or sellers conditional on a transaction taking place, whereas in the latter, if the platform wants to monetize on at least one side, it has to charge for participation or some proxy for a transaction taking place (e.g., a per-click fee). This distinction thus affects the price instruments available to the platform (see, in particular, Chapter 5). Also, since a transaction platform can more easily monitor trade, it may be subject to a different liability regime. It has also been claimed that the distinction is relevant for market definition purposes in competition cases – in this book, we do not enter into the debate of market definition.[32]

Platform Audiences

Another way to classify platforms is to consider which kind of audiences a platform is catering to. Some platforms only have businesses as users; this obviously holds for so-called B2B (business-to-business) platforms. Some two-sided platforms have businesses on one side and users on the other; this applies to B2C (business-to-consumers) platforms. Yet other platforms cater only to consumers. This applies to ad-free dating platforms, for example; it also applies to C2C (consumer-to-consumer) – or P2P (peer-to-peer) – platforms in the sharing economy.

---

[31] See, e.g., Filistrucchi et al. (2014).
[32] One of the authors has expressed his views on this topic, e.g., in Franck and Peitz (2019).

Platform Functions

Our last classification is based on the functionality offered by a platform. This serves to illustrate the wide variety of platforms in the real world and thus the importance of platforms in market economies – in particular, with the increasing importance of digital markets. We provide an incomplete and nonexclusive list (arguably, some of the following examples may belong to different categories).

- *Hardware/software systems*
    - Function: Allow application developers and end users to interact.
    - Examples: Operating systems for computers, smartphones, or videogame consoles (Android, Linux, Mac OS, PlayStation, Tencent Games); standardized formats (DVD, MPEG, VHS).[33]
- *Matchmakers*
    - Function: Help members of one group to find the right "match" within another group; these are pure interaction platforms.
    - Examples: Dating platforms (Baihe, Tinder); job boards (Monster, 51jobs); peer-to-peer platforms in the sharing economy for cleaning services, baby, dog or cat sitting; publishers (Cambridge University Press, Wiley, Wikipedia); MOOC platforms (Coursera, EDX); yellow pages; real estate portals; price search engines.
- *Exchanges*
    - Function: Help "buyers" and "sellers" search for feasible contracts and for the best prices; although many of these platforms also feature matching as an important function, they differ from matchmakers by allowing transactions to be conducted on the platform.
    - Examples: Flea markets; trade fairs; shopping malls; stock exchanges;[34] real estate agents, hotel booking platforms (Booking, Expedia, Tuoniu as well as, for travel agents and airlines, Amadeus); food delivery platforms (Deliveroo, Delivery Hero, Just Eat Takeaway, Meituan, Uber Eats); B2C and C2C online shopping portals (Alibaba Group's Taobao, Amazon Marketplace, Dangdang, eBay); B2B procurement platforms (Alibaba, DHgate, eWorldTrade, Global Sources); crowdfunding platforms (Indiegogo, Kickstarter, LendingClub, Ulule).
- *Peer-to-peer marketplaces*
    - Function: Facilitate the exchange of goods and services between "peers"; these platforms can be seen as specific combinations of exchanges and matchmakers that operate in the so-called "sharing economy"; that is, they facilitate the sharing of resources by letting the owners of underused resources make these resources available to other individuals.

---

[33] Other examples are the modem standards for end-user internet access in the 1990s, as empirically investigated by Augereau, Greenstein, and Rysman (2006).

[34] One way to view stock exchanges as two-sided platforms is that they allow companies to list their shares and traders to trade these stocks. Network effects arise since traders benefit from many stocks being traded and companies are attracted by exchanges that offer a lot of liquidity.

- Examples: Airbnb, Didi, Etsy, Eatwith, Grab, TaskRabbit, Uber, Xiaozhu.
- *Media and entertainment platforms*
  - Function: Provide content to users and audience to content providers. Advertising is a common monetization strategy: The platform sells users' attention to advertisers.
  - Examples: Newspapers, radio and TV broadcasters; social networks (Facebook, LinkedIn, Renren, TikTok); online media portals; news aggregators.[35]
- *Payment systems*
  - Function: Provide a method for payment to facilitate transactions between buyers and sellers.
  - Examples: AliPay, American Express, Apple Pay, Bitcoin, Mastercard, PayPal, Visa, WeChat Pay, YouTrip.

Key Insights from Chapter 1

- We define **platforms** as *entities that bring together economic agents and actively manage network effects between them.*
- **Network effects** are themselves defined as *the impacts that an additional user of a product or service, or an additional participant to some interaction, has on the value that other users or participants attach to this product, service, or interaction.* Network effects can be positive or negative. When platform users can be identified as belonging to distinct groups, it is useful to distinguish between network effects that arise inside a given group of users (*within-group network effects*) and those that a user of some group exerts on users of another group (*cross-group network effects*).
- Positive within-group network effects give rise to an *attraction loop*. The combination of positive cross-group network effects in two directions give rise to an *attraction spiral*. Environments in which cross-group network effects are positive in one direction but negative in the other direction generate an *attraction/repulsion pendulum*.
- To be considered a platform, an entity must facilitate the interaction between users who are linked by some form of network effects *and* must manage these network effects in an active way. Whether a particular entity meets these two requirements is often a question of degree and focus.
- Platforms can be classified in many different ways. For our purpose, we build a typology by answering two questions: How does the platform *create* economic value? How does the platform *capture* economic value?

---

[35] Some software applications may become platforms in their own right; for example, some online video games become platforms as they may connect viewers to professional players (e.g., League of Legends, which is owned by Tencent) and may provide advertising and other marketing opportunities.

2 Ratings, Recommendations, and the Use of Big Data

In the initial chapter, we defined *network effects* as the impacts that an additional user of a product or service has on the value that other users attach to this product or service, and *platforms* as entities that bring together economic agents and actively manage network effects among them. We also made a distinction between network effects according to whether they arise within a particular group of users or across different groups of users.

Regarding the distinction between the two types of network effects, we noted that it may sometimes be unclear, as the attractiveness of a platform may increase primarily with the volume of interaction that this platform manages; in that case, network effects are jointly generated by all users, irrespective of the group they belong to. A case in point is when platforms collect and use big data. Participation and use by other users may matter because their active evaluation of products and services or the information contained in their actions either provides guidance for a user's action or enables the platform to provide better services or add specific offerings.

To actively manage such interaction, platforms can implement *rating and recommender systems*. How are rating and recommender systems instrumental in producing network effects? Consider, for instance, the case of Amazon, which publishes product reviews and average ratings. Arguably, the more consumers that are active on Amazon, the more informative are the reviews and ratings, thus allowing consumers to make better-informed decisions. Amazon also provides recommendations by matching product descriptions with consumers' interests. Similarly, the more consumers that are active on the platform and the larger the volume of transactions they generate, the better the data that Amazon has about consumer characteristics and, so, the better the matches it can suggest; the quality of recommendations increases thus with the number of consumers, which in many cases will lead to a higher expected net consumer benefit. These mechanisms point to positive within-group network effects.

On two-sided platforms, positive cross-group network effects might arise. For instance, a high-quality seller thinking of participating on eBay, Taobao, Amazon Marketplace, or some other B2C platform cares about the ease with which it can build its reputation. The more buyers active on the platform, the more precise the information about the seller type at a given point in time (assuming truthful consumer ratings). Thus, there is a positive cross-group network effect from buyers to high-quality sellers. Similarly, the more buyers on a platform, the better the matching between buyers and sellers (in terms of horizontal characteristics). This, in particular, reduces the expected number of products returned to the sellers. Thus, thanks to the recommender system, there is a positive cross-group external effect from buyers to sellers. This effect is strengthened by more detailed data on each consumer and each seller, as this improves the expected match quality.

Ratings are intended to help consumers make choices based on the quality or value-for-money dimension. Recommendations can also serve this purpose; they have the potential to address buyer heterogeneity if they are personalized. This does not mean that some degree of personalization is impossible in the context of a rating system. In fact, several platforms offer the option of personalization – by, for instance, showing ratings and reviews only of buyers with certain profiles. Such rating selection can provide better guidance because what is good for one group of buyers is not necessarily good for others. For example, a business traveler may have different needs and preferences than a family on vacation and, thus, may prefer to see only reviews and ratings by fellow business travelers.

In the rest of this chapter, we analyze the economics behind the use of big data and in particular, ratings, reviews, and recommendations that have become mainstream on digital platforms. We start in Section 2.1 by analyzing rating and review, systems. These systems provide platform users with information about either products or their counterparties to a transaction. Of crucial importance is, of course, the informativeness of these systems, which depends on the users' actions.[1] We then turn, in Section 2.2, to recommender systems, which aim to reduce users' search cost by pointing them towards transactions that may better match their tastes. Besides the ability of such systems to generate network effects, we also discuss their effects on the distribution of sales between "mass-market" and "niche" products.[2] Finally, in Section 2.3, we complement the analysis of ratings and recommender systems by uncovering additional channels through which big data may generate network effects and other self-reinforcing processes on platforms.

2.1   Ratings and Reviews

Ratings and reviews are prevalent on digital platforms. Platforms acting as vertically integrated retailers (such as Amazon or JD) generally ask buyers to rate products or services and often give buyers the chance to write reviews. In such a case, we speak of *product ratings* and *product reviews*. For platforms that host buyers and sellers (such as Amazon Marketplace or Taobao Marketplace), users on either side are often asked to rate and comment on the counterparty to the transaction. These we call *seller* (or *buyer*) *ratings* and *reviews*.

---

[1] As we analyze it in Chapter 6, it also depends on the specific design chosen by the platforms.

[2] In Chapter 6, we investigate the incentives that platforms may have to reduce the informativeness of recommender systems. In general, this chapter focuses on platform decisions regarding rating and recommender systems under the presumption that they are done with the intent to improve the users' experience; potential conflicts with a platform's monetization incentives will be explored in detail in Chapter 6. Sections 2.1 and 2.2 closely follow Belleflamme and Peitz (2018a).

Before analyzing the economics of these two types of rating and review systems (2.1.2 and 2.1.3), we consider their significance for digital platforms. We argue that by responding to asymmetric information problems, ratings and reviews become an important source of network effects, which makes them instrumental in platforms' efforts to gain market shares (2.1.1). Finally, we question a crucial aspect of ratings and reviews for platform users – namely, their informativeness (2.1.4).

2.1.1   A Source of Network Effects

Asymmetric information problems are prominent on platforms that facilitate the trade of experience goods, as buyers typically have less information than sellers about the quality of the goods or services offered for sale.[3] Rating and review systems are instruments that platforms can use to address asymmetric information problems, as they facilitate the circulation of trade-relevant information among the parties.[4]

Importantly, rating and review systems become more effective instruments the larger the number of transactions that the platforms facilitate. Indeed, the ability of these systems to tackle information problems faced by buyers (and possibly sellers) increases with the volume, variety, and velocity of the data that platforms can collect about their users and the transactions they conduct.[5] As a result, ratings and reviews can be an important source of network effects: The more users that are active on a platform – and, thus, the more ratings and reviews that are available – the better-informed other users are prior to making their purchase decisions.

In what follows, we will clearly identify the various forms that these network effects can take. What we want to stress here is that, although users often have access to ratings and reviews whether or not they purchase on a particular platform, network effects tend to be "platform-specific" for a number of reasons.

(1) Some users may not consider purchasing on a platform different from the one on which they obtain information. In this case, even if a featured product is available on multiple platforms, it matters on which platform better information is available. For instance, in the early 2000s, buyers in the USA may have accessed ratings and reviews available on books at Amazon and then purchased the book from Barnes & Noble. However, as we discuss in this chapter, the positive sales effect of high ratings is more pronounced on the same platform than across platforms. This suggests that a substantial fraction of buyers took note of reviews and ratings only on the platform on which they terminated their purchase.

---

[3] We argue in Section 2.2 that asymmetric information problems may also apply to search goods. In this case, even if buyers can ascertain quality before purchase, they may lack information prior to investing time and effort to obtain relevant product information. Here, platforms can use ratings and reviews (on top of other instruments) to lower buyers' search costs and to improve the match between buyers and products/sellers.

[4] In Chapter 4, we examine other instruments that platforms can use, such as insurance, certification, guarantees, and warranties.

[5] The veracity of the data is also crucial, as we discuss in Section 2.1.4.

(2) When buyers rate sellers on a two-sided platform, a seller may (at least partially) condition its behavior on the distribution channel picked by the user. In this case, the seller's reputation is actually conditional on the transaction on a platform. For example, a hotel may be more accommodating to the wishes and requests of a guest who booked on a particular platform. To give another example, a seller may exert particular effort to speedy delivery of a product ordered through a particular platform.

(3) The identity of a seller may be platform-specific, or it may be costly for the user to identify the same seller across platforms. For instance, it may be difficult to verify that the seller name on eBay or Amazon Marketplace corresponds to the seller name on some other distribution channel. If this is the case, network effects are, by construction, platform-specific. For all these reasons, we can safely record the following finding:

LESSON 2.1   *Because they generate platform-specific network effects, rating and review systems fuel self-reinforcing mechanisms that, other things being equal, make successful platforms even more successful, at the expense of their smaller rivals.*

We now turn to an in-depth analysis of rating and review systems applied to products and services and to transaction counterparties.

2.1.2   Product Rating and Review Systems

Many online retailers have established rating and review systems (or "rating systems" for short) that allow buyers to rate and comment on particular products. Absent such a rating system, we would not classify an online retailer as a platform, since, given prices, a buyer's purchase intention would not be affected by other buyers' purchases. However, the presence of a rating system renders the retailer a platform, as it is a source of network effects, and its design affects the strength of network effects. We record this point in the following lesson, and we illustrate it through a simple model (which less mathematically oriented readers may prefer to skip).

LESSON 2.2   *Product rating systems have the potential to solve asymmetric information problems. In an e-commerce context in which buyers rate products, as more buyers on a platform make the average product rating more informative, a platform with a product rating system features positive within-group network effects among buyers.*

In other words, product rating systems can be the source of an attraction loop.

A simple model We consider a firm that carries products sourced at marginal cost c and sold at price p. Neither the firm nor the buyers know the quality of any product prior to consumption. What is known is that quality q may be either high ($q = H$) or low ($q = L$) with probability $1/2$, and that this probability is drawn independently across products. Buyer valuations for high and low quality (respectively, v_H and v_L) satisfy $v_H > c > v_L$ and $(v_H + v_L)/2 > c$. The first set of inequalities tells us that if information were complete, only high-quality products would be traded (as buyers value the low quality below its marginal cost). The second inequality tells us that when buyers are uninformed, trade will nevertheless take place, as the average valuation of a product is above the marginal cost.

Suppose that there are k buyers, who arrive in random order at each product. Each buyer is inclined to leave a review (if the firm provides a rating system) with some probability ρ, which is independent of the actual quality of a product. Furthermore, suppose that buyers perfectly observe product quality after purchase and report this quality truthfully if they write a review.

Absent a product rating system, a monopoly firm sets its price equal to the average valuation, $p = (v_H + v_L)/2$, and all buyers make a purchase. With a product rating system and under the assumption of a uniform price, the firm has to set the price such that buyers buy the product even when no review is available. This price is the same as without a rating system, as a buyer who does not observe any review is willing to pay up to the average valuation – that is, $(v_H + v_L)/2$.

At such a price, a buyer buys the product as long as no review of low quality has been posted (i.e., if either no review is available, or if only positive reviews are available). If the product is of high quality, regardless of the order in which buyers appear, there will be no negative review posted. If the product is of low quality, a buyer in position k encounters with probability $(1 - \rho)^{k-1}$ that none of the previous $k - 1$ buyers left a review. Thus, the overall probability that a buyer in a market with a total of n_b buyers does not see a negative review is $P_H + P_L$, where $P_H = 1/2$ is the probability that the product is of high quality (and it does not matter then whether or not buyers wrote a review), and $P_L = \sum_{k=0}^{n_b-1}(1 - \rho)^k/(2n_b) = [1 - (1 - \rho)^{n_b}]/(2\rho n_b)$ is the cumulative probability that none of the previous buyers left a review and the product is of low quality. Importantly, P_L decreases as the number of buyers, n_b, increases (it converges to 0 as n_b tends to infinity). The expected surplus of a buyer is then equal to $U^e = P_H(v_H - p) + P_L(v_L - p)$. As $p = (v_H + v_L)/2 > v_L$, it follows that $U^e = (P_H - P_L)(v_H - v_L)/2$, which is *increasing* in n_b. Thus, a platform with a product rating system is more informative the larger the number of buyers and, therefore, exhibits positive network effects.

Note that in this example, a monopoly firm makes a lower profit with a rating system, because it sells at the same price to fewer buyers. However, if buyer participation necessitates an up-front fixed cost for buyers, there is a hold-up problem absent a rating system. In this case, establishing a rating system limits the hold-up problem and, in equilibrium, may lead to higher profits, since the market would break down absent a rating system. In this case, a monopoly firm has the incentive to establish a rating system.

In the above example, the rating system generates positive within-group network effects. Does this imply that retailers with a rating system do not feature two-sidedness? In general, one- or two-sidedness is often a matter of the concrete circumstances. This is also the case with rating systems, as we now show with three simple models.

(1) Consider a stylized two-period setting in which some users simultaneously make purchase decisions in period 1, and other users simultaneously make purchase decisions in period 2. Suppose that a fraction of the former group posts a rating. Thus, period-2 buyers can make better-informed decisions, as the number of period-1 users increases. This means that due to the ratings system, there are positive cross-group network effects from period-1 users to period-2 users.

(2) Consider another stylized setting that features two types of buyers. For the first type, products are experience goods (quality is observed with some noise after purchase), and for the second type, they are credence goods (quality is not observed, even after consumption). Suppose that only users who get to know the quality of the product leave a rating (and do so truthfully). If users buy different products over time and base their decisions on average ratings, they benefit from a retailer attracting more type-1 buyers, as additional rankings allow for better-informed choices. Thus, there exist positive within-group network effects for type-1 buyers and positive cross-group network effects from type-1 to type-2 buyers. To the extent that type-1 buyers can draw on their own previous experience, informative ratings are less essential than for type-2 buyers, and, thus, the cross-group network effects generated by type-1 buyers are stronger than their within-group network effects.

(3) Consider now that, depending on the group a buyer belongs to, they leave reviews with different probabilities; let λ_j denote the review probability in group j. If n_j^i buyers of group j participate on platform i, the expected number of reviews on platform i is $m^i = \lambda_1 n_1^i + \lambda_2 n_2^i$. More reviews make a platform more attractive to buyers. This benefit can be captured by an increasing and concave function $f(m^i)$. In this setting, there are positive within-group network effects for each group of buyers. In addition, there are positive cross-group network effects between the two groups of different strength (if $\lambda_1 \neq \lambda_2$).

As just argued, rating systems help buyers make better-informed choices. With a rating system in place, the empirical prediction is that a more highly rated product should see its sales increase compared to a less highly rated product. To test this hypothesis, Chevalier and Mayzlin (2006) analyze the effect of book reviews on the sales patterns of the two leading online booksellers in the USA (at that point in time), Amazon and Barnes & Noble, which both offer buyers the opportunity to post book reviews on their site.[6] Using a "difference-in-differences" approach (i.e., they take differences between the relative sales of a book at the two retailers to control for possible effects of unobserved book characteristics on book sales and reviews), the

---

[6] For a deeper account of this paper, see Case 23.2 in Belleflamme and Peitz (2015).

authors show that an additional positive (respectively negative) report on Amazon leads to an increase (respectively decline) in sales at Amazon relative to the sales at Barnes & Noble.[7]

Interestingly, the study by Chevalier and Mayzlin (2006) shows that it is not just the number of reviews (or some summary statistics) that matters but also the length and content of the reviews. One interpretation is that buyers want to evaluate how much to trust a particular review or because there is uncertainty with respect to the fit of the match, which is buyer-specific. Case 2.1 reports three studies that point at other important aspects of reviews or of the way they are presented.

CASE 2.1 WHAT DETERMINES THE POWER OF REVIEWS?

Chintagunta, Gopinath, and Vekataraman (2010) analyze the link between box office performance of movies and review data from the Yahoo! Movies website (sixteen months of data from 2003 to 2005). Their identification strategy builds on the fact that movies are released sequentially across geographic markets and, thus, user reviews must stem from areas in which a movie has previously been released. They find that the composition of positive versus negative reviews and not the overall number of reviews drives box office performance.

Chakraborty, Deb, and Öry (2019) document that the rating behavior of users may depend on the type of service or service provider: Restaurant ratings on Yelp feature 40 percent negative reviews (one or two stars) for chain restaurants and 20 percent negative reviews for independent restaurants. Clearly, this may be due to chain restaurants suffering from more quality problems than independents. Chakarborty, Deb, and Öry advance a different explanation based on different distributions of prior beliefs. The motive for users to leave ratings is that they affect purchase and consumption decisions of future users. As they formally show, if prior beliefs are homogeneous, users tend to decide to give a review only after a negative experience. By contrast, if beliefs are heterogeneous, users are inclined to leave reviews also after positive experiences. This implies that in the former case only negative reviews will be made, while there will be a mix of positive and negative reviews in the latter case. If users hold homogeneous prior beliefs for chain restaurants but not for independent restaurants, this is consistent with the empirical observations.

Vana and Lambrecht (2019) use product review data from an UK online retailer. They identify the effect of the content of individual reviews, since the position at which reviews are placed is exogenous in their setting (placement by the date of being posted). When a new review appears, all existing reviews are shifted downward by one position. This shift occurs regardless of the content and rating of any review. As the authors show, the ratings of the first displayed reviews have a strong effect on purchase likelihood. In particular, if these reviews come with a high rating (four or five stars out of five), the estimated purchase probability increases significantly.

2.1.3   Seller Rating Systems

We now focus on rating systems of B2C and C2C platforms, which bring sellers and buyers together. Compared to online retailers, these platforms allow buyers not only to rate products (as discussed in the previous section) but also to

---

[7] There is also some evidence that an additional negative review is more powerful in decreasing book sales than an additional positive review is in increasing sales (measured by the sales rank).

rate sellers. This is simply because a particular product may be provided by multiple sellers.[8]

The key issue here is trust: Should buyers trust the quality claims that sellers make about their products and services on offer? In a bilateral relationship between buyers and sellers, such trust problems can be solved through repeated interaction. But in anonymous markets, alternative solutions need to be found. Rating and review systems (or "reputation systems") provide such an alternative: They serve as a substitute for personal experience by letting individual buyers draw on the collective experience of other buyers. Case 2.2 illustrates how a rating system makes the asymmetric information problem faced by occasional buyers less severe and, thus, serves as a partial substitute to reputation within a bilateral relationship.

CASE 2.2 RATINGS ON EACHNET: BEFORE AND AFTER

Some platforms started off without a rating system. For instance, the Chinese auction site EachNet operated initially (1999–2001) without such a system. A certain degree of bilateral trust between seller and buyer was established through communication between the two parties, which eventually led to a physical meeting. Thus, the buyer could inspect the product before paying and the seller could make sure that the buyer made the payment. While this does not resolve all asymmetric information problems ex ante, some of the most unpleasant surprises for buyer and seller could be avoided even without a rating and review system. In 2001, EachNet introduced a rating and review system. Cai et al. (2014) empirically investigate how a seller's "reputation" affects outcome, depending on whether a rating and review system is in place. A seller's reputation is approximated by the cumulative success rate of its listings. A seller's listing is successful if it led to at least one transaction. One may expect that if a buyer and a seller successfully complete a transaction, they may be more likely to interact again in the future. This may hold, in particular, for "reputed" sellers (i.e., those with a high cumulative success rate). Indeed, Cai et al. (2014) find a positive correlation between sellers' cumulative success rate and the fraction of repeat buyers. The important finding here is that this correlation weakens after the introduction of the rating system. This confirms our conjecture: EachNet's rating system has alleviated the asymmetric information problem faced by occasional buyers and has thus complemented the existing reputation of sellers within their bilateral relationship with buyers.

Rating systems can address adverse selection and moral hazard problems. Think, for instance, of Airbnb: Accommodations that suffer from some unexpected problems can be singled out by reviews and ratings. To the extent that these unexpected problems are inherent to the property, this reveals the quality of the accommodation and resolves adverse selection problems. Yet, unexpected problems can also arise if the seller decides not to exert effort; here, ratings and reviews can help to solve the associated moral hazard problem.[9]

---

[8] Apart from that, both types of platforms have a lot in common regarding ratings and reviews: They may use ratings as a full or partial substitute for active quality control; they also have to balance their reliance on user feedback and internal expertise.

[9] Many sellers plan to be active for a long term and have no or few returning buyers. Thus, sellers repeatedly face a moral hazard problem of the sort that if they provide effort, it is likely that consumers have a good experience. However, even with seller effort, there is some probability that a consumer will have a bad experience. Consumers can report their experience and the resulting rating may sustain seller effort. In such a context, a seller may have some private information about the

It is also important to stress that trust problems may also exist the other way round. To continue with the example of Airbnb, hosts (i.e., sellers) may have difficulties in entrusting guests (i.e., buyers) the task of taking good care of their flat; that is, moral hazard also exists on the buyer side. Hence, alongside one-sided rating systems, there also exist two-sided rating systems. For instance, Amazon Marketplace has a one-sided rating system according to which buyers rate sellers. In contrast, the initial eBay system was two-sided, and so are the systems of Airbnb and Uber. Here, each transaction partner can rate, and leave a review about, the partner on the other side.

As above, we argue that seller ratings generate various sorts of network effects. The network effects among buyers are quite similar to the ones generated by product reviews. What is novel here is that network effects also exist for sellers, though in less obvious ways.

Within-Group Network Effects on the Buyer Side

If reviews and ratings are noisy, a platform with few transactions per seller does not provide very reliable information. Given the number of sellers, the more buyers that are active on the platform, the more precise is the information on any seller, since the average valuation tends to converge on the true valuation. This suggests that there exist positive network effects on the buyer side – we will discuss and qualify this finding in the next section, as the informativeness of the ratings depends on their truthfulness.

For a given number of buyers, the rating system's informativeness tends to increase with the response rate of buyers. Here, the rating system may be designed to encourage buyers to leave a review or rating. Response rates may depend positively on the ease of use of the platform and on the community feeling that it creates. The platform may also provide nonmonetary or monetary incentives to leave reviews. As an example of the former, Tripadvisor awards a number of badges depending on review activity. Regarding the latter, Fradkin, Grewal, and Holtz (2017) ran a field experiment on Airbnb in which they provided monetary incentives for leaving reviews and showed that this can be effective. A seller reputation system may also suffer from low response rates by buyers who are afraid to rate a seller after a bad experience (more on this later in the chapter when we discuss the informativeness of ratings and reviews). In general, we can state the following lesson:

LESSON 2.3 *Seller rating systems have the potential to solve asymmetric information problems. In a buyer-seller context in which buyers rate sellers, as more buyers*

quality of the experience. As a limit case, the seller may observe the realized quality prior to offering a product or service for sale. A platform may offer sellers the opportunity to make quality claims when offering their products. As Jullien and Park (2019) show, (in the "best" equilibrium) the seller's claims will be truthful if the platform features a well-functioning rating system. Given such a rating system, allowing the seller to make quality claims improves on the outcome that resulted if the platform did not provide such a communication opportunity to the seller. More precisely, Jullien and Park (2019) consider a repeated moral hazard problem with cheap talk. Their key finding is that cheap-talk communication can help solve the seller's moral hazard problem. With cheap talk consumers can reward the seller's effort provision without delay.

on a platform make the rating system more informative, a platform with a rating system features positive within-group network effects on the buyer side.

In other words, seller rating systems can be the source of an attraction loop on the buyer side.

Network Effects on the Seller Side

We have just concluded that buyers positively affect one another by leaving reviews and ratings about sellers on two-sided platforms. But how are sellers affected? It seems clear that all sellers are not necessarily affected in the same way. For one, as rating systems alleviate hidden information problems, "good" sellers should benefit more than "bad" sellers (who should even suffer). But sellers also differ along other dimensions that determine how rating systems affect them, compared to alternative reputation mechanisms. We discuss these issues in turn.

Separate the Wheat from the Chaff

A number of empirical works have shown that more reputable sellers are more successful – that is, reputation pays. Reputable sellers may be able to ask for a premium and/or they may enjoy higher transaction volumes – in particular, they may also be able to successfully sell products that buyers a priori deem to be risky to buy.

Resnick et al. (2006) run a controlled field experiment to investigate the price premium of reputation: They sell a number of identical products (collectible postcards); some of them are randomly assigned to an established seller with a good record and some to a seller with little track record. They estimate an 8 percent price premium for a seller with 2,000 positive and one negative ratings, compared to a seller with ten positive and zero negative ones. Cabral and Hortacsu (2010) collect a large data set of seller histories on eBay. Unfortunately, they do not observe the number of a seller's past completed transactions and assume that the frequency of a seller's feedback is a good proxy for the frequency of actual transactions.[10] According to their estimates, a seller's weekly sales growth rate drops from a positive rate of 5 percent to a negative rate of 8 percent upon receiving their first negative rating.[11]

The introduction or redesign of a rating system may have an impact on the sellers' decision about whether to join a platform (and on the scale of its activities). For instance, if the rating system leads to better-informed buyers, low-quality sellers may abstain from participating. It might also affect the behavior of sellers beyond whether (and with what intensity) to participate. For instance, if a misrepresentation of product quality is punished through a negative rating that is easily observable to potential buyers, a seller may be more careful in drafting their announcements.

---

[10] This assumption may seem innocuous. However, as discussed below, buyers are likely to give reviews and ratings with different rates to different seller types.

[11] A potential drawback is that they do not include price effects, but they may actually be small. Other early empirical work on auction sites includes McDonald and Slawson (2002), Melnik and Alm (2002), Livingston (2005), and Jin and Kato (2006). For a summary of this and other work, see Bajari and Hortacsu (2004) and Tadelis (2016).

In short, a rating system may affect participation (and, thus, affect the amount of adverse selection), as well as behavior, given participation (and, thus, the degree to which the moral hazard problem plays out). Case 2.3 gives some indications along these lines.

CASE 2.3 THE IMPACTS OF THE REDESIGN OF EBAY'S RATING SYSTEM

Klein, Lambertz, and Stahl (2016) investigate the effects of eBay's redesign of its rating system in May 2008, when eBay introduced one-sided feedback that is not subject to retaliation and, thus, can be seen as more accurately reflecting a buyer's experience (we come back to the issue of retaliation later). Since, prior to that date, in May 2007, eBay introduced an anonymous detailed seller rating (DSR) on top of its rating system, Klein, Lambertz, and Stahl could use this DSR before and after the change to a one-sided rating system as a measure of buyer satisfaction. Buyers can give feedback through DSRs in four service dimensions at least partly under the control of the seller – namely, "item as described," "communication," "shipping time," and "shipping and handling charges" – by assigning one to five stars. The authors found a significant increase in buyer satisfaction with the introduction of the one-sided rating system, but did not observe a significant change in the sellers' exit rate. This can be seen as evidence that, in this instance, the redesign of the rating system was successful in reducing moral hazard but did not significantly affect the composition of sellers. In the case of eBay, this seems conceivable, as a low-quality product may find its buyer even if quality is revealed, since there may be a market for such low-quality products. The effect of the redesign of the rating system would then encourage truthful announcements by sellers but would not remove their incentive to participate. Using internal eBay data, Hui, Saeedi, and Sundaresan (2019) confirm the finding by Klein, Lambertz, and Stahl (2016) that low-quality sellers do not exit more often after the policy change. However, they sell fewer items, which implies that buyers obtain a higher quality on average.

To sum up, empirical studies confirm that seller rating systems generate cross-group network effects from buyers to sellers: The more buyers leave reviews and ratings, the more sellers are affected. It also appears that network effects differ along two important dimensions: the quality of the sellers ("good" or "bad") and the type of asymmetric information problem that ratings address (adverse selection/hidden information or moral hazard/hidden action), as stated in the next lesson:

LESSON 2.4 *In the case of hidden-information problems, sellers are affected differentially by seller rating systems: High-quality sellers enjoy a positive cross-group network effect from more buyers leaving ratings, while low-quality sellers suffer a negative cross-group network effect from more buyers leaving ratings. In the case of hidden-action problems, all sellers may benefit, as buyers understand that the system disciplines sellers.*

Seller Ratings in the Presence of Existing Reputation

When joining a two-sided platform, sellers may start out in quite different situations. Some sellers may have established a strong reputation, relying on a strong brand, while others may lack consumers trust. A rating system offers the latter a chance to overcome the asymmetric information problem.[12] Sellers without brand recognition

---

[12] If sellers of initially unknown quality arrive sequentially, meaning that new sellers have to decide
whether to enter and existing sellers whether to continue, then the optimal design of a rating system is

can then be expected to disproportionately benefit from rating systems. This may lower reputational barriers to entry for such sellers. This is indeed the finding by Hollenbeck (2017, 2018) in the context of hotel ratings. He finds that the revenue premium enjoyed by chain hotels over independent hotels has decreased over the period 2000–2015 with the increasing popularity of Tripadvisor and hotel booking portals.[13]

On the other hand, sellers who join a platform without an established "outside" reputation face a so-called cold start problem, as they have to start interacting with buyers without any past feedback. Li, Tadelis, and Zhou (2016) show how allowing sellers to reward buyers for leaving ratings may solve this problem, on top of offering any seller a way to signal high quality. They analyzed the impacts of Taobao's introduction, in May 2012, of the Rebate-for-Feedback (RFF) mechanism, whereby sellers were allowed to give rebates to buyers leaving an informative feedback after purchasing an item (Taobao used a machine learning algorithm to ensure the quality of feedback). Their empirical analysis establish that the introduction of RFF had three marked impacts. First, it was used as a signal of high quality, as high-quality sellers self-selected into choosing to use the RFF feature. Second, buyers understood correctly the signaling aspect of the RFF feature, as sellers increased by 30 percent the sales of the items exhibiting with this feature. Finally, the RFF feature appeared as a substitute to established reputation, as less experienced sellers were more likely to use it.[14]

In a similar vein, rating systems may also lead to a change in business models chosen by sellers. For instance, umbrella branding can be a strategy to build brand recognition and trust among consumers. A well-functioning rating system may remove the incentives to engage in such a branding strategy.

In the context of app stores, app developers often release new versions. A platform design decision is whether ratings from earlier versions are carried over to the new version. There are pros and cons from the perspective of providing information to app users. If the upgraded version may contain bugs, then a fresh start may be the design that is more informative to buyers. If, however, it is clear that the new version works at least as well as the old version (and is, therefore, a true upgrade), more information can be transmitted to buyers if app developers have at least the option to

intricate. This issue is analyzed by Vellodi (2019). If the rating system is fully transparent, buyers go for the highest-rated seller. This leads to low entry rates and to early exit of some high-quality firms. The welfare-maximizing platform design is not to provide fully transparent ratings (and, thus, to use obfuscation in the rating system) because, for dynamic reasons, the rating system has to provide incentives for high-quality firms to enter and remain active. To do so, the optimal rating system suppresses good reviews about highly rated firms, which is formally shown by Vellodi (2019).

[13] Hollenbeck, Moorthy, and Proserpio (2019) find that ratings and advertising are substitutes. In particular, they find that independent hotels react more strongly to negative reviews on Tripadvisor than chain hotels by increasing advertising spending. This is compatible with the view that brand recognition provides some protection against negative reviews.

[14] An RFF may also help to resolve the seller's moral hazard problem, as a lack of effort is more likely to be punished by buyers in the presence of RFF; see Li (2010) and Li and Xiao (2014). This applies to new and established sellers alike.

carry over the rating they gained with the old version to the new version; otherwise, at least highly rated app developers have an incentive to forego or postpone an upgrade so as to continue benefiting from their established reputation. Thus, if new versions do not perform worse than old versions, one should expect that at least highly rated apps (that obtain their reputation on the platform) will see less innovation than in the alternative system in which rating information is not lost from one app version to the next. This is indeed the finding of Leyden (2020) using data about Apple's App Store: From 2008 until 2017, rating information could not be carried over from one app version to the next; Apple changed its policy allowing app developers to choose whether to start fresh or to carry over the rating from the old version to the new.

Seller Ratings and Discrimination

Absent a rating system, in the presence of hidden information, users may rely on observables that are correlated with a hidden variable that drives quality. This may give rise to "statistical" or "nonstatistical" discrimination. For instance, in the sharing economy, users on one side may refuse to interact with users on the other side if the latter have observables that are seen in an unfavorable light.[15] For example, guests with African American names may be more likely to be rejected by landlords in the USA (for evidence, see Edelman, Luca, and Svirsky, 2017). To the extent that this is due to statistical discrimination, a good track record reflected by a very positive rating may solve the underlying asymmetric information problem. Also, in case of nonstatistical discrimination (i.e., if users assign biased probabilities depending on certain characteristics such as gender or ethnicity), a reputation system may mitigate such biases. In an empirical assessment of discrimination for long-distance carpooling on Blablacar, Lambin and Palikot (2018) find evidence that discrimination is less pronounced in the group of drivers with a good record than in the group of drivers who have not yet established a good record.

We record the previous findings in Lesson 2.5.

LESSON 2.5 *The cross-group network effect that buyers exert on seller by leaving ratings is more likely to be positive for sellers without an existing reputation or who may suffer from discrimination absent a rating system.*

2.1.4 The Informativeness of Ratings and Reviews

Rankings and reviews can be relevant for buyers only if they contain relevant information. Clearly, if they are informative about the (price-adjusted) quality of a product, buyers must, at least to some degree, have a common perception of the (price-adjusted) quality and must be able and willing to report their experiences with the product.

---

[15] If the former hold correct beliefs about the probability distribution of different subpopulation, discrimination may be called "statistical"; if they are based on wrong beliefs, they may be called "nonstatistical." The distinction becomes blurred when ex ante incentives to invest in certain skills are relevant, as biased perceptions (in either group of users) can become self-confirming prophecies.

We identify three sets of reasons why the informativeness of ratings and reviews may be limited due to decisions by buyers and sellers: (i) noisy ratings and reviews; (ii) strategically distorted ratings and reviews; and (iii) asymmetric herding behavior.[16] We discuss these reasons in turn, before examining how platforms can act to make rating systems more – or less – informative.

Noise

We describe here four reasons that buyers may leave noisy ratings and reviews: bad understanding, idiosyncratic tastes, uncontrollable shocks, and price variations.

Bad Understanding

Buyers may leave noisy ratings and reviews simply because they fail to understand what they are asked. While this is often easily identified after reading a review, buyers who rely on summary statistics may not be able to identify that ratings are based on irrelevant experiences. For instance, this applies to product ratings on Amazon. Here, some reviewers do not base their rating on the quality and characteristics of the product they bought but on such factors as Amazon's delivery service, which can be considered orthogonal to the product sold by Amazon. For example, the 2010 edition of our textbook *Industrial Organization: Markets and Strategies* received a five-star rating by one reviewer on Amazon.com with the following review: "It's my first time to buy used books. And it has definitely met my expectation. Well kept just few marks. Like it very much."[17] While we are happy that the reviewer gave a five-star rating, we are not so sure if this actually reflects their quality assessment of the book rather than the physical appearance of the used copy.

Idiosyncratic Tastes

Ratings may also be noisy for potential buyers because of idiosyncratic tastes. While rating systems are supposed to capture the quality of a product or seller, reviewers may comment on horizontal characteristics or on vertical characteristics for which they have heterogeneous willingness to pay. In other words, ratings that aggregate tastes of other buyers may not strongly correlate with one's own taste. For instance, a reviewer may give a negative product rating because they do not like the color of the product, but other potential buyers may not share this negative feeling.

Uncontrollable Shocks

Similarly, there may be shocks that are not under the seller's control. If a reviewer leaves a negative seller rating because of late delivery, this may not have been under the seller's control if, say, the transport company did not deliver in time. One would expect that such shocks to product and service satisfaction wash out if there are a

---

[16] For other overviews, see Aral (2001) and Tadelis (2016).

[17] As Tadelis (2016, p. 328) notes, confusion is likely with multiple review targets: "Multiple review targets may create an inference problem that confuses between the seller's quality of executing the sale and the quality of the product."

large number of reviewers. Thus, the informativeness increases with the number of fellow users, a source of the network effects mentioned above. Shocks may affect the experience of a consumer and, thus, the review, as in the above example. Reviews may also reflect the mood a consumer experiences when considering whether to write a review. For example, being in a bad mood on a particular day may affect the probability and content of reviews.[18] As the reviewers' mood is random, the informativeness of ratings and "average" reviews increases with the number of fellow users.

Price Variations

Product and seller reviews are often likely to be based on how satisfied a buyer is when taking into account how much they paid.[19] However, products may be sold at different prices over time and space. Thus, what looks like a rather bad deal at a high price may be a good deal at a low price. Therefore, with price variation (over time and space), the informativeness of ratings suffers. This is clearly an issue for products or services featuring price dispersion.

Strategic Distortions by Buyers or Sellers

Buyers or sellers may take actions that systematically distort seller or product ratings. Clearly, since sellers benefit from a positive reputation, they may pay others to leave positive reviews and ratings about their offers; they may also pay others to leave negative reviews about the offers of close competitors. First, we examine such "fake reviews," and then we consider the specific problems that may emerge from "two-sided rating systems," in which both counterparties to a transaction are invited to rate one another.

Fake Reviews

The unsuspecting reader may think that fake reviews are an issue cooked up by economists who believe in incentive theory (and, in particular, moral hazard). However, there is evidence that fake reviews are widespread and that markets for such fake reviews have been created (see, e.g., Xu et al., 2015, and He, Hollenbeck, and Proserpio, 2021).[20] Generating such fake reviews is costly. Costs and benefits from

---

[18] Brandes and Dover (2018) provide evidence that weather conditions in the review phase affect the review probability and content of consumers who stayed in a hotel booked through a hotel booking platform. In particular, they find that rainy weather increases the likelihood of providing a review and decreases the rating of a hotel that accompanies such a review.

[19] For an empirical investigation on the effect of price on restaurant rating on Yelp, see Luca and Reshef (2020).

[20] He et al. (2021) study the use of fake reviews on Amazon that are sold by reviewers in private Facebook groups who are then paid via PayPal. They find that products' average ratings fall after firms stop buying fake reviews. They see this as evidence that fake reviews are mostly used for low-quality products. Since fake reviews are costly to generate, a more benign view of the use of positive, paid-for reviews and ratings is that they can be seen as a seller's costly advertising and may be used as a signal of high quality – on the theory of advertising as a quality signal, see Nelson (1974), Kihlstrom and Riordan (1984), and Milgrom and Roberts (1986). For an empirical analysis of Taobao facilitating such signaling, we refer again to Li, Tadelis, and Zhou (2016).

fake reviews depend on the particular site. As Ott, Cardie, and Hancock (2012) argue in the case of hotels, the costs of a fake review are high if a user is required to purchase a product prior to reviewing it. For instance, hotel booking platforms Booking and Expedia require an actual purchase, whereas Tripadvisor (which, as a referral website, does not monitor transactions) allows anyone who claims to have made a booking to post reviews about a hotel. Thus, fake reviews are more costly on Booking and Expedia than on Tripadvisor. A number of firms also offer sellers the purchase of positive reviews, as illustrated in Case 2.4.

CASE 2.4 BUYING POSITIVE REVIEWS

In 2019, Fivestar Marketing posts the following prices for a review in Germany: on Google 12.95 Euro; on Tripadvisor 14.95 Euro; and on Amazon 22.95 Euro.[21] Fivestar Marketing operates as a two-sided platform where sellers buy reviews on one side and reviewers are paid for their service on the other side. The vacation portal HolidayCheck has sued Fivestar Marketing because it claims that it can show that reviewers did not stay in the hotels that received the reviews. In a related earlier case, Amazon sued a seller of positive reviews. The court decided in favor of Amazon and prohibited the publication of purchased product reviews unless it is explicitly mentioned that these reviews were purchased (here presumably the reviewer tested the product for review).[22]

The expected benefit of a purchase review depends on the attention that a particular review attracts. Everything else being given, the expected benefit is greater on a website with many visitors but smaller on a website with many other reviews. Hence, in an environment in which the ratio of reviews to traffic is the same across websites, it is not clear on which website the expected benefit is the largest. We note that posting a fake review on a website with a quickly growing visitor base and a small stock of reviews is particularly attractive. Instead of buying positive fake reviews for itself, a seller may prefer to buy negative fake reviews about competing sellers; this makes consumers more likely not to visit the competitor. Some of that lost attention may be captured by the seller paying for the fake review. Incumbent sellers may have invested quite some effort which may be undermined by copycats buying fake negative reviews. If these incumbent sellers operate on a shoestring, they may be pushed out of the market.[23] This undermines ex ante incentives for sellers on the platform. If the problem becomes widespread on the whole platform, this also undermines the attractiveness of the platform itself. This suggests that newcomer platforms must think hard about how to design their rating system right from the start.

---

[21] See https://fivestar-marketing.net/bewertungen/

[22] See press release by OLG Frankfurt on March 5, 2019, "Amazon kann sich gegen 'gekaufte' Produktbewertungen wehren" ("Amazon can defend itself against 'bought' product reviews"), available at https://ordentliche-gerichtsbarkeit.hessen.de/pressemitteilungen.

[23] Some sellers did so on Amazon Marketplace, as reported by James Clayton, "Amazon's murky world of one-star reviews," BBC News, September 7, 2020: www.bbc.com/news/technology-54063039.

Even powerful platforms such as Amazon are reported to have difficulties removing fake negative reviews effectively. As for providing systematic evidence on the extent of fake reviews, it is obviously hard (because actual fakes are difficult to spot) but not impossible, as laid out in Case 2.5.

CASE 2.5 EXPEDIA, TRIPADVISOR, AND FAKE REVIEWS

To estimate the extent of fake reviews, Mayzlin, Dover, and Chevalier (2014) exploit different policies by hotel information and booking sites about who can leave feedback: Expedia requires the reviewer to have booked a hotel on its site, while Tripadvisor does not (as it only refers to booking sites). Thus, we would expect to see more fake reviews on Tripadvisor. Consider a geographic area in which hotels compete for business travelers. It is in the strategic interest of any hotel in this area to improve its ranking relative to that of competing hotels in the same area. A hotel can achieve this by inflating its own rating with fake positive reviews and by deflating the rating of hotels in its vicinity with fake negative reviews.

Mayzlin, Dover, and Chevalier argue that independent hotels are more likely to sponsor fake reviews, as their cost from being detected is less severe than if such a review was sponsored by a hotel belonging to a chain. Thus, the prediction is that hotels in the vicinity of such independent hotels have more negative reviews on Tripadvisor relative to Expedia, and independent hotels have more positive reviews on Tripadvisor relative to Expedia. These predictions are confirmed in their data set. And fake reviews are not unique to hotels; for instance, Luca and Zervas (2016) analyze fake restaurant reviews on Yelp.

Platforms have responded to these issues by trying to detect fake reviews, remove them, and punish the party responsible for the fake reviews. In the case of negative reviews posted on competitors' sites, it is clearly harder to find the responsible party, but the presumption is that a positive fake review stems from the party offering a particular product or service. For instance, hotels have an interest in improving their ratings on a hotel booking platform and sellers have an incentive to improve their ratings on Amazon or eBay. If a hotel or seller pays for a positive review, there is the risk that this reduces the informativeness of the rating system. Amazon uses text recognition software trying to spot suspicious reviews on its marketplace. It may punish suspicious sellers by removing them from the platform. This arguably reduces the incentive of sellers to pay for positive fake reviews, as sellers critically rely on Amazon to connect to buyers. However, Amazon's policy opens the door for competitors to harm a successful seller. Instead of paying for fake negative reviews about this seller, they may now pay for fake positive reviews. While it is rather costly to generate *credible* fake positive reviews, it is rather cheap to generate *suspicious* fake positive reviews. Such suspicious fake positive reviews are easily detected by the platform. If it then attributes these fake reviews to the successful seller, it may drop this seller from the platform to the benefit of the seller's competitors. As documented in Dzieza (2018), this appears to be the strategy chosen by some ruthless competitors.

One might suspect that a welfare-maximizing platform would engage in costly activities to improve the precision of the rating system. However, it does so only up to a point. Obviously, when improving the precision (e.g., by removing erroneous or false reviews and ratings) the platform compares expected welfare gains to the effort cost. Even if the effort cost were zero, a welfare-maximizing platform may allow for some buying of reviews so as to encourage users to try out new and untested products. In other words, the rating system may be made less informative to encourage users to engage in experimentation, which, with a more informative system, would be privately not optimal for any given user.[24]

Two-Sided Rating Systems

Problems of systematic misrepresentation and, possibly, underreporting of negative experiences may arise with two-sided rating systems in which both buyer and seller leave feedback. Such two-sided ratings appear to be desirable if both parties have private information and/or choose private actions. In its early days, eBay used a two-sided system, arguably because sellers would like to know which buyers to trust. In particular, a buyer may place the highest bid but then refuse to make the promised payment. With developments in electronic payments, this risk for the seller could be eliminated. This has removed the main reason to use two-sided ratings on eBay. Although two-sided rating systems do not necessarily distort ratings, Case 2.6 shows that the past system on eBay did.

CASE 2.6 THE PROBLEMS WITH THE "OLD" EBAY RATING SYSTEM

The eBay rating system had the design feature that buyers and sellers had a time window during which they could leave feedback. When one party left feedback, it was disclosed to the other party. This opened up the possibility of retaliation for a negative rating. Bolton, Greiner, and Ockenfels (2013) analyze rating behavior on the old eBay and document that the two ratings in buyer-seller pairs are highly positively correlated. They also document that sellers typically wait for the buyer to leave a rating and respond promptly. This supports the view that sellers use their feedback as an implicit threat to leave a negative rating if they receive a negative one. This makes it more painful for buyers to give negative ratings and, effectively, distorts the distribution of ratings received by sellers.[25] Indeed, as Nosko and Tadelis (2015) report, using internal eBay data, a buyer is three times more likely to complain to eBay's customer service than to give a negative rating. This suggests a severe underreporting of negative experiences. As mentioned above, eBay eventually switched to a one-sided rating system.

Other platforms continue to employ two-sided rating systems. This applies, in particular, to platforms in the sharing economy because here, not only the payment, but also the way a buyer uses a product, matter to the seller. For instance, somebody renting out an apartment on Airbnb may worry about whether the renter will create a mess or damage some furniture. This is why Airbnb has a two-sided rating system.[26] Initially, reviews were immediately made public, allowing the possibility of retaliation. Fradkin, Grewal, and Holtz (2017) run field experiments and find that

---

[24] Che and Hörner (2018, section V) propose a formal model with public recommendations in which the welfare-maximizing platform received a signal about the quality of the new product and encourages some users to experiment even when the platform received a bad signal.

[25] There is, of course, an easy way for the platform to avoid such retaliation possibilities: Ratings may be disclosed only after the other party has provided the rating, or the time window to leave ratings has closed.

[26] For descriptive statistics on Airbnb's rating system, see Zervas, Proserpio, and Byers (2015).

those who do not provide reviews tend to have worse experiences than those who do. They conclude that strategic reviewing behavior has occurred on Airbnb, although the overall bias appears to be small. Also, since buyer and seller may interact socially, they may be less inclined to leave negative reviews.

Airbnb no longer makes reviews public as long as the counterparty still has the option of posting a review and has not yet done so. While one party does not observe the counterparty's review prior to uploading their own review, there remain reasons for strategically underreporting negative experiences (in addition to the social interaction reason given above). Reviews are not anonymized, so somebody who rents out a flat can check the track record of somebody wanting to rent the flat. If that person tends to leave negative reviews, a future landlord may be less inclined to confirm the request. Anticipating this, the potential renter may be less harsh and leave positively biased reviews or no review at all.

A platform has various design options that affect the response rate and the informativeness of review and rating systems. For our purposes, we summarize the insights obtained so far by the following finding.

LESSON 2.6   *Rating systems may suffer from a lack of informativeness due to noise and bias introduced through the actions of buyers and sellers. In particular, platform users may game the system. This tends to reduce the strength of network effects.*

Asymmetric Herding Behavior

A tendency to provide positive feedback, but to refrain from providing negative feedback, does not necessarily arise due to strategic considerations or independent mistakes by reviewers. It may also be the result of asymmetric herding behavior. Muchnik, Aral, and Taylor (2013) conduct a randomized field experiment with fake ratings of comments on posted articles on a news website and analyze the dynamics of future feedback. They observe an asymmetric response to a fake positive rating compared to a fake negative rating. They find that a fake positive rating increases the probability of accumulating positive herding by 25 percent. While a fake negative rating also increases subsequent negative votes, this was neutralized by offsetting positive votes. Thus, there is herding on positive but not on negative ratings – Muchnik, Aral, and Taylor call this a "social influence bias."

These results were obtained in a news setting and not in shopping contexts, but they are suggestive of reviewer behavior also in the latter contexts. This suggests that paid-for fake positive reviews can generate positive herding on B2C and C2C platforms. Thus, the damage done from a positive fake review would not be corrected if the fake report were not removed immediately but at some later time (see Aral, 2001). As pointed out, there are other reasons that ratings and reviews do not provide accurate information. This may also give rise to long-term effects thanks to herding. Further issues arise in platform design by a for-profit platform – this is analyzed in Chapter 6.

2.2   Recommendations

As we discussed in the previous section, buyers can obtain valuable information from reviews and ratings by other buyers. In this case, the role of the platform is twofold: First, it invites buyers to evaluate various offers that have proved successful or popular with others; second, it organizes the exchange of the information across users (possibly combined with some policing so as to ensure that abuses are contained and mistakes are corrected). Since buyers actively provide and access the information, we may consider ratings and reviews as part of a platform's *information-pull* strategy.

In this section, we examine an alternative strategy of platforms, which consists of making recommendations to specific buyers. Such recommendations, based on popularity and on other sources of information, are an attempt to reduce search costs. Hence, platforms pursue an *information-push* strategy, as they advertise specific products to buyers based on their characteristics and observed behavior. Naturally, information pull-and-push strategies are not mutually exclusive – quite the contrary, as ratings and reviews often serve as inputs for recommendation algorithms. For instance, Amazon makes product suggestions, and buyers then access additional information before making their purchase decision.

In what follows, we first analyze how recommender systems (in a similar way as rating systems) generate network effects (2.2.1). Second, we examine how recommender systems affect the distribution of sales (2.2.2): Do they contribute to making popular products even more popular, or do they drive consumers to discover niche products?

2.2.1   Product Recommender Systems and Popular Products

We argue here that product recommender systems are the source of positive network effects. This insight is easily established when buyers have homogeneous tastes and make mistakes, and the recommender system is based on the popularity of a product – this is the issue we consider here. Suppose that there are two products that can be ranked by their attractiveness. Product A is more attractive than product B; more specifically, suppose that product A gives a net benefit of 1 and product B of -1. Consumers arrive sequentially and can be of two types: "amateur" or "expert." An amateur consumer bases their decision on popularity, while an expert consumer acquires information about product features and makes a purchase based on that information.

To construct a numerical example, suppose that 50 percent of buyers follow a recommendation if they receive one and otherwise do not buy, while the remaining 50 percent collect information and, with 80 percent probability, make the right choice – that is, with 20 percent probability, they erroneously choose the inferior product. The recommender system recommends the product that is purchased more. We will show that the last buyer is better off if there are more fellow buyers. Let us start with two buyers. If buyer 2 is an amateur, they make an expected benefit $0.5(0.8 - 0.2) = 0.3$,

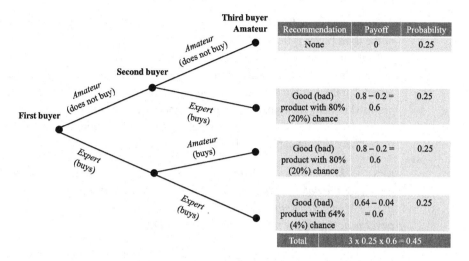

First buyer

Second buyer

Third buyer

Recommendation	Payoff	Probability
None	0	0.25
Good (bad) product with 80% (20%) chance	0.8 − 0.2 = 0.6	0.25
Good (bad) product with 80% (20%) chance	0.8 − 0.2 = 0.6	0.25
Good (bad) product with 64% (4%) chance	0.64 − 0.04 = 0.6	0.25
Total	3 x 0.25 x 0.6 = 0.45	

Figure 2.1 Recommender systems and network effects – a numerical example

as, with 50 percent probability, buyer 1 was an expert – i.e., buyer 1 purchased and, thus, indirectly recommended the "good" product with 80 percent probability and the "bad" product with 20 percent probability. If buyer 2 is an expert, they make an expected benefit of $0.8 - 0.2 = 0.6$. Hence, the expected benefit of buyer 2 is 0.45 (i.e., the average of 0.3 and 0.6, as they have equal chances of being either type).

Now consider the case with three buyers. If the third buyer is an expert, their expected benefit continues to be 0.6 as the recommender system has no influence on their decision. If the third buyer is an amateur, they purchase only if the recommender system points them to the most popular product. For this to happen, the two previous buyers must have purchased one product more than the other. Let us examine when this does and does not happen. Four cases have to be distinguished according to the type of the successive buyers; each case has the same probability of occurrence – and thus 25 percent (see Figure 2.1 for a depiction of these four cases). The first case is the succession of two amateurs: As neither of them purchased, the recommender system remains silent, and the third buyer does not purchase either, yielding them a benefit of zero. Second, if the first buyer is an amateur (who, therefore, did not purchase) and the second is an expert, then the system recommends the good product with an 80 percent probability, and the bad product with a 20 percent probability, yielding the third buyer an expected benefit of $0.8 - 0.2 = 0.6$. Third, if the first buyer is an expert and the second an amateur, the configuration is similar to the previous one (as the second buyer follows the recommendation resulting from the first buyer's purchase decision); the expected benefit of the third buyer is again equal to 0.6. Finally, if there is a succession of two experts, both must have made the same choice for the recommender system to be informative (and so for the third buyer to purchase); this is so if they both decide to buy the good product (with 64 percent probability) or the bad product (with 4 percent probability); the third buyer's benefit in this case is then equal to $0.64 - 0.04 = 0.6$. In sum, if the third buyer is an amateur, their expected benefit is $0.25 \times 0 + 3 \times 0.25 \times 0.6 = 0.45$. Hence, the expected benefit of the third buyer is $0.5 \times 0.6 + 0.5 \times 0.45 = 0.525$.

Comparing the two cases, we observe that the last of three buyers has a larger expected benefit (0.525) than the last of two buyers (0.45). Hence, we have established that the last buyer benefits if more previous buyers are around and that buyers, prior to knowing their position in the sequence, are also better off if more fellow buyers are present. In this example, amateurs benefit from more buyers, as it becomes more likely that an expert has been around previously.

LESSON 2.7   *By recommending more-popular products, product recommender systems have the potential to provide purchase-relevant information to amateur buyers. In an e-commerce context, they have the potential to generate network effects, as a buyer is better off the more fellow buyers that are around.*

A platform may have information that a new product is of high quality (good signal) or it may not be sure, in which case users would need to experiment to generate information (bad signal). The platform may then recommend the new product instead of an established product with intermediate uniform quality to some users; that is, it occasionally spams users by recommending a product after receiving a bad signal. By doing so, it encourages user experimentation which generates learning externalities.[27]

A recommender system may also help to reduce the search cost. Suppose that there are several products, some of which are considered clear failures and a few that can be considered serious options. Absent recommendations based on popularity, a consumer may have to inspect quite a large number of products. With such recommendations, the consumer can restrict their search to the subset of serious options and, thus, reduce their expected search costs.

LESSON 2.8   *Product recommender systems have the potential to reduce search costs. In an e-commerce context, they have the potential to generate network effects, as a larger number of buyers provides more reliable information about which products are serious options.*

If some consumers are frequent shoppers, while others buy only occasionally, the former make larger contributions to the functioning of the recommender system than the latter. As an illustration, suppose that frequent shoppers buy several products from a large set, whereas occasional buyers buy only one. The shopping behavior of frequent buyers allows the recommendation system to help other frequent shoppers to more easily find other products of interest. Thus, the recommender system generates positive within-group network effects among frequent shoppers.

---

[27] Che and Hörner (2018) characterize the dynamics of spamming. In the welfare maximum, the platform uses spamming very cautiously immediately after a product is released, gradually increases its frequency, and stops it completely when it has become sufficiently pessimistic about the product quality. As they show, such private recommendations lead to a welfare-superior outcome compared to public recommendation that may take the form of a rating system.

If the recommender system can access additional information on occasional shoppers (e.g., that they are close to certain frequent shoppers in a friendship network), information gathered on frequent shoppers may also allow for useful recommendations to casual shoppers. In this case, there is a positive cross-group network effect from frequent shoppers to occasional shoppers. By contrast, information on purchase decisions by occasional shoppers is of little or no help in making better recommendations to other shoppers. More generally, not only the total number of users but the composition of the recommendation network matter for the functioning of the recommender system.

Recommender systems can also be important on *two-sided* platforms. Here, the platform can make recommendations to both sides with the aims of reducing search costs and improving expected match quality. These recommendations may be based not only on observables of the two individual users on either side but also on the behavior of other users on both sides.

LESSON 2.9   *Partner recommender systems have the potential to reduce search costs. In a two-group matching context, they have the potential to generate positive cross-group network effects, as more participation by one group generates the chance for the platform to propose matches that are more attractive for members of the other group, and vice versa.*

We note that while both sides tend to benefit from such cross-group external effects, the benefits may vary depending on the terms of transaction between users on both sides. These terms of transaction for a particular user may also depend on participation levels on the same side. For instance, if buyers for collectibles receive better recommendations, they may drive up the price and, thus, receive a smaller fraction of the generated surplus.

Some platforms operate recommender systems that provide the same recommendations to all users and help them in finding high-quality content. An example are news aggregators that recommend media content from different news providers depending on the content categories. Absent a news aggregator, users have to choose a media outlet that best fits their taste and then consume low- and high-quality content from this outlet. The role of the news aggregator is to always recommend the high-quality content in case one of the outlets provides high-quality, while the other does not. This makes the news aggregator attractive at least to those users who do not hold strong views about which media outlet they prefer if the quality were the same. Thus, these users go to the news aggregator and those that hold strong views about the outlets bypass the news aggregator. If outlets' revenues depend on quality provision, the presence of a news aggregator affects the media outlets' incentives of quality provision. As Jeon and Nasr (2016) show in a specific setting, media outlets may specialize their high-quality provision, average quality on each media outlet may go up, and all users may benefit from the presence of a news aggregator.[28]

---

[28] Jeon and Nasr (2016) postulate that there is a continuum of content categories with content located at the extreme points of the Hotelling line. Users obtain content for free and outlets monetize through

Adding users here affects the average quality available on the aggregator compared to the one available on a media outlet. Thus, there may be an attraction spiral that operates through higher quality provided by the media outlets.

2.2.2   Product Recommender Systems and the Long Tail

In many internet markets, a limited number of items (often a few hundred) account for the bulk of sales, while the vast majority of items (which constitute the tail of the distribution) sell only very few units. It has been argued that internet markets have a longer tail in the sales distribution than traditional markets.[29] The question we address in this section is how recommender systems affect the distribution of sales: Do they reinforce the skewness of the distribution, or do they make the tail longer, or thicker? We first discuss the main effects that recommender systems can have; next, we review recent empirical work.

Heterogeneous Tastes and Recommendations

Buyers often do not have homogeneous tastes. However, a recommender system reporting only the popularity of different products may provide useful information even to buyers who have strong tastes for specific products. In particular, some buyers may be aware that they have a taste for niche products in a certain product category, whereas others may realize their preference for the standard products that cater to the taste of the mass market. Consider a recommender systems based on popularity information – that is, information displaying in relative terms how often a product has been purchased. As a fictional example, consider a supermarket selling different types of cheese and providing popularity information. If you are new to the store and know that you like to avoid unpleasant surprises, you may opt for the popular cheese varieties. However, if you know that you like new taste experiences, you may opt for cheese varieties that are bought less frequently. In such a situation, the fact that a product has or has not been sold often provides valuable information to new buyers. A buyer with a niche taste may buy products that sold little in the past, whereas a buyer with a mass-market taste will purchase products that sold a lot in the past.

In practice, buyers may encounter products with mass or niche appeal and, in addition, suffer from not being able to judge product quality ex ante. It may then appear to be difficult to disentangle popularity information as a proxy for quality from popularity information as an indication of whether a product is a mass-market product – one that provides a good fit to the taste of many buyers – or a niche market product – one that provides a good fit to the taste of only few buyers.

There are two borderline cases. In the first, all buyers have the same taste and care only about quality. High quality proves to be more "popular" and accounts for a larger volume of sales if some consumers are informed about the product quality

---

advertising. To give incentives for costly high-quality content, it is assumed that high-quality content generates higher ad revenues than low-quality content. For a short formal presentation of the analysis of Jeon and Nasr (2016), see Peitz and Reisinger (2016).

[29] For an informal account, see Anderson (2006).

and buy only high quality, whereas others are not and, thus, have to randomize over several products of different qualities. Higher quality, then, turns out to be more popular. To resolve the asymmetric information problem, a platform may want to resort to a rating system, as analyzed in the previous section. Thus, the effect of such a rating system is to divert demand from a low-quality product to a high-quality product. In the other borderline case, buyers are uncertain only about whether the product better serves the mass or the niche market, leading to this outcome.

A different situation arises if buyers observe whether a product is meant to cater to the mass or to the niche market, but they do not observe the product quality. To address the role of popularity information in guiding buyer behavior in such a situation, we present a simple model in which firm behavior is treated as exogenous – in particular, the prices of all products are fixed.[30] As we will show, in such a scenario – in which consumers know in advance whether some product features fit their taste but are not fully informed about a quality dimension of the product – a recommender system reporting the popularity of a product may also provide valuable information to consumers. Tucker and Zhang (2011) provide support for this theory in a field experiment. A website that lists wedding service vendors switched from an alphabetical listing to a popularity-based ranking in which offers are ranked by the number of clicks the vendor receives. The authors measure vendors when located in towns with a large population as having broad appeal and when located in small towns as having narrow appeal. Tucker and Zhang find strong evidence that narrow-appeal vendors receive more clicks than broad-appeal vendors when ranked similarly in the popularity-based ranking.

We record these findings in the following lesson. We then provide a more detailed account of the model, which less mathematically oriented readers may want to skip.

LESSON 2.10   *Product recommender systems reporting product popularity may affect mass-market and niche products differently. Given a similar ranking, niche products tend to do relatively better with such a recommender system.*

The model goes as follows. Suppose that consumers face a choice problem of buying one unit of two products offered by two different sellers; they may buy none, one, or both. Prices are fixed throughout the analysis. With probability $\lambda > 1/2$, a consumer thinks more highly of product 1 than of product 2; consequently, product 1 can be called a mass-market product and product 2 a niche product. Each product can also be of high or low quality with equal probability.

The consumer's utility depends both on the quality of the product and on whether the product matches their taste. A high-quality product that provides the wrong match is assumed to give net utility $v_H = 1$ and a low-quality product, $v_L = 0$. A product with the right match gives the previous net utilities augmented by t. These utilities are gross of the opportunity cost z that a consumer incurs when

---

[30]   The model exposition is, in large part, identical to the one in Belleflamme and Peitz (2015, chapter 15). It is based on Tucker and Zhang (2011).

visiting a seller (e.g., clicking onto its website). A consumer knows their match value and receives a noisy private signal about quality. The noisy quality signal may come from noisy information in the public domain, such as publicly revealed tests. The ex ante probability of high quality is assumed to be $1/2$. The probability that the signal provides the correct information is ρ, which, for the signal to be informative but noisy, lies between $1/2$ and 1. Hence, with a positive signal realization, the posterior belief that the product is of high quality is ρ. It follows that if a consumer who prefers product i receives a high-quality signal and buys from seller j, they obtain expected utility $U_{Hg} \equiv \rho + t - z$ if $i = j$ (i.e., if seller j offers the product that matches consumer i's taste), and $U_{Hb} \equiv \rho - z$ if $i \neq j$. Correspondingly, with a low-quality signal, expected utility is $U_{Lg} \equiv (1-\rho) + t - z$ if $i = j$ and $U_{Lb} \equiv (1-\rho) - z$ if $i \neq j$. Table 2.1 displays the four possible levels of expected utility.

Table 2.1 Expected utility according to signal and match

	Good match	Bad match
High-quality signal	$U_{Hg} \equiv \rho + t - z$	$U_{Hb} \equiv \rho - z$
Low-quality signal	$U_{Lg} \equiv (1-\rho) + t - z$	$U_{Lb} \equiv (1-\rho) - z$

For a given match, $\rho > 1/2$ implies that the consumer is better off with a high-quality signal: $U_{Hk} > U_{Bk}$ for $k = g, b$. Also, for a given signal, $t > 0$ implies that the consumer prefers to have a good match: $U_{Kg} > U_{Kb}$ for $K = H, L$. What is unclear is how the consumer balances the quality of the match with the quality of the signal. The consumer finds the quality of the match more important if $U_{Lg} > U_{Hb}$, which means that they are better off with a low-quality signal and a good match than with a high-quality signal and a bad match. This is so if $1 + t > 2\rho$. Otherwise, the quality of the signal outweighs the quality of the match.

We first consider the product choice of a single buyer – this is the situation encountered by buyers when no recommender system is available. A buyer purchases the product independently of the signal realization and match value if $U_{Lb} > 0$; that is, the opportunity cost of visiting a seller is sufficiently small, $z < z_{Lb} \equiv 1 - \rho$. By contrast, if the opportunity cost is too large, the consumer will never buy. This is the case if $U_{Hg} < 0$, or, equivalently, if $z > z_{Hg} \equiv \rho + t$. Hence, we focus on the intermediate range where $z \in [z_{Lb}, z_{Hg}]$. A product with a good match but a low-quality signal is bought if $U_{Lg} \geq 0$, or, equivalently, if $z \leq z_{Lg} \equiv 1 - \rho + t$. A product with a bad match but a high-quality signal is bought if $U_{Hb} \geq 0$ or $z \leq z_{Hb} \equiv \rho$.

As indicated above, two scenarios are possible. In the first scenario, the buyer sees the quality of the match as more important; the inequality $U_{Lg} > U_{Hb}$ is equivalent to $z_{Lg} > z_{Hb}$, which becomes $1 + t > 2\rho$. Thus, for this scenario to apply, consumer tastes must be sufficiently heterogeneous (t large) and signals sufficiently noisy (ρ small). In the second scenario, the quality of the signal matters more; we have $U_{Lg} < U_{Hb}$, or, equivalently, $z_{Lg} < z_{Hb}$. Thus, for this scenario to apply, consumer tastes must be sufficiently homogeneous (t small) and signals sufficiently informative (ρ large). Consumer choice can be fully described depending on whether $z_{Lg} > z_{Hb}$ or the reverse inequality holds. For $z_{Lg} > z_{Hb}$, we obtain that a product is bought by a consumer who does not observe a low-quality signal and a bad match if $z \in (z_{Lb}, z_{Hb})$; it is bought by a consumer who observes a good match if $z \in (z_{Hb}, z_{Lg})$; and it is bought by a consumer who observes a good match and a high-quality signal if $z \in (z_{Lg}, z_{Hg})$. For $z_{Lg} < z_{Hb}$, we obtain that a product is bought by a consumer who observes neither a low-quality signal nor a bad match if $z \in (z_{Lb}, z_{Lg})$; it is bought by a consumer who does not observe a low-quality signal if $z \in (z_{Lg}, z_{Hb})$; and it is bought by a consumer who observes a good match and a high-quality signal if $z \in (z_{Hb}, z_{Hg})$. Interestingly, in the first scenario, if $z \in (z_{Hb}, z_{Lg})$, consumer choice is determined purely by the match quality, whereas in the second scenario, if $z \in (z_{Lg}, z_{Hb})$, consumer choice is determined purely by the signal realization.

Second, we analyze buyer behavior in the presence of a *recommender system* that provides popularity information. For a recommender system to have any impact, we need at least another consumer who makes their choice after obtaining the information generated by the first consumer's choice. The recommender system here simply reports the choice of the first consumer. The second consumer knows the parameters of the model but neither the signal realization nor the type of the first consumer. We assume that all random variables are i.i.d. across consumers (concerning the quality signal, this is conditional on true quality).

To analyze whether a recommender system favors mass-market products or niche products, we consider two cases: $z \in (z_{Lb}, \min\{z_{Hb}, z_{Lg}\})$ and $z \in (\max\{z_{Hb}, z_{Lg}\}, z_{Hg})$. In addition, there are two intermediary cases – that is, $z \in (z_{Hb}, z_{Lg})$ for $1 + t > 2\rho$ and $z \in (z_{Lg}, z_{Hb})$ for $1 + t < 2\rho$. In the first case, in which $z \in (z_{Hb}, z_{Lg})$, the first consumer's choice does not reveal anything about their private signal. Hence, the recommender system does not contain any valuable information for the second consumer. In the second case, where $z \in (z_{Lg}, z_{Hb})$, the first consumer's choice is determined solely by the signal realization. The second consumer will then use the information provided by the recommender system to update their beliefs: They update their quality perception upwards if a particular product has been bought (purchase data) or if the seller has been visited (click data). This implies that a previous visit or purchase increases the chance of subsequent visits and purchases. Here, the recommender system favors the sale of high-quality products. The former case is characterized by a relatively low cost of visiting sellers. Here, a consumer who observes a good match with a particular product always visits the corresponding seller. The consumer visits the seller of the product with a bad match only in case of high-quality information. This implies that click and purchase data still contain some useful information for the second consumer. The second consumer knows whether they have a taste for the niche product or the mass-market product. Hence, if they have a taste for the niche product, they know that it is unlikely that the first consumer had the same taste. Therefore, it is quite likely that the first consumer's visit or purchase was driven by a positive realization of the quality signal. The opposite reasoning applies to a consumer who has a taste for the mass-market product. Here, click and purchasing data are less informative, thus implying that sellers of niche products benefit more from information on visits or purchases.

In the latter case, in which $z \in (\max\{z_{Hb}, z_{Lg}\}, z_{Hg})$, information on a *lack* of visits or purchases hurts the seller of the mass-market product more. While niche sellers are at a disadvantage matching consumer tastes, this disadvantage becomes an asset when it comes to consumer inferences about product quality. It increases the benefit due to favorable popularity information and reduces the loss due to unfavorable popularity information. An interesting question, which we do not analyze here, is the possibility of rational herding. This is a situation in which consumers ignore their private information and rely fully on the aggregate information provided by the system. This means that learning stops at some point.[31]

A prominent mix of various recommender systems is in place at Amazon. Perhaps the most notable example (at least in product categories in which consumers do not search among product substitutes) is that, when listing a particular product, Amazon recommends other products that consumers have purchased together with the displayed product. The economics of such a recommender system are different from a system that merely reports the popularity of products. It allows consumers to discover products that serve similar tastes and, thus, is likely to produce good matches at low search costs. Such a recommender system is based on previous sales and appears to be particularly useful in consumer decision-making for products that enjoy complementary relationships. It implies that products with no or limited sales will receive little attention. This reasoning suggests that recommender systems may work against the long tail, an argument in contrast to the view that people discover better matches on recommender systems. The latter view is based on the observation that consumers with very special tastes more easily find products that provide a good match to their tastes, so that they do not need to resort to very popular products or buy at random.

However, these two views are not necessarily contradictory. While the long-tail story refers to the diversity of aggregate sales, the discovery of better matches refers to diversity at the individual level. It might well be the case that people discover better matches through recommender systems but that they discover products that are already rather popular among the whole population. Hence, sales data in the presence of recommender systems may show more concentration at the aggregate level.[32]

---

[31] A seminal paper on rational herding is Banerjee (1992). Tucker and Zhang (2011) also address herding in the present context.

[32] This point is made in the numerical analyses of Fleder and Hosanagar (2009). However, in their model, the recommendation network essentially provides information about the popularity of a product and does not allow for more-fine-tuned recommendations.

Empirical Work on Recommender Systems

While the previous discussion brings interesting insights, empirical analyses will have to show whether recommender systems lead to more concentrated or more diverse sales. Diversity may be enhanced by the directed search that is inherent in recommender systems: As it reduces their search costs, users may feel more encouraged to search outside of known products that they like, with the effect that more diverse sales are observed at the aggregate level. Indeed, as can be shown formally, if the consumer population is characterized by taste heterogeneity, a recommender system that provides personalized recommendations may lead to a "thicker" tail in the aggregate, meaning that less popular products receive a larger share of sales after the introduction of a recommender system.[33] A likely outcome, then, is that more niche products will be put on the market and that product variety in the market will, therefore, increase, as suggested in Case 2.7.

CASE 2.7 COPURCHASE LINKS ON AMAZON AND THE LONG TAIL

Oestreicher-Singer and Sundararajan (2012a) and Oestreicher-Singer and Sundararajan (2012b) shed some light on this issue.[34] They collected a large data set, starting in 2005, of more than 250,000 books from more than 1,400 categories sold on Amazon. They restrict their analysis to categories with more than 100 books, leaving them with more than 200 categories. For all the books, they obtain detailed daily information, including copurchase links – that is, information on titles that other consumers bought together with the product in question (and which Amazon prominently communicates to consumers). These copurchase links exploit possible demand complementarities. Since these links arise from actual purchases and not from statements by consumers, they can be seen as providing reliable information about what other consumers like. By reporting these links, Amazon essentially provides a personalized shelf for each consumer according to what they were looking at last. This allows consumers to perform a directed search based on their starting point. Oestreicher-Singer and Sundararajan (2012b) find that if a copurchase relationship becomes visible, this leads, on average, to a threefold increase in the influence that complementary products have on each others' demand.

The question, then, is how these copurchase links affect sales. In particular: Which products make relative gains in such a recommendation network? Are these the products that already have mass appeal (because they are linked to other products) or, rather, niche products? To answer this question, one must measure the strength of the links that point to a particular product. For this, it is important to count the number of links pointing to a product and to know the popularity of the products from which a link originates. Hence, a web page receives a high ranking if the web pages of many other products point to it or if highly ranked pages point to it. This is measured by a weighted page rank based on Google's initial algorithm. Oestreicher-Singer and Sundararajan (2012a) construct the Gini coefficient for each product category as a measure of demand diversity within a category. They regress this measure of

---

[33] See Hervas-Drane (2015) for a formal analysis.

[34] Other relevant empirical work has been done by Brynjolfsson, Hu, and Simester (2011) and Elberse and Oberholzer-Gee (2007). Brynjolfsson, Hu, and Simester (2011) compare online and offline retailing and find that online sales are more dispersed. While compatible with the hypothesis that recommender networks lead to more-dispersed sales, other explanations can be given. Elberse and Oberholzer-Gee (2007), comparing DVD sales in 2005 to those in 2000, find that the tail had got longer in 2005. However, they also find that a few blockbusters enjoy even more sales; this is like a superstar effect. Again, the role of recommender systems is not explicit.

demand diversity on the page rank (averaged within a category), together with a number of other variables. In their thirty-day sample, they find that categories with a higher page rank are associated with a significantly lower Gini coefficient. This means that in a product category in which, on average, recommendations play an important role, niche products within this category do relatively better in terms of sales, whereas popular products perform relatively worse than in a product category where this is not the case. This is seen as evidence in support of the theory of the long tail.[35]

The finding that a recommender system favors products in the long tail suggests that such a system may encourage participation on the seller side, as it becomes more attractive for niche players to become active. Since an increase in the number of buyers improves the granularity of the recommender system, a platform with a well-designed recommender system features positive cross-group network effects from buyers to marginal sellers.

Recommender systems may use information that is different from the actual purchases, such as information related to purchase intentions. For instance, Amazon can recommend products based on clicking behavior. If many people who looked at one product also took a close look at another product, this may suggest that the two products are closely related (as substitutes or complements) and that potential buyers benefit from cross-recommendations. We note that recommender systems may also have a future in physical retailing, provided that shoppers use a device that can provide personalized recommendations. For instance, in-shop displays may make personalized recommendations based on a shopper's history and the histories of fellow shoppers.

A profit-maximizing platform may have an incentive to distort the recommender system or make it less informative. We investigate this issue in Chapter 6 under the heading of search engine bias and quality degradation.

2.3   Self-Reinforcing Effects of Big Data

While we do not need a precise definition of the point at which a data set becomes "big," big data often means that there are a lot of observations (volume), possibly of different sources and types (variety), and that new data arrive frequently (velocity). Many platforms (but also other firms) continuously collect large amounts of data. These data are part of a data value chain, which may bring multiple advantages to data users. The value of data is generated by a number of complementary activities. It includes data generation, data storage, data preparation, and data analysis. While it may be useful to imagine this as a sequential chain, it is often an ongoing endeavor, in which existing data are analyzed and at the same time new data are generated and stored. Figure 2.2 represents the data value chain.

---

[35] To take into account possible unobserved heterogeneity in the data, Oestreicher-Singer and Sundararajan (2012a) also construct a panel data set. The estimation results are confirmed with panel data techniques.

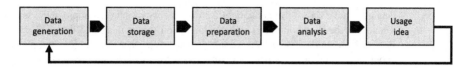

Figure 2.2 Data value chain

One important element in the data value chain that may be forgotten is the usage idea. Data become valuable because they contain information that can be used to deliver a product or service generating value for some parties. Moreover, because volume and variety matter, the more data can be collected – and from more varied sources – the larger the value that can be generated. Self-reinforcing effects are thus at work, as more users and transactions on the platform generate more data, which contributes to make the platform more attractive for other users. As a consequence, platforms may be able to achieve a competitive advantage through the collection and exploitation of data. How much so? This depends on a number of factors, which we discuss in this section.

2.3.1   Network Effects or Not?

A first question is whether the data-driven self-reinforcing effects can be qualified as network effects or not. As we explained in the previous chapter, network effects occur when the decision of one user affects the well-being of another user. Implicit behind this definition is that other things are supposed to be equal, in particular prices and other strategies that platforms could choose. This is so, for instance, in the case of recommender systems described in the previous section. These systems make use of big data by exploiting correlations between consumers' choices (such as purchases, wish lists, and clicks) to make recommendations. Hence, data from additional users allow a firm to provide better recommendations to any user and, thus, a higher quality of its service. Network effects are present because, given the prices set by the platform and given the initial investment it made (in designing the recommendation algorithm), the data collected from one user contribute to make the platform more attractive for other users.

Big data also generate network effects when, for a given number of participants, richer data lead to better matches by making statistical correlations more detailed. Case 2.8 provides an illustration of such a process.

CASE 2.8 HOW DATA GENERATE NETWORK EFFECTS ON WAZE

We refer back to the case of Waze presented in the previous chapter to illustrate network effects as a result of data. Traffic data from its users allows Waze to navigate drivers in such a way that they save time compared to those drivers not using Waze. Clearly, the more users have Waze, the more up-to-date information each user has about routes. If some roads are typically not taken, Waze may encourage some users to "experiment" by directing them to these roads. As the amount of traffic tracked by Waze increases in a time interval, Waze can lower the rate of experimentation and, thus, is able to reduce the average travel time of users. Here, data generate a short-term network effect if only very recent data improve the service quality. Then, it is the data volume in a particular period that matters and data can be treated as a flow variable. In the case of Waze, some data are rather short-lived – for example, information about congestion levels at peak hour traffic – whereas others such as additional traffic lights because of roadworks may be more long-lived if this construction requires some time such as repairs of a bridge.

In the previous two examples, data are the source of network effects because more data imply better services and, thus, higher quality. When these services or quality are provided by the platform, this constitutes a data-driven attraction loop; when they are provided by independent providers on the platform, users experience data-enabled network effects and the associated attraction spiral operates through quality on the provider side (see Section 1.2.1).

On other platforms, more data allow for better logistics and, thus, lower costs (e.g., fewer returns because items arrive on time). While better logistics may directly increase user benefits, it also does so indirectly through cost reductions if some of these cost savings are passed on to consumers and, thus, consumers benefit from the associated scale economies. In such cases, we cannot speak of network effects per se because, when users benefit indirectly from cost savings, it is because prices have decreased (a pecuniary externality); that is, scale economies operate on the supply side (via costs) and not on the demand side (via willingness to pay). Network effects are also absent when the learning that data enable is specific to each user, as the data from one user does not benefit other users. Self-reinforcing effects may nevertheless be present if the improved quality of the service induces each user to increase their engagement on the platform, thereby generating even more data.

LESSON 2.11   *Data may generate self-reinforcing effects: As more users join the platform, they generate more data, which can be exploited to make the platform more attractive for other users.*

Behind what may appear to be a semantic or conceptual distinction, the important questions are: How strong and long-lasting are these self-reinforcing effects? How costly is it for platforms to generate them? In sum, to what extent do they allow platforms to flourish and possibly gain a competitive advantage?

2.3.2   Short-Term or Long-Term Effects?

We argue here that data-enabled self-reinforcing effects are more likely to be a source of competitive advantage the longer these effects can play. Long-term effects may arise for two reasons: either because past data stay relevant for quite some time or because algorithms are self-learning and trained by data. We examine these two reasons in turn.

Long-Lived Data
In Case 2.8, we saw that the data-enabled network effects rely both on short-lived data (such as information about congestion levels) and long-lived data (such as

information about substantial roadworks). Only the latter stay relevant in the long run and may produce long-term effects. The same goes when some users generate content that is consumed by other users. For example, contributions by users to improve Wikipedia entries increase users' benefits in the long term if the associated entry remains relevant and information does not change frequently. If you read the article on "merchants" on Wikipedia, most of the information provided by users is likely to stay relevant for many years. In contrast, information about some active rapper needs to be regularly updated. In sum, Wikipedia's set of articles constitutes a stock of data whose value depreciates over time and may be replenished by recent additions and corrections.

To evaluate whether and to what extent long-term effects are present, we need to see if the length of storage should matter. That is, the testable hypothesis is the following: The larger the stock of data, the higher the quality of the service offered to users. In the case of search engines, Chiou and Tucker (2017) empirically estimate the impact of a change of the platforms' data-retention policies in response to public pressure by the European Commission on search quality. Search quality is presumed to decrease if the number of repeat searches on the search engine goes up. Chiou and Tucker find little evidence that reduced storage negatively affected search quality. This suggests that in the market under investigation, the most recent three to six months of data provide as good search quality as data covering more than one year.

Self-Learning Algorithms

While past data may no longer be of any direct relevance to the quality of a platform's service, the fact that a platform had access to data in the past may have allowed it to develop an algorithm superior to the one used by a competitor, even if both platforms had access to the same data more recently. Such a situation is similar to learning-by-doing effects resulting in dynamic efficiency gains (lower cost or higher quality for users). The strength of learning-by-doing here depends on the number of users and their level of engagement. Case 2.9 provides an illustration.

CASE 2.9 LONG-TERM DATA-ENABLED SELF-REINFORCING EFFECTS ON PLAN-TIX/PEAT

Plantix is an app that allows farmers to obtain a quick response to detect plant diseases and pests. It is widely used in India, and its use is spreading in many other countries. A farmer only needs to take a picture of the plant, upload it, and learn about the identified disease or pest (or nutrient deficiency) and how it can be treated. As of April 2018, Plantix is able to identify more than 240 plant diseases. PEAT, the startup behind Plantix, does not yet have a revenue model, but the success of the app partly relies on positive network effects, as farmers upload photos to obtain help and automatically contribute to enriching the existing database. As PEAT states on its website: "Every picture improves Plantix image recognition. By uploading pictures, you can help farmers all over the world grow smart."[36] As the database grows and the AI algorithms improve, more diseases will be detected and the the probability of correct identification of the disease or pest will increase.

---

[36] See https://plantix.net; last accessed March 2019.

In the latter case, as in other cases, the reason users benefit from a lot of other users' activities in the past can be twofold: First, the larger stock of data is useful by itself; second, it enabled the platform to improve the precision of the information service it provides to users, as it could train its algorithm with additional data. In either case, there are dynamic network effects and the quality of the service depends on the data collected from the total number of users served in the past, possibly discounted by $\delta \leq 1$ if data become less useful as they age. Then, for a given price of the platform service, consumers derive a higher utility in period T the more users the platform served in the past (N_t in period $t < T$); i.e., $U(\sum_{t=-\infty}^{T-1} \delta^{T-1-t}N_t)$ increasing in N_t for all $t \in \{-\infty, \ldots, T-1\}$. As a result, a newcomer who does not have access to such past data would be at a disadvantage.[37]

LESSON 2.12   *In some cases, a deeper data pool allows a platform to improve its quality. Then, better data in the past generate a competitive advantage for a platform.*

2.3.3   Cost of Collecting and Analyzing Data

So far, we have focused on the benefits that a platform can gain from collecting more data as a by-product of a particular service: By enlarging its data pool, the platform is able to improve the service quality. However, data are not a manna from heaven. Collecting them often necessitates costly efforts. Even when data can be used for "free" (i.e., without incurring any opportunity cost), its analysis and interpretation can be costly. Platforms may then limit the use of data (e.g., by analyzing only a subsample). This means that even though self-reinforcing effects may arise thanks to a data value chain, platforms may not have an unlimited demand for data, as they have to balance the extra value from data that they can extract and the opportunity cost of the use of these data.

In many markets, self-reinforcing effects due to more available data are likely to be nonlinear – that is, they are positive but eventually become weaker as the size of the pool becomes sufficiently large. Then, a large firm may strive for a deeper data pool not because this makes this firm's offer much more attractive but because it deprives a smaller competitor from building up its data pool to offer services of comparable quality.[38] Note that a firm collecting data because of a completely different user activity may use the data pool to offer attractive services for other user activities. Whether this is a possibility depends on the type of data collected and their usefulness – for example, to provide better recommendations for different user activities.[39]

[37] Hagiu and Wright (2020a) consider such dynamic network effects in a model with two competing platforms and show that if one of them wins in one period T, it will enjoy an increasing advantage and, therefore, be able to win the competition in all subsequent periods.

[38] We return to this issue in Chapter 3 where we discuss incumbency advantages with network effects.

[39] In the same spirit, what appears to be conglomerate activities may be driven by obtaining a more detailed and real-time picture of a particular person (e.g., by tracking people across different websites).

Another reason why data may be costly to collect is that platforms may have to compensate consumers for offering their data. They may do so by a monetary payment or, as is more common, by providing a service free of charge if the consumer accepts the privacy policy of the platform. A rational consumer's decision about whether to opt in is driven by their private benefits from obtaining the service relative to the opportunity cost of providing those data (which may consist in higher prices or intrusive advertising). However, due to economies of scale in data collection, the information provided by other consumers allows a platform to predict consumer characteristics based on limited knowledge about this consumer (e.g., even if the consumer in a social network does not reveal a certain characteristic, their position in the social network may be highly informative).[40] Thus, there are information externalities. The more consumers have agreed to reveal information, the better a platform can predict certain characteristics of a consumer even if this consumer does not allow the platform to obtain access to their characteristics (or user behavior that predicts such behavior). In this case, a rational consumer is willing to reveal information for a small compensation. The larger the platform, the smaller is the compensation the consumer receives. Also, the overall compensation by the platform may be decreasing (even if this consists in monetary payments to each agreeing consumer;[41] more straightforwardly, if there is a nonmonetary payment in the form of a digital service that has a large fixed cost component and negligible variable costs). Hence, including such compensations, a platform enjoys self-reinforcing effects in generating information.

LESSON 2.13   *A platform that provides a payment or a service in return for consumers to provide their personal data may enjoy positive self-reinforcing effects in information acquisition: The larger its user base, the less costly it is to obtain the data from its users.*

To sum up, when do data-enabled self-reinforcing effects lead to long-lasting competitive gains for the platforms that generate them? Hagiu and Wright (2020b) identify the following conditions: (i) The value added by user data must be high and long-lasting, (ii) data must be proprietary (i.e., not shared with or easily accessible by competing platforms) and must lead to hard-to-imitate service improvements, and (iii) network effects are generated (i.e., users realize that their benefits increase thanks to the data collected from other users).

---

[40] For example, as shown in a study by MIT students, men's sexual orientation can be predicted by an analysis of a social network site such as Facebook. Since homosexual men tend to have a higher share of gay friends than straight men, a man's sexual orientation can be predicted based on the sexuality of their direct links in the social network. See Johnson (2009).

[41] For a formal analysis on the generation of information through individual data, see Bergemann, Bonatti, and Gan (2019). As formally investigated by Choi, Jeon, and Kim (2019), negative information externalities can explain the privacy paradox; that is, consumers express concerns about a loss of privacy but are willing to provide their personal data for a small compensation.

Key Insights from Chapter 2

- One cannot understand the functioning of prominent digital platforms (such as Airbnb, Amazon, Booking, Taobao, eBay, Google Shopping or Uber) without taking proper account of the functioning of rating and recommender systems, and the use of big data.
- Rating and recommender systems are crucial for the performance of digital platforms because potential buyers incur an opportunity cost in evaluating how products and services fare in terms of quality and how they fit their tastes; thus, they appreciate ratings, reviews, and recommendations because knowing what other buyers did in the past helps them to make better-informed decisions.
- When two-sidedness is an essential feature of a digital platform, users are often keen to infer information about the reliability of the counterparties to the transactions that they may conduct on the platform. Here, rating systems can possibly steer buyers away from low-quality sellers and can discourage sellers from misbehaving. Conversely, thanks to rating systems, sellers can stay clear of problematic buyers, and buyers may have a stronger incentive to behave properly.
- Rating and recommender systems make heavy use of big data and are the source of positive within-group and cross-group network effects. As big data also allow platforms to generate other forms of self-reinforcing effects, they are, in many cases, a key driver allowing a platform to attract many buyers (and, if applicable, sellers), which is a source of competitive advantage in markets with competing platforms.

3   An Economic Primer on Network Goods

In Chapter 1, we extensively described the different types of network effects that may be at work on platforms, distinguishing between cross-group and within-group network effects; we also illustrated how positive network effects give rise to attraction loops and spirals; and it is in this spirit that we defined platforms as entities that bring together economic agents and actively manage network effects between them. In Chapter 2, we elaborated on some particular sources of network effects, namely, rating, review, and recommender systems; we argued that these systems have the potential to generate attraction loops and spirals because the value they create for users is likely to increase with the number of users on the platform.

A central feature that emerges from the previous two chapters is that users affect one another through the decisions they make on platforms: By joining a platform or by increasing the intensity of their participation on the platform, a user makes it more (or, sometimes, less) interesting for other users to participate as well; likewise, they take into account the (observed and/or expected) participation of other users when making their own decision. In sum, users' decisions on platforms are *interdependent*.

As a result, platform users cannot make their decisions in isolation from the decisions made by other users. This situation stands in sharp contrast with the consumers' decisions that we usually analyze in markets in which network effects are either inexistent or negligible. Think, for instance, of the market for potatoes. When you consider buying a bag of potatoes, you do not care about the decisions that other consumers may make on this market, as these decisions have no bearing whatsoever on the utility you can obtain from this bag of potatoes. You can thus safely ignore the behavior of other consumers when making your own choices. But you may have second thoughts if you were choosing, say, some communication device instead of potatoes; here, to be able to communicate with many other people, you would tend to choose a device that has already been adopted – or you expect to be so in the near future – by many other users. That is, the decisions of other users enter your utility function and affect your demand behavior. If you are the one everybody wants to talk to, it may be enough if you move first, but don't fool yourself: For most of us, it does not work this way.

In this chapter, we formalize this demand interdependence and, more broadly, seek to understand key economic consequences of network effects. We first analyze the impacts that network effects have on the demand for participation on a platform (Section 3.1). The main lesson we draw is that the interdependence between individual demands leads to unconventional aggregate demands; in particular, we show that a given price for accessing the platform may be compatible with several levels of participation. This is due to the fact that the aggregate demand for participation may exhibit upward-sloping segments: Because of positive network effects, a larger price is associated with *more* demand for participation. On this basis, we explore the pricing of access to a platform (Section 3.2). The previous discussion suggests that the presence of network effects makes pricing significantly more complex than in other markets. There are three interrelated reasons for that: First, as just discussed, different demand levels may result from a given price and, thus, it may be difficult to predict demand after observing the price; second, the price that a platform can set depends on the expectations that users form about other users' participation; third, small differences in prices may lead to the tipping of the market with either all potential users or none of them joining the platform.

To manage network effects, platforms combine pricing with other strategic decisions (Section 3.3). In particular, a platform has to decide the extent to which its services are compatible with alternative services. The trade-off behind this decision is the following. On the one hand, incompatibility makes network effects platform-specific; that is, users must join the same platform to enjoy the benefits of positive network effects; as a consequence, attraction loops or spirals confer a competitive advantage as they do not spill over to rival platforms. On the other hand, compatibility amplifies network effects (as it allows users of different platforms to interact) and, thereby, the users' willingness to pay. The timing of strategic decisions is also crucial in the presence of network effects. Because past market shares impact current ones, prices must be set in a dynamic way. To seed the market, it may then be profitable to start with low, introductory, prices; making sure to launch a platform before rivals do may also be favorable. But these strategies have some downsides that need to be carefully gauged.

Throughout this chapter, we focus on platforms catering to one group of users who benefit from within-group network effects. In other words, we focus on attraction loops. In each section, we introduce the main intuition through simple models, which we then enrich to gain a better understanding of the mechanisms at work.

3.1   Demand for Network Goods

In this section, we explain why the demand for network goods behaves quite differently from the demand for goods that do not exhibit network effects. Here is how we proceed. We first build our intuition with the simplest model: Two users have to choose whether or not to purchase a network good (Section 3.1.1); we then dig a bit deeper by extending the model to a continuum of users (Section 3.1.2); finally, we refine our analysis by introducing additional considerations within the model (Section 3.1.3).

3.1.1   A Simple Model with a Single Good and Two Users

To get a first intuition about the impacts of network effects on demand, let us take a very simple example. Suppose that there are only two users, Xena and Yuri. They are both interested in buying at most one unit of a particular product. Their interest in the product is measured by an intrinsic valuation, which we note r_x for Xena and r_y for Yuri. We assume that Xena is more interested in the product than Yuri: $r_x > r_y$. The good is sold at some fee A (which we take as given for the moment).

If the product we consider does not generate any external effect from one user on the other, then each user can take their decision regardless of what the other user decides. The decision rule is extremely simple: Buy the good as long as the fee does not exceed one's valuation (otherwise, the net benefit would be negative and the alternative of not buying, which leaves a net benefit of zero, would be preferable). It is then very easy to construct the demand function – that is, to map with each possible fee the quantity purchased, which is equivalent here to the number of buyers. Denoting the number of buyers n and recalling our assumption that $r_x > r_y$, we find the following demand function: If $A > r_x$, then $n = 0$ (both Xena and Yuri find the good too expensive); if $r_y < A \leq r_x$, then $n = 1$ (only Xena finds the good cheap enough); if $A \leq r_y$, then $n = 2$ (both users are happy to buy). This simple example confirms two standard features of demand: (i) The quantity demanded is an inverse function of the fee (this is the Law of Demand applied to a single product), and (ii) each fee A corresponds to a unique quantity n.

Let us now add network effects into the picture. Network effects, in this simple example, can be represented as some additional benefit that each user obtains when the other user also purchases the good. For instance, Xena and Yuri may want to store some photos on Dropbox. They derive an extra benefit if they can share their folder with the other user. Similarly, Xena and Yuri may enjoy streaming on Spotify. They derive an extra benefit if they can access each other's playlists.

Let $\beta > 0$ denote this "network benefit," which we assume to be identical for Xena and Yuri. A user's willingness to pay for the good is now made of their intrinsic valuation (which comes from the stand-alone utility of the good), possibly augmented by the network benefit. The key difference with the previous case (where network effects were absent) precisely lies in the term "possibly": When buying the product, the additional network benefit is *conditional* on the decision of the other user. As a result, the decisions of the two users become interdependent: Whether or not it is in their best interest to purchase the good may depend on the decision of the other user. The decision rule therefore becomes more complex, as different scenarios have to be considered. Here, each user must answer two questions: Should I buy or not if I believe that the other is *not* going to buy? Should I buy or not if I believe that the other *is* going to buy? As each user faces a binary decision problem, that leaves us with four possibilities, which we can represent in a 2x2 matrix (see Table 3.1).

Let us put the choices of Xena vertically and those of Yuri horizontally; within the four cells of the matrix, we write the net benefits of the two users, starting with Xena's. For instance, in the top left cell (which corresponds to the case where both

Table 3.1 Adoption of a network good by two users

		Yuri	
		Buy	Don't buy
Xena	Buy	$r_x + \beta - A, r_y + \beta - A$	$r_x - A, 0$
	Don't buy	$0, r_y - A$	$0, 0$

users buy the good), the net benefits are, respectively, $r_x + \beta - A$ and $r_y + \beta - A$: Both users enjoy the network benefit as they both purchase the good. In contrast, when only Xena buys the good (in the top right cell), Xena obtains only $r_x - A$ (while Yuri has a net benefit of zero).

Now, to determine the demand function, we need to solve the game played by X and Y. In particular, we determine the Nash equilibrium of the game played by the two users – that is, we look for situations that are mutually optimal for the two users (each one making the choice that maximizes their net benefit, while anticipating correctly that the other user will do so as well). Let us consider the four possibilities in turn:

- For which fees would both users decide to buy the good? If they both buy, we are in the top left cell of the matrix and we need to make sure that no user wants to "deviate" – that is, they decide not to buy under the belief that the other user is buying. This is so for Xena if $r_x + \beta - A \geq 0$ and for Yuri if $r_y + \beta - A \geq 0$. As we assume that $r_x > r_y$, both conditions are satisfied if $A \leq r_y + \beta$.
- For which fees would only Xena choose to buy? Xena must be better off buying when Xena believes that Yuri is not buying ($r_x - A \geq 0$), while Yuri must prefer not buying when Yuri believes that Xena is buying ($0 \geq r_y + \beta - A$). For the two conditions to be simultaneously met, the fee must be such that $r_y + \beta \leq A \leq r_x$, which is only possible if $r_x > r_y + \beta$ or, equivalently, $\beta < r_x - r_y$.
- Applying the same reasoning, it is easy to show that there does not exist any fee such that only Yuri would want to buy (this would require $r_x + \beta \leq A \leq r_y$, which is clearly impossible as $r_x > r_y$ and $\beta > 0$).
- Finally, for which fees do both users prefer not to buy? Deviations from the bottom right cell are not profitable if $0 \geq r_x - A$ and $0 \geq r_y - A$, which are both satisfied if $A \geq r_x$ (given that $r_x > r_y$).

Putting everything together, we see that we need to distinguish between two cases according to whether the network benefit (β) is smaller or larger than the difference in valuations ($r_x - r_y$). Consider first the case where $\beta < r_x - r_y$. That is, users get small extra benefits when they both buy the good and/or they are rather heterogeneous in terms of intrinsic valuations for the good. In that case, the demand function is relatively similar to the one we obtained absent network effects: $n = 0$ for $A \geq r_x$, $n = 1$ for $r_y + \beta \leq A \leq r_x$, and $n = 2$ for $A \leq r_y + \beta$. The only impact of

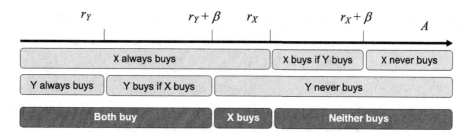

Figure 3.1 Demand with two users and weak network effects

network effects, here, is to enlarge the set of fees for which both users buy the good. Figure 3.1 shows how the demand function is built.

The alternative case, with $\beta > r_x - r_y$, is more interesting. When network effects are stronger (compared to user heterogeneity), the demand "function" (or correspondence to be correct) looks as follows: $n = 0$ for $A \geq r_y + \beta$; $n = 0$ and $n = 2$ for $r_x \leq A \leq r_y + \beta$; and $n = 2$ for $A \leq r_x$. We observe two major changes. First, there is no longer any fee such that only one user buys the good. We already know that this user would be Xena, but Xena being the only buyer would require $r_y + \beta \leq A \leq r_x$, which is impossible given that $\beta > r_x - r_y$. So, either both users buy the good or neither of them does. The second transformation is even more striking: For fees comprised between r_x and $r_y + \beta$, there are two equilibria: $n = 0$ (no one buys) or $n = 2$ (both buy). In other words, the same fee gives rise to two different demanded quantities. This is because the good is found, at the same time, too expensive if one believes that the other user will not buy (meaning that the network benefit will not materialize) *and* cheap enough if one believes that the other user will buy (which would guarantee the added network benefit). The two equilibria conform with a *self-fulfilling prophecy*: If both users believe that no one will buy, they find the fee too high, and, thus, they optimally decide not to buy, thereby verifying their initial belief; conversely, if they both believe that everyone will buy, they find the fee low enough, they both buy, and they confirm again their initial belief.[1] Figure 3.2 illustrates how the demand function is built when network effects are stronger.

A direct consequence of the existence of multiple equilibria is *unpredictability*: For these intermediate fees, it is a priori impossible to say if the two users will buy the good or not. Another consequence is *potential inefficiency*. If $A \leq r_y + \beta$, it is clear that both users are better off in the situation where they buy than in the situation where they do not buy. Yet, for $A \geq r_x$, it could be that no user buys at equilibrium, which would be inefficient.

---

[1] In an alternative formulation of the problem, we could assume that Xena and Yuri have the same intrinsic valuation for the product (which we note v) but differ in their valuation of the network benefit: β_X for Xena and β_Y for Yuri. Assuming $\beta_X > \beta_Y$, we let you check that we have again two equilibria for any price p comprised between v and $v + \beta_Y$. Even more generally, when the two users differ in their valuations of both the intrinsic and the network benefits, multiple equilibria are observed for prices such that $\max\{v_X, v_Y\} \leq p \leq \min\{v_X + \beta_X, v_Y + \beta_Y\}$.

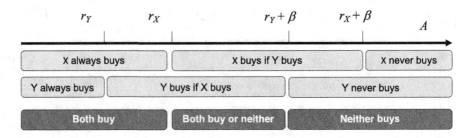

Figure 3.2 Demand with two users and strong network effects

One could argue that these two features hinge on our (implicit) assumption that users decide simultaneously so that they possibly fail to coordinate their beliefs and do not buy. Indeed, if decisions were made sequentially (with the second user observing the choice of the first), the first user would be more willing to buy the product, anticipating that the second user would follow suit. In particular, for any fee such that Yuri would be happy to buy if Xena buys as well (i.e., for $A \leq r_y + \beta$), both users will end up buying the good even if Xena would not buy when knowing to be the sole potential buyer (i.e., for $A \geq r_x$). This would be efficient. Then, we would have a unique demand for each fee. Yet, this argument relies on another strong assumption – namely, that both users know the intrinsic valuation of the other user. If users do not know exactly how much interest the other user has in the product, it can be shown that the unpredictability and potential inefficiency due to multiple equilibria may arise again.

We record our findings in the following lesson.

LESSON 3.1   *Network effects make users' purchasing decisions interdependent. As a result, there can be several levels of demand for the same fee, making it hard to predict a priori what users will decide and giving rise to potential inefficiencies, as users may fail to purchase the product although this would make them all better off.*

In the following section, we generalize our analysis by considering the arguably more realistic situation with a large number of potential users. Inevitably, we will need to build a model that is slightly more involved and requires some mathematical formalization. If you prefer to skip this section, here are the main findings that we can draw from this model:

(1) We generalize the results outlined in Lesson 3.1: We show that there can be up to *three* different demand levels for some fees, each of them corresponding to a self-fulfilling prophecy; thus, unpredictability and potential inefficiency are even more acute problems in this more general setting.

(2) The model allows us to explain that the multiplicity of demand levels results from the existence of an upward-sloping portion in the demand "function"; that is, the quantity demanded of the good may *increase* with the fee of the good. This is so because the impact of the Law of Demand (according to which

the quantity demanded decreases with the fee) is more than compensated by the network effect (which increases the users' willingness to pay as demand expands).

3.1.2   Demand for a Network Good with Many Users

Suppose now, more realistically, that there is a very large number of potential users who, like Xena and Yuri in the previous model, simultaneously decide whether or not to join a particular network (or, equivalently, to buy one unit of a product that exhibits network effects).[2] Formally, we identify a particular user by a real number taken between 0 and 1; there is thus a continuum of users, with a total mass of 1. Furthermore, to simplify our computations, we assume that any number (or "type") can be drawn with equal probability (i.e., we assume a uniform distribution of the user types). It follows that the mass of users with types below some threshold $\beta < 1$ represents exactly a share β of the total population of users.

A direct consequence of assuming a continuum of users is that the decision of any particular user has a negligible effect on the aggregate behavior. This contrasts with the previous simple model where any player realized that by adopting the network good, they were increasing the size of the network; for instance, if Xena expected Yuri to adopt the good, Xena knew that by adopting as well, this would increase the network size from 1 to 2. Here, users do not take such impact into account, simply because the huge number of users makes this individual impact so tiny (it is like a drop in the ocean). That is, users consider that their decision whether to adopt or not has no impact on the network size.

As choices are simultaneous (i.e., there is no way to observe the choices of others before making one's own choice, nor is it possible to commit to one's future choice), each user has to form *expectations* about the combined choices of other users. In particular, when what matters is the number of users joining the network (and not their identity), users base their decision on the expected size of the network, which we write n^e. In the following analysis, we will restrict attention to equilibria in which users form the same expectations and these expectations turn out to be correct; that is, at equilibrium the actual network size is equal to the expected one ($n = n^e$), meaning that *expectations are fulfilled*; we call this a fulfilled-expectations equilibrium, or FEE.

We now develop two specific settings. In both settings, we assume (like in the previous example) that a user's gross utility is the addition of a stand-alone benefit and a network benefit that increases linearly with the expected size of the network: $r + \beta n^e$. In the first setting, the user type is their valuation of the stand-alone benefit while, in the second, it is their valuation of the network benefit. We normalize to 0 a user's utility from not joining the network. Hence, if the access fee is A, a user

---

[2] For an early formalization of demand for a network good, see Artle and Averous (1973). We propose here a simplified version of the models developed in Belleflamme and Peitz (2015, section 20.2.1) and Belleflamme and Peitz (2018b). See also Economides (1996).

of type r (first case) or of type β (second case) joins the network if and only if $r + \beta n^e - A \geq 0$.

The latter formulation encompasses cases in which the outside option generates network benefits, provided that these network benefits increase linearly as well. Take, for instance, the case of Waze, the GPS navigation app that we described in Chapter 1. As we argued, nonadopters also benefit from an increased adoption of Waze, yet to a lesser extent than adopters. The utility of not joining Waze could then be expressed as γn^e, with $\gamma < \beta$ and n^e denoting the expected number of adopters of Waze. For a user to join Waze, we would then need $r + \beta n^e - A \geq \gamma n^e$, or $r + (\beta - \gamma)n^e - A \geq 0$; denoting $(\beta - \gamma)$ by β' drives us back to our formulation. Similarly, in Section 3.2.3, we will consider cases in which the outside option is to join another free network. Let the network under consideration be network 1 and the outside option be network 2. If the total mass of users is set to unity, a user's net utility is $r_1 + \beta_1 n_1^e - A$ on network 1 and $r_2 + \beta_2(1 - n_1^e)$ on network 2. It follows that a user joins network 1 if and only if $(r_1 - r_2 - \beta_2) + (\beta_1 + \beta_2)n_1^e - A \geq 0$, which is equivalent to our formulation if we set $r \equiv r_1 - r_2 - \beta_2$ and $\beta \equiv \beta_1 + \beta_2$.

Heterogeneous valuations of stand-alone benefits

We assume here that users differ in their valuation of the stand-alone benefit of the product but value the network benefits in the same way. That is, the user type is their valuation of the stand-alone benefit r (which, as indicated above, is drawn from a uniform distribution on the interval $[0, 1]$). As for the network benefit, it increases linearly with the expected size of the network, with an intensity β that is the same across users.

For a given n^e, the indifferent user between joining or not joining the network has a type r_0 such that $r_0 + \beta n^e - A = 0$ or $r_0 = A - \beta n^e$; users with $r \geq r_0$ (resp. $r \leq r_0$) join (resp. do not join) the network. As types are comprised between 0 and 1, there are three possible scenarios according to whether $r_0 \leq 0$, $r_0 \geq 1$, or $0 < r_0 < 1$. In the first scenario, $r_0 \leq 0$ such that all users join the network; as we impose fulfilled expectations, we have $n^e = n = 1$, so that $r_0 \leq 0$ is equivalent to $A \leq \beta$. The second scenario is the mirror image of the first: If $r_0 \geq 1$, then no user joins the network, meaning that $n^e = n = 0$ and $r_0 \geq 1$ is equivalent to $A \geq 1$. Finally, if $0 < r_0 < 1$, the share n of users joining the network is found by solving the system of equations $n = n^e = 1 - r_0$, which gives $n = (1 - A) / (1 - \beta)$.

As in the simple model of the previous section, there are two cases to distinguish. First, if $\beta < 1$, the network effects are weak with respect to the heterogeneity of intrinsic valuations (equal to 1 here). In that case, there is a unique network size for every fee: If $A \geq 1$, no user joins the network; if $\beta \leq A \leq 1$, a strict subset of users joins the network; the size of this subset is $n = (1 - A) / (1 - \beta)$, which decreases with the access fee A; if $A \leq \beta$, all users join the network.

In the second case, the network effects are strong compared to user heterogeneity ($\beta > 1$). Here, for any fee A such that $1 < A < \beta$, three FEE coexist: Either no user joins the network, or all of them do, or just a share of them do; in the latter case, the network size is equal to $(A - 1) / (\beta - 1)$ and *increases* with the access fee.

Heterogeneous valuations of network benefits

Alternatively, we can suppose that all users have the same valuation for the stand-alone benefit but differ in their valuation of the network benefit; that is, it is now β that is drawn from a uniform distribution on $[0, 1]$, while r is the same for all users. Here, a user decides to join the network if $r + \beta n^e \geq A$. We immediately see that if all users expect no user to join the network ($n^e = 0$), it is indeed an equilibrium for none of them to do so if $r \leq A$. Now, if $n^e > 0$, the user who is indifferent between joining and not joining is of type β_0 such that $r + \beta_0 n^e - A = 0$ or $\beta_0 = (A - r) / n^e$. To have a fulfilled-expectations equilibrium such that all users join the network, we need to have $\beta_0 \leq 0$ with $n^e = 1$; this is so if $A \leq r$.

The remaining possibility is to have only a fraction of users joining the network. This fraction is found by solving $n = n^e = 1 - \beta_0$. Solving for A, we find $A = r + n(1 - n)$. Such a demand curve was derived by Rohlfs (1974). Interestingly, this inverse demand for joining the network is a bell-shaped function of n, which reaches a maximum at $n = 1/2$, where $A = r + 1/4$. That is, the inverse demand first increases (for $n < 1/2$) and then decreases (for $n > 1/2$) with the network size. This is due to the twofold role that n plays under our restriction of fulfilled expectations. On the one hand, there is the Law of Demand: An increase in n (seen as the actual size of the network) has a negative impact on the fee, which needs to go down to convince more users to join the network. On the other hand, there are the network effects: An increase in n (seen now as the *expected* size of the network) raises all users' willingness to pay, meaning that higher fees are compatible with larger networks. In this setting, the latter effect outweighs the former for small network sizes ($n < 1/2$), thereby generating an upward-sloping inverse demand; the reverse applies for larger network sizes ($n > 1/2$) where the law of demand dominates. As a result, any A such that $r < A < r + 1/4$ generates three equilibrium network sizes: $n_n = 0$, $n_s = \frac{1}{2} - \frac{1}{2}\sqrt{1 - 4(A - r)}$ and $n_l = \frac{1}{2} + \frac{1}{2}\sqrt{1 - 4(A - r)}$. We observe that a fee decrease makes the network smaller at the "small" equilibrium (n_s) and larger at the "large" equilibrium (n_l); at the limits, we have $n_s = 0$ and $n_l = 1$ for $A = r$, and $n_s = n_l = 1/2$ for $A = r + 1/4$.

Figure 3.3 depicts the multiplicity of equilibria for the two models we just considered (heterogeneous intrinsic valuations in the left panel; heterogeneous network valuations in the right panel).

Collecting the previous results, we can generalize the observations made in Lesson 3.1 as follows:

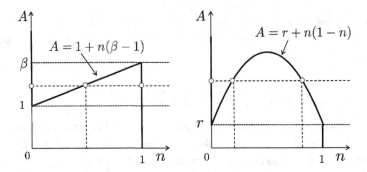

Figure 3.3 Multiple demand levels for network goods

LESSON 3.2   *For products exhibiting network effects, the demand may contain upward-sloping segments (where higher demand levels give rise to higher fees); this arises when the demand-expanding impact of network effects dominates the Law of Demand. As a result, up to three levels of demand may coexist for the same fee (with one of them being the zero level).*

As in the simple model, the coexisting demand levels stem all from *self-fulfilling prophecies* insofar as they correspond to network sizes that generate utilities such that the combined purchasing decisions of the users exactly match the expectations on which these decisions were based. As a result, both a "small" and a "large" network can be compatible with the same fee: On the one hand, the fee is sufficiently low to convince a few users with high network valuations to join, despite a small expected network size; on the other hand, even if a larger expected network size could command a larger fee, this large number of users can only materialize if the fee is low enough to convince users with lower network valuations to join.

At this point, we are left with a possible multiplicity of equilibria, which hampers our ability to predict how the market will exactly behave. In the next section, we argue that one of the multiple equilibria is less reasonable than the other, although it is very significant from an economic point of view.

3.1.3   Dynamic Behavior, User Expectations, and Equilibrium Stability

We assumed so far that all users make their adoption decision at the same time, which is to say that none of them is able to observe the choices of other users before making their own decision. We also assumed that users hold self-fulfilling expectations – that is, that they make predictions about the size of the network that turn out to be correct. This is equivalent to saying that for a given access fee A, users play an anonymous game and that we solve for the Nash equilibrium of this game. This appears as a natural assumption when decisions are taken simultaneously.

In reality, it takes time for networks to build and it is thus reasonable to posit that adoptions decisions are made in a sequential way, with later users observing the current size of the network when deciding whether or not to join. Such dynamic behavior leads us to envision alternative ways in which users form their expectations. A reasonable assumption (especially in settings where users have limited information) is that users have *myopic* expectations, in the sense that they base their decision on the current network size but fail to anticipate how their decision will affect the future network size. In other words, they expect the future to look like the present.[3]

In this context, it is logical to assume that users can easily change their mind about participation in the network, whose size may thus increase or decrease from one period to the next. That is, period t users observe some network size n_t, which they use to evaluate their net utility of joining the network; based on this evaluation, a fraction of users decides to join the network, thereby generating a new network size, noted n_{t+1}. The process is then repeated in period $t + 1$, with users confirming or revising their decision upon the observation of n_{t+1}. We are interested in the sequence of such myopic user decisions. We say that a fulfilled-expectations equilibrium (FEE) is *stable* if myopic expectations produce a sequence of adoptions that converge to this equilibrium (when starting from a network size in the vicinity of but different from the network size in an FEE). In other words, our notion of stability refers to the following thought experiment: Take a network size corresponding to a FEE; suppose that users are slightly wrong in predicting this network size and that a sequence of myopic decisions starts on the basis of this incorrect expectation; then, for the FEE to be seen as stable, the sequence of decisions should converge back to the correct network size. We apply this concept to the last model of the previous section, in which users differ in their valuation of the network benefits (but share the same valuation of the intrinsic benefit). Recall that three equilibria can coexist in this model, which we called the "null," the "small," and the "large" network equilibria. Before developing the argument formally (less technically oriented readers may want to skip the exposition), we summarize the main insights in the following lesson.

LESSON 3.3   *The "null network" and "large network" equilibria are stable, whereas the "small network" equilibrium is unstable. The size of the network in this unstable equilibrium can then be seen as a* critical mass *of users that needs to be reached for the successful buildout of the network.*

In the model where users differ in their valuation of the network benefits, a user of type β has a net utility of joining the network that is given by $r + \beta n^e - A$, where we recall that n^e is the shared expectations of all users regarding the size of the network. As $\beta \le 1$, we see that any expected network size n^e such that $n^e \le A - r$ leads to an actual null network (as $r + \beta n^e - A \le 0$ for all users). At the other extreme, we have that whenever $A \le r$, all users join the network ($n = 1$) irrespective of the expected network size (as even for the less eager user, $\beta = 0$, $r + \beta n^e - A \ge 0$). It follows that for $A > r$ and $n^e > A - r$, the actual network size is comprised between 0 and 1. In sum, the actual network size n for some expected size n^e is obtained as follows:

$$n\left(n^e\right) = \begin{cases} 0 & \text{if } n^e \le A - r \\ 1 & \text{if } A \le r \\ 1 - (A - r)/n^e & \text{otherwise.} \end{cases} \quad (3.1)$$

---

[3] This analysis borrows from Easley and Kleinberg (2010, chapter 17).

Let us focus on the case where $A > r$. As we showed above, as long as $A < r + 1/4$, three FEE coexist: $n_n = 0$, $n_s = \frac{1}{2} - \frac{1}{2}\sqrt{1 - 4(A - r)}$ and $n_l = \frac{1}{2} + \frac{1}{2}\sqrt{1 - 4(A - r)}$. We call them, respectively, the "null network," the "small network," and the "large network" equilibria. We can use expression (3.1) to confirm that expectations are fulfilled at these three equilibria: (i) If $n^e = 0$, then we see from the top line that $n(0) = 0$; (ii) if $n^e = n_s$, simple computations establish that $n(n_s) = 1 - (A - r)/n_s = n_s$; (iii) it is also the case that $n(n_l) = n_l$.

Now, what happens if all users expect a network size different from 0, n_s or n_l and behave in a myopic way? We assume that adoptions take place over two consecutive periods (e.g., days or weeks) and we focus on user choices in the second period. Suppose that the first period ($t = 1$) ended with a fraction n_1 of users deciding to join the network; to make the exercise interesting, take $n_1 > A - r$. At the next period ($t = 2$), users have the opportunity to confirm or revise their previous decision, expecting the future network size to be the same as the one they currently observe; that is, $n^e = n_1$, which implies that the actual network size at the end of period 1 is $n_2 = n(n_1)$. As $n_1 > A - r$, we derive n_2 from the bottom line of expression (3.1): $n_2 = 1 - (A - r)/n_1 > 0$. What we want to characterize is the adoption path that these myopic decisions generate. Formally, we are interested in the sign of $n_2 - n_1$: If it is positive (resp. negative), the network expands (resp. contracts) from one period to the next. Simple computations establish that:

$$n_2 - n_1 = 1 - \frac{A - r}{n_1} - n_1 = \frac{1}{n_1}(n_1 - n_s)(n_l - n_1).$$

It follows that the network expands ($n_2 - n_1 > 0$) if the initial network size (n_1, which is also the initial expectation) is between n_s and n_l; otherwise (i.e., if $n_1 < n_s$ or $n_1 > n_l$), the network contracts.

What does this tell us about the *stability* of the three FEE? That is, starting from any FEE and supposing that users wrongly predict this network size, does the ensuing sequence of myopic decisions converge back to the FEE or not? Imposing this stability requirement to the "small network" equilibrium n_s, we see that it is not satisfied: Any expectation taken in the vicinity of n_s (but different from it) drives the sequence of myopic decisions *away* from n_s (the network shrinks if one starts with expectations below n_s or grows if one starts with expectations above n_s). The small network FEE is thus unstable. In contrast, the other two FEE are stable. First, any expected network size slightly above zero drives the dynamics of myopic adoptions back to zero. Second, expectations below n_l make the network expand, while expectations above n_l make it contract: In both cases, the process converges back to n_l.

We illustrate our findings in Figure 3.4. Assuming $A > r$, we draw the function $n(n^e)$, which maps the actual network size against the shared expectation of the users. We see that $n(n^e)$ crosses the 45° line at three points, which correspond to the three FEE (as $n = n(n^e) = n^e$). The arrows indicate in which direction the sequence of myopic decisions evolve when one moves away from a FEE:

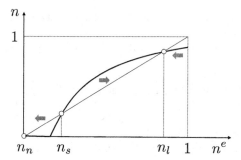

Figure 3.4 Stability and instability of fulfilled-expectation equilibria

If $n(n^e) > n^e$, the network expands (right arrow); if $n(n^e) < n^e$, the network contracts (left arrow). It is then clear that the process converges to n_n and n_l, the two stable FEE, but moves away from the vicinities of n_s, the unstable FEE.

This analysis teaches us important economic insights for the supply of network good, which we address in the next section. First, the "null network" equilibrium is definitely a trap that any producer of network good has to deal with: If users expect that the network will not grow – or will grow just a little – then the network is doomed to failure. Success requires that users expect a network of a larger size than the "small network" equilibrium; if users act myopically, it is the actual size of the network that has to go beyond that point. We can therefore say that the successful buildout of a network needs the attraction of a *critical mass* of users. Then, once this critical mass is passed, the network is likely to snowball, up to reaching the stable "large network" equilibrium. The next case perfectly illustrates this point.

CASE 3.1 THE MILLION DOLLAR HOMEPAGE[4]

In 2005, Alex Tew, an English student, had a daring idea to finance his university education. He decided to set up a website and to sell the space on this site. More precisely, he conceived the home page as a 1000 × 1000 pixel grid, thereby creating a million pixels, which he offered for sale at $1 apiece in 10 × 10 blocks. Anyone purchasing pixel blocks would then be able to display a clickable image on them. Naturally, Alex was hoping to sell all the pixels on his page and so, to raise a million dollars of income.

At first glance, his plan looked like wishful thinking: As his home page had no visibility whatsoever to start with, why would anyone be willing to pay to advertise there? It is not as if Alex was proposing to put a billboard on a strategic spot in a busy street, with a regular flow of potential viewers. His page was lost in the immensity of the web and the probability that anyone would visit it was thus close to zero.

Yet, for Alex, there was no reason to believe that his project was stillborn. It was just a matter of generating the right expectations: If he could make people expect his project to succeed, then it would indeed succeed. In fact, if advertisers bought pixels expecting that other advertisers would do so as well, the site would attract visitors, which would make all advertisers right in their decision to buy pixels in the first place: a self-fulfilling prophecy.

[4] Source: Garone (2016).

In more technical terms, Alex had in mind a mechanism of indirect network effects, which would be fueled by the viewers' curiosity about who would want to advertise, and which would thereby make the utility of an advertiser depend positively on the number of fellow advertisers.

To kick-start this attraction spiral, Alex asked family and friends to buy the first pixels, and sent out a press release, which the BBC and The Register (a technology news website) picked up. This turned out to be a clever move, as the process quickly started to snowball: It took the Million Dollar Homepage one month to receive $250,000, two months to receive $500,000, and four months to raise $999,000; by that time, hits from 25,000 unique visitors were counted on the page every hour. The remaining 1,000 pixels were auctioned on eBay for $38,100.

After this amazing achievement, Alex Tew's launched a number of spinoffs of the Million Dollar Homepage. Unfortunately for him, none of them succeeded the way he hoped. This serves as a cruel reminder of how difficult it is for any provider of a network good to escape the trap of the "null network equilibrium."

3.2   Pricing of a Network Good

In the previous section, we took the fee of network goods as given. We now endogenize the choice of fee, focusing on the pricing behavior of a single network (or platform) operator. We start by supposing that there is only a single network good for purchase (or a single network to join); the main issue here is how the interdependency among users' adoption decisions affects the monopoly platform's pricing decision. We first reconsider our simple model with two users (3.2.1) and next, extend the analysis to a continuum of users (3.2.2). We suppose then that users have free access to a second network good; the platform must take into account that the users' outside option is now endogenous (3.2.3).

3.2.1   Pricing to Two Users

As we did before, we first draw some insights from a simple case with two users. In the next section, we consolidate and enrich our findings by considering a continuum of users. Our two users, Xena and Yuri, are assumed to have different valuations for the stand-alone benefits of the network good (respectively r_x and r_y) but to share the same valuation for the network benefits (β), which they obtain when they both purchase the good. Because of the network effects, their net utilities are contingent on their combined decisions, which places them in the 2x2 game of Table 3.2.

We recall from the previous analysis that the form of the demand function depends on the strength of the network effects. Noting $N(A)$ the number of buyers at fee A, we can summarize our previous results as follows:

If $\beta < r_x - r_y$,

$$N(A) = \begin{cases} 0 & \text{if } A \geq r_x, \\ 1 & \text{if } r_y + \beta \leq A \leq r_x, \\ 2 & \text{if } A \leq r_y + \beta. \end{cases}$$

If $\beta > r_x - r_y$,

$$N(A) = \begin{cases} 0 & \text{if } A \geq r_y + \beta, \\ 0 \text{ or } 2 & \text{if } r_x \leq A \leq r_y + \beta, \\ 2 & \text{if } A \leq r_x. \end{cases}$$

Table 3.2 Demand for a network good by two users

| | | Yuri | |
		Buy	Don't buy
Xena	Buy	$r_x + \beta - A, r_y + \beta - A$	$r_x - A, 0$
	Don't buy	$0, r_y - A$	$0, 0$

Suppose that the network good is provided by a monopoly platform, which faces a constant marginal cost $f \geq 0$ to deliver the good to an extra user (or to connect an extra user to the network). We assume that $f < r_x$ so that even selling only to Xena is profitable. We want to characterize the optimal pricing behavior of this intermediary.

We start with the case of *weak network effects* ($\beta < r_x - r_y$). As already explained, there is a single quantity demanded for each fee in this case. The platform faces thus the alternative of either setting a high fee ($A = r_x$) and selling only to Xena, or to lower the fee (to $A = r_y + \beta$) so as to sell to Yuri as well. Selling a single unit is more profitable than selling two if and only if $r_x - f > 2\left(r_y + \beta - f\right)$, which is equivalent to $\beta < r_x - r_y - \frac{1}{2}\left(r_x - f\right)$. Now, from a welfare point of view, it would be desirable to have both users buying the good, instead of just Xena, if $r_x + r_y + 2\beta - 2f > r_x - f$, or $\beta > \frac{1}{2}\left(f - r_y\right)$. As $r_x > r_y$ implies that $r_x - r_y - \frac{1}{2}\left(r_x - f\right) > \frac{1}{2}\left(f - r_y\right)$, there exist values of the parameter β that satisfy the previous two conditions, meaning that the monopoly intermediary may find it profitable to limit the network size in a welfare-detrimental way. This is so in spite of the intermediary's ability to internalize, via its choice of fee, the network effect that users exert on one another.

Let us move now to the case of *strong network effects* ($\beta > r_x - r_y$). Here, there is no fee that would generate an equilibrium where only one user joins the network. The intermediary is thus looking for the highest fee compatible with both Xena and Yuri joining the network. The problem here is that there exist fees for which the intermediary cannot be sure of what the users will decide: If $r_x \leq A \leq r_y + \beta$, they both adopt the good or neither of them does according to the expectations they form regarding the other user's decision. If the intermediary is pessimistic about the users' chances of coordinating on the adoption equilibrium, then the safe option is to set $A = r_x$; the corresponding profit is $\pi_{pes} = 2\left(r_x - f\right)$, where the subscript "*pes*" stands for "*pessimistic*." At the other extreme, if the intermediary is very optimistic, it believes that setting the high fee $A = r_y + \beta$ still leads both users to adopt the good, thereby generating a profit of $\pi_{opt} = 2\left(r_y + \beta - f\right)$, with the subscript "*opt*" standing for "*optimistic*."[5]

---

[5] We have implicitly assumed so far that the intermediary is not able to price discriminate. In Chapter 5, we will consider this possibility when the platform intermediates between distinct groups of users, which makes price discrimination feasible.

3.2.2   Pricing to a Continuum of Users

We now generalize the analysis to a large number of users.[6] To keep things simple, we consider a pure communication technology that generates only network benefits (the stand-alone benefits are nil for all users). As we did previously, we assume that there is a unit mass of users, identified by their valuation β of the network benefits, which can take any value between 0 and 1. Here, β can be interpreted as the value that a particular user attaches to the possibility of communicating with each additional user. So, if a fraction n^e of users is expected to adopt the communication technology and if the fee of the technology is A, then user β enjoys a net utility of $\beta n^e - A$. Following the methodology developed in previous sections, we compute the inverse demand for network participation, under the requirement of fulfilled expectations, as $A = n(1 - n)$. As far as supply is concerned, we let the total cost of providing this communication technology to n users be given by the twice continuously differentiable function $f(n)$, with $f'(n) \geq 0$. In what follows, we compare the network sizes that prevail under monopoly, perfect competition, and welfare maximization.

Starting with the monopoly, let us assume for now that the platform chooses how many users to connect to the network: that is, the value of n that maximizes $n^2(1 - n) - f(n)$. In this scenario, the platform is able to control network effects directly (we will comment on this later). The network size that the monopoly chooses, which we note n^m, corresponds to the largest intersection between the marginal revenue and marginal cost curves, which is characterized by $n^m(2 - 3n^m) = f'(n^m)$.

In contrast, the network size that would prevail under perfect competition, which we note n^c, corresponds to the largest intersection between the demand function and the marginal cost curve, which implies that $n^c(1 - n^c) = f'(n^c)$. Recalling that the maximum value of $A = n(1 - n)$ is reached for $n = 1/2$ and is equal to $1/4$, we can show a first important result: If $f'(1/2) \leq 1/4$, then $n^m < n^c$ — that is, a smaller network size emerges under monopoly than under perfect competition. That is, despite its ability to internalize network effects (which competitive firms lack), a monopoly platform restricts the network size (i.e., the quantity) below the perfectly competitive level. To see this, refer to Figure 3.5 and note first that if $f'(1/2) \leq 1/4$, then the marginal cost curve intersects the schedules $n(1 - n)$ and $n(2 - 3n)$ at values of n that are strictly larger than $1/2$; to complete the proof, note that $n > 1/2$ implies that $n(2 - 3n) < n(1 - n)$. Let us illustrate this result with two specific examples. First, let $f'(n) = f$, with $f < 1/4$; in this case, we find that $n^m = (1 + \sqrt{1 - 3f})/3$ and $n^c = (1 + \sqrt{1 - 4f})/2$; we quickly see that $n^c = 1$ for $f = 0$ and $n^c = 1/2$ for $f = 1/4$; more generally, it is easily checked that $n^m < n^c$ for $f < 1/4$. Second, take $f'(n) = \phi n$, with $\phi < 1/2$; here, $n^m = (2 - \phi)/3$ and $n^c = 1 - \phi$; we find that $n^m - n^c = (2\phi - 1)/3 < 0$ for $\phi < 1/2$.

---

[6] This exposition follows Belleflamme and Peitz (2018b).

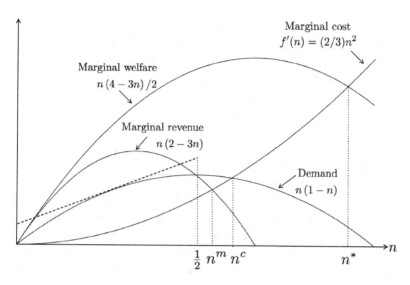

Figure 3.5 Insufficient provision of network goods

Finally, let us compute the welfare-maximizing network size, which we note n^*. Total surplus is computed as $TS(n) = \int_{1-n}^{1} \beta n \, d\beta - f(n) = \frac{1}{2}n^2(2-n) - f(n)$. From the first-order condition, we see that n^* satisfies $n^*(4-3n^*)/2 = f'(n^*)$. It is easily seen that $n(4-3n)/2 > \max\{n(1-n), n(3-2n)\}$. As the marginal cost curve is assumed to be increasing in n, it follows that n^* is necessarily larger than n^c and n^m. We check in the above two examples that $n^* = 1 > n^c, n^m$. In words, in the presence of network effects, both perfect competition and monopoly fail to achieve the first best. Network effects are the main source of the market failure: When joining the network, users do not internalize the positive consumption externality that they exert on the other users. Figure 3.5 depicts graphically the relationship between n^m, n^c and n^*; in this figure, we set $f'(n) = (2/3)n^2$. Lesson 3.4 summarizes our main findings.

LESSON 3.4   *In general, a monopolist (who cannot resort to fee discrimination) supports a smaller network and charges a higher fee than perfectly competitive firms. Both a monopoly and a perfectly competitive industry tend to provide the network good in insufficient quantity with respect to what would be socially desirable.*

In the previous lesson, we were careful not to overstate the comparison between monopoly and perfect competition. Our analysis can indeed be qualified in a number of ways. First, the condition $f'(1/2) < 1/4$ is sufficient but not necessary; if $f'(1/2) > 1/4$, it is possible to find cost functions that lead to larger network sizes under monopoly than under perfect competition. Take, for example, $f'(n) = 1/25 + n/5$, which is such that $f'(1/2) = 0.26$; then, it can be checked that $n^c = 0.4 < n^m = 0,491$ (this function is represented by the dotted line in Figure 3.5).

Second, and more importantly, we could assume that the monopoly platform sets the access fee to the network instead of choosing directly the number of users. In the absence of network effects, this would not make any difference but in the presence of network effects, it does: When the monopoly sets the fee, it faces the multiplicity of equilibria problem.[7] For the fee and quantity decisions to lead to the same outcome, we would need to impose that for any fee that the platform chooses, it is the largest equilibrium network size compatible with that fee that is selected; otherwise, the platform could end up with a null or a small network. As competitive firms face the same multiplicity of equilibria problem, it is not clear how the monopoly solution compares with the perfectly competitive one in the case of fee setting. If both market structures lead to the same equilibrium (i.e., the small or the large one), then Figure 3.3 suggests that the previous result still holds: The monopoly leads to a smaller network size. Yet, one can argue that a monopoly platform is better equipped than competitive platforms to deploy additional strategies to ensure that the largest equilibrium network size eventually emerges. Let us briefly discuss two such strategies (we fully address these strategies in the next three chapters). First, the monopoly could boost the growth of the network through "partial vertical integration" – that is, by generating some network effects on its own or by investing upfront in the intrinsic quality of the network good (e.g., in Case 3.1, we saw that Alex Tew had friends and family buying the first pixels on the Million Dollar Homepage). Second, the platform may be in a position to practice differential pricing and so, be able to pay early adopters, which is another way to kick-start network growth.

3.2.3   Pricing in the Presence of an Alternative Network Good

So far, we considered situations in which there is only one network good available. In such situations, the outside option that users face is exogenous and thus *constant*: What they obtain if they do not purchase the good (or do not join the platform) is independent of their behavior and, for that matter, of the behavior of other users. This changes when users can choose among several network goods or platforms, as is the case in many markets. In particular, if the available networks are incompatible, then network benefits are specific to each network good. As a result, the outside option of buying a particular network good becomes *endogenous*, in the sense that the value of the outside option depends on the users' choices.

To see this, suppose that a given set of users are already interacting via an existing network and contemplate joining a newly established platform offering a different network good. From the point of view of the new platform, the users' outside option is what they obtain if they stay on the existing network. Because network effects are specific to each network good, we have that the value of the outside option decreases as more users join the new platform; this is because fewer users stay on the existing network, which reduces the network benefits that users can enjoy there. Consequently, attraction loops become more powerful because the gap in network benefits between the new platform and the existing network widens as more users switch. On the other hand, attraction loops are also harder to set in motion, as the

---

[7] An additional issue, which we address in the next section, is whether the price affects users' expectations or not.

outside option of staying on the existing network is the largest when no user has moved yet to the new platform.

This discussion suggests that faced with incompatible network goods, users may coordinate on a single network – that is, the market may "tip." In contrast, if platforms are compatible, each user generates network benefits for any user of any network good alike; it is as though a single – "global" – network existed that encompasses both networks. In that case, the models we analyzed here are still relevant, as they allow us to derive the demand for access to the "global" network. The new platform then aims to attract a share of this demand. A priori, if the two networks' cost structures are reasonably similar, they should coexist at equilibrium.

It appears thus that users' choices – and therefore platform pricing – become more complex when several network goods are available, and that compatibility is a key strategic dimension for platform operators. In this section, we focus on the pricing behavior of a platform competing against an alternative network with an exogenous price. We first extend our previous model to fit two network goods; second, we examine the new platform's pricing decision when the two networks are incompatible (we analyze the impacts of compatibility in the next section).

Model

We extend our previous analysis by introducing a second network good. We suppose that a fixed set of users view the two network goods as horizontally differentiated: If the two goods offer the same value, each good attracts some users. We assume that the horizontal differentiation between the two network goods stems from the users' heterogeneity in terms of stand-alone benefits. We model this in the Hotelling fashion by assuming that the two network goods are located at the extreme points of the unit interval (the new platform at 0 and the established network good at 1), while a unit mass of users are located uniformly on the interval.[8] Seeing the unit interval as the space of stand-alone benefits that a platform can offer and a user's location as their definition of the stand-alone benefit that is the most valuable for them, we have that users incur a disutility when accessing a network that does not correspond to what is ideal for them. This disutility takes the form of a "transport cost" that increases linearly with the distance that separates the user's location from the location of the network good that they decide to consume.

Network goods are different along three other dimensions. First, we assume that the new platform can set its access fee A_1 to its network, while the access fee to network 2 is fixed. To simplify the exposition, we assume that both network goods are provided at a marginal cost of zero and that access to network 2 is free (i.e., it is priced at marginal cost). Second, we assume that the intensity of network effects may differ across the two platforms. Finally, we assume that the new platform offers a network good of higher quality; in particular, platform 1 provides all users with larger stand-alone benefits than platform 2. A scenario that fits with this description is the

---

[8] We adapt the model of Griva and Vettas (2011). We also borrow from Doganoglu and Wright (2006) when addressing the effects of compatibility in the next section.

following: All users are interacting on the legacy network before the new platform enters the market with a superior network good; users must then decide whether to pay the fee A_1 to join the new platform or to keep using the legacy network at no cost (for instance, because they have already sunk the access fee for this network).

Against this backdrop, we write the net utility function of a user located at $x \in [0, 1]$ when the new platform sets fee A_1 as:

$$U(x) = \begin{cases} r + q - \tau x + \beta_1 n_1^e - A_1 & \text{if joining the new platform} \\ r - \tau(1 - x) + \beta_2 n_2^e & \text{if staying on the legacy network} \\ 0 & \text{if not joining any platform} \end{cases}$$

Let us detail all the elements of this function. First, $r > 0$ is the (gross) stand-alone benefit that accrues to a user at the ideal location; in what follows we assume that r is large enough so that all users will join one or the other network (i.e., the third option of not joining any network is never exercised and the market is said to be "fully covered"). Second, $q \geq 0$ is the extra (gross) stand-alone benefit that the new platform offers relative to the legacy network. We can see q as a quality difference between the two network goods and so, call network good 1 "superior." Third, τ measures the "transport cost" (or the user's reduction in stand-alone benefit) per unit of distance; hence, the total transport cost for user x is τx if they join network 1 or $\tau(1 - x)$ if they join network 2. Finally, network benefits for network i are computed as $\beta_i n_i^e$, where β_i measures the strength of the network effects (which is assumed to be the same for users of the same platform but may differ across platforms) and n_i^e is the expected size of network i.

From the utility function, we can identify the user who is indifferent between the two networks as the user located at x_0 such that $r + q + \beta_1 n_1^e - \tau x_0 - A_1 = r + \beta_2 n_2^e - \tau(1 - x_0)$, which is equivalent to:

$$x_0 = \frac{1}{2} + \frac{q + \beta_1 n_1^e - \beta_2 n_2^e - A_1}{2\tau}. \tag{3.2}$$

As long as x_0 lies between 0 and 1, and under our assumption that the market is fully covered, all users located at the left of x_0 join the new platform and all users to the right join the legacy network. It follows that $n_1 = x_0$ and $n_2 = 1 - x_0$. We observe thus that network benefits create an additional term in the vertical dimension: Other things being equal, a network that is expected to attract more users obtains a larger market share ($\partial n_i / \partial n_i^e > 0$).[9] Here, the quality difference between network goods is endogenous, insofar as it results from the decisions of the users themselves (and not from some outside force, like q). As we see in expression (3.2), stronger network effects (i.e., a larger β_i) make this source of quality difference more consequential. This can lead to a point where one network captures the whole market (which is then said to "tip"). For this to happen, network effects must be "strong enough" relative to the degree of horizontal differentiation between the platforms: The more users

---

[9] This is no longer true when network goods are fully compatible, as we discuss subsequently.

see network goods as differentiated (i.e., the more they care for a particular network goods), the stronger network effects need to be to convince all users to join the same network.

The endogenous quality difference also depends on the way users form their expectations about the network sizes. As before, we require expectations to be fulfilled at equilibrium and we assume that expectations can be influenced by the fee set by the new platform. The latter assumption seems appropriate when the platform cannot change its fee easily; this may be due to technological, institutional, or regulatory reasons that impose costs and/or delay when modifying fees. Then, it makes sense to assume that users first observe the fees (and believe that they will not change) and then form their expectations; we call such expectations "responsive."[10]

Pricing in the Presence of Incompatible Networks

We suppose here that the network goods are incompatible with one another; this means that a user of network i cannot interact with a user of network j and that network benefits are therefore specific to the particular network good. Under responsive expectations (i.e., the platform can manage users' expectations through its choice of fee), x_0 indicates the location of the indifferent user (if one exists) for a fee A_1, when all users expect that a share x_0 of users will indeed connect to network 1. A given fee A_1 may give rise to three possible fulfilled-expectation equilibria (FEE). First, all users may connect to network 1; for this situation to be a FEE, the user located at 1 must be better off connecting to network 1 than to network 2 when $n_1^e = 1$: $r + q + \beta_1 - \tau - A_1 \geq r$ or $A_1 \leq q + \beta_1 - \tau$. Second, to have a FEE with all users joining network 2, the user located at 0 must be better off joining network 2 than network 1 when $n_1^e = 0$: $r + q - A_1 \leq r + \beta_2 - \tau$ or $A_1 \geq q - \beta_2 + \tau$. Finally, to derive an interior FEE, we set $x_0 = n_1$, $n_1^e = n_1$ and $n_2^e = 1 - n_1$ in expression (3.2), and we solve for n_1, which gives:

$$n_1 = \frac{q + \tau - \beta_2 - A_1}{2\tau - \beta_1 - \beta_2}. \tag{3.3}$$

We see in this expression that the sign of $(2\tau - \beta_1 - \beta_2)$ determines how n_1 varies with the fee of platform 1. If $(\beta_1 + \beta_2)/2 < \tau$, then the market share of network 1 decreases with its own fee; here, the Law of Demand applies because the average network effects (measured by $(\beta_1 + \beta_2)/2$) exert a weaker force than horizontal differentiation (measured by τ) does. In contrast, if $(\beta_1 + \beta_2)/2 > \tau$, then the new platform gains a larger market share when it *increases* its fee. In other words, the demand for access to the new platform is downward-sloping when $(\beta_1 + \beta_2)/2 < \tau$ but contains an upward-sloping portion when $(\beta_1 + \beta_2)/2 > \tau$, which leads to multiple levels of demand for some prices (as we saw above). Before examining these two cases in more detail, we can already draw the following general lesson:

---

[10] Alternatively, we could consider situations in which the platform finds it easier to change fees. Then, users would have no reason to base their expectations about network size on the announced fee, either because they cannot observe it or because they believe that the announced fee can be modified later on; such expectations are then called "passive" – using the terminology of Hurkens and Lopez (2014). We do not consider this alternative scenario here.

LESSON 3.5   *In situations in which a platform sets a fee for access and users can, alternatively, join for free another incompatible network, the market structure depends on the balance between two opposite forces: On the one hand, horizontal differentiation leads users to adopt the network that is a better fit to their tastes; on the other hand, network effects drive users to adopt the same network, as this allows them to enjoy higher network benefits. It follows that if horizontal differentiation weighs more than network effects, then there is room for two networks; otherwise, it is possible that only one network will be used.*

"Weak" Network Effects

When network effects are not too strong – that is, when $(\beta_1 + \beta_2)/2 < \tau$ – then each fee A_1 gives rise to a unique FEE: $n_1 = 0$ for $A_1 \leq q + \beta_1 - \tau$; n_1 is defined by expression (3.3) for $q + \beta_1 - \tau \leq A_1 \leq q - \beta_2 + \tau$; and $n_1 = 1$ for $A_1 \geq q - \beta_2 + \tau$. Facing this "demand function," platform 1's profit-maximization program is:

$$\max_{A_1} \frac{q + \tau - \beta_2 - A_1}{2\tau - \beta_1 - \beta_2} A_1 \text{ subject to } A_1 \geq q + \beta_1 - \tau.$$

Solving for the first-order condition of the unconstrained program, we find:

$$A_1^* = \frac{q + \tau - \beta_2}{2}.$$

The size of platform 1's network is then computed as:

$$n_1^* = \frac{1}{2} \frac{q + \tau - \beta_2}{2\tau - \beta_1 - \beta_2}.$$

In what follows, we assume that $0 < n_1^* < 1$, which is equivalent to $\beta_2 - \tau < q < 3\tau - 2\beta_1 - \beta_2$. (We note that $q < 3\tau - 2\beta_1 - \beta_2$ guarantees that $A_1^* > q + \beta_1 - \tau$, meaning that the constraint of this maximization program is satisfied.) Under these assumptions, we compute platform 1's profit as:

$$\pi_1^* = \frac{(q + \tau - \beta_2)^2}{4(2\tau - \beta_1 - \beta_2)}. \tag{3.4}$$

We now assess how platform 1 is affected by the network effects present on platform 2. We first note that *an increase in β_2 drives platform 1 to reduce its profit-maximizing fee* $(\partial A_1^*/\partial \beta_2 < 0)$.[11] An increase of β_2 has thus two contrasting effects on the size of platform 1's network. On the one hand, for a given A_1, fewer users choose platform 1 when network effects become stronger on platform 2. On the other hand, platform 1 reacts to an increase in β_2 by lowering its fee, which attracts more users. To assess the balance between these two effects, we compute:

$$\frac{\partial n_1^*}{\partial \beta_2} = \frac{q - \tau + \beta_1}{2(2\tau - \beta_1 - \beta_2)^2} > 0 \Leftrightarrow \beta_1 > \tau - q.$$

We observe thus that, *if network effects are strong enough on platform 1, then platform 1 attracts more users when network effects become stronger on platform*

---

[11] We let β_2 increase from 0 to $2\tau - \beta_1$, keeping the average network effects "weak."

2. The total effect of an increase in β_2 on platform 1's profit is thus ambiguous as the "price effect" is negative while the "quantity effect" may be positive. Deriving π_1^* with respect to β_2, we obtain:

$$\frac{\partial \pi_1^*}{\partial \beta_2} = \frac{(q + \tau - \beta_2)(q - 3\tau + 2\beta_1 + \beta_2)}{4(2\tau - \beta_1 - \beta_2)^2}.$$

As we assume that $q + \tau - \beta_2 > 0$ (to guarantee $n_1^* > 0$), we see that *an increase in β_2 may be beneficial for platform 1 if it offers strong enough network effects*, namely if $\beta_1 > (3\tau - q - \beta_2)/2$. Interestingly, the latter condition is more likely to be satisfied if (i) platform 1 has a large quality advantage (large q) and (ii) network effects are strong on platform 2 (high β_2). To understand the latter result (which may seem surprising at first glance), let us go back to expression (3.2), which identifies the user who is indifferent between the two platforms. Given that all users join one or the other platform, we have that $n_2^e = 1 - n_1^e$; it follows that $\partial^2 x_0 / (\partial n_1^e \partial \beta_2) = 1/(2\tau) > 0$; that is, as we noted above, the attraction loop that benefits platform 1 $(\partial x_0 / \partial n_1^e)$ gets stronger as β_2 increases.

"Strong" Network Effects

We now briefly consider the case in which $(\beta_1 + \beta_2)/2 > \tau$. As suggested by our previous analysis with a single available platform, "strong" network effects may lead to a multiplicity of FEE for a given pair of fees. In particular, we observe the following demand configuration: For $A_1 \geq q + \beta_1 - \tau$, the unique FEE is $n_1 = 0$; for $q - \beta_2 + \tau \leq A_1 \leq q + \beta_1 - \tau$, three FEE coexist: n_1 is either equal to 0 or 1, or it is defined by expression (3.3) and lies between 0 and 1; for $A_1 \leq q - \beta_2 + \tau$, the unique FEE is $n_1 = 1$. Therefore, platform 1 faces a "demand function" that contains an upward-sloping portion, which looks like the one depicted in the left panel of Figure 3.3. This implies that if the platform chooses an intermediate fee, it cannot know a priori which of the three possible network sizes will result. As one of them may be $n_1 = 0$ (which obviously implies $\pi_1 = 0$), the platform may prefer to make sure to avoid this risk by setting $A_1 = q - \beta_2 + \tau$, so as to guarantee that $n_1 = 1$ is the unique equilibrium.

If platform 1 adopts the latter strategy (which we will discuss in more detail in the next chapter), an *increase in β_2 has two detrimental effects on platform 1*: First, for given values of β_1 and τ, a larger value of β_2 makes it more likely that the condition $(\beta_1 + \beta_2)/2 > \tau$ is satisfied, leading to a potential multiplicity of FEE; second, the platform's profit being equal to $q - \beta_2 + \tau$, it is clearly decreasing in β_2.

3.3 Strategies for Network Goods

As we saw in the previous section, the presence of network effects makes fee setting a rather complex exercise, because (i) pricing is affected by – and may affect – users' expectations, (ii) multiple equilibria may result from a given combination of fees, and (iii) pricing may be "a matter of life or death," as markets may tip when network effects are strong. Platforms must thus carefully factor in network effects in their choice of pricing strategy. Network effects also drive platforms to design specific strategic instruments, which we start studying in this section.[12] As hinted in the previous section, a platform has first to decide whether or not to be compatible with the other network that their potential users could join (3.3.1). Then, if the platform opts for incompatibility, it must try to make network effects work to their advantage. To do so, it may use introductory fees to build an early installed base of users and, thereby, preempt its rivals (3.3.2). It may also try to take an early lead in the competition (3.3.3).

3.3.1   Compatibility Decisions

To analyze the incentive for a platform to be compatible with a competing network, we return to the model we analyzed in the last part of the previous section.[13] Recall that we extend the Hotelling model of product differentiation to two network goods featuring positive (within-group) network effects; network good 1 is located at 0, network good 2 is located at 1 and a mass 1 of users are uniformly located between these two extreme points. To simplify our analysis, we assume that the strength of network effects is the same on both networks, namely that $\beta_1 = \beta_2 = \beta$. We focus on the case where network effects are weak and the new platform does not find it profitable to attract all users; that is, we assume $\beta < \tau$ and $q < 3(\tau - \beta)$.

Pricing Under Compatibility
We suppose now that the two networks are fully compatible. This implies that all users can interact with one another, irrespective of the network they have decided to connect with; as a result, we have that $n_1^e = n_2^e = 1$. It follows that users do not care anymore about the expected sizes of the two networks when choosing which network to join, as they can enjoy the exact same network benefits on either network. That is, the user who is indifferent between the two networks is such that $r + q + \beta - \tau x_0 - A_1 = r + \beta - \tau(1 - x_0)$, which is equivalent to $x_0 = (\tau + q - A_1)/(2\tau)$. As all users located on the left of x_0 choose network 1, we have that $n_1 = x_0$. Hence, the new platform chooses A_1 to maximize $A_1 n_1 = A_1(\tau + q - A_1)/(2\tau)$. The profit-maximizing fee is easily found as $A_1^c = (\tau + q)/2$ (with the superscript c for *compatibility*). At this fee, the platform attracts $n_1^c = (\tau + q)/(4\tau)$ users and achieves a profit of:

$$\pi_1^c = \frac{(\tau + q)^2}{8\tau}. \tag{3.5}$$

---

[12] We will develop our analysis in the next chapters.

[13] Starting in the 1980s, the industrial organization literature has explored the incentives of firms to opt for compatibility in oligopoly contexts. Seminal papers by Katz and Shapiro (1985), Katz and Shapiro (1986), Farrell and Saloner (1985), and Farrell and Saloner (1986) investigate the link between users' adoption and platforms' compatibility decisions.

Platform's Compatibility Choice

To assess whether the platform prefers compatibility or incompatibility, we compare profits in the two regimes – that is, expression (3.5) and expression (3.4) where we set $\beta_1 = \beta_2 = \beta$ and assume $\beta < \tau$ for network effects to be "weak." We compute:

$$\pi_1^c - \pi_1^* = \frac{(\tau + q)^2}{8\tau} - \frac{(q - \beta + \tau)^2}{8(\tau - \beta)} = \beta \frac{\tau^2 - \beta\tau - q^2}{8\tau(\tau - \beta)} > 0 \Leftrightarrow q < \sqrt{\tau(\tau - \beta)} \equiv \hat{q}.$$

We observe thus that the platform's preference for compatibility basically depends on the size of the quality advantage it has over the alternative network: If this advantage is small (i.e., if $q < \hat{q}$), then the new platform can achieve a larger profit by making its network good compatible with the other network; the reverse applies when the new platform's quality advantage is large (i.e., if $q > \hat{q}$).

To understand the intuition behind this result, note that compatibility has two major implications for the new platform. On the one hand, compatibility increases the users' willingness to pay, as users prefer to join a "common" large network rather than having to choose between two potentially smaller networks; this effect is positive as it allows the new platform to raise its fee: $A_1^c = (\tau + q)/2 > A_1^* = (\tau + q - \beta)/2$. On the other hand, compatibility decreases the endogenous quality difference between the networks, as users' adoption decision no longer depends on relative network sizes. Whether this second effect is positive or negative for the new platform depends on the size of its network under incompatibility: The level playing field that compatibility creates makes a platform with a small network better off and a platform with a large network worse off. Here, the new platform's network size under incompatibility, with $\beta_1 = \beta_2 = \beta$, is equal to $n_1^* = (q + \tau - \beta)/4(\tau - \beta)$; it is larger than $1/2$ (meaning that the size of the new platform's network is larger than the one of the legacy network) if $q > \tau - \beta$.

Observing that $\hat{q} > \tau - \beta$, we have thus the following three cases: (1) For $0 \leq q \leq \tau - \beta$, the new platform benefits from the two effects of compatibility; (2) for $\tau - \beta \leq q \leq \hat{q}$, the new platform suffers from the "level playing field effect," but this is more than compensated by the users' larger willingness to pay, meaning that compatibility remains the preferred option; (3) for $\hat{q} \leq q \leq 3(\tau - \beta)$, the negative "level playing field effect" becomes dominant and the new platform therefore prefers incompatibility.

Users' Preferences Regarding Compatibility

To examine users' preferences, we consider the total consumer surplus and ignore distributional effects between different users (i.e., because of user heterogeneity, users may be affected differentially). Consumer surplus is the addition of the following four components:

(1) **Total stand-alone benefits** All users obtain r and the users joining the new platform get the extra value q; the total stand-alone benefits are thus equal to $r + n_1 q$; they are *larger under incompatibility* because the new platform – which is superior – attracts more users under incompatibility ($n_1^* \geq n_1^c$).

(2) **Total network benefits** Under incompatibility, the n_1^* users of the new platform enjoy network benefits of βn_1^*, while the $(1 - n_1^*)$ users of the legacy network enjoy network benefits of $\beta (1 - n_1^*)$; under compatibility, all users enjoy network benefits of β; as $\beta - \left[\beta \left(n_1^* \right)^2 + \beta \left(1 - n_1^* \right)^2 \right] = 2\beta n_1^* \left(1 - n_1^* \right) > 0$, we see that total network benefits are *larger under compatibility*.

(3) **Total transport costs** We need to subtract the total users' disutility of not being able to join their ideal network; given that the network goods are located at the extreme points of the interval, total transport costs decrease the more symmetric the networks' market shares are; as $n_1^* \geq n_1^c$, total transport costs are *smaller under compatibility*.

(4) **Total fees** Finally, we also need to subtract the total fees that users have to pay to join the new platform, $n_1 A_1$; as this is equivalent to the new platform's profit in this example, we already know that total fees are *smaller under incompatibility for small values of q*.

As compatibility has contrasting effects on the four components of consumer surplus, we cannot say a priori what users prefer. We can, however, figure out that *users prefer compatibility when the platforms are relatively similar*. Indeed, when $q = 0$, the new platform attracts the same number of users in the two regimes ($n_1^* = n_1^c = 1/4$ for $q = 0$); it follows that the total stand-alone benefits and transport costs are the same in the two regimes; total network benefits, with $n_1^* = 1/4$, are higher under compatibility by $3\beta/8$; as for the total bill, given $n_1^* = n_1^c = 1/4$, $A_1^c = \tau/2$ and $A_1^* = (\tau - \beta)/2$, it is larger under compatibility by $(1/4)\left(A_1^c - A_1^* \right) = \beta/8$. So, consumer surplus is larger by $\beta/4$ under compatibility when $q = 0$. By continuity, this holds true for small values of q. This implies that *the new platform and users have aligned preferences for compatibility when the quality advantage of the new platform is small*.

Do the new platform and users still agree for larger values of q? We know that the new platform gets the same profit under compatibility and incompatibility at $q = \hat{q}$; from the users' viewpoint, this means that the total bill is the same: $n_1^c A_1^c = n_1^* A_1^*$. The difference in consumer surplus comes thus from the differences in the other three components. Yet, incompatibility yields larger stand-alone benefits whereas compatibility yields larger network benefits and smaller transport costs. We thus need to compute the difference in consumer surplus to assess the net effect:

$$CS^c - CS^* \big|_{q = \hat{q}} = \beta \frac{2\sqrt{\tau (\tau - \beta)} + (2\tau - 3\beta)}{16 (\tau - \beta)}.$$

The latter expression is positive for $\tau > (9/8)\beta$. If so, when the new platform's quality advantage becomes large enough to drive it to choose incompatibility, this choice goes against the preferences of the users, as they would be collectively better off under compatibility.

Lesson 3.6 collects our findings:

LESSON 3.6   *A fee-setting platform facing competition from a free legacy network prefers to be compatible with this network if it is relatively similar to it in terms of intrinsic quality. However, if the new platform has a sufficiently large quality advantage, it prefers to be incompatible with the free network, which may hurt users, who would collectively prefer compatibility.*

In the above analyses, we did not introduce compatibility costs. However, by choosing compatibility with the legacy network, the new platform may have to forego higher-quality provision. This makes compatibility less attractive for the new platform and users alike. To see this, suppose that the new platform has to forego its quality advantage q if it chooses compatibility. Hence, with $q = 0$, the profit under compatibility becomes $A_1^c = \tau/8$. We can then compute that for the platform to prefer compatibility, the quality advantage that it enjoys under incompatibility (q) must be lower than $\hat{q} - (\tau - \beta)$. We check thus that the platform is less inclined to make its network compatible with the legacy network if compatibility comes at the cost of losing the quality advantage it has under incompatibility.[14]

The following case illustrates the pros and cons of compatibility (or standardization) when network owners have idiosyncratic preferences over the choice of standard (or even randomize over different standards failing to anticipate future compatibility issues) and the value from network size changes over time.

CASE 3.2 THE COMPATIBILITY OF RAILWAY TRACK GAUGES

Puffert (2002) documents and tries to explain the historical selection of regional standards for railway track gauge (i.e., the distance between a pair of rails). When two railway companies or administrations adopt the same standard, they both benefit from greater profits, as they can exchange traffic more easily and, thereby, lower their costs and improve their services. Hence, network effects are present and they induce standardization on a unique gauge. However, regional histories show that actors in the railway value chain (builders, operators, or regulators) have had idiosyncratic preferences over which gauge to select, based on the respective technical performance of different standards; this has been a source of variety in gauge choices. The relative importance of these two conflicting forces has evolved through time. As Puffert writes (p. 291), "[h]istorically, an interest in compatibility was often relatively weak in the early years of railways. Railway builders did not foresee the future value of long-distance railway transport, and thus they placed little value on compatibility with previous lines, except for those nearby. As time went on, railway builders placed an increasing value on compatibility."[15] The geographical position of a country also explains its preference

---

[14] When two or more firms decide whether to keep a common standard or go separate paths, this can be formalized as firms playing a standardization game. If at least one firm prefers incompatibility, the outcome can be called forking. If firms were both better off under a common standard but cannot agree on which of the alternatives to pick, the outcome can be called fragmentation. See Simcoe and Watson (2019) for a classification and case studies.

[15] Simcoe and Watson (2019) speak of splintering, when an excessive variety of incompatible standards survive. As they write, in the case of railway gauges, this arguably happened because of "a combination of initial experimentation, path-dependence, and decentralized decision-making. As regional networks grew and merged, the costs of incompatibility became clear" (Simcoe and Watson, 2019, p. 292). Put differently, initially there were separate markets with a single standard. Thus,

regarding standardization vs. variety: "The variant gauges of Russia and Spain remain to this day, as these more peripheral countries had little exchange of traffic with the core of Europe until their common-gauge networks – and potential conversion costs – had grown relatively large" (p. 288).

3.3.2   Dynamic Pricing of Network Goods

The static framework that we developed in the previous section does not provide us with the necessary tools to analyze how platforms compete in a situations of incompatibility.[16] As users typically arrive on the market sequentially, platforms need to develop dynamic strategies that incorporate the effects of current fees on future market shares. Because of the reinforcing power of network effects, platforms may indeed want to set lower fees today, so as to increase their chances of winning the standards war and, thereby, be able to set higher fees later on (as users will be willing to pay more to join a larger – or the only remaining – network).

To analyze this kind of issues, we need to adopt a dynamic framework, where platforms and users make decisions over consecutive periods. In such a setting, the platform that leads the race at some point in time faces what can be called the "harvest/invest conundrum." On the one hand, this platform is tempted to set higher fees so as to "harvest" the higher willingness to pay that users have for its network. On the other hand, the platform is also tempted to set lower fees in order to "invest" in the future size on its network because the gains from increasing network size are typically larger for a large than for a small platform. As these short-term and long-term incentives go in opposite directions, it is a priori not clear which one will dominate. As a result, the sequence of fees that a platform will set through time may increase or decrease.

To explore this point a bit further, let us briefly describe a model of dynamic competition between platforms producing incompatible network goods.[17] Users are assumed to live for potentially many periods (i.e., they die and are replaced with a constant hazard rate). As assumed so far, users derive stand-alone and network benefits from the network good that they choose. The stand-alone component is received once the user joins a network and its value is supposed to be the user's private information; the network component is received each period that a user is still alive. A newborn user chooses one of the two existing networks and stays with it until death. This decision is assumed to be made in a rational, forward-looking way. This means that users are able to anticipate all future decisions so as to estimate correctly the evolution of network sizes. In each period, the two platforms compete for new users to join their network by setting the fee of their network good (fees below marginal costs are allowed).

initially there was no coordination issue. However, when these regional markets became one larger national or multinational market, the resulting incompatibility was costly.

[16] In the static framework we confined ourselves to a setting in which the price of one of the network goods is fixed. Here, we discuss what happens with two platforms pricing dynamically.

[17] We follow here the exposition of Cabral (2011) given in Belleflamme and Peitz (2018b).

Although the pricing equilibrium is symmetric, market shares are generally asymmetric because of the stochastic appearance of new users. So, there are two questions of interest: (i) Does the large network attract a new user with higher probability than the small network? (ii) Does the large network increase its size in expected value? The answer to the first question is yes. As for the second question, the answer is yes as well, as long as network effects are sufficiently strong and the big firm is still shy of holding 100 percent of the market.

The previous results suggest that getting a head start may prove valuable in situations with incompatible platforms. However, as we discuss in the next section, the current analysis abstracts away a number of factors that may reverse this statement.

3.3.3   First- or Second-Mover Advantage in Standard Wars?

What are the factors that could mitigate the first-mover advantage that seems to characterize the competition between incompatible network goods? In other words, how could a platform that enters the competition later than a rival compensate for its handicap in terms of network size (knowing that this handicap is meant to grow, other things being equal)? On a related note, what could go wrong for a platform that builds an early installed base of users?

Intrinsic Quality

A first factor to take into account is the intrinsic quality of the product or the service that the competing platforms provide. In the dynamic model that we sketched in the previous section, it was assumed that both platforms had the same, fixed, intrinsic quality (as measured by the value that users attach to the stand-alone benefits). This was clearly a simplifying assumption as product qualities result from firms' investments in R&D and are likely to improve over time (because of knowledge spillovers and/or users' feedback). Platforms may then face the following trade-off when deciding to enter early on the market: They may secure a head start, but they may also have to compromise on the quality of their product; a later entrant with a better product would then be able to overcome an initial disadvantage. This applies if it is more costly to upgrade quality over time than to start with a fresh design at some later point in time.

Backward Compatibility

A second issue concerns compatibility across periods: By posing that users can collect network benefits during their whole life, the previous model implicitly assumed that new versions of the network goods are backward compatible with old ones. In reality, firms may decide against backward compatibility. One reason is that firms may want to force old users to buy a new version of the network good (because, if they stick to the old version, they will not enjoy network benefits from users of the new, incompatible, version). This form of "planned obsolescence" is commonplace in user electronics markets. Another reason, which is hard to disentangle from the previous one, is that backward compatibility often constrains a platform in its effort to improve its products; to reach the full potential of technological advancement, it may thus decide to introduce a new version that is incompatible with the previous one. Abandoning backward compatibility clearly modifies the incentives to build an early installed base of users.

Expectations Management

Finally, when users are not as fully rational as they are supposed to be in the previous framework, there may exist less costly ways to get a head start (or to catch up if one is lagging behind) than through low introductory fees. If users form their expectations in a nonrational way, platforms have the potential to influence these expectations in their favor, thereby creating self-fulfilling prophecies: If users are made to believe that a particular platform will become dominant, then they will adopt the network good of that platform, thereby helping it to become dominant and confirming the initial beliefs. A salient way to manage expectations is to announce a new good well in advance of actual market availability. The objective is to deter users from buying the existing good of a competing platform, thereby slowing down the growth of this platform. However, this tactic of "product preannouncement" may prove to be a double-edged sword, as it might also freeze the sales of the current generation of the platform's own good.

The next case illustrates the three issues that we have just discussed.

CASE 3.3 TIMING IS KEY WHEN COMPETING WITH INCOMPATIBLE PLATFORMS

Intrinsic quality As an illustration of why taking an early lead may not be the best tactic, consider the observation that Hagiu and Rothman (2016) make about the competition between marketplaces (i.e., platforms that facilitate trade between suppliers and buyers): "Entrepreneurs should really focus on being the first to create a liquid market in their segment. The winning marketplace is the first one to figure out how to enable mutually beneficial transactions between suppliers and buyers – not the first one out of the gate. Indeed, many prominent marketplaces were not first movers: Airbnb was founded more than a decade after VRBO; Alibaba was a second mover in China after eBay; and Uber's UberX copied Lyft's peer-to-peer taxi business model."

Backward compatibility Consider the controversy that arose around Apple iPhones end of 2017 (see Kottasová, 2017): "Tech analysts and angry customers have reported in recent days that operating system updates had caused older iPhones to slow considerably, with some suggesting that Apple could be using the tactic to encourage fans to buy new phones. Apple insists the updates were made with a different goal in mind: It said the performance of lithium-ion batteries degrades over time, which can sometimes cause phones to suddenly shut down in order to protect their components."

Expectations management To illustrate the potential perverse effects of product preannouncement, let us just quote this telling title of an article published in May 2017: "Customers Waiting on New iPhones Crimp Apple's Profits " (Goel, 2017).

Key Insights from Chapter 3

- Because network effects make users' purchasing decisions interdependent, the same fee may give rise to several levels of demand, which correspond to different self-fulfilling prophecies.
- A monopolist generally supports a smaller network and charges a higher fee than perfectly competitive firms, but even a perfectly competitive industry fails to reach the network size what would be socially desirable.
- When network effects are strong enough, competition between incompatible platforms may lead to market tipping: A single platform attracts all users.

4 Growing a Platform

We explained how platforms follow a two-step process to generate economic value: First, they *bring together* economic agents and, second, they *actively manage network effects* among these agents. The first step – bringing agents together – is a prerequisite for network effects to materialize: For agents to benefit from interacting, they must somehow be in the presence of one another. Although this looks like a truism, it is often an impossible task for agents to coordinate this common presence by themselves. This is where the platform comes into play: It provides a venue and often an infrastructure that enables the interaction among affiliated agents. The second step is then to manage the network effects – that is, to put in place the conditions for agents to benefit the most (or suffer the least) from their common presence on the platform. In the previous chapter, we looked at a platform that caters to one group of users; in the subsequent chapters we will focus on two-sided platforms.

Chapters 5 and 6 will examine the strategies that two-sided platforms can deploy to manage network effects (using prices and other instruments). But first, in this chapter, we focus on the first step of the value-creation process. We start by going one step further back and asking whether establishing a two-sided platform is a good idea in the first place. We address this existential question in Section 4.1, where we explore the economic trade-offs for a firm of choosing a (two-sided) platform model rather than alternative modes of organization. For firms adopting the two-sided platform model, we then expose the difficulties that they will inevitably face when trying to bring two groups of agents together. In fact, the potential existence of network effects is not sufficient to have agents affiliate with the platform: They first need to be convinced that they will find other agents on the platform, with whom they can interact. The key question is thus how to convince them. In Section 4.2, we formalize what is known as the "chicken-and-egg-problem" and show how an adequate choice of strategies may solve it. In Section 4.3, we discuss the strategies that platforms can implement to increase the level of trust among users, thereby securing their participation and, possibly, intensifying the network effects. Finally, in Section 4.4, we examine why and how a platform may decide to expand the range of services that it offers.

4.1 Platform or Not Platform?

Up to a few decades ago, the travel and hospitality industry was almost entirely organized in a traditional – vertically integrated – way, with services being provided by firms owning their means of production (means of transport, accommodations) and hiring service providers (drivers, hoteliers, etc.). An intermediary sector complemented the industry, with distributors selling seats and rooms, and helping travelers find their way through the multiple alternatives. Airlines partly owned airline reservation systems that connected airlines to travel agents. The airline reservation systems subsequently became independent two-sided platforms. Nowadays, while most of these intermediaries have moved online, a whole new breed of intermediaries has emerged, providing travelers with similar services as vertically integrated firms, yet in a completely different way. Two prominent examples of these new intermediaries are Airbnb in the short-term accommodation sector and Uber in the point-to-point transportation sector. The two companies share the common feature of not owning the means of providing their service (no property for Airbnb, no fleet of cars for Uber). Instead, they operate as platforms: They do not control the production of a service, but they enable it by facilitating the interaction between those who want to consume a service (travelers) and those who can perform it (who act mostly as independent contractors).

Similar changes take place in other industries. As the heated competition between Walmart and Amazon illustrates so well, retailers, who are the traditional vertical link between producers and consumers, now compete with platforms that operate marketplaces. As with Airbnb versus hotel chains, or Uber versus taxi companies, the opposition is between *enabling* a transaction (here, setting up an infrastructure through which producers and consumers can interact directly to exchange goods) or *controlling* a transaction (here, buying and reselling goods). Putting the "enable mode" (platform) at one extreme, and the "control mode" (vertical integration or resell) at the other, it is possible to define a whole spectrum of business models that companies can choose from. In reality, firms often adjust their business model by moving along this spectrum, as illustrated in Case 4.1.

CASE 4.1 HYBRIDIZATION OF BUSINESS MODELS IN THE HOSPITALITY INDUSTRY

In 2017, Airbnb started to move a little away from a pure platform model by partnering with the real estate industry to design "Airbnb-friendly leases." For instance, in France, the real estate company Century 21 helps Airbnb promote contractual agreements between landlords and tenants, whereby tenants are allowed to sublet their apartment on the platform; the proceeds of the short-term rentals are then divided between all the parties. Airbnb even went one step further in Florida by partnering with Newgard Development Group to develop "Airbnb-branded apartments." The annual leases also allow tenants to rent these apartments on Airbnb; moreover, each property also has a sort of concierge, who helps with check-in or cleaning, while rooms are suited for guests with secure storage and keyless doors. At the other end of the spectrum, Accorhotels took a step away from pure vertical integration in 2015 by transforming its Accorhotels.com distribution platform into a marketplace open to a selection of independent hotels.[1]

As far as online travel intermediaries are concerned, they operate either as referrals or agents (i.e., they set up a platform that refers travelers to hotels, who then interact directly) or as merchants (i.e., they book rooms from hotels and resell them to travelers). Condorelli et al. (2018) report the following: "Priceline makes most of its revenue through the referral mode and the rest from acting as a merchant. Priceline's subsidiary Booking.com is an agency-based business, whereas its subsidiary Agoda is a merchant-based business. Expedia operates mainly under the merchant mode receiving roughly 75 percent of its revenue through the merchant mode and some 21 percent through the referral mode. Expedia expanded its business by acquiring the agency-based online hotel business Venere. Orbitz's net revenue stems fairly evenly from its air and hotel businesses (34 and 29 percent respectively), with its revenue from the hotel business coming mainly from the merchant mode."

We will consider hybrid business models of that sort in more detail in Section 4.2.4. But we need first to highlight the main economic trade-offs that firms face when moving closer to one or the other extreme.

4.1.1   The Basic Trade-Off: Enabling vs. Controlling

As we just discussed, when a firm is organized as a platform, it makes it possible for sellers (or service providers) and buyers (or customers) to interact directly; it therefore leaves the residual control rights over the provision of the service (or the sale of the product) to independent professionals. In contrast, when a firm is vertically integrated or when it operates as a reseller, it keeps the residual control rights for itself. The basic choice is thus between enabling and controlling; that is, between allowing independent professionals to provide goods to customers over the platform and employing professionals to produce the goods (or to buy the goods from these professionals) so as to provide them to customers.

According to Hagiu and Wright (2015a,b, 2019), a firm that contemplates the choice between these two options faces a fundamental trade-off between motivation and adaptation on the one hand, and coordination on the other hand. *Motivation* refers to the ability to drive professionals to exert costly efforts that lead to improving the customers' experience. Arguably, motivation is easier to achieve in the enabling than in the controlling mode, for the simple reason that professionals have more incentives to exert effort when they themselves control the transactions with customers, and are thus able to capture the full returns of their investment. *Adaptation* concerns the capacity to adjust decisions to private information that professionals may have. Again, by letting professionals interact directly with customers, the enabling mode also lets them make decisions that are adapted to their private information; in contrast, in the controlling mode, the firm may take inadequate decisions, as it does not have access to the professionals' private information. Finally, *coordination*

[1] Sources: J. Hempel, "Airbnb's newest weapon against regulation: The real estate industry," *Wired*, July 3, 2018; D. Meyer, "Airbnb apartment complex in Florida is designed for homesharing. But that means sharing profits, too," *Fortune*, October 13, 2017; *HNN Newswire*, "Accor rebrands, opens distribution platform" June 3, 2015.

has to do with the internalization of potential spillovers; for instance, the goods or services provided may be substitutes or complements to one another, which implies that selling more of one good decreases (substitutes) or increases (complements) the demand for the other good; similarly, individual professionals or suppliers may exert, through their actions, positive or negative externalities on one another (think, e.g., of persuasive advertising, which may have a negative, business-stealing, effect). Here, the controlling mode has a clear advantage over the enabling mode, as the firm is in a position to adjust decisions so as to take the various spillovers into account. We summarize this discussion in the next lesson:

LESSON 4.1   *The enabling mode (platform) fares better in terms of motivation (inducing professionals to exert efforts) and adaptation (letting professionals adjust their actions according to their private information). The controlling mode (vertical integration, resell) fares better in terms of coordination (internalizing externalities across professionals, goods and services).*

Naturally, there exist tools that firms can use to alleviate the inherent drawbacks of the mode they have chosen. A platform that can monitor the transactions may charge independent professionals a variable fee proportional to the volume of trans-actions that they conduct. Thereby, the platform may coordinate better the activities of the affiliated professionals. Typically, the platform will set a positive usage fee if spillovers are negative, so as to induce professionals to choose a lower level of harmful activities; by the same token, negative usage fees are meant to make pro-fessionals intensify beneficial activities when spillovers are positive. The same logic applies when the goods or services provided on the platform are substitutes (calling for increased fees) or complements (calling for reduced fees).

A vertically integrated firm may use incentive schemes to address the moral haz-ard problem that it faces in terms of motivation. For instance, by linking bonuses or commissions to the number of customers attracted, the firm may induce the professionals it employs or its suppliers to exert more effort.

Hagiu and Wright (2015b) build a model that incorporates all the previous ele-ments. The key ingredients of the model are the following: First, there is a set of professionals who can either interact directly with customers (enabling mode) or be employed by the firm (controlling mode). Second, professionals take two types of action, which both impact positively the customers' demand for their product or service: One action is transferable (i.e., the control over this action can be trans-ferred from the professional to the firm), while the other action is not (i.e., the firm cannot control it); the former can be some advertising or marketing action, while the latter is some unobservable effort made by the professional; it is the latter type of actions that generate a moral hazard problem. Third, the exact impact of transferable actions on demand is unknown to the firm but known to the professional when the action is taken; it is here that professionals have private information. Finally, trans-ferable actions generate positive or negative spillovers across professionals. Solving the model, the authors show that the firm will prefer the enabling mode (i.e., the platform) provided that the magnitude of the spillover parameter is sufficiently small relative to the importance of moral hazard and professionals' private information. This condition is more likely to be satisfied if usage fees can be used in the enabling mode but less likely to be satisfied when bonuses can be used in the controlling mode.

4.1.2   Other Trade-Offs

We have focused so far on situations in which asymmetric information is to the disadvantage of the firm, either because professionals have private information about how their actions affect the consumers' willingness to pay or because the firm cannot observe the efforts that they exert. However, the reverse may also happen. First, the firm may have some private information about the way some activities (e.g., marketing or advertising) affect customers. This information could come from the exploitation of large volumes of transaction data, to which individual professionals have no access. In such instances of two-sided private information, Hagiu and Wright (2015a) argue that the residual control rights should rest with the party whose private information is more valuable to design demand-enhancing activities; this implies that a platform is more effective in dealing with the professionals' private information insofar as this information is more important than the firm's private information. Second, moral hazard can be present on the professionals' as well as on the firm's side; that is, both the firms and professionals may make investment decisions that cannot be monitored by the other side. For instance, in point-to-point transportation, drivers invest in their knowledge of the routes and in the quality of their service, while firms (Uber or taxi companies) invest in advertising and in the quality of the technological infrastructure (dispatch and payment systems).[2] Here, this additional source of moral hazard tends to reinforce the advantage of the enable mode with respect to the control mode.

The two organization modes also involve major differences in terms of cost structures. As platforms rely on independent professionals to produce goods or to provide services, they trade off production costs for coordination costs. Compared to vertically integrated firms or to resellers, platforms do not need to acquire and transform inputs, but they have to attract both professionals and customers, and to facilitate their interaction. Also, platforms do not exploit economies of scale or scope, but within-group and cross-group network effects. One may be tempted to think that platforms face lower costs than vertically integrated firms as they do not produce anything by themselves, but as we will discuss in the next section, the cost of acquiring participants may be extremely large.

The quality of the products and services offered to the consumers in the two modes may also differ. In particular, because platforms rely on independent professionals, they are more flexible than integrated firms or resellers (which are bound by their previous production choices and past investments). As mentioned previously when referring to adaptation, platforms can focus more easily on products and services that

---

[2] See Hagiu and Wright (2019) for other examples.

match the consumers' tastes, and adjust them fast whenever necessary. Moreover, by using digital technologies, platforms can make their products and services more convenient to use.

4.1.3   How to Choose?

As already indicated, enabling or controlling is not necessarily a black and white decision: Firms may well combine the two modes (we return to this later). Yet, the question remains as to which aspects of a business should be better organized under one mode or under the other. In their analyses, Hagiu and Wright (2015a,b) propose some guidelines, which they confront with real cases. As reported in Case 4.2, their predictions seem relevant in view of Amazon's choices.

CASE 4.2 WHEN DOES AMAZON ENABLE AND WHEN DOES IT CONTROL?

Amazon acts nowadays both as a reseller (controlling mode) and as a marketplace (enabling mode). As stated in Lesson 4.3, the enabling mode is more likely to be favored when the necessity to adapt to changing market conditions is important (thanks to the private information they possess, professionals may indeed adjust their decisions more efficiently than an integrated reseller would do). Applying this argument, we expect that for products that change relatively fast (typically electronics), Amazon relies proportionately more on its marketplace whereas, for products that change relatively slowly (typically books), Amazon sells a larger proportion as a reseller. The empirical analysis of Hagiu and Wright (2015a) lends credence to this hypothesis. They show indeed (using high-level data collected from Amazon's website in January 2014) that Amazon was listed as a seller for 54 percent of the 20.5 million new books, but for only 1 percent of the 25.8 millions new "electronics" items it had in stock.

4.2   The Chicken-and-Egg Problem

After pondering the various trade-offs presented in the previous section, a firm may decide that the platform mode of organization is better suited to its business. However, before jumping in with both feet, the firm needs to realize that launching a platform is fraught with a major difficulty, known as the *chicken-and-egg problem*.[3] We start this section by describing the nature of this problem (4.2.1). We then explore how a nascent two-sided platform should design its price structure to try and circumvent the problem, first in a static context (4.2.2) and next in a dynamic context (4.2.3). Finally, we discuss how strategies aiming at kick-starting a two-sided platform may lead, at least temporarily, to hybrid modes of organization that combine features of platforms and other business models (4.2.4).

Note that in what follows, we will most of the time identify the two groups participating in a two-sided platform as "buyers" and "sellers." Although this formulation is restrictive, we believe that giving generic names to the two groups of users will facilitate the exposition (otherwise, we would quickly struggle with complex combinations of letters and numbers). We will use other denominations when dealing

---

[3] It is also sometimes referred to as the mutual baiting problem.

with platforms for which this formulation is clearly inappropriate (think of a dating website, for instance, or any platform that does not organize transactions).

4.2.1   Chicken or Egg: Which Should Come First?

To understand the nature of the chicken-and-egg problem, recall from Chapter 3 that network effects create an interdependence between the users' decisions to participate in a particular platform. This is so because the value that any user attaches to the platform depends on whether – and possibly to which extent – other users also participate in the platform. When a user cannot observe what other users decide (which is generally the case in large anonymous markets), they have to base their own decision on the expectations that they form about what the participation level in the platform could be. As a result, it is often the case that several equilibria coexist in the game that users play when deciding whether or not to join a given platform. These equilibria are brought about by self-fulfilling prophecies, insofar as the expectations that users form lead them to make decisions that, when combined, confirm the initial expectations. Among these *fulfilled expectations equilibria*, there is the so-called null equilibrium, such that no user participates in the platform. This equilibrium logically follows from users having pessimistic expectations about the platform's ability to attract membership: If (potential) users believe that no one will join the platform, they attach very little value, if any, to joining; as a result, if there is a cost (even small) to participating in the platform, all users refrain from doing so, which validates their initial expectations.

Quite obviously, the challenge for any platform business is to overcome the null equilibrium. In Chapter 3, we examined this issue in situations with direct network effects – that is, network effects that emerge within a single group of users. We showed that the challenge there is to attract a sufficient number of initial users, a socalled *critical mass*, so as to generate optimistic expectations that would eventually lead to a stable equilibrium with a large number of users. The trick is thus to convince a sufficient number of early users, who will then naturally attract new users thanks to the attraction loop that network effects nourish.

Getting the better of the null equilibrium seems even more challenging for two-sided (or worse, multi-sided) platforms featuring an attraction spiral. Here, network effects arise across various groups of users (we talk of "cross-group network effects"). Typically, users in group A value the platform because it allows them to interact with users of group B, and vice versa.[4] Expectations have thus to be formed regarding the participation of users in the other group. Here, the null equilibrium arises when users expect that the platform will not be able to attract any counterparty from the other group (and does not offer a sufficiently large stand-alone utility to at least some users of a group). Think, for instance, of a platform that organizes the exchange of secondhand goods: If, as a seller, I believe that this platform will

[4] Their valuation of the platform may also depend on the participation of other users of their own group, as we saw in Chapter 1.

not attract any buyer, I have no reason to set up a shop trying to sell my old stuff there; likewise, as a buyer, if I believe that this platform will not attract any seller, I will not go there looking for good bargains. In a nutshell, a platform that does not manage to attract any "sellers" (or group A users) will not attract any "buyers" (or group B users), and if it does not attract any buyers, it will not be able to attract any sellers. The chicken-and-egg problem refers to this vicious circle, as we record in Lesson 4.2:

LESSON 4.2   *The chicken-and-egg problem for a two-sided platform describes the fact that users in one group will not participate unless they expect users in the other group to participate, and vice versa.*

4.2.2   Divide-and-Conquer Strategy

As a two-sided platform serves two different groups of users, it is in a position to set a different tariff for each group.[5] In the next chapter, we will look more deeply into the various tariff instruments that platforms can use. Here, we focus for simplicity on access fees – that is, a fixed fee that users have to pay (once and for all) to participate in the platform. Our main point in this section is that the ability for a platform to set different fees for the different groups of participants is key for solving the chicken-and-egg problem. Moreover, the platform may have to set a fee for one group of users that is below its cost of serving these users, thereby *subsidizing* their participation. We record this finding in the following lesson:

LESSON 4.3   *To overcome the chicken-and-egg problem, platforms may resort to a "divide-and-conquer" strategy, whereby they set a low fee for one group and a high fee for the other group. To apply such a strategy, platforms must be allowed to set different fees to different groups and possibly below-cost fees.*

Divide and Conquer in a Platform Model
We now establish the result more formally.[6] Consider a platform that tries to attract buyers and sellers. For simplicity, we assume that there are N_b identical buyers and N_s identical sellers (with N_b and $N_s \geq 2$). If n_b buyers and n_s sellers join the platform (with $0 \leq n_b \leq N_b$ and $0 \leq n_s \leq N_s$), then their respective net surpluses are given by:

$$v_b = r_b + \beta_b n_s - A_b \text{ and } v_s = r_s + \beta_s n_b - A_s.$$

This formulation of surpluses resembles the one we used in the previous chapter when dealing with within-group network effects. As before, a user net surplus is

---

[5] This can be seen as price discrimination when the platform offers the same service to the two groups, e.g., a matching service. However, in many instances, one cannot really talk of price discrimination, as the platform has distinct offerings for the two groups; for instance, a gaming platform sells a console to end users (the buyers in our terminology), and licences development tools to game developers (the sellers in our terminology). In any case, platforms are able to observe which user belongs to which group and so make them distinct offerings.

[6] We follow section 4.3 in Belleflamme and Toulemonde (2009).

made of three components: an intrinsic benefit, (r_b, r_s), a network benefit, and, in deduction, an access fee paid to the platform (A_b, A_s). The only difference is that network benefits stem now from interactions *across* groups rather than within a group, which leads to an attraction spiral. Here a buyer gets a benefit β_b from each seller they interact with, yielding a total network benefit of $\beta_b n_s$; the parameter β_b measures thus a buyer's valuation of interacting with an additional seller or, equivalently, the intensity of the cross-group network effect that sellers exert on buyers. Similarly, each seller gets a total network benefit of $\beta_s n_b$.

To complete the description of the model, we make the following assumptions. First, we suppose that users who decide not to join the platform have an outside option whose value is constant (think of the value of not interacting with any user of the other group); we note these values v_b^0 and v_s^0.[7] Second, the platform faces no fixed cost when launching its operations; as for the marginal costs that it incurs when accommodating an extra buyer or seller, we set them at zero; the access fees can then be reinterpreted as margins above (if positive) or below (if negative) the respective marginal cost. Finally, we consider a two-stage game: In the first stage, the platform sets the fees A_b and A_s; in the second stage, upon observing these fees, the N_b buyers and the N_s sellers simultaneously decide whether or not to join the platform. We look for the subgame-perfect equilibria of this game. Our main question is, of course, whether and how the platform is able to cover its launching costs (which is the same as making a profit under our assumptions).

Working by backward induction, we start with the second stage of the game. Given A_b and A_s, what do buyers and sellers decide? Because users are identical and because their outside option is independent of their choice, all users within a group make the same decision: Either they all join the platform or none of them does; we can make the exact same argument for sellers. This leaves us with four possible equilibrium configurations: (n_b, n_b) can be equal to (N_b, N_s), $(0,0)$, $(N_b, 0)$, or $(0, N_s)$. We consider them in turn.[8]

- If (N_b, N_s) is an equilibrium, then it must be that any buyer is better off interacting with all sellers on the platform than staying out and keeping their (the buyer's) outside option: $r_b + \beta_b N_s - A_b \geq v_b^0$; similarly, for any seller, we must have $r_s + \beta_s N_b - A_s \geq v_s^0$.
- If $(0,0)$ is an equilibrium, then any user prefers staying out than joining the platform that no user of the other group is joining: $v_b^0 > r_b - A_b$ (for buyers) and $v_s^0 > r_s - A_s$ (for sellers).
- If $(N_b, 0)$ is an equilibrium, then any buyer prefers to join the platform even if no seller joins it $(r_b - A_b \geq v_b^0)$, while any seller prefers to stay out although all buyers join the platform $(v_s^0 > r_s + \beta_s N_b - A_s)$. Inverting the roles of buyers and

sellers, we find the conditions for $(0, N_s)$ to emerge as the equilibrium configuration.

We summarize the conditions for the four configurations as follows (and we represent them in Figure 4.1):

$$(N_b, N_s) \text{ if } \begin{cases} A_b \leq r_b - v_b^0 + \beta_b N_s \\ A_s \leq r_s - v_s^0 + \beta_s N_b \end{cases} \qquad (0,0) \text{ if } \begin{cases} A_b > r_b - v_b^0 \\ A_s > r_s - v_s^0 \end{cases}$$

$$(N_b, 0) \text{ if } \begin{cases} A_b \leq r_b - v_b^0 \\ A_s > r_s - v_s^0 + \beta_s N_b \end{cases} \qquad (0, N_s) \text{ if } \begin{cases} A_b > r_b - v_b^0 + \beta_b N_s \\ A_s \leq r_s - v_s^0 \end{cases}$$

As was the case with within-group network effects, *cross-group network effects may generate multiple equilibria*. In particular, if the platform sets fees such that $r_b - v_b^0 < A_b \leq r_b - v_b^0 + \beta_b N_s$ and $r_s - v_s^0 < A_s \leq r_s - v_s^0 + \beta_s N_b$, then both (N_b, N_s) and $(0,0)$ are equilibria (see the middle area in Figure 4.1). For such fees, the platform may attract all users of both groups, but may also fail to attract any. If the platform wants to resolve the chicken-and-egg problem for sure, it has to sets its fees so that $(0,0)$ is not an equilibrium. That is, it must either set $A_b \leq r_b - v_b^0$ or $A_s \leq r_s - v_s^0$, so as to convince all users in one group that it is profitable for them to join the platform *even in the absence of any interaction with users of the other group*. The platform thus "compels" the participation of one group and then monetizes this participation by raising the fee for the other group: When observing the low fee set to, say, buyers, sellers unequivocally anticipate that all buyers will join and are then willing to pay as much as $r_s - v_s + \beta_s N_b$ to join as well. In sum, to avoid the null equilibrium, the platform applies a *divide-and-conquer strategy*, setting a low (possibly negative) fee for one group ("divide") and making it up by setting a high fee for the other group ("conquer").

In other words, the platform needs to choose a "subsidy side" and a "money side." How? Intuitively, it is more profitable for the platform to forego profits on the group

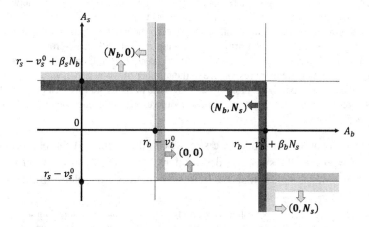

Figure 4.1 Multiple equilibria when launching a platform

that exerts the largest cross-group network effect on the other group, as this determines how much money can be raised on the other side. Here, if buyers are on the subsidy side, profits are $N_b \left(r_b - v_b^0\right) + N_s \left(r_s - v_s^0 + \beta_s N_b\right)$, while if they are on the money side, profits are $N_b \left(r_b - v_b^0 + \beta_b N_s\right) + N_s \left(r_s - v_s^0\right)$. Clearly, the former option is more profitable than the latter if $\beta_s > \beta_b$ – that is, if buyers exert a larger network effect on sellers than sellers do on buyers. Interestingly, to choose which group to subsidize (and which group to "monetize"), the platform does not care about the number of agents in each group (N_b and N_s). It is therefore wrong to think that platforms should monetize the group with the largest number of agents (shopping malls provide an illustration of this principle, as they charge retailers and give free access to shoppers, although the latter group is much larger in size than the former). We record our result in Lesson 4.4 and illustrate it in Case 4.3.[9]

LESSON 4.4   *When applying a divide-and-conquer strategy, a monopoly platform subsidizes the group that exerts the largest cross-group network effect on the other group, and monetizes the other group (irrespective of the relative size of the groups).*

CASE 4.3 PRICING ACCESS TO NIGHTCLUBS

In the offline world, nightclubs may serve as dating platforms, which may help explain a skewed pricing structure, taking the form of gender-specific prices: Women pay a lower entrance fee than men; sometimes they can enter for free, or even for a "negative" price if they are offered a free drink.[10] For instance, Holland (2007) reports the following pricing for a number of nightclubs in Johannesburg, South Africa, during April 2007: The Voodoo Lounge charged a cover charge of SAR 200 for men but only SAR 100 for women on Fridays and Saturdays; the same ratio applied to Catwalk, Fourways, where men paid entrance fees of SAR 100 while women paid only SAR 50. In relative terms, somewhat more attractive to men was the Manhattan Club charging an entrance fee of SAR 70 for men and SAR 60 for women. Two other hot spots were Café Vacca Matta, with an entrance fee of SAR 60 for men and SAR 40 for women, and Panache Café, with an entrance fee of SAR 50 for men and SAR 30 for women.

One may explain this phenomenon merely by different price elasticities for men and women. An additional insight can be obtained taking into account cross-group network effects. Even if men and women have the same willingness to pay for a visit to a nightclub, a profit-maximizing nightclub may charge different prices to men and women. As a matter of fact, the nightclub can be seen as a platform in a matching market with cross-group external effects: The utility functions of men and women depend positively on the number of visitors of the opposite sex. If men are more responsive to the number of women than women to the number of men, the profit-maximizing price structure has the property that women pay less than men. This suggests that nightclubs are concerned about getting the gender balance right and adjust prices accordingly.

Coming back to our model, we stress two other points. If the platform chooses group $k = b, s$ as the subsidy side and if $r_k < v_{k0}$ (i.e., if users in group k value more their outside option than the intrinsic benefits on the platform), then $A_k < 0$:

---

[9] Chan (2019) establishes this result more generally by showing that this equilibrium should be selected among the set of multiple equilibria when applying the concept of *potential-maximizer selection*.

[10] This case is taken mostly verbatim from Belleflamme and Peitz (2015, p. 665).

Users in group k are subsidized and the platform makes losses on that side (as we set the marginal cost for each group to zero). Note also that if the platform was forced to set the same fee for both sides (e.g., because price discrimination was prohibited), then both fees would be below cost and the platform would not be profitable.[11] Finally, being able to solve the chicken-and-egg problem is not a guarantee for profit. In general, the platform makes a positive profit provided that $\max\{\beta_b, \beta_s\} > (v_b^0 - r_b)/N_s + (v_s^0 - r_s)/N_b$. The latter condition is more likely to be satisfied – that is, the launch of the platform is more likely to be successful – (i) the stronger the total cross-group network effects (i.e., the larger β_b, β_s, N_b and N_s), (ii) the larger the intrinsic benefits that the platform provides its users with (r_b and r_s), and (iii) the smaller the value that users can secure when not joining the platform (v_b^0 and v_s^0).

Divide and Conquer with Multiple Platforms

In our previous model, we focused on the entry of a single platform. We kept a potentially alternative platform in the background (through the users' outside option), but we did not consider the potential strategic reactions of this other platform. In this book, we decided to focus on economic environments with only one platform. However, here we make an exception to see how a divide-and-conquer strategy plays out when a competing platform is around. More specifically, we model the competition between two identical platforms, vying for attracting the same groups of buyers and sellers. Think, for example, of two ride-hailing platforms that want to enter a given city, with fixed populations of potential drivers and of riders. We also enrich our previous setting by allowing platforms to set usage fees on top of participation fees.[12] As this model is more complex, we state its main result in Lesson 4.5 for readers who would prefer to skip the exposition.

LESSON 4.5   *When undifferentiated two-sided platforms compete in prices, they both follow a divide-and-conquer strategy and the outcome is such that the market tips in favor of a single surviving platform, which is potentially left with no profit.*

The model goes as follows. There is a group of buyers and a group of sellers, each consisting of a continuum of mass 1. Each user needs the intermediation service of a platform to find their "match" – that is, the unique member of the other group with whom they can trade. Two platforms, noted 1 and 2, compete to offer this matching service. These platforms are incompatible and multihoming (i.e., registering with both platforms) is not possible. As a result, to have a chance of finding one another, matching partners need to register with the same platform. So, if n_b^i buyers and n_s^i sellers register with platform i ($i = 1, 2$), then the probability for a

---

[11] The alternative would be to set two positive prices but then, no user would join.
[12] This model is adapted from Caillaud and Jullien (2003). We follow the exposition of Belleflamme and Peitz (2018b).

buyer and the probability for a seller to find their match on platform i are respectively equal to λn_s^i and λn_b^i, where λ is the probability that two matching partners find each other when they register with the same platform. The gross gain from a successful match is equal to $1/2$ for each partner (gains of trade are normalized to one and are supposed to be equally shared among trading partners after some efficient bargaining process). The net gain is then $1/2\left(1-a^i\right)$, where a^i is the transaction fee that platform i charges. Because we assume constant gains from trade and efficient bargaining, transaction fees are nondistortionary. As a result, it is only the total fee that matters (i.e., a^i) and not the way it is split between the trading partners. Given that platforms also set participation fees A_k^i, the expected net utilities for a buyer and for a seller when registering with platform i along with n_s^i sellers and n_b^i buyers are respectively equal to $v_b^i = \lambda n_s^i \frac{1}{2}\left(1-a^i\right) - A_b^i$ and $v_s^i = \lambda n_b^i \frac{1}{2}\left(1-a^i\right) - A_s^i$.

We analyze the following game. In the first stage, platforms set their price structure to maximize their profit; that is, platform i chooses the triple $\left(A_s^i, A_b^i, a^i\right)$ to maximize $\Pi^i = n_s^i A_s^i + n_b^i A_b^i + \lambda n_s^i n_b^i a^i$ (where we continue to set to zero the marginal cost of providing services to agents of any group). In the second stage, agents choose which platform (if any) to register with; we assume singlehoming on both sides (agents register with at most one platform) and we normalize to zero the outside option of not registering with any platform.

As in the previous simple model, platforms resort to a "divide-and-conquer" strategy, which consists first in "dividing" by subsidizing one group of users to convince them to join and next in "conquering" the users of the other group, who have no better option than to join the platform as well. To be sure of attracting the group of, say, buyers, platform i must offer them a better deal than platform j, even in the worst-case scenario where buyers hold the pessimistic belief that they will find no seller on platform i; that is, it must be that $-A_b^i > \lambda\frac{1}{2}(1-a^j) - A_b^j$. If this condition is met, buyers will join platform i and sellers will follow suit (whatever their beliefs), thereby generating maximal aggregate surplus λ, which platform i can capture by setting the transaction fee at its maximal level ($a^i = 1$). Platform i finds this strategy profitable as long as $\lambda + A_s^i \geq -A_b^i$. Yet, as platform j can follow the exact same strategy, competition through divide-and-conquer strategies will drive profits to zero and allow only one platform to remain active. At equilibrium, the remaining platform subsidizes full participation, charges the maximal transaction fee ($a^i = 1$) and makes zero profit ($A_s^i + A_b^i = -\lambda$). As the presence of positive cross-group network effects makes it efficient to have all agents register with the same platform, the equilibrium is socially desirable.

If one platform (the incumbent) could play before the other (the entrant), the same equilibrium would prevail, with the incumbent deterring the entry but foregoing all profit. The surviving platform may, however, achieve positive profits at equilibrium when transaction fees are not feasible (e.g., because agents, when matched, could bypass the platform to trade). This result is reminiscent of what we already observed in the previous chapter when dealing with within-group network effects: When cross-group network effects are strong (which is the case here, as platforms are undifferentiated), a winner-takes-all situation emerges at equilibrium; in other words, the market tips.

4.2.3   Seeding Strategies

The previous models share two simplifying assumptions: Users are homogeneous within each group, and they decide simultaneously whether or not to join the platform. More often than not, however, users of the same group differ along several dimensions, and affiliation to the platform takes place over time. We briefly describe here how a platform may try to exploit these two features to its advantage in order to solve the chicken-and-egg problem.

As the proverb says, Rome was not built in a day. The same applies to platforms: They can be effectively built stage by stage. The idea is to start small by attracting, say, a few sellers, who will serve as "bait" to win over some buyers; these buyers will then be used as a bait to attract some more sellers, starting a domino chain reaction. The hope is to reduce costs by subsidizing only a small group of early users. But for this strategy to work, this group of users must be sufficiently important to generate optimistic expectations and a feedback loop.

Even if a platform can attract users in a sequential way, it still faces the same fundamental question: Who should it target first? To answer this question, we can apply the same logic as previously, when we distinguished the "subsidy side" from the "money side." The basic principle is that the platform should aim at targeting in priority those users who generate large cross-group network effects, while not being too costly to attract in the first place.

Users who generate large network effects for the other side are called *marquee users*; typical examples are large buyers generating sizable sales for sellers (e.g., a government) or sellers of popular products who are likely to win over many buyers (e.g., popular games on a gaming console, marquee brands in a shopping mall, or opinion leaders on digital media). Having marquee users on board allows a platform to attract relatively more users from the other side; it also contributes to generating positive expectations on both sides regarding the future growth of the platform. The returns of attracting marquee users are thus likely to be high, but so is the cost of attracting them. Marquee users are indeed courted by competing platforms, which places them in a position to extract most of, if not all, the benefits that their presence on a platform generates. In other words, platforms are likely to compete away the returns of having marquee users on board.[13] Case 4.4 illustrates how platforms may combine the strategy of marquee users with a divide-and-conquer pricing scheme to try and kickstart their activity.

---

[13] This issue deserves closer consideration in the context of exclusivity agreements and homing decisions when platforms compete. We do not include them in this book, as this requires a careful analysis of strategic interaction between platforms.

CASE 4.4 HOW PLEX IS DEALING WITH THE CHICKEN-AND-EGG PROBLEM

In an article entitled "Plex strikes deal to offer free Warner movies on its platform" (*The Inquirer*, August 30, 2019), Chris Merriman describes the strategies that the media streaming platform Plex uses to launch its operations. We reproduce part of the article here, emphasizing the parts that illustrate what we discussed previously.

"Media streaming stalwart Plex *has signed a deal with Warner Brothers, which will see classic titles made available to users, at no charge.* Plex has traditionally been more focused on giving users a way of collecting their personal collections of videos, photos and music from multiple hard drives, NAS devices and PCs. But with the streaming wars expected to go completely bonkers in 2020, it's clear that Plex has a strategy. Last year, *it introduced integration with Tidal for music streaming*, and thanks to its deal with WB, it has a streaming video service of its very own too. The company is already well aware of the landscape before it, and *will start offering more paid subscription services next year*, in the hope of creating a 'one-stop-streaming shop'. Plex has no plans to launch a formal streaming service of its own. ... Plex wants to be squeaky clean (and, we can't emphasise enough, isn't doing anything illegal – it's you lot) and *getting some big-name streaming services into its channel library* (BBC iPlayer has been available for years) *might be the lure that people have been waiting on*, especially if they can subscribe right from the Plex app. The issue could be whether (say) Disney+ wants to be seen on Plex – its all very chicken and egg. We won't really know the outcomes of all this until more of these proposed services come online."[14]

Alternatively, instead of focusing on the intensity of cross-group external effects, platforms may target primarily those users who can be attracted – and retained – at relatively lower costs. It may be users with lower outside options (e.g., because they are still unattached to any platform), users with higher valuations for the platform services (e.g., early adopters), users who put a greater weight on stand-alone than on network benefits (e.g., gamers who value more the console performance than the possibility of playing multiplayer games), or more loyal users (who are less likely to churn once they are on the platform). We summarize our discussion in the following lesson.

LESSON 4.6   *To solve the chicken-and-egg problem, platforms may want to attract users in a sequential way and thus implement a seeding strategy. They should then target in priority those users who present the highest ratio between the positive network effects they generate for other users, and the cost that needs to be incurred to attract them.*

Three comments in relation with Lesson 4.6: First, the previous argument also applies for platforms that manage direct network effects. It is crucial to identify the most influential early adopters, so as to kick-start the network as effectively as possible and get the attraction loop going. Second, the strategies that we have considered so far can only work if the actions that the platform deploys on one side (or for early users) are observed and correctly understood by users on the other side (or by later users). For instance, a platform may try to attract more buyers by lowering the membership fee for sellers. The idea is simple: Buyers are more willing to join the platform if they expect that more sellers will be present; however, for buyers to form

---

[14] Source: www.theinquirer.net, last accessed September 2019.

such an expectation, they must be able to observe that sellers do indeed pay a lower fee, which may not be easy in many contexts; at its early stage, a platform may thus need to publicize the decisions it makes so as to increase their visibility.[15]

Finally, all sequential seeding strategies imply that platforms have to sustain losses (or at least an absence of revenues) in the early stages of their existence, and hope to recoup this "investment" later on. Case 4.5 illustrates how risky this strategy can be.

CASE 4.5 LAUNCH OF THE XBOX GAMING PLATFORM

Microsoft's Home and Entertainment Group reported a total loss of $4 billion for the four years after the launch of the Xbox gaming console. The largest part of these losses was due to the subsidization of the Xbox (which sold at a price below its manufacturing cost). Yet, the Xbox eventually became a success, which made Ed Fries, former head of Microsoft Game Studios, declare: "I wouldn't say we lost $4 billion. I'd say we spent $4 billion building the Xbox brand and business." It is too early to say if the same strategy will pay for Uber. From its founding in 2009 to 2017, the company raised $17.3 billion and spent $10.7 billion (estimates by Bloomberg News); in 2018, Uber reported adjusted losses of $304 million and $404 million in the first and second quarters.[16]

Platforms need thus to have sufficiently deep pockets to start their operations. In this respect, financial sources (banks, business angels, venture capitalists, family and friends, crowdfunders) should be seen as yet another group of participants that platforms need to get on board when launching their activities. Important cross-group network effects are at work here as well: Investors must expect sufficient future activity on the platform to agree to fund it; participants are more likely to join the larger the value for money the platform can offer (and the more advertising it can make), which clearly depends on its funding. Relying on external funding may thus exacerbate the chicken-and-egg problem. This may decide firms to take some distance, at least temporarily, with the platform model, as we discuss in the next section.

4.2.4   Initial In-House Production

The previous section illustrated the difficulties raised by the chicken-and-egg problem. Sometimes, these difficulties may be insurmountable, so that the platform business model becomes, at least in the short term, unworkable. A would-be platform may then want to start its operations by controlling transactions and try to enable them later. This can be done, for instance, by providing customers with in-house – first-party – products or services instead of relying on third-party independent providers. Then, third-party providers can be invited to join at a later stage once a solid customer base has been built. This strategy can be seen as a nonprice version of the divide-and-conquer scheme described previously: The participation of

---

[15] As we discuss it in the next chapter, a monopoly platform has incentives to disclose prices. See also Jullien and Pavan (2019) who study the key trade-offs that platforms face when designing their information management policies.

[16] See https://bit.ly/2xCU0EZ for the declaration of Ed Fries, https://bloom.bg/2D4bdaa for Bloomberg News estimates, and https://bit.ly/2NAY7LK for numbers about Uber.

one group is secured not through subsidies but through direct provision of what this group is looking for; the next step is then similar, given that the other group can be attracted more easily once the first group is firmly on board.

A quick look back at history reveals that several well-established and successful platforms followed this integrated route in their early days and exploited network effects only later. The first gaming consoles initially came bundled with in-house games before independent game developers were allowed to write games for them; Apple launched several of its devices (personal computers, smartphones) in a vertically integrated way by supplying its own array of complementary products before opening them to third-party software or apps; Amazon started as a pure reseller before creating its marketplace and opening it to third-party sellers.

More generally, firms having adopted the pipeline business model from the start may, at some later stage, decide to expand their activities by using a platform business model. Here, although the motivation is often not to overcome the chicken-and-egg problem (as the pipeline business model was the natural start), it can be argued that the preexistence of a solid and long-lasting pipeline firm facilitates the launch of a new service organized as a platform (we return to this issue in Section 4.4). In this "product-to-platform scenario," the pipeline company leverages its existing product to develop a platform around it, while maintaining its own production of this product.[17] As an illustration, the hotel chain Marriott International launched in 2019 Home and Villas, a peer-to-peer rental platform focused on the segment of premium and luxury homes. As Mody et al. (2020, p. 708) explain: "One of Marriott's objectives was to keep loyal customers within the Marriott ecosystem and allowed its loyalty program members to redeem their points for Homes and Villas stays. Furthermore, the added platform was asset-light, allowed rapid scaling, plus could accommodate much higher asset heterogeneity compared to its existing hotel room inventory while still ensuring quality."

4.3   Building Trust among Users

As we explained in Section 4.1.1, platforms enable transactions instead of controlling them, like vertically integrated firms do. As a result, platforms facilitating trade rely on external and independent sellers to deliver goods and services to buyers. Similarly, on platforms that facilitate matchmaking, users from different groups cocreate the match thanks to the infrastructure provided by the platform. In both cases, transactions will take place on the platform only if users sufficiently trust one another. Otherwise, users will form pessimistic expectations about the participation

[17] Hagiu and Altman (2017) describe how companies can achieve this in practice. Hagiu, Jullien, and Wright (2020) study the "hosting rivals" strategy, whereby a pipeline turns itself into a platform by letting rivals sell their products or services alongside the firm's core product. The benefit of this strategy is that it enhances the demand for the core product (as users enjoy the convenience of one-stop shopping); the downside, however, is that it also intensifies competition with rivals for noncore products.

of other users and it is then very likely that no users will actually participate – the self-fulfilling prophecy of the "null equilibrium," described in Section 4.2.

Building trust among potential users is thus a strong prerequisite for launching a platform. As transactions are largely anonymous and one-off (users rarely meet before or after the transaction takes place), this is anything but an easy task. In this section, we first recast this issue in more general terms, using the theory of asymmetric information (4.3.1). Then, we present a number of strategies that platforms can deploy to address asymmetric information problems (4.3.2) and discuss how these strategies also affect the strength of network effects on the platform (4.3.3).

4.3.1   Asymmetric Information Problems on Platforms

As we already explained in Chapter 2, asymmetric information problems are common on platforms. It is indeed rare that users know one another before interacting on a platform. As a result, users ignore many important aspects of their potential counterparts that are relevant for their valuation of the platform: What is their willingness to participate to the interaction? How will they behave during the interaction? Will they respect the terms of the transactions? And so on. These problems are particularly prominent on platforms that facilitate the trade of goods, as buyers typically have less information than sellers about the quality of the goods or services offered for sale (either because this information is hidden or because it is costly to search). Case 4.6 provides an illustration of asymmetric information problems arising on platforms.

CASE 4.6 MY TAILOR MAY BE RICH, BUT IS SHE RELIABLE?

In Nigeria, people of all conditions strive to wear made-to-measure clothes. There is thus a large demand for tailors and, consequently, a large – and diverse – supply of them (more than 100,000 tailors are registered). The problem is that information is highly asymmetric: Buyers have very little means to check beforehand whether the tailor they contract with is trustworthy or not. As reported in an article published in *The Economist* in 2019, "many customers have tales of tailor despair, from bespoke clothes that are paid for but never delivered, to sleeves falling off at the seams."[18] Given that the base of smartphone users is fast growing in Nigeria, local entrepreneurs decided to address this market failure by launching *Fashion map*, a platform that connects customers and tailors (and other professionals of the fashion industry such as fashion designers). The platform allows tailors to increase their client base by providing them with location-based visibility. More importantly, it allows customers to make better-informed choices by checking the designs that tailors propose, and by reading the reviews and ratings written by other customers.

Problems of asymmetric information arise in two typical situations: *hidden information* (leading to adverse selection problems) and *hidden actions* (leading to moral hazard problems). We briefly review these two situations and the specific problems that they involve for platforms.

---

[18] See *The Economist*, "Why an 'Uber for tailors' is gaining ground in Lagos," September 26, 2019.

Hidden Information

The parties to a transaction may differ in their access to the information relevant for that transaction. Typically, some information is not accessible to one party. For instance, on crowdfunding platforms (such as Kickstarter or Prosper), funders can hardly ascertain the quality of the projects presented on the platform, as well as the reliability of the entrepreneurs proposing them. Similarly, on job boards, job seekers have information about their competences that is largely unknown to employers. In such cases, the price that buyers are willing to pay for a given transaction is proportional to what they believe is the average quality offered to them. But this price may fall short of what sellers of high-quality goods or services (who face higher costs) would require to accept selling. As they figure this out, buyers would revise downward their estimate of the average quality for sale, which could then scare away even medium-quality sellers. At the end of this unraveling process, only low-quality goods or services will be for sale, making the platform largely unattractive for any user.

Hidden Actions

Problems may also arise because the quality of a transaction depends on actions that one and/or the other party takes. If these actions cannot be controlled and are taken after the transaction price is set, then the parties may have insufficient incentives to invest time and energy in improving the quality of the transaction. For instance, on carpooling platforms (such as BlaBlaCar), the quality of the transaction depends on the level of effort, attention, and care exerted mostly by the driver, but also by the traveler. As the two parties will probably not meet again in the future, they may not care too much about behaving nicely. As such opportunistic behaviors are likely to damage the quality of the transaction, the parties may just refrain from engaging in this transaction altogether, another source of inefficiency for the platform.

4.3.2   Strategies to Address Trust Issues on Platforms

A traditional instrument to address asymmetric information problems is the use of *certification* and *warranties*. When a seller wants to transact with a buyer, third parties may provide certification, and platforms are a natural candidate for such certification services. Certification is an ex ante solution to asymmetric information problems, as it may ensure a minimum quality provided on the platform; lower-quality sellers are not admitted or worse-performing sellers are expelled from the platform. Certification can be mandatory or voluntary. For instance, Uber checks the records of its drivers to make sure that they are eligible to drive; such certification is mandatory. Airbnb offers the sellers of accommodation services the option to certify the authenticity of photos of the announced property, thus reducing the risk of unpleasant surprises for the buyer; such certification is voluntary. As for warranties, they may, in principle, be provided by sellers themselves, but platforms are often in a better position to provide them, since they interact more frequently and directly with buyers.

As these measures may lead to the removal of underperforming sellers from the platform, their impacts on the potential competition among sellers must be taken into account. Absent asymmetric information, reducing seller competition makes the platform less attractive for buyers, everything else given. However, with asymmetric information, removing underperforming sellers may actually make the platform more attractive for buyers, since the expected quality that will be consumed is increased. Thus, for example, security checks for apps on Google Play or certification by Apple may be in the mutual interest of platform and buyers.

Note that buyers are often heterogeneous with respect to seller quality. For instance, some buyers may require fast delivery, whereas others care less about delivery speed. In this case, a platform may establish two market segments for sellers: In one segment, they have to promise a certain quality, while in the other, they do not. For example, Amazon hosts premium sellers with guaranteed fast delivery and standard sellers without that guarantee.

Asymmetric information problems can also be addressed ex post through *insurance* and *guarantees*. For instance, Airbnb insures sellers against vandalism by buyers. Another example is eBay's guarantee to buyers (introduced in 2010) to compensate them if the seller does not deliver as advertised (see Hui et al., 2016). Rating and review systems, which we described in Chapter 2, complement these classic instruments.

4.3.3   Trust and Network Effects

By alleviating asymmetric information problems, these strategies affect the strength of cross-group network effects among users.[19] For an illustration, think of platforms that allow for advance bookings; these platforms may impose specific cancellation policies as a way to affect the network benefits that different groups of users get from a transaction, as described in Case 4.7.

CASE 4.7 CANCELLATION POLICIES ON AIRBNB AND BOOKING

Landlords who wish to offer their rental property for short-term accommodation choose preferably online platforms that attract large numbers of users. As of 2020, the two largest platforms in many countries are Airbnb and Booking. Since its creation, Airbnb has operated as a platform that connects landlords (or "hosts") with travelers (or "guests"). As for Booking, it used to focus on the matching between hotels and travelers but started, more recently, to attract landlords to rent out fully furnished flats. It is interesting to compare the policies that the two platforms apply when either a guest or a host cancels a reservation. What happens when a guest cancels is quite similar on the two platforms, insofar as they both let hosts choose what they deem as the most appropriate cancellation policy. On Airbnb, the choice of cancellation policy goes from Flexible (free cancellation until 24 hours before check-in) to Super Strict 60 Days (50 percent refund for cancellation at least 60 days before check-in). Here is the advice that

---

[19] We will have a more general look at the interplay between platforms' price and nonprice strategies in Chapter 6.

Booking gives to its hosts: "Let guests know if they can cancel their bookings free of charge, and, if so, until when. Generally speaking, we recommend allowing guests to cancel for free until 1 or 2 days before check-in. Alternatively, you can select non-refundable policies where guests won't get their money back if they cancel." On the other hand, the two platforms apply different rules when a host cancels a reservation. On Airbnb, a host who cancels a reservation must pay a penalty (whose amount depends on how soon before check-in the cancellation took place), while the guest receives their money back and is invited to find a different place on the platform or elsewhere. In contrast, a host who cancels a reservation on Booking must provide a good substitute and bear the potential additional costs that the guest would face (e.g., because still available offers of similar quality are more expensive). It is thus reasonable to state that the governance model of Airbnb is more seller-focused, whereas the governance model of Booking is more buyer-focused. This means that β_s tends to be higher and β_b lower on Airbnb compared to Booking.

Cancellation policies are just one of many platform design decisions that platforms can take to improve trust among users. We now provide a partial list of other decisions of that sort. We distinguish between the decisions that are likely to increase network benefits across the board from those that are likely to affect different groups of users in opposing ways. As we just saw, the fine-tuning of cancellation policies by home rental platforms falls into the second category. To fix ideas, we return to the formulation we used above, with the net surpluses of buyers and sellers being respectively given by:

$$v_b = r_b + \beta_b n_s - A_b \text{ and } v_s = r_s + \beta_s n_b - A_s.$$

In this formulation, β_b measures a buyer's valuation of interacting with an additional seller or, equivalently, the intensity of the cross-group network effect that sellers exert on buyers; similarly, β_s measures the intensity of the cross-group network effect that buyers exert on sellers.

Design Decisions with Positive Impacts on All Users
Some design decisions that platforms make tend to increase (at least weakly) the network benefits for both buyers and sellers. Here are some examples:

(1) Platforms design *matching algorithms* that determine how well a proposed partner fits. The better the algorithm, the larger the cross-group network effects β_b and β_s tend to be. A particular instance of such matching is *targeted advertising*. The expected benefit from a buyer-seller match increases as the targeting technology improves. If targeting simply allows a firm to avoid making impressions on consumers who will never buy from this firm, this increases β_s (for given ad volume). If both parties benefit from such an improvement, the network effect increases with this technology for a given number of participants on the other side.

(2) A buyer and a seller may form different expectations about a transaction or an interaction. As this may prevent the transaction from taking place or lead to ex post disagreement, the platform may find it profitable to offer *dispute settlement mechanisms* and default policies. Such decisions are likely to enhance the value

of transactions for both parties (from an ex ante and an ex post perspective), meaning that both β_b and β_s should increase.

(3) Platforms can also take ex ante measures to address quality issues. In particular, they may impose a *minimum quality standard* on the products available on the platform and may develop their own (possibly noisy) *certification system*. A quality standard may not only apply to traded products but also to products or interactions that are not remunerated between the two sides. For example, as we discuss in the next chapter, academic journals use reviews to help in the selection of journal articles (the platform may pay reviewers, but there is no direct payment from authors to reviewers). These measures should raise the average quality of products and, thereby, increase β_b. As for sellers, those who meet the quality requirements should benefit from the buyers' higher willingness to pay, meaning that β_s increases as well. In contrast, the sellers who do not meet the quality requirements (or violate some code of conduct) may have their visibility on the platform reduced or be removed altogether from the platform; for those sellers, β_s is decreased, possibly to zero.

(4) A platform may provide *insurance* against certain risks. If insurance is provided to buyers, β_b is increased, while β_s may go up or down. For instance, a platform that protects buyers against sellers of fraudulent products increases the expected benefit from more variety on the platform from the buyers' perspective; that is, β_b is larger the better the protection buyers enjoy. In this case, β_s is likely to go up for sellers of legitimate products since they avoid demand dilution. If, on the other hand, return rights provide an insurance to buyers in case the product turns out to be a bad fit, β_b is larger the more generous the return rights (for given retail prices), while β_s is smaller (this situation fits into the next category of examples). Endogenizing retail prices affect β_b and β_s, and may change their sign.

(5) Another form of insurance concerns the *payments* that buyers make to sellers. A platform may offer its own payment system or keep payments temporarily on its own accounts to reduce the risks of fraud for both parties to the transaction. The objective is to make sure that buyers pay before taking possession of the product or service, while sellers get paid only after delivery. Compared to upfront payment, this benefits buyers and facilitates refunds. Compared to ex post payments, this benefits sellers, as they know that the payment has already been made and will be transferred if the product or service is delivered. In sum, both β_b and β_s are increased in the process.

Design Decisions with Contrasted Impacts

We review now design decisions that are likely to affect buyers and sellers in conflicting ways.

(1) Platforms address adverse selection and moral hazard problems on the seller side by imposing *return policies* on sellers that negatively affect β_s and positively β_b. If sellers are heterogeneous in meeting the buyers expectations, the

negative effect on β_s is larger for underperforming sellers than for sellers who perform well.

(2) A platform that redesigns its *seller rating system* to be more informative increases the expected benefit users obtain from using the platform for given participation levels of sellers and fellow buyers; that is, β_b increases.[20] The impact for sellers is ambiguous as it depends on the relative consequences of good and bad reviews, and on a seller's intrinsic quality.

(3) Yet another measure is to impose some *liability rules*. For instance, a landlord on a home rental platform who cancels a reservation may be obliged to provide compensation, as documented in Case 4.7. If such a measure is imposed upon sellers, then β_s is decreased and β_b increased.

LESSON 4.7   *A platform imposes trading rules that make the interaction on the platform less risky for at least one group of participants and thus create a more favorable environment for user interaction.*

A platform thus becomes a private regulator that may impose rules on how trade is carried out, it provides ancillary services (such as insurance), it may establish a conflict resolution scheme, and, as an extreme measure, exclude participants of certain types or certain behaviors from the platform.[21] While the rules that govern the trading environment develop over time, initial rules may be essential when launching a platform.

4.4   Platform Expansion

So far in this chapter, we have mainly been concerned with the early – and perilous – stages of a platform's life. Before examining the strategies of platforms that have successfully overcome the hurdles of the launch phase (see the next two chapters), we now make a sort of flash-forward by looking at expansion strategies that an established platform can resort to.

We think, in particular, of strategies aiming at expanding the range of services that the platform offers. On top of facilitating interactions and building trust, a platform may indeed want to create more value for its users by offering them additional products or services and to open the platform to further user groups. To understand why and how a platform may do so, it is useful to distinguish the new products and services according to whether they are substitutes or complements to those offered by the third-party providers that are active on the platform. Developing in-house production corresponds to the former case, while expanding to adjacent markets corresponds to the latter. We consider the two cases in turn.

---

[20] We refer back to Chapter 2 for details on seller rating systems.

[21] Of course, private incentives of the platform may not coincide with those of a social planner. Therefore, public policies may restrain platform decision-making. In this book, we do not elaborate on the interplay between regulatory policy and rule making by private platforms.

4.4.1 In-House Production: The Return

As discussed in Section 4.2.4, choosing a hybrid model that combines platform-like and pipeline-like features may help platforms to roll their operations out when the chicken-and-egg problem is particularly costly to solve. We argue here that a hybrid model may also help platforms to expand their operations at a later stage of their existence.[22] It is indeed not rare to observe that businesses operating as platforms start at some point to produce their own products or services, thereby increasing their control on the transactions conducted on the platform. Zhu (2019) identifies two main motivations behind platforms' entry into the space of their third-party providers. A first motivation is *value capture*: The platform substitutes its own products to some of its providers offering, so as to appropriate directly the value that these products generate. A second motivation is *quality enhancement*: The idea here is to use in-house production in order to make the platform globally more attractive by replacing third-party providers that perform poorly or by catering to a segment that is not well taken care of by third-party providers. Also, integration may simply offer more convenience; in other words, users value having access to the bundled service more than combining the different services themselves. Case 4.8 provides examples for these the two motivations.

CASE 4.8 WHY DO PLATFORMS OFFER THEIR OWN PRODUCTS OR SERVICES?

Value capture (1) It has been showed that Amazon is more likely to sell its own branded version of products sold by third-party sellers when these products have proved successful. (2) Google was found guilty by the European Commission of giving an illegal advantage to its own comparison shopping service, thereby demoting those of competitors.[23]

Quality enhancement (1) JD (a large Chinese e-commerce platform) seems to introduce its own products in market segments that are more exposed to counterfeiting. (2) Google's decision to produce its own flashlight app could be explained by users raising privacy concerns about existing third-party flashlight apps. (3) It is argued that Intel decided to enter product spaces where the quality of third-party products was poor and where increased competition was likely to enhance the providers' incentives to innovate.[24]

Clearly, when first-party products or services are introduced to enhance the quality of the platform, all stakeholders are likely to benefit (except, perhaps, those poorly performing sellers that would be kicked out). In contrast, when the platform enters to capture the value of highly performing sellers, these providers lose part (or all)

---

[22] This may also help *pipelines* to expand, as we illustrated previously with the case of Marriott International venturing into the peer-to-peer rental market.

[23] See CASE AT.39740 – Google Search (Shopping), 27/06/2017. We return to potential search engine biases in Chapter 6.

[24] Most of these examples are taken from Zhu (2019) and Hagiu and Spulber (2013). Further examples can be found in Evans, Hagiu, and Schmalensee (2006). As they explained for software platforms: "Where exactly the tasks performed by software are accomplished is a matter of business and design decisions. Many tasks that used to be performed by stand-alone applications have become integrated into other applications (such as spell checkers, which originally were sold separately from word processing programs) or into the software platform itself" (Evans, Hagiu, and Schmalensee, 2006, p. 52).

of their revenues. They may then reduce their investments in the quality of their offering, or leave the platform altogether. Other providers may do likewise, as they fear the platform's entry in their segment as well. As for the direct impact on consumers, it is a priori ambiguous: On the one hand, the previous chain of events is going to hurt them, but, on the other hand, they will benefit from the products and services now offered by the platform itself. The platform will take these direct impacts into account when optimizing its fee structure. So, price effects need also to be factored in to ascertain whether introducing first-party products is profitable for the platform and how it affects third-party providers and consumers.

We now extend the model we introduced in Section 4.2.2 to put some structure on the analysis. As less mathematically inclined readers may prefer to skip this part, we summarize our main results in the following lesson.

LESSON 4.8   *When a platform introduces in-house production that competes with the offering of third-party providers, the value generated by the interaction of buyers and sellers is reduced. Hence, for this strategy to be profitable, the consumers' valuation of the in-house production must be sufficiently high. This does not guarantee, however, that consumers will be better off. As for sellers, they are likely to be worse off.*

Recall that we express the net surpluses of buyers (consumers) and sellers (providers) respectively as follows:

$$v_b = r_b + \beta_b n_s - A_b \text{ and } v_s = r_s + \beta_s n_b - A_s,$$

with n_b and n_s denoting the numbers of buyers and sellers that join the platform. Now, instead of supposing as before that there is a fixed number of identical agents in each group, we assume instead that a mass of Z buyers and of Z sellers have an outside option that is uniformly distributed on $[0, Z]$, with Z large. Hence, for given A_s and A_b, the equilibrium number of buyers and sellers is characterized by $n_b = r_b + \beta_b n_s - A_b$ and $n_s = r_s + \beta_s n_b - A_s$. Solving this system of two equations in two unknowns, we obtain:

$$n_b = \frac{r_b - A_b + \beta_b (r_s - A_s)}{1 - \beta_b \beta_s} \text{ and } n_s = \frac{r_s - A_s + \beta_s (r_b - A_b)}{1 - \beta_b \beta_s}.$$

Assuming that network effects are positive and not too strong (so that $\beta_b \beta_s < 1$), these two expressions can be seen as "demand functions for participation": They express the number of agents joining the platform as a decreasing function of the fee that the platform charges these agents, but also of the fee that the platform charges to agents of the other group.

We will analyze this model in detail in the next chapter. Here, we just develop a special example. The situation we have in mind is the following: Each buyer makes one transaction with each seller present on the platform; the value of a transaction is β_b for a buyer and β_s for a seller. To fix ideas, we set numerical values to the parameters of the model: Let $r_b = 110$, $r_s = 0$, $\beta_b = \frac{1}{2}$

and $\beta_s = \frac{1}{4}$. Substituting these values into the demand functions, we have $n_b = \frac{4}{7}(220 - 2A_b - A_s)$ and $n_s = \frac{2}{7}(110 - A_b - 4A_s)$. The platform chooses A_b and A_s to maximize its profit $\Pi = A_b n_b + A_s n_s$ (where we assume for simplicity that the platform faces no fixed or variable cost). The first-order conditions for profit maximization yields $440 - 8A_b - 3A_s = 0$ and $110 - 3A_b - 8A_s = 0$. The solution to this system gives the platform's optimal fees, namely $A_b = 58$ and $A_s = -8$. Note that in this setting, sellers (who exert the strongest cross-group network effects, as $\beta_b = \frac{1}{2} > \beta_s = \frac{1}{4}$) are subsidized. We can now compute the platform's profit and the agents surpluses at the optimum as:

$$\Pi^0 = 3520, \ v_b^0 = 64 \text{ and } v_s^0 = 24. \tag{4.1}$$

Suppose now that the platform introduces its own products and that these products compete with the offering of the third-party sellers. This has two effects on the value created on the platform. First, as buyers value the platform's products, their surplus is increased by some amount $\alpha > 0$. Second, the competition exerted by the platform's products decreases the value that buyers and sellers can extract from their transactions; in particular, the sum $\beta_b + \beta_s$ is reduced by some amount δ, which we set to $\frac{1}{5}$. Redoing the previous computations under these new assumptions, we find:

$$\Pi^1 = \frac{400}{1479}(110 + \alpha)^2, \ v_b^0 = \frac{800}{1479}(110 + \alpha) \text{ and } v_s^0 = \frac{220}{1479}(110 + \alpha). \tag{4.2}$$

Comparing the values in (4.1) and (4.2), we can identify the threshold on α (which measures the buyers' valuation of the platform's products) for the introduction of first-party products to benefit the platform, the buyers and the sellers. The results are summarized in Table 4.1. Unsurprisingly, sellers are more likely to be hurt (i.e., much higher values of α are needed to make them better off). What is more striking is that the platform may benefit from in-house production while buyers (and sellers for that matter) are made worse off. This is so, in our simple example, if $4.1 < \alpha < 8.3$.

Table 4.1 Impacts of the introduction of first-party products

	$0 < \alpha < 4.1$	$4.1 < \alpha < 8.3$	$8.30 < \alpha < 51.3$	$\alpha > 51.3$
Platform profit:	*Lower*	**Higher**	**Higher**	**Higher**
Buyer surplus:	*Lower*	*Lower*	**Higher**	**Higher**
Seller surplus:	*Lower*	*Lower*	*Lower*	**Higher**

The previous analysis focused on short-term responses by the different players. In the medium term, third-party sellers may design other strategies to mitigate the negative impacts of the platform's entry into their product space. As Zhu (2019) reports, one strategy consists in reallocating resources so as to avoid head-to-head competition with the platform's in-house production; this can be done, for instance, by moving to more differentiated product segments or by rescheduling the release of products.[25] Another strategy is to form closer ties with the platform, so as to share (and potentially grow) the value created and, thereby, reduce the risk of expropriation. Here, the stronger the outside option of the seller, the larger his bargaining power. The presence of competing platforms (which may strategically commit not to compete with their sellers) is thus key to determine what outside option is available. What is also crucial in this regard is the size and importance of the seller. Large sellers have, obviously, less to fear from competition coming from the platform. If they feel that this competition becomes too strong, they may credibly threaten to leave the platform and, if needs be, create their own competing platform. The decision by Disney to take its content out of Netflix (as of 2020) and launch its own streaming platform is a case in point.

4.4.2   Growing in Adjacent Markets

A platform may also want to broaden its offering by introducing new products or services that do not compete with those offered by the third-party providers that it hosts. Growth thus takes place in markets that are adjacent to the platform's initial market. The decision to expand a platform's operations into adjacent markets may result from the presence of economies of scope on the supply or on the demand side. We examine them in turn.

Supply-Side Economies of Scope
Supply-side economies of scope exist if it is cheaper to provide the existing and the new products or services jointly rather than separately. In other words, the platform leverages its current operations to enter the adjacent market at a lower cost than another firm would do if it was active only in that market. This is mainly due to the existence, in the initial market, of some spare capacities of inputs that the platform can use in a productive way in the adjacent market (or a nonrivalry of the use of these inputs). These spare capacities can be of several forms:

- *Software*: Elements of software can be reused across different services; Condorelli and Padilla (2020b, p. 154) give the example of Facebook and Instagram that sell advertising slots through a common online facility. Similarly, Uber deploys the logistics technologies that it developed for its ride-hailing platform in the adjacent markets of freight brokerage (Uber Freight) or food delivery (Uber Eats).
- *Data*: The data that the platform is collecting regarding its initial services can be exploited to provide additional services in a more efficient way. For example, when an e-commerce platform offers warehousing services to its sellers, sales information in one geographic market can inform optimal stocking decisions in other geographic markets and allow a reduction of the overall delivery and warehousing cost.

---

[25] See also Wen and Zhu (2019).

- *User base*: A larger user base on at least one side of the platform with the initial services may lead to a lower cost of introducing or operating adjacent services. For example, the opportunity cost of advertising a new service may well be reduced compared to a new stand-alone service since some users of the initial service may receive targeted ads.

Demand-Side Economies of Scope

Economies of scope often arise on the demand side insofar as the users' total willingness to pay for different products or services increases when they are available on the same platform rather than on different platforms. Again, this makes it more profitable for a single platform to provide these products and services than it is for distinct platforms or firms to do so. Demand-side economies of scope can stem from different sources.

- *Complementarities*: A platform may find it profitable to introduce complementary products and services that increase the value of products and services that are already provided on the platform (either by third-party providers or by the platform itself). For instance, by introducing Xbox Live online gaming system, Microsoft enhanced the value to users of third-party developers' games for the Xbox console. Another example is the launch of Trips by Airbnb in 2016, a feature that suggests travel guides and activities for guests using the platform. Similarly, several marketplaces have bundled payment facilities with their services. For instance, Alibaba added Alipay and Apple added Apple Pay. They both followed the footsteps of eBay, which acquired PayPal in 2002; eBay's aim at the time was to "help both customers and the company's bottom line by speeding up the payment process."[26] However, in 2014, eBay spun off PayPal into a separate company. A potential explanation behind this separation could be eBay's failure to create a sufficiently large ecosystem (like Alibaba or Apple managed to do).
- *Convenience*: Complementarity arises when a group of users finds it more convenient to access different products and services via a single platform; one can think of several reasons why "one-stop shopping" generates benefits for users: reduction of transaction costs, single billing, easier use (e.g., because of common layouts or transferable user experience across services), interoperable or interconnected features (e.g., single password, reuse of payment information, transferability of files).[27]

---

[26] See Margaret Kane, "eBay picks up PayPal for $1.5 billion," August 18, 2002, www.cnet.com /news/ebay-picks-up-paypal-for-1-5-billion/ (last accessed November 19, 2020).

[27] Complementary services and increased convenience may also help the platform to retain its users. A platform may indeed see its users leaving and completing their transactions outside the platform (a phenomenon known as "bypass," "platform leakage," or "disintermediation"). This risk is more acute when the platform mainly acts as a matchmaker and, as we discuss in the next chapter, when it sets transaction fees (i.e., if users have to pay for each effective transaction they conduct on the platform); the temptation is then high for users to use the platform to find a suitable match and then conclude the transaction outside the platform so as to avoid the payment of fees. To counteract this tendency, a

- *Trust*: The existing user base on the initial market may facilitate entry into the adjacent market by generating positive expectations about the future success of the new service. For instance, Google launched in 2019 a new service, called Pigeon, that allows commuters to help one another by reporting issues that may arise on public transports (such as delays or overcrowding); like Waze (which we described in Chapter 1), this service exploits direct network effects, which makes the chicken-and-egg problem particularly acute; clearly, Google's reputation (and also its large user base) is conducive to reassure potential Pigeon users that the service will attract many other users and will therefore be valuable. The geographical expansion, one city after the other, of ride-hailing platforms (like Uber or Lyft) and food-delivery platforms (like Deliveroo or DoorDash) follows the same logic: By observing the platform's success in other cities, users should be convinced that the platform is also likely to operate successfully in their city; moreover, platforms can achieve demand-side economies of scope in building brand awareness via (inter)national advertising campaigns. Let us also recall the early days of Facebook, which we described in Chapter 1: The first target group, students in one university, was used as a showcase for the social network's ability to reach other user groups.[28] The regular expansion of Google's and Apple's portfolio of services (or "ecosystems") clearly follows this logic.
- *Building on a user base*: A motivation for platforms to expand their portfolio of services is to manage network effects across different markets, by building on the installed base of one of the user groups in the initial market. For example, Uber introduced in April 2020 a new parcel delivery service called Uber Direct; because the same couriers that already deliver food through Uber Eats can also deliver parcels through Uber Direct, the positive cross-group network effects that couriers exert on the groups of restaurants and diners can be extended, at little cost, to the groups of parcel senders and receivers. Belleflamme, Omrani, and Peitz (2015) provide an another example: Some crowdfunding platforms attract expert investors on top of unsophisticated "crowdfunders" because the former, through their larger ability to assess the reliability of entrepreneurs, generate positive cross-group network effects for the latter.[29]

To understand the implications of such an expansion, think of the two groups initially connected by the platform as groups *A* and *B*, the new group as group *C*,

platform may want to develop services that enhance the value of completing transactions on the platform (the payment facilities that we just discussed are an obvious example) and offer management tools that allow sellers to streamline the transactions they conduct on the platform with their own business processes (e.g., invoicing, scheduling, or inventory management); the same goes for the services aiming to increase trust among users (such as insurance) that we described in Section 4.3.3.

[28] The argument is here the same as the way umbrella brands can be bearers of reputation; see e.g. Wernerfelt (1988) and Cabral (2000). We note that not necessarily the same consumers have to consume the portfolio of products or services under the umbrella. Instead, it is sufficient that consumers of the services disclose their experience to some consumers of other services (or in other geographic markets).

[29] Building on an existing base on (at least) one side, also helps to resolve the chicken-and-egg problem.

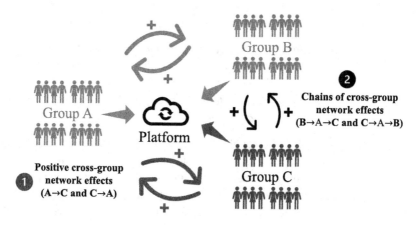

Figure 4.2 Platform expansion by building on a user base

and group *A* as the pivotal group.[30] As illustrated in Figure 4.2, the expansion to group *C* first generates a new attraction spiral between groups *A* and *C*. Then, even if there is no direct interaction between groups *B* and *C*, users of group *B* indirectly care about participation by users of group *C*; this is because the participation level of group *C* affects the participation level of group *A*, which enters the utility of users of group *B*. By the same token, users in group *C* indirectly care about the participation in group *B*. Hence, the platform expansion generates a chain of cross-group network effects from *B* to *A* and from *A* to *C* and in reverse. The resulting indirect network effects are more complex than the ones we described in Chapter 1 (see Section 1.2.1). The consequence of the platform's leveraging of group *A*'s pivotal role is that the new attraction spiral between groups *C* and *A* turbocharges the existing attraction spiral between groups *B* and *A*.

- *Data*: Network effects across markets may be data-enabled. Here, the data collected on the initial market contribute to improve services on the adjacent market and possibly vice versa. That is, there exist complementarities in using data as an input on several markets; a clear illustration is Facebook's entry in the dating market in 2020 (with Facebook Dating). The idea here is that Facebook is able to suggest better matches thanks to the data it has accumulated. In general, data in the initial market may allow improvement in the expected value for users from joining the adjacent market and, at the same time, increase the revenues of the platform relative to a platform that would start from scratch.[31]

---

[30] In our examples, couriers and entrepreneurs are group *A*; diners/restaurants and crowdfunders are group *B*; parcel senders/receivers and sophisticated investors are group *C*.

[31] Chen et al. (2020) consider targeted offers and personalized prices in the adjacent market that are enabled by the data collected in the initial market. Users may still benefit if the benefits from increased match quality dominates the higher expenses due to personalized prices. Condorelli and Padilla (2020a,b) describe the strategy of "privacy policy tying" whereby a platform links its privacy policies in its initial market and an adjacent market; the idea is to make users accept the combined

The next lesson summarizes what we have learned in this section:

LESSON 4.9 *Platforms may decide to expand their operations into adjacent markets to take advantage of supply-side economies of scope (the joint provision of several services is cheaper than their separate provision) or demand-side economies of scope (the users' willingness to pay for the joint consumption of several services is larger than for their separate consumption).*

We acknowledge that supply-side and demand-side economies of scope cannot always easily be separated. For example, in the case of data, more data and better analytics allow Amazon to better predict demand. This leads to lower costs, but also to higher consumer benefits if better predictions give rise to shorter delivery times. On a two-sided platform, if the seller does the warehousing and the platform provides better demand predictions to the seller, the seller can reduce its warehousing costs and, therefore, enjoys network benefits. On a hybrid platform such as Amazon (including Amazon Marketplace), better data and data analytics may therefore lead to supply-side economies of scope, as well as demand-side economies of scope on the seller and the buyer side. Thus, when Amazon expands its operations to additional product categories or geographic markets, multiple economies of scope may be at play.

Note that Lesson 4.9 only lists incentives for expansion for a given market structure. As Condorelli and Padilla (2020b) stress, platforms may also have incentives to implement expansion strategies aiming at reducing competition in their initial market and/or in the adjacent markets they enter.[32]

commercial exploitation of the data generated in the two markets; they also analyze the potential anticompetitive impacts of such a strategy. In a similar vein, de Cornière and Taylor (2020) study "data-driven mergers," that is, mergers between firms active on adjacent markets such that the data generated on one market can be used on the other market; here as well as in Chen et al. (2020), the focus is on the pro- or anticompetitive effects of mergers, a topic that we will address in our second book.

[32] Expansion may indeed be used to leverage market power from the initial market to the adjacent ones or to protect market power in the initial market. See also the previous footnote. We postpone further discussion of these issues to our second book.

Key Insights from Chapter 4

- Platforms *enable* transactions, while vertically integrated firms *control* transactions. The former mode of organization fares better when it comes to inducing professionals to exert efforts and let them take advantage of their private information. The latter mode is more efficient in internalizing externalities across professionals, goods, and services.
- Two-sided platforms face a chicken-and-egg problem because users in one group will not participate unless they expect users in the other group to participate, and vice versa. Platforms may overcome this problem by subsidizing one group and monetizing the other, and thus follow a *divide-and-conquer strategy*. Platforms choose to subsidize the group that exerts the largest cross-group network effect on the other group.
- Another way out of the chicken-and-egg problem is to attract first those users who present the highest ratio between the positive network effects they generate for other users, and the cost that needs to be incurred to attract them.
- By introducing in-house production that competes with the offering of third-party providers, a platform reduces the value generated by the interaction of buyers and sellers. Such a strategy can only be profitable if consumers find the in-house production attractive enough. If so, this strategy can allow a platform to alleviate the chicken-and-egg problem or to expand at a later stage. Expansion can also be achieved through the exploitation of supply-side and demand-side economies of scope.

5   Platform Pricing

In this chapter, we examine how a platform, which has passed the launch phase, prices its services. We already gained some insights about pricing in the previous chapter when dealing with the chicken-and-egg problem; we learned that one way to solve the problem is to have a low price on one side (the "subsidy side") and a high price on the other (the "money side"), the subsidy side being the one exerting the strongest cross-group network effect. But the model we used was extremely simple, with homogeneous users in each group. In this chapter, we extend this intuition to more realistic settings in which users are heterogeneous, with the consequence that reducing the price on one side also leads to more participation on that side; that is, a demand expansion effect has to be taken into account.

A number of features make platform pricing inherently complex. First, the presence of various groups of users opens the possibility for differential pricing, at least across users of different groups (not necessarily within a particular group). Second, differential pricing is desirable to tackle the interdependence between the users' decisions, which results from the presence of network effects; in the presence of heterogeneous users, the price structure will then be jointly determined by the price elasticities and the network effects. Third, prices can be used to regulate both the access to the platform and the intensity of participation on the platform.

We address all these issues in this chapter. In Section 5.1, we provide a general introduction to platform pricing by describing the different types of prices that a platform might choose, by going through a simple numerical example, and by discussing why the platform's decisions may diverge from what would be optimal from a social point of view. We then address, in Section 5.2, the platform pricing problem in a general way. Our goal is to understand how the platform optimally chooses prices so as to manage network effects, and why this often leads to pricing structures such that different groups of users end up paying quite different prices; we also address the question whether platforms should charge users only for accessing the platform or also for the transactions they conduct on the platform. In the last two sections, we address a number of advanced issues related to platform pricing. In Section 5.3, we extend the analysis of the first two sections (which focuses on two-sided platforms setting a different fee on each side) in several directions; we study what happens when the platform is restricted to set a single fee, when within-group network effects are present, and when a one-sided platform can practice differential pricing. Finally, in Section 5.4, we examine the link between pricing and the way users form their expectations regarding the participation of other users; these expectations may vary according to what users can observe and what the platform can commit to. As set out in the introduction, we focus in this book on the strategy of a single platform that does not need to worry about the strategic choices of other firms.

5.1 Platform Pricing: The Basics

This section aims at introducing, in a less formal way, our analysis of the pricing problem of a monopoly platform. We start by presenting the various types of prices that a platform may choose and by identifying the roles that these prices play (5.1.1). We then walk you through a simple numerical model; the objective is to gain some intuition about platform pricing (5.1.2). Finally, we discuss how the platform's profit-maximizing price structure differs from the socially optimal one (5.1.3).

5.1.1 Prices? What Prices?

Two-sided platforms can set two types of fees. On the one hand, *membership fees* (a.k.a. subscription fees) are paid once or renewed on a regular basis. By regulating the access to the platform, they determine the size and composition of the groups of users that interact on the platform during a given period of time. On the other hand, *transaction fees* (a.k.a. usage fees) are paid per effective transaction, either as a per-unit or per-transaction fee or as a share of the transaction price (commission). Hence, transaction fees regulate the activity on the platform, as the total bill that users end up paying depends on the number and value of the transactions that they conduct; they may also have an impact on the participation decision.

Ideally, a profit-maximizing platform would balance the advantages of these two types of fees. For instance, by decreasing the transaction fees, the platform can increase the volume of transactions and, thereby, the value that users attach to the platform; it is then possible to capture this increased value by raising the membership fees. Yet, the optimal balance between the two types of fees heavily depends on the environment in which the platform operates, as it may condition which fee can effectively be charged.

- Regarding membership fees, imposing them may be challenging for a platform that starts its operations because of the chicken-and-egg problem (see Chapter 4). If users are not confident of finding counterparts in the other group, they may be reluctant to pay a membership fee up front, as they may not be able to conduct any transaction once they are on the platform; this risk disappears with transaction fees, as they are only paid if an effective transaction takes place.
- As for transaction fees, they obviously make it necessary that the platform observes the transaction. Also, transaction fees may induce users to visit the platform just of finding counterparts and, once they have found them, to complete the transaction outside the platform – and thus to bypass the stage at which a

transaction fee is paid leading to "platform leakage." This scenario becomes more likely the harder it is for the platform to monitor transactions outside the platform, and the easier it is for users to bypass the platform to finalize transactions. Platforms may then want to choose nonprice strategies that make bypassing more difficult, so as to restore their capacity to set transaction fees or, if possible, charge a referral fee if a transaction was initiated on the platform but finalized outside of the platform.[1]

5.1.2   A Motivating Numerical Example

To get a better understanding of the profit-maximizing price structure of a monopoly platform, we first construct a numerical example (we explore the issue more systematically in the next section).[2]

Setting
We consider here the case in which the platform sets a price per transaction: It sets a transaction fee a_s on the seller side and a transaction fee a_b on the buyer side. Both sides of the market have a certain number of market participants. Buyers and sellers receive gross surpluses that depend positively on the number of market participants on the other side of the market. Thus, there are mutual positive cross-group network effects. For this example, we set the number of buyers and sellers to six and we denote by n_s and n_b the number of sellers and of buyers who decide to join the platform (with $0 \leq n_s, n_b \leq 6$). We make the following assumptions:

- Each buyer either asks for no or exactly one unit from each seller. Thus, if trade occurs, sellers pay $a_s n_b$ and buyers $a_b n_s$ to the platform.
- The buyer side is homogeneous: Every buyer obtains a gross surplus of $6n_s$. We can think of each seller setting the price charged to buyers, leaving each of them with a gross surplus of 6. Even if all buyers are (ex ante) homogeneous, sellers may not be able to extract the full surplus because buyers draw their willingness to pay from a distribution – the seller knows the distribution but not the realization.
- Sellers are heterogeneous in the following way: Seller $i \in \{1, 2, 3, ..., 6\}$ obtains a gross surplus of $n_b(i - 3)$. This is compatible with the following scenario: For each transaction, seller i obtains a revenue equal to i and incurs a cost of 3 (e.g., to bring its product to the marketplace). Note that in this example, sellers 1 and 2 are not willing to join the platform even if access is free (i.e., even if their transaction fee, a_s, is equal to zero).[3]

---

[1] We analyze nonprice strategies in the next chapter. For a formal analysis of the use of transaction and referral fees, see Hagiu and Wright (2021).

[2] We extend the example developed in Peitz (2006, pp. 326–328).

[3] We could also apply this example to the context of ad-financed media, with advertisers on side b and, say, readers on side s. Think of readers consuming a web page that contains some content, along with as many ads as there are advertisers registered with the platform. Advertisers all obtain a benefit of 6 per view of the web page, while readers are heterogeneous in the way they value the presence of an ad on the platform: Readers $i \in \{4, 5, 6\}$ are "ad-lovers" (as they get a positive surplus for each ad they

- The buyers' and sellers' gross surpluses are assumed to be independent of the transaction fees charged by the platform; this is the case if sellers cannot internalize changes in the fee structure and adjust the prices they charge to buyers accordingly.[4]

Pricing

The platform chooses the transaction fees a_b and a_s to maximize its profits, which can be expressed as follows: $\Pi = \pi_b + \pi_s = a_b \times n_b(a_b, a_s) \times n_s(a_b, a_s) + a_s \times n_b(a_b, a_s) \times n_s(a_b, a_s)$, where π_k is the profit obtained on side k and $n_k(a_b, a_s)$ is the number of agents of side k joining the platform as a function of the transaction fees that the platform charges (with $k \in \{b, s\}$). Note that, for the sake of simplicity, we assume that the platform has no variable costs.

In this simple example, the optimal fee for buyers is easily found. As the buyer side is homogeneous, the platform has no better choice than setting $a_b = 6$ – that is, the highest fee compatible with the participation of the six buyers (as long as at least one seller participates).

Finding the optimal fee for sellers requires, however, some more thinking. As a first approximation, the platform may focus on the profits to be made on the seller side, π_s, given the participation of the six buyers. The platform would then compute its profit for different fees, as done in Table 5.1. As a result, it would set $a_s = 2$, attract two sellers and achieve a profit on the seller side of $\pi_s = a_s \times n_b(6, 2) \times n_s(6, 2) = 2 \times 6 \times 2 = 24$. The resulting profit on the buyer side would be $\pi_b = a_b \times n_b(6, 2) \times n_s(6, 2) = 6 \times 6 \times 2 = 72$, yielding a total profit of $\Pi = 96$.

Yet, this approach is short-sighted because it ignores the positive cross-group network effect that sellers exert on buyers. Reducing the fee on the seller side does indeed decrease profits on that side but contributes, through the larger seller participation, to increase profits on the buyer side. To evaluate the net benefits of such

Table 5.1 Profits on the seller side

a_s	n_s	n_b	$\pi_s = a_s n_s n_b$
3	1	6	18
2	2	6	24
1	3	6	18
0	4	6	0
−1	5	6	−30
−2	6	6	−72

view), reader 3 is not affected by ads, and readers $i \in \{1, 2\}$ are "ad-haters" (as they get a *negative* surplus for each ad they view).

[4] A reason for this could be that each seller also sells to (many) other buyers outside the platform and it has to set a uniform price to all buyers, no matter whether or not they buy via the platform. An example is the no-surcharge rule in payment systems according to which buyers pay the same price to the seller irrespective of their means of payment.

Table 5.2 Profits on both sides

a_s	n_s	n_b	$\pi_s = a_s n_s n_b$	$\pi_b = a_b n_s n_b$	$\pi = \pi_s + \pi_b$
3	1	6	18	36	54
2	2	6	24	72	96
1	3	6	18 ⤵ −6	108 ⤵ +36	126 ⤵ +30
0	4	6	0 ⤵ −18	144 ⤵ +36	144 ⤵ +18
−1	5	6	−30 ⤵ −30	180 ⤵ +36	150 ⤵ +6
−2	6	6	−72 ⤵ −42	216 ⤵ +36	144 ⤵ −6

move, one needs to look at the computations reported in Table 5.2. We see that each extra seller that joins the platform generates an additional profit of 36 on the buyer side (as each of the six buyers pays a fee of 6 for the transaction they conduct with the extra seller). This increase in profits on the buyer side outweighs the loss incurred on the seller side up to the fifth seller (attracting the sixth one would reduce total profits). The optimum for the platform is thus to set $a_s = -1$ and to attract five sellers. Total profit is then equal to $\Pi = (a_b + a_s) \times n_b(6, -1) \times n_s(6, -1) = 5 \times 6 \times 5 = 150$ (recall that under the previous – myopic – approach, the platform's profit was limited to 96).

The main lesson we can draw from this example is that *it may be optimal for the platform to subsidize the participation of some users.* In the absence of cross-group network effects, it would not make sense for the platform to pay sellers to participate; but here, as additional sellers allow the platform to collect larger profits from buyers, subsidizing seller participation becomes profitable.[5] Another important finding is that *the price structure is not neutral* – that is, the allocation (and total surplus) is affected not only by the total fee for a transaction $a_s + a_b$, but also by how much of it is borne by buyers and sellers respectively. Finally, the example shows that prices on the two sides of the platform jointly depend on price elasticities *and* on the strength of the cross-group network effects. Lesson 5.1 states more precisely how.

LESSON 5.1   *A for-profit two-sided platform sets a relatively low price (possibly below cost) for the group of users that is more sensitive to price changes and/or exerts a stronger cross-group network effect.*

The principle stated in the previous lesson echoes what we learned in the previous chapter when dealing with the chicken-and-egg problem: When the platform resorts to a divide-and-conquer strategy, it tends to subsidize the group that exerts the stronger network effects.

Social Optimum
How does the privately optimal price structure differ from the socially optimal one? If there are positive cross-group network effects, it is easy to understand that it cannot be socially optimal to set the price for participation and usage in platforms equal

---

[5] In the context of ad-financed media, this means that it may be profitable to attract readers/viewers who dislike advertising.

to the marginal cost (i.e., zero in our example). As we just showed, if we lower the fee on one market side, additional participants will appear on this side of the market. This leads to a higher surplus on the other side of the market due to the positive cross-group network effect enjoyed on this side, which in turn leads to a positive feedback effect on the other side of the market (this is the attraction spiral described in Chapter 1). Thus, it cannot be socially optimal to set prices equal to marginal cost. Instead, in general, it is socially optimal to subsidize both sides of the market.

In our numerical example, it was optimal for the platform to subsidize sellers with €1 per transaction. Taking the social viewpoint (i.e., taking the surplus of all participants into account, as well as the profit of the platform), we see that it is also socially optimal to subsidize the seller side, but the welfare-maximizing subsidy is even more pronounced; in the example, it is €2 per transaction. To see this, note that for any $a_b \leq 6$, the six buyers join and their aggregate gross surplus is equal to $U_b = 36n_s$. On the seller side, given that six buyers join, the aggregate gross surplus is equal to $U_s(5) = (3 + 2 + 1 + 0 - 1) \times 6 = 30$ if five sellers (i.e., sellers 2 to 6) join, or to $U_s(6) = (3 + 2 + 1 + 0 - 1 - 2) \times 6 = 18$ if all sellers join. As fees are a pure transfer from users to the platform, total welfare is equal to $W(5) = 36 \times 5 + 30 = 210$ if five sellers join and to $W(6) = 36 \times 6 + 18 = 234$ if six sellers join.

As shown in Table 5.2, setting $a_s = -2$ is not optimal for a profit-maximizing platform. However, in this example, a not-for-profit platform could implement the socially optimal outcome by setting $a_s = -2$ and $a_b = 2$, while avoiding losses.[6] This illustrates the more general finding that the solution to this Ramsey problem is to subsidize the market side whose demand is particularly resilient and which exerts a particularly strong cross-group network effect on the other side of the market.[7] We pursue this discussion in the next section.

5.1.3 Pricing Distortions by a Monopoly Platform

Four reasons drive a platform to choose a price structure that differs from the one that would maximize total surplus. The first distortion is observed in any monopolized market, while the other three result from the presence of cross-group network effects. We describe them in turn.

Market-Power Distortion
A monopolist exerts its market power by restricting output, which drives prices above their efficient level.

---

[6] A not-for-profit platform would not maximize the total value for its users if it were completely free (i.e., with $a_s = a_b = 0$). To maximize value, it is necessary to incentivize all sellers to participate, which requires a subsidy for sellers and a corresponding positive fee for buyers.

[7] See Armstrong (2006).

Spence Distortion

This distortion is analogous to a well-known result about a monopolist's choice of quality due to Spence (1975): A monopolist chooses too low a quality with respect to the social optimum. The reason is that the monopoly (maximizing profit) cares about the impact of enhanced quality on marginal consumers (those who enter the market last for a given price of the product), whereas a benevolent planner (maximizing social welfare) cares about the impact on the *average* valuation of consumers. In the present two-sided context, the quality dimension that matters for buyers is the sellers' participation rate, and vice versa. Because the profit-maximizing platform internalizes only cross-group network effects to marginal users rather than all participating users, it sets participation rates that differ from the social optimum ones. In particular, the "Spence distortion" (as named by Weyl, 2010) induces the monopoly two-sided platform to set its price too high (too low) for, say, buyers when the average seller values the interaction with buyers more (less) than the marginal seller does (and similarly for the seller price).

Displacement Distortion

As we saw in the simple numerical example here (and as we will soon confirm more generally), platforms adjust prices downward on one side to take into account the positive cross-group network effect that users on this side exert on the other side. That is, the profit-maximizing price on one side reflects the valuation of the interaction by the marginal users on the other side. Yet, the valuation of the interaction is usually different in the monopoly outcome than in the socially optimal outcome. If the monopoly price for, say, buyers is above the efficient price, then the marginal buyers (those who join the platform the last) value more highly the interaction with sellers in the monopoly outcome than in the socially optimal outcome. As a result, the monopoly platform charges sellers below the efficient level. There is, as Tan and Wright (2018a) call it, a negative "displacement distortion."

Scale Distortion

Finally, Tan and Wright (2018b) identify a fourth reason for which the monopoly platform may depart from the social optimum; they call it the "scale distortion." The profits that a monopoly platform can extract from, say, sellers depend on how much sellers can interact with buyers and, hence, on the buyers' participation rate. Yet, this rate generally differs in the monopoly and the socially optimal outcomes. It follows that the incentives for a monopoly platform to increase its price for buyers also differs from the incentives for a benevolent planner.

Depending on the various costs that the platform faces and on the users' standalone benefits, the last three distortions may reinforce or counterbalance the market-power distortion on either side of the platform. Lesson 5.2 summarizes what we have learned so far:

LESSON 5.2   *The fee structure chosen by a profit-maximizing monopoly platform differs from the socially optimal structure for a number of reasons: The monopoly platform restricts output (market-power distortion), cares about marginal users rather than about average users (Spence distortion), induces different interaction benefits (displacement distortion), and different participation rates (scale distortion). Depending on the specifics of the environment (strengths of the cross-group network effects, costs, and stand-alone benefits), the combined impact of these distortions may lead the monopoly platform to set prices that are below or above the efficient level on either side.*

5.2   The General Platform Pricing Problem

We now want to gain a deeper understanding of the price structures on a two-sided platform. Before doing so, let us recall that potential platform users face the general problem that they have to form expectations about participation levels on the other side. We described this problem in Chapter 4 in the context of the launch of a platform. In particular, we stressed that multiple equilibria may occur for given fees and that one of these equilibria may involve no participation whatsoever (the so-called null equilibrium). Indeed, if fees are larger than the stand-alone benefits and if, on each side, users expect no participation on the other side, then it is an equilibrium for no user to participate. This problem is still present after the launch phase. In this section, we will somehow abstract it away by assuming that users manage to coordinate their decisions (potentially with the help of the platform) so as to avoid the null equilibrium. Obviously, if the platform can commit about participation levels (for instance, by auctioning a number of slots), it can select the most profitable equilibrium in case of multiple equilibria; we consider this possibility in the next section.

To fix ideas, the platform we consider is a marketplace that links buyers to sellers.[8] We assume that every buyer has demand for exactly one unit from each seller, and that there are positive gains from trade: The benefit of a transaction is β_b for the buyer and β_s for the seller (these benefits may be heterogeneous on each side). Buyers and sellers also enjoy a stand-alone benefit r_b and r_s, respectively (which only depends on the side a user belongs to). The platform sets, on each side, a membership fee (noted A_k) and a transaction fee (noted a_k, $k \in \{b, s\}$). In sum, when n_b buyers and n_s sellers join the platform, the net utility of a buyer is $v_b = r_b + (\beta_b - a_b)n_s - A_b$ and the net utility of a seller is $v_s = r_s + (\beta_s - a_s)n_b - A_s$. Implicit in this formulation is that there is zero pass-through, as a change in the transaction fee does not affect the gross benefit of a transaction on either side.

Both buyers and sellers have heterogeneous opportunity costs to participate in the market. Buyers with v_b greater than their opportunity cost of joining the platform will participate given the level n_s, and all sellers with v_s greater than their opportunity cost

---

[8] This setting follows Rochet and Tirole (2006, Section 5).

of joining the platform will participate given the level n_b. The platform incurs a cost f_k, $k \in \{b, s\}$, per participant from side k and a per-transaction cost c. Suppose that participants observe fees a_b, a_s, A_b, and A_s. The buyer demand N_b is then a function of a_b, A_b and n_s, while the seller demand N_s is a function of a_s, A_s and n_b. Suppose that for any set of fees, there is a unique solution (n_b, n_s) with $n_b = N_b(a_b, A_b, n_s)$ and $n_s = N_s(a_s, A_s, n_b)$ that maximizes the volume of trade $n_b n_s$.

The platform's profit can be written as:

$$\Pi = (A_b - f_b)n_b + (A_s - f_s)n_s + (a_b + a_s - c)n_b n_s$$
$$= \left[\left(\frac{A_b}{n_s} + a_b \right) + \left(\frac{A_s}{n_b} + a_s \right) - \frac{f_b}{n_s} - \frac{f_s}{n_b} - c \right] n_b n_s,$$

where $A_b/n_s + a_s$ and $A_s/n_b + a_s$ are the average fees per transaction respectively for a buyer and for a seller, and where $P \equiv A_b/n_s + a_b + A_s/n_s + a_s$ can be seen as the fictitious price per transaction or the revenue that each transaction generates for the platform. This formulation allows us to get a first view of the platform's maximization problem. If $f_b = f_s = 0$, the platform can be thought of first choosing the fictitious price per transaction and then determining the price structure that applies to each side. At the second step, the platform chooses a_b, a_s, A_b, and A_s to maximize $n_b n_s$ under the constraint that $A_b/n_s + a_b + A_s/n_s + a_s \equiv P$. This gives a derived demand for a fictitious transaction service $Q(P)$. The price level for a transaction is determined according to the standard Lerner formula:

$$\frac{P - c}{P} = \frac{1}{\eta}.$$

where $\eta = -PQ'(P)/Q(P)$ is the inverse price elasticity of the derived demand for transaction services. In what follows, we refine the analysis by focusing in turn on environments in which the platform sets only transaction fees or only membership fees.

5.2.1   Transaction Fees on a Two-Sided Platform

For a platform to charge transaction fees, it must be able to monitor transactions and prevent users from bypassing the platform by completing transactions elsewhere (see the discussion in Section 5.1.1). Arguably, digital technologies have allowed platforms to fare considerably better on these two fronts, which explains why transaction fees have become a very popular type of fees. This is especially so among online marketplaces, which charge a commission from the transactions on their platform. Who do they charge? It depends, as Case 5.1 illustrates.

CASE 5.1 HOW DO PLATFORMS SPLIT TRANSACTION FEES? DOES IT MATTER?[9]

Many platforms facilitating the interaction between buyers and sellers (or customers and providers) choose to take commissions from sellers only. For instance, in the ride-hailing sector, Uber and Lyft both charge drivers a commission of about 20 percent; Fiverr, an online marketplace for freelance services, also charges freelancers a transaction fee that hovers

[9] The numbers given in this case were collected early 2020.

around 20 percent. Product marketplaces also charge sellers, but set lower fees: an average of about 10 percent on eBay and Amazon, 3.5 percent on Etsy (on which handmade items and craft supplies are traded). Some platforms choose, however, to charge both sellers and buyers. Airbnb, for example, takes a commission of 3-5 percent from hosts, and a commission of 6-12 percent from guests. Buyers may sometimes be charged negative transaction fees; this practice is common in the credit card industry. As an illustration, just before writing these lines, one of the authors received a phone call from his bank, proposing him a deal whereby he would receive cash back of 3 percent on any transaction that he would pay with the credit card issued by this bank.

In some cases, it may not really matter which side pays the commission; yet, in other cases, this may make a real difference. To understand what motivates the variety of fee structures described in the previous case, we consider here the special case in which buyers and sellers are heterogeneous with respect to transaction benefits but all have a zero opportunity cost of joining the platform. We suppose furthermore that $r_k = f_k = 0, k \in \{b, s\}$. In this case, it is sufficient to consider transaction fees.[10] We note that as long as buyers and sellers cannot internalize a change in the fee structure in their contractual relationship, the fee structure matters for them; that is, the way the total transaction fee is split between buyers and sellers is relevant. This is so because users base their participation decision on the fee they are charged (and not on the total fee).

In particular, a buyer is active if $\beta_b \geq a_b$, and a seller is active if $\beta_s \geq a_s$. It follows that the number of active buyers is $N_b(a_b) = \Pr(\beta_b \geq a_b)$; correspondingly, the number of active sellers is $N_s(a_s) = \Pr(\beta_s \geq a_s)$. The platform profits are $(a_b + a_s - c)N_b(a_b)N_s(a_s)$. Assuming that N_b and N_s are logconcave (i.e., the logarithm of these functions are concave in their argument), the first-order conditions of profit maximization characterize the solution to the maximization problem. Taking the derivative of logarithmic profits and rearranging gives:

$$\frac{1}{a_b + a_s - c} = -\frac{N_b'}{N_b} \text{ and } \frac{1}{a_b + a_s - c} = -\frac{N_s'}{N_s}.$$

Hence the optimal price structure has to satisfy $\frac{N_b'}{N_b} = \frac{N_s'}{N_s}$, which also obtains from maximizing $N_b(a_b)N_s(a_s)$ subject to $a_b + a_s \equiv P$. Let us denote the buyers' price elasticity of demand by $\eta_b = -\frac{N_b'}{N_b}a_b$ and the sellers' price elasticity of demand by $\eta_s = -\frac{N_s'}{N_s}a_s$. Then we can rewrite the previous two equations as:

$$\frac{a_b - (c - a_s)}{a_b} = \frac{1}{\eta_b} \text{ and } \frac{a_s - (c - a_b)}{a_s} = \frac{1}{\eta_s}.$$

These equations correspond to the monopoly pricing formula (or Lerner index) adjusted to a two-sided platform. The difference with the monopoly pricing absent cross-group network effects is the following. Here, the platform charges two prices per transaction instead of just one. As a result, the opportunity cost of a transaction on one side is the cost c *decreased* by the price charged on the other side. By basing its

---

[10] Our exposition follows Rochet and Tirole (2003).

choice of prices on these opportunity costs, the platform internalizes the cross-group network effects. Rearranging the two equations, we find:

$$a_b + a_s - c = \frac{a_s}{\eta_s} = \frac{a_b}{\eta_b}, \text{ which implies } \frac{a_s}{a_b} = \frac{\eta_s}{\eta_b}.$$

LESSON 5.3   *When users are heterogeneous only with respect to transaction bene-fits β_k, $k \in \{b, s\}$, the profit-maximizing price structure has the property that the ratio of transaction fees is equal to the ratio of demand elasticities.*

In other words, if buyers are rather insensitive to price changes (low price elas-ticity), they will face a rather low transaction fee. This insight stands in contrast to the pricing formula applied to separate monopoly markets: The Lerner formula tells us that holding marginal costs constant across markets, consumers have to pay a *higher* price if they are less price elastic. The reason that we obtain a very different result is that both markets are linked, as it is the overall volume of transactions that is maximized for a given total price P.

5.2.2   Membership Fees on a Two-Sided Platform

We now look at situations in which the platform only sets membership fees. As explained, membership (or subscription) fees are the only option for platforms that have a hard time monitoring transactions or preventing users from getting around their payment system. Most offline platforms share these characteristics and focus thus on membership fees; think, for instance, of trade fairs and shopping malls. As for online platforms, some prefer to rely on membership fees, even though transaction fees would be feasible. Case 5.2 provides some illustrations.

CASE 5.2   RELIANCE ON MEMBERSHIP FEES IN OFFLINE AND ONLINE PLATFORMS

Batibouw, the biggest trade fair in Belgium for construction, renovation, and home improve-ment, is a two-sided platform connecting professionals and the general public. Users on both sides are charged a membership fee: For the 2020 fair, visitors had to pay an entrance ticket of €15, while exhibitors were charged a fixed fee of €580, plus €150 per square meter for their stand.[11] Interestingly, trade fairs often allow exhibitors to offer a certain number of free tickets to visitors of their choosing (usually, their most important customers). This is the case, for instance, at ISPO Munich, a trade fair for sports businesses. This trade fair also takes a number of measures to make visits "easier, more efficient, and more cost-effective" (e.g., by offering special deals for traveling and accommodation).[12] This contributes to reducing the net entrance cost for visitors, possibly making it negative. Negative membership fees for buy-ers are also often practiced by shopping malls, under the form of free parking and gifts (such as gift cards and cash back).[13]

---

[11] See www.batibouw.com; last accessed February 20, 2020.
[12] See www.ispo.com/en/markets/ticket-debate-ispo-munich-plans-new-pricing-structure; last accessed February 20, 2020.
[13] Gao (2018) gives the example of Macy's (a well-known department store in New York), which offered saving passes, entitling visitors redeeming the pass in person to 10 percent off merchandise purchases.

In the online world, Maker's Row, an American B2B platform that connects manufacturers with SMEs, charges users a monthly or yearly membership fee and does not take any commission from the transactions. Another example is TrustedHousesitters, a peer-to-peer platform that connects pet owners with "house sitters" – that is, people who come live in the owners' place while they are away to take care of their pets. The platform charges owners and sitters an annual membership fee and no transaction fee.[14]

Another common practice for online platforms is to charge sellers a listing fee. A listing fee is a fixed fee to be paid for each product or service that the seller wishes to list on the platform. This sort of fee is popular with classified advertisements platforms, in B2C (e.g., Craigslist) and in B2B (e.g., Mascus) contexts. The total membership fee for a seller then depends on the number of listed products or services. This is akin to the fee that exhibitors pay in trade fairs in proportion of the size of their stand.

To understand how a platform sets membership fees, we proceed in two steps. We first derive the monopoly pricing formula adjusted to a two-sided platform in a rather general setting. We then adopt a more specific model to obtain some further results. This second model is also the one that we will use in the next two sections to study a number of related issues.

The Two-Sided Monopoly Pricing Formula

As before, let us assume that users derive no stand-alone benefit from the platform: $r_b = r_s = 0$. Yet, in contrast to the previous case, we assume that users are homogeneous in their valuation of the cross-group network effects. Under these assumptions, the net utility of a buyer is $v_b = \beta_b n_s - A_b$ and the net utility of a seller is $v_s = \beta_s n_b - A_s$, when n_b buyers and n_s sellers join the platform.[15] If $\beta_b > 0$ and $\beta_s > 0$, we have an attraction spiral; if one of the two parameters is strictly positive and the other zero, an attraction spillover; and if one is strictly positive and the other strictly negative, we have an attraction/repulsion pendulum.

Users have heterogeneous opportunity costs for joining the platform. The actual number of users on each side is then determined by a free-entry condition: The lower the membership fee, the larger the number of users who join, everything else being equal. We capture this relationship by writing the number of buyers on the platform as a function of the buyers' net utility: $n_b = N_b(v_b)$. Similarly, we express the number of sellers on the platform as a function of the sellers' net utility: $n_s = N_s(v_s)$.

The platform's profit is $\Pi = n_s(A_s - f_s) + n_b(A_b - f_b)$. Using the definitions of v_b and v_s, we can express membership fees as functions of net utilities, $A_s = \beta_s N_b(v_b) - v_s$ and $A_b = \beta_b N_s(v_s) - v_b$. This allows us to write the platform's profit as a function of the net utilities offered to buyers and sellers:

$$\Pi(v_s, v_b) = (\beta_s N_b(v_b) - v_s - f_s)N_s(v_s) + (\beta_b N_s(v_s) - v_b - f_b)N_b(v_b).$$

[14] See https://makersrow.com/plans and www.trustedhousesitters.com/pricing/; last accessed February 20, 2020.

[15] We follow here Armstrong (2006, section 3) and Belleflamme and Peitz (2015, chapter 22).

The first-order conditions for profit maximization are:

$$
\begin{cases}
\dfrac{\partial \Pi}{\partial v_s} = (\beta_s N_b(v_b) - v_s - f_s)N'_s(v_s) - N_s(v_s) + \beta_b N_b(v_b)N'_s(v_s) = 0, \\[2ex]
\dfrac{\partial \Pi}{\partial v_b} = \beta_s N_s(v_s)N'_b(v_b) - N_b(v_b) + (\beta_b N_s(v_s) - v_b - f_b)N'_b(v_b) = 0.
\end{cases}
$$

This can be written as:

$$
\begin{cases}
(A_s - f_s)N'_s(v_s) - N_s(v_s) + \beta_b N_b(v_b)N'_s(v_s) = 0, \\[1ex]
\beta_s N_s(v_s)N'_b(v_b) - N_b(v_b) + (A_b - f_b)N'_b(v_b) = 0.
\end{cases}
$$

Hence, the profit-maximizing membership fees satisfy:

$$
A_s = f_s - \beta_b n_b + \frac{N_s(v_s)}{N'_s(v_s)} \quad \text{and} \quad A_b = f_b - \beta_s n_s + \frac{N_b(v_b)}{N'_b(v_b)}.
$$

Monopoly membership fees are equal to the cost of providing access adjusted *downward* by the network benefit exerted on the other side of the platform, and adjusted *upward* by a factor related to the sensitivity of participation on the platform. Note that for a given number of participants on the other side of the platform, the demand elasticities for access can be expressed as:

$$
\eta_s(A_s|n_b) = A_s \frac{N'_s(\beta_s n_b - A_s)}{N_s(\beta_s n_b - A_s)} \quad \text{and} \quad \eta_b(A_b|n_s) = A_b \frac{N'_b(\beta_b n_s - A_b)}{N_b(\beta_b n_s - A_b)}.
$$

We can thus rewrite the equation for profit-maximizing membership fees as:

$$
\frac{A_s - (f_s - \beta_b n_b)}{A_s} = \frac{1}{\eta_s(A_s|n_b)},
$$

$$
\frac{A_b - (f_b - \beta_s n_s)}{A_b} = \frac{1}{\eta_b(A_b|n_s)}. \tag{5.1}
$$

As in the previous case with transaction fees, we have expressed the monopoly pricing formula (or Lerner index) adjusted to a two-sided platform using membership fees. Since the platform has monopoly power on both sides of the market, the formula applies to buyers and sellers. Furthermore, the platform internalizes cross-group network effects. This is reflected by the downward adjustment of the cost by the network benefit on the buyer side, $\beta_b n_b$, in the pricing formula for the sellers' membership fees and, similarly, by the network benefit on the seller side, $\beta_s n_s$, in the pricing formula for the buyers' membership fees. We observe that markups are set as if there were lower costs: $f_s - \beta_b n_b$ and $f_b - \beta_s n_s$, respectively.

In the special case that elasticities are constant and of the same size on both sides of the platform and that costs for granting access are the same, the group which exerts the larger network benefit enjoys the lower membership fee. This membership fee may even be zero or negative – that is, one side of the market receives a payment for joining. The main insight of our analysis is stated in the next lesson.

LESSON 5.4 *Consider a platform that charges membership fees so as to maximize profits. It tends to charge a lower membership fee to the group of users that exerts the larger network benefit on the other. It may even subsidize this group so as to generate a higher volume of trade and, thus, extract higher profits from the other group of users.*

If the platform incurs positive costs for serving users, subsidization is compatible with positive prices. For example, the cost of producing and selling a flashy magazine may be larger than the cover price. Subsidization of readers (i.e., below marginal-cost pricing) may be worthwhile to make the magazine more attractive for advertisers.

A Specific Model with Linear Cross-Group Network Effects

To obtain explicit expressions for prices and profit, we redo the analysis in the case of a uniform distribution of the outside option that is symmetric on both sides of the market; we also include a stand-alone benefit of the platform for the two groups of users ($r_k \geq 0$ on side k).[16] We assume that there is a unit mass on each interval of length 1 in the range $[0, V]$, where V is sufficiently large such that some participants on each side do not participate in the solutions we are going to consider. Hence, all sellers with an outside option of less than $v_s = r_s + \beta_s n_b - A_s$ will pay the membership fee if they expect a participation level of n_b, and all buyers with an outside option of less than $v_b = r_b + \beta_b n_s - A_b$ will pay the membership fee if they expect a participation level of n_s. Since buyers and sellers are uniformly distributed, we have $n_s = v_s$ and $n_b = v_b$. For given membership fees, participants play an anonymous game and we solve for the Nash equilibrium of this game; the expected number of participants on each side has to be equal to the actual number. Hence, we solve the system of two linear equations in two variables, n_s and n_b, and obtain:

$$n_s = \frac{r_s - A_s + \beta_s(r_b - A_b)}{1 - \beta_s \beta_b} \text{ and } n_b = \frac{r_b - A_b + \beta_b(r_s - A_s)}{1 - \beta_s \beta_b}. \quad (5.2)$$

We assume that $\beta_s \beta_b < 1$ (i.e., cross-group network effects are not too strong), so that the numbers of agents registering on the platform are decreasing functions of the membership fees.

Because of the uniform distribution of the outside option, demand by group b can be written as $N_b(n_s, A_b) = r_b + \beta_b n_s - A_b$ and demand by group s as $N_s(n_b, A_s) = r_s + \beta_s n_b - A_s$; we observe thus that the demand function of each group is a linear function of the price for this group, for a given participation level on the other side. Since cross-group network effects are linear, demand functions are linear functions of parameters β_b and β_s respectively. Users on both sides observe A_b and A_s and make their participation decisions. Figure 5.1 depicts the demand functions depending on participation levels on the other side for given prices. Function $N_b(\cdot, A_b)$ expresses how side b would react to the participation level on side s; correspondingly for $N_s(\cdot, A_s)$. The Nash equilibrium of the anonymous game is then the intersection of these two "reaction" functions. If cross-group network

---

[16] The analysis is taken from Belleflamme and Peitz (2018b). In what follows, we consider the case of an attraction spiral; that is, we take $\beta_b > 0$ and $\beta_s > 0$; the results can, however, be easily transposed into situations of attraction spillover and attraction/repulsion pendulum.

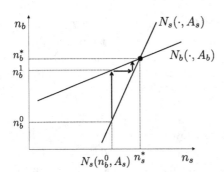

Figure 5.1 Demands for participation on a two-sided platform

effects are not too strong, the unique equilibrium is stable in the sense that starting from any participation level on one of the two sides (e.g., n_b^0), after an iteration
$n_b^1 = N_b(N_s(n_b^0, A_s), A_b)$ the participation level moves closer to the equilibrium participation level on side b, n_b^*. This continues to hold for subsequent iterations, and
there is convergence towards the equilibrium participation level, as illustrated in
Figure 5.1. This graphically illustrates the attraction spiral.

Starting from the equilibrium at membership fees (A_b, A_s), we will now analyze
what happens if the membership fee on one side is changed – for example, an
increase of A_s from A_s^0 to A_s^1. This implies that there is a parallel shift of $N_s(\cdot, A_s)$
to the left. Denoting the equilibrium at the participation stage given (A_b^0, A_s^0) by
(n_b^{*0}, n_s^{*0}) – as illustrated in Figure 5.2 – we can now analyze how participation
levels adjust on one side given the participation level on the other side. Starting
in (n_b^{*0}, n_s^{*0}), after the change in membership fee and given participation level n_b^{*0},
fewer users on side s decide to participate; this number is given by $N_s(n_b^{*0}, A_s^1)$. In
response, fewer users on side b will participate (namely, $N_b(N_s(n_b^{*0}, A_s^1), A_b^0)$. Considering subsequent reactions, this process converges to the new equilibrium (n_b^{*1}, n_s^{*1}),
as shown in Figure 5.2. This tells us how participation decisions adjust to changes in
membership fees.

We can now solve the platform's maximization problem. The first-order conditions with respect to A_s and A_b can be written respectively as:

$$\begin{cases} A_s = \frac{1}{2}(f_s + r_s) - \frac{1}{2}(\beta_s + \beta_b)A_b + \frac{1}{2}(\beta_s r_b + \beta_b f_b), \\ A_b = \frac{1}{2}(f_b + r_b) - \frac{1}{2}(\beta_s + \beta_b)A_s + \frac{1}{2}(\beta_b r_s + \beta_s f_s). \end{cases}$$

We observe that the presence of positive cross-group network effects affects the
platform's choice of fees in two ways. First, positive cross-group network effects
generate a negative relationship between the two fees; because participations on the
two sides are complementary to one another, lowering the fee on one side drives the
platform to raise the fee on the other side.[17] Second, the cross-group network effects

---

[17] In that regard, two-sided platforms bear some resemblance with multiproduct firms. Yet, as Rochet
and Tirole (2003) point out, end users internalize the corresponding externalities in a multiproduct
setting but not in a multi-sided setting.

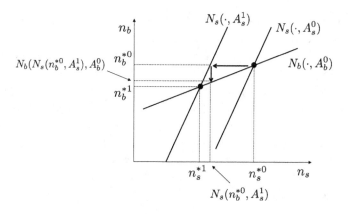

Figure 5.2 Impacts of fee changes on participation on a two-sided platform

make the optimal fee on one side depend also on features pertaining to the other side (cost and stand-alone benefit). This is another consequence of the complementarity between the two sides: The opportunity cost of attracting, say, an additional buyer is lower than the marginal cost (f_b) because this additional buyer will entice extra participation on the seller side and hence, extra revenues and costs for the platform on that side (which depend on r_s and f_s). In general, because of cross-group network effects, revenues and costs cannot be easily allocated to one side or the other.

We can now proceed by solving the previous system to obtain the privately optimal fees.[18] We introduce the following notation: Let $\mu_k \equiv r_k - f_k$ denote the difference between the stand-alone benefit (r_k) and the marginal cost (f_k) on side k ($k = s, b$). We can then write:

$$
\begin{cases}
A_s^* - f_s = \frac{1}{2}\mu_s + \frac{1}{2}\frac{\beta_s - \beta_b}{4 - (\beta_s + \beta_b)^2}\left(2\mu_b + (\beta_s + \beta_b)\,\mu_s\right), \\
A_b^* - f_b = \frac{1}{2}\mu_b + \frac{1}{2}\frac{\beta_b - \beta_s}{4 - (\beta_s + \beta_b)^2}\left(2\mu_s + (\beta_s + \beta_b)\,\mu_b\right).
\end{cases}
\tag{5.3}
$$

We have expressed the privately optimal margins (i.e., the optimal fee minus the marginal cost) as the sum of two terms. The first term is the margin that platforms would set absent cross-group network effects (i.e., for $\beta_s = \beta_b = 0$); in that case, the margin on each side would only depend on costs and willingness to pay on that side (it is as though the "platform" was selling two independent services to two separate groups of customers). The second term depends on the intensity of the cross-group network effects and on parameters pertaining to both sides. In this linear model, this second term vanishes in the special case where the marginal cross-group network effects are equal across sides ($\beta_s = \beta_b$). In contrast, if $\beta_s > \beta_b$ – that is, if sellers value more highly the interaction with buyers than buyers value the interaction with sellers – we see that the platform chooses to have a larger margin on the seller side and a lower

---

[18] To satisfy the second-order conditions for profit maximization, we need to impose a more stringent condition than $\beta_s \beta_b < 1$, namely $\beta_s + \beta_b < 2$.

margin on the buyer side (with respect to what would prevail in the absence of cross-group network effects). The intuition is simple: As the two sides are complementary, the platform can attract more agents on one side by lowering its fee on the other side; when, for instance, $\beta_s > \beta_b$, this "leverage strategy" is more effective when applied on the buyer side; it is thus profitable for the platform to lower the buyer fee and to capture the extra value created on the seller side by increasing the seller fee. This reasoning may even lead the platform to set a negative margin on the buyer side: It can be checked that for $\beta_s > \beta_b$ and $\mu_s/\mu_b > (2 - \beta_s(\beta_b + \beta_s))/(\beta_s - \beta_b)$, we have $A_b^* < f_b$. The exact reverse logic applies in the case where $\beta_b > \beta_s$.[19]

Finally, we compute the profit-maximizing participation levels and the platform's profit at its maximum as:

$$n_b^* = \frac{2\mu_b + (\beta_b + \beta_s)\mu_s}{4 - (\beta_b + \beta_s)^2}, \quad n_s^* = \frac{2\mu_s + (\beta_b + \beta_s)\mu_b}{4 - (\beta_b + \beta_s)^2} \quad \text{and}$$

$$\Pi^* = \frac{\mu_s^2 + \mu_b^2 + \mu_s\mu_b(\beta_s + \beta_b)}{4 - (\beta_s + \beta_b)^2}. \tag{5.4}$$

We see clearly in the latter expression that the platform's profit increases with the intensity of the positive cross-group network effects (i.e., β_b and β_s), as a larger β_k increases the surplus created by transactions between the two sides, and the monopolist can extract part of that increase.

We close this section by discussing the case of academic journals, which can be seen as platforms choosing membership fees, as explained in Case 5.3.

CASE 5.3 PRICING OF ACADEMIC JOURNALS

Academic journals (online and offline) are instances of two-sided platforms with authors on one side and readers on the other side. Arguably, reviewers constitute a third side, but, for simplicity, we consider quality control of the platform as given. Traditional journals charge a subscription fee (discriminating between institutional subscribers and individuals). Authors often have to pay a submission fee. For example, the *Journal of Finance* (owned by the American Finance Association and published by Wiley) charges a submission fee of US$300 for authors from high-income countries and a subscription fee of US$44 for individual subscription (through membership in the American Finance Association) and of up to around US$1,000 for institutional subscribers (print and online); the *Journal of Financial Economics* (published and owned by the commercial publisher Elsevier) charges a submission fee of US$1,000 and a subscription fee of around US$200 for individual subscribers and of US$6,000 for institutions (print only).[20]

There are positive cross-group effects in both directions. Since authors want to be read, they care about a large number of subscribers, as this increases the expected impact of their paper (the reputation of the journal is arguably what they care about most). Viewers care about the number and composition of articles. An increase in average quality happens if the journal makes a more informed selection among the submitted papers.

---

[19] A social planner would choose membership fees that are lower than those chosen by the profit-maximizing platform. Both first-order condition for welfare maximization are indeed negative when evaluated at A_s^* and A_b^*.

[20] All fees have been collected from the publishers' websites on February 6, 2020.

The typical pricing structure has been challenged by open-access journals. Here, authors are the only paying side, whereas readers obtain access for free. Also, traditional journals offer the option for authors to publish their articles as open access articles, in which case they have to pay a publication fee. For example, the *Journal of Finance* charges a fee of US$3,500; the *Journal of Financial Economics* charges a fee of US$1,800 to make the article open access.

In line with the previous case, McCabe and Snyder (2005) take the view that the quality of an academic journal is determined by the ability of its editors. Reading an article is a costly activity. Good articles give the reader positive surplus; bad articles do not. Since readers do not observe the quality of an article before reading it, they benefit from the guiding hand of an able editor, who is likely to reject bad articles. When submitting their work, authors are assumed not to know the quality of what they have written. They are assumed to care only about whether their paper is published (and do not mind the average quality of the journal). McCabe and Snyder (2005) provide comparative statics with respect to the editors' ability. In particular, they use a two-sided pricing model to study the impacts of a change in the editors' ability on the profit-maximizing subscription price. They find that for given prices, authors suffer while readers gain as the editors' ability increases. The direct loss to an author is that their article is less likely to be published: Since all articles are identical ex ante, they know that the fact that editors make a better informed decision also applies to them and thus their article is more likely to be rejected. Readers benefit from an increase in the editors' ability because they end up reading fewer bad papers. The profit-maximizing journal responds to this change in benefits and losses by reducing authors' submission fees and increasing readers' subscription fees.

5.3 Network Effects and Pricing Instruments

So far, we have focused on platforms that serve two distinct groups of users and are able to set a different (transaction or membership) fee on each side; moreover, we only considered cross-group network effects. In this section, we want to extend the analysis by considering other situations that may occur in reality. First, we examine what happens when a monopoly two-sided platform can only use a single fee to maximize its profit (5.3.1). Second, we discuss how pricing is affected when within-group network effects are also present (5.3.2). Finally, we look at situations in which all users are seen to belong to a unique group (as we assumed in Chapter 3), but we add the possibility for the platform to price discriminate among sub-groups of users (5.3.3).

5.3.1 Constrained Two-Sided Pricing

In our previous analyses, we assumed that the platform was facing no constraint of any sort when setting its transaction and/or membership fees. However, constraints of several types may prevent platforms from choosing their optimal fees. First, negative fees (such as cash backs, discounts on other services or in kind payments) may not be feasible or below-cost pricing may be prohibited (because, e.g., of a strict application of competition rules); in this case, a platform that would have optimally set a fee below zero (or the marginal cost) for one group, would be forced to set this fee equal to zero (or to the marginal cost); obviously, if the platform's marginal cost is zero, the two restrictions become equivalent. Second, the platform may be constrained to set a fee of zero on one side because even positive prices are not feasible; this may be due to the nonexcludable nature of the service that the platform provides (think, e.g., of free-to-air broadcasting) or to the lack of cost-effective micropayment technologies (which make zero fees dominate small but positive fees). Finally, platforms may be forced to charge all users the same fee, whatever the group the users belong to; for instance, a few states in the United States forbid gender-based price discrimination, which constrains the pricing of heterosexual nightclubs and dating platforms.

In all these instances, a platform would have to deviate from its privately optimal fee structure and would therefore achieve suboptimal profits. The question of interest is how these constraints impact the well-being of the various groups of participants. To answer this question, we consider in turn the cases in which the platform only controls a single price (the other one being constrained), and the case in which the platform is forced to set the same fee on both sides.

Two Sides but One Price

Suppose, without loss of generality, that fees are regulated on the buyer side. We consider here the case in which the platform sets transaction fees (but the same reasoning can be made when the platform sets membership fees). As we assumed in Section 5.2.1, the platform provides no stand-alone benefits and faces no cost to accommodate users ($r_k = f_k = 0$; $k = b, s$). Then, a buyer is active if $\beta_b \geq a_b$, and a seller is active if $\beta_s \geq a_s$, meaning that the number of active buyers is $N_b(a_b) = \Pr(\beta_b \geq a_b)$, while the number of active sellers is $N_s(a_s) = \Pr(\beta_s \geq a_s)$. If the buyer fee is exogenously set at $\bar{a}_b$, the platform chooses a_s to maximize $\Pi = (\bar{a}_b + a_s - c) N_b(\bar{a}_b) N_s(a_s)$. From the first-order condition, we can express the profit-maximizing seller fee as a function of the regulated buyer fee: $\hat{a}_s = \phi(\bar{a}_b)$. Because cross-group external effects are positive, it is intuitive that $\hat{a}_s$ is a decreasing function of $\bar{a}_b$: An increase in the regulated fee on the buyer side induces buyers, and consequently sellers, to leave the platform; to mitigate this negative impact, the platform reacts by decreasing the fee on the seller side.[21] If the platform was able to set both a_s and a_b, it would choose a_s^* and a_b^*, as characterized in Section 5.2.1.

---

[21] Formally, differentiating the first-order condition for profit-maximization with respect to a_s and $\bar{a}_b$ gives: $da_s/d\bar{a}_b = \left(-\frac{\partial^2 \Pi}{\partial a_s \partial \bar{a}_b}\right) / \left(\frac{\partial^2 \Pi}{\partial a_s^2}\right)$. Evaluated at $\hat{a}_s$, the denominator is negative (from the second-order condition) and the numerator is equal to $-\frac{dN_s}{da_s} N_b(\bar{a}_b)$, which is positive. We have thus that $da_s/d\bar{a}_b < 0$.

As $a_s^* = \phi\left(a_b^*\right)$ and $\phi\left(\cdot\right)$ is a decreasing function, it follows that if $\bar{a}_b < a_b^*$ then $\hat{a}_s > a_s^*$, and if $\bar{a}_b > a_b^*$ then $\hat{a}_s < a_s^*$.[22]

In words, if the constrained fee for buyers is lower than the fee that the platform would optimally set (if it could control that fee), then the platform sets a higher fee for sellers (compared to the one it would set were it able to control both fees). This happens, for instance, if the platform is constrained to set a fee of zero to buyers, although the optimum would have been to set a small positive fee. In that case, sellers will be charged more because of that constraint. As a consequence, more buyers but fewer sellers join the platform.

The exact opposite results are obtained if the constrained fee for buyers is *larger* than the unconstrained one. A case in point could be that the platform would optimally charge buyers a negative fee but cannot find a feasible way to do so: The buyer fee is then raised to zero (which decreases the buyers' participation) and, as result, the seller fee is set below its optimal level (which increases sellers' participation).

In both cases, the net effect on the users' surplus is ambiguous: Those users who pay less meet fewer users on the other side, while those users who pay more meet more users on the other side. To gain some more insights, we solve the previous model under a number of specific assumptions (less mathematically oriented readers may want to skip the technical details). We show (in this specific example) that *when the platform is forced to set a zero fee for buyers, sellers are always hurt while buyers may benefit (compared to the unconstrained situation)*; a precondition for buyers to benefit is that the platform would charge them a positive fee if it were not constrained.

Assume that there is a unit mass of buyers and a unit mass of sellers, β_b is uniformly distributed on the interval $[0,1]$, and β_s is uniformly distributed on the interval $[0,\sigma]$. It follows that $N_b\left(a_b\right) = 1 - a_b$ and $N_s\left(a_s\right) = \left(\sigma - a_s\right)/\sigma$. For given fees a_s and a_b, the surplus of buyers and sellers are respectively computed as:

$$U_b = \int_{a_b}^{1}\left((\beta_b - 1)\frac{\sigma - a_s}{\sigma}\right)d\beta_b = \frac{1}{2\sigma}\left(\sigma - a_s\right)\left(1 - a_b\right)^2,$$

$$U_s = \int_{a_s}^{\sigma}\left((\beta_s - a_s)(1 - a_b)\right)\frac{1}{\sigma}d\beta_s = \frac{1}{2\sigma}\left(1 - a_b\right)\left(\sigma - a_s\right)^2.$$

If the platform is unconstrained, it chooses a_s and a_b to maximize $\left(a_s + a_b\right)\left(1 - a_b\right)\left(\sigma - a_s\right)/\sigma$ (where c, the cost that the platform faces per transaction, is set equal to zero). Solving the system of first-order conditions yields the optimal fees $a_s^* = \left(2\sigma - 1\right)/3$ and $a_b^* = \left(2 - \sigma\right)/3$.

Consider now the case where the platform is constrained to charge buyers a fee of zero ($\bar{a}_b = 0$). Note that this forces the platform to lower the buyer fee if

---

[22] For general functions $N_s\left(a_s\right)$ and $N_b\left(a_b\right)$, the argument is valid in the vicinity of the optimal fees (i.e., if regulated fees are not too different from the optimal ones). Yet, for the linear functions that we have been using so far, the argument holds everywhere.

$\sigma < 2$ (i.e., if $a_b^* > 0$) or to raise it if $\sigma > 2$ (i.e., if $a_b^* < 0$). The platform now chooses a_s to maximize $a_s(\sigma - a_s)/\sigma$. The optimal fee is easily found as $\hat{a}_s = \sigma/2$. We check that $\hat{a}_s > a_s^*$ if $\sigma < 2$, i.e., if $\bar{a}_b = 0 < a_b^*$, and vice versa. We also check that, as expected, the constraint hurts the platform: $\Pi^* - \hat{\Pi} = (\sigma + 1)^3/(27\sigma) - \sigma/4 = (4\sigma + 1)(\sigma - 2)^2/(108\sigma) > 0$. Now, comparing the users' surpluses, we find:

$$\hat{U}_s - U_s^* = \frac{-1}{216\sigma}(\sigma - 2)^2(4\sigma + 1) < 0,$$

$$\hat{U}_b - U_b^* = \frac{1}{108\sigma}(2 - \sigma)\left(10\sigma + 2\sigma^2 - 1\right).$$

We observe the constraint always makes sellers worse off. As for buyers, the constraint may make them better off if $\left(3\sqrt{3} - 5\right)/2 \simeq 0.1 < \sigma < 2$.

Nondiscriminatory Pricing

If the platform is constrained to charge the same fee on both sides, one expects the common constrained fee to be set somewhere between the two unconstrained fees. This means that, inevitably, users one on side will be charged a higher fee, while users on the other side will be charged a lower fee. As these changes in the price structure will affect participation levels, it is a priori not clear how the users' surpluses will be affected.

To shed light on this issue, we return to the model of Section 5.2.2 in which the platform sets membership fees on both sides (a similar argument can be made in the case of transaction fees). For readers who may prefer to skip the mathematical developments, we summarize the main findings we derive in this setting: *The imposition of a common nondiscriminatory fee always hurts the group that would have paid a lower fee absent this constraint; interestingly, the other group may be worse off as well: Although this group pays a lower fee, it suffers from the reduced participation on the other side of the platform.* Applying these insights to the case of heterosexual dating platforms, we can conjecture that a non-discriminatory fee would make women worse off (as they typically pay lower fees than men when such distortions are allowed), and potentially men as well (as the advantage of a lower fee may be outweighed by the disadvantage of meeting fewer women on the platform).[23]

Recall that the surplus of a buyer is $v_b = r_b + \beta_b n_s - A_b$ and the surplus of a seller is $v_s = r_s + \beta_s n_b - A_s$ when n_b buyers and n_s sellers join the platform. Assuming that the users' outside options are uniformly distributed, expression (5.2) gives us the participation levels on both sides as a function of the two prices. We consider

[23] Our simple model only captures some features of a matching platform. Trégouët (2015) develops a richer matching model in which, prior to matching, men and women invest in a costly signal that determines their belief about the types of their potential partners; in this setting, a ban on gender-based price discrimination may be welfare-enhancing.

here a special case in which users obtain the same stand-alone benefits on both sides ($r_s = r_b = 1$) and the platform faces no cost when registering users ($f_b = f_s = 0$). These assumptions do not affect the nature of the results we present here but greatly simplify the exposition. Setting $r_s = r_b = 1$ and $f_b = f_s = 0$ in expression (5.3), we obtain the optimal–unconstrained–fees as:

$$A_s^* = \frac{1 - \beta_b}{2 - \beta_b - \beta_s} \text{ and } A_b^* = \frac{1 - \beta_s}{2 - \beta_b - \beta_s}.$$

Recall that the second-order conditions impose $\beta_b + \beta_s < 2$. We observe thus that (i) $A_s^* > 0 \Leftrightarrow \beta_b < 1$, (ii) $A_b^* > 0 \Leftrightarrow \beta_s < 1$, (iii) $A_s^* > A_b^* \Leftrightarrow \beta_s > \beta_b$, and (iv) $A_s^* + A_b^* = 1$. Recall also that in this model, $v_s = n_s$ and $v_b = n_b$. It follows that we can express the sellers' and buyers' surplus as $U_s^* = n_s^* v_s^* = \left(n_s^*\right)^2$ and $U_b^* = n_b^* v_b^* = \left(n_b^*\right)^2$. Plugging the above values of A_s^* and A_b^* into expression (5.2), we can compute the equilibrium participation level on both sides, n_s^* and n_b^*, so as to find:

$$U_s^* = U_b^* = \frac{1}{(2 - \beta_b - \beta_s)^2}.$$

Suppose now that some regulation imposes that the same fee, A, be charged on both sides. The platform's maximization problem then becomes:

$$\max_A A \left[n_s(A) + n_b(A) \right] = \frac{2 + \beta_s + \beta_b}{1 - \beta_s \beta_b} A(1 - A).$$

The profit-maximizing fee is easily computed as:

$$\tilde{A} = \frac{1}{2} = \frac{1}{2} \left(A_s^* + A_b^* \right).$$

We observe thus that in this linear model, a monopoly platform that must set the same membership fee on both sides, chooses a fee that is just equal to the average of the fees that it would have set without this constraint. If $\beta_s > \beta_b$ – that is, if sellers value more the interaction on the platform than buyers do, which implies $A_s^* > A_b^*$ – then sellers are charged less and buyers are charged more once the platform must set a common nondiscriminatory fee; the reverse applies when $\beta_b > \beta_s$. Yet, participation levels are affected as well. To derive the net effects on all participants, we first derive the equilibrium participation levels $\tilde{n}_s$ and $\tilde{n}_b$ by plugging the value of $\tilde{A}$ into expression (5.2); from there, we can compute the sellers' and buyers' surplus as $\tilde{U}_b = \tilde{n}_b \tilde{v}_b = (\tilde{n}_b)^2$ and $\tilde{U}_s = \tilde{n}_s \tilde{v}_s = (\tilde{n}_s)^2$. Doing so, we find the following values:

$$\tilde{U}_s = \frac{(1 + \beta_s)^2}{4(1 - \beta_b \beta_s)^2} \text{ and } \tilde{U}_b = \frac{(1 + \beta_b)^2}{4(1 - \beta_b \beta_s)^2}.$$

Comparing surpluses in the two cases, we find:

$$U_s^* > \tilde{U}_s \Leftrightarrow (1 - \beta_s)(\beta_b - \beta_s) > 0 \text{ and } U_b^* > \tilde{U}_b \Leftrightarrow (1 - \beta_b)(\beta_b - \beta_s) < 0.$$

Let us first show that it is impossible to have both $\tilde{U}_s > U_s^*$ and $\tilde{U}_b > U_b^*$; supposing $\beta_b > \beta_s$, these two inequalities would impose $\beta_s > 1$ and $\beta_b < 1$, which is clearly incompatible with $\beta_b > \beta_s$; similarly, supposing that $\beta_s > \beta_b$, we would need $\beta_s < 1$ and $\beta_b > 1$, another incompatibility. It follows that *some users will inevitably be hurt when a common fee is imposed.*

There are then two possible cases. On the one hand, *all users may be worse off*; this is so if both $U_s^* > \tilde{U}_s$ and $U_b^* > \tilde{U}_b$, which is possible in two instances: Either $\beta_b > 1 > \beta_s$ or $\beta_b < 1 < \beta_s$. On the other hand, *one group may suffer while the other benefits*; this is so if cross-group network effects are relatively weak, so that $\beta_b, \beta_s < 1$; the group that benefits is the one that is charged less under a common fee (i.e., buyers if $\beta_s > \beta_b$, so that $A_s^* > \tilde{A} > A_b^*$, and buyers otherwise).

We close this section by recording our main results in Lesson 5.5:

LESSON 5.5   *Platforms may be restricted to set fees on one side only or to charge the same fee on both sides. Such constraints are detrimental for the profits of a monopoly platform and for the welfare of at least one group of participants (the other group may benefit from the constraint if it leads to lower fees for this group).*

5.3.2   Within- and Cross-Group Network Effects

We have focused so far on cross-group network effects. However, many platforms also have to manage within-group network effects on one or both sides. That is, they must take into account that more participation or interaction in one group not only affects users of the other group but also users of that same group. One simple way to extend our setting to incorporate such effects is to add a component in a user's gross utility that varies (linearly) with the number of users of the same group:

$$v_b = r_b + \beta_b n_s + \gamma_b n_b \text{ and } v_s = r_s + \beta_s n_b + \gamma_s n_s. \tag{5.5}$$

The parameters γ_k ($k = b, s$) measure how a user of group k values the interaction with an extra user of their own group; if $\gamma_k > 0$, then within-group network effects are positive (they are negative otherwise). This formulation supposes that cross-group and within-group network effects are additively separable. Whether this separability assumption is reasonable depends on the particular environment that is considered, as discussed in Case 5.4.

CASE 5.4 WITHIN-GROUP NETWORK EFFECTS ON TWO-SIDED PLATFORMS

On *ride-hailing platforms* (such as, Uber, Lyft, or DiDi), there are clear positive cross-group network effects between riders and drivers, as each group benefits from more participation on the other side of the platform. There also exist negative within-group network effects in each group: For a given number of riders, having more fellow drivers increases each driver's waiting time; the same goes for riders (excluding the service of sharing the ride with other parties, which some ride-hailing apps provide). In this case, both γ_s and γ_b are negative. As long as the platform sets the price of a ride, the cross-group and within-group network effects are independent of one another in their intensity, meaning that our model is a good approximation. In contrast, if drivers set the price of a ride, more intense competition among drivers (i.e., a more negative γ_s) would lead drivers to reduce their price, which would increase a rider's valuation of interacting with drivers (i.e., β_b would increase).

In *open rodeo competitions* (which are quite popular in the western United States), positive cross-group network effects are present: The more contestants sign up, the more excitement for the audience; the larger the audience, the more visibility for the contestants. There are also negative within-group network effects among contestants, as the more numerous they are, the lower their probability of winning the prize. As for the audience, it can be argued that when it comes to enjoy a show, the more spectators there are the more fun it gets for all of them; within-group network effects would then be positive. If we let contestants be group s and spectators be group b, we would then have $\gamma_s < 0 < \gamma_b$. Given that the competition among contestants and the increasing fun among spectators do not induce any change in prices, our separability assumption seems adequate.

A similar configuration is observed on *video game platforms*: Positive cross-group network effects from game developers to gamers, and vice versa; negative within-group network effects (i.e., competition) among game developers; and positive within-group network effects among gamers (through multi-player games); however, it is not clear whether these various effects can be separated from one another.

A final example is *social networks* like Facebook. Here, as explained in Chapter 1, network effects are primarily found within the group of end users (and are positive) generating an attraction loop; yet, for monetization purposes, advertisers are added to the platform, which creates a mix of positive and negative cross-group network effects (advertisers value the presence of more users, whereas users tend to dislike an increase in advertising, thereby generating an attraction/repulsion pendulum); negative within-group network effects are also likely to arise among advertisers, as they compete for the users' attention.

The question of interest is how a monopoly platform adjusts its price structure to account for within-group network effects. To fix ideas, we refer to the case in which the platform sets a membership fee on each side and cross-group network effects are positive (as in Section 5.2.2). Suppose that, initially, within-group network effects are inexistent (as we assumed before). Now introduce positive within-group network effects among buyers. As a result, an additional buyer contributes to attract more buyers. How does this change affect the platform's choice of fees? This is not clear a priori because two forces work in opposite directions. On the one hand, as users are keener to join the platform than before, it is less costly for the platform to "use" buyers to attract sellers; this leads the platform to invest by lowering A_b and recoup this investment by increasing A_s; this tactic is all the more interesting in that sellers value the presence of buyers – that is, as β_s is large. On the other hand, the platform realizes that more revenues can be gained on the buyer side than before (because buyers now also enjoy the presence of fellow buyers); it thus pays to attract more sellers by decreasing A_s, so as to attract more buyers, and to reap the additional revenues by increasing A_b; this tactic pays more the more buyers value the presence of sellers (i.e., the larger β_b). We understand therefore that the impact of within-group network effects on the fee structure depends on the balance between the cross-group network effects.

Regarding equilibrium participation levels, even if fees are likely to move in opposite directions (as we just explained), we expect positive within-group network effects in one group to lead the platform to attract more users of that group and, by ricochet, more users of the other group as well. For that reason, we also expect the platform to make higher profits when positive within-group network effects appear in one group. Negative within-group network effects would have the exact opposite impacts. We confirm these results by developing the linear model of Section 5.2.2 with the utility formulation (5.5). We present the detailed computations below (which less mathematically oriented readers may want to skip); for now, we record the following findings:

LESSON 5.6   *Suppose that a monopoly platform serves two groups with positive cross-group network effects and sets membership fees. The presence of positive within-group network effects in one group leads the platform to attract more users of both groups and allows it to make larger profits (compared to the situation in which these within-group network effects are absent). The opposite prevails in the presence of negative within-group network effects. In any case, the platform raises one fee and lowers the other; whether the group that exhibits within-group network effects ends up paying less or more depends on the balance between the cross-group network effects.*

Given than $n_k = v_k$ in this model ($k = b, s$), we find from expression 5.5 that $A_b = r_b + \beta_b n_s - (1 - \gamma_b) n_b$ and $A_s = r_s + \beta_s n_b - (1 - \gamma_s) n_s$. We will show in Section 5.4.2 that the same equilibrium allocation is found whether the platform chooses participation levels or membership fees. As it can be checked that this result still holds in the present setting, we assume that the platform chooses participation levels (which simplifies the exposition). The maximization program of the platform can thus be written as (assuming for simplicity that $f_s = f_b = 0$):
$\max_{n_s, n_b} \Pi = (r_s + \beta_s n_b - (1 - \gamma_s) n_s) n_s + (r_b + \beta_b n_s - (1 - \gamma_b) n_b) n_b$. Solving the system of first-order conditions, we find the optimal participation levels (where the subscript w refers to within-group network effects):

$$n_s^w = \frac{2(1 - \gamma_b) r_s + (\beta_b + \beta_s) r_b}{4(1 - \gamma_s)(1 - \gamma_b) - (\beta_b + \beta_s)^2} \text{ and } n_b^w = \frac{2(1 - \gamma_s) r_b + (\beta_b + \beta_s) r_s}{4(1 - \gamma_s)(1 - \gamma_b) - (\beta_b + \beta_s)^2}.$$

The second-order conditions require $\gamma_s < 1$, $\gamma_b < 1$, and $4(1 - \gamma_s)(1 - \gamma_b) > (\beta_b + \beta_s)^2$. Under these restrictions, it can be shown that both n_s^w and n_b^w increase with γ_s and γ_b. This means that compared to the situation without within-group network effects, introducing positive (resp. negative) effects within one group raises (resp. reduces) equilibrium participation in both groups.

Using n_s^w and n_b^w, we can derive the optimal fees:

$$A_s^w = \frac{[2(1 - \gamma_s)(1 - \gamma_b) - \beta_b(\beta_b + \beta_s)] r_s + (1 - \gamma_s)(\beta_s - \beta_b) r_b}{4(1 - \gamma_s)(1 - \gamma_b) - (\beta_b + \beta_s)^2},$$

$$A_b^w = \frac{[2(1 - \gamma_s)(1 - \gamma_b) - \beta_s(\beta_b + \beta_s)] r_b + (1 - \gamma_b)(\beta_b - \beta_s) r_s}{4(1 - \gamma_s)(1 - \gamma_b) - (\beta_b + \beta_s)^2}.$$

Deriving these expressions with respect to γ_s and γ_b, we can show that an increase in either γ_s or γ_b leads to an increase in A_s^w and a decrease in A_b^w if and only if $\beta_s > \beta_b$.

Finally, we compute the platform's maximal profit as:

$$\Pi^w = A_s^w n_s^w + A_b^w n_b^w = \frac{(1 - \gamma_s)\,r_b^2 + (1 - \gamma_b)\,r_s^2 + (\beta_b + \beta_s)\,r_b r_s}{4\,(1 - \gamma_s)\,(1 - \gamma_b) - (\beta_b + \beta_s)^2}.$$

Differentiating with respect to γ_s and γ_b, we check that Π^w increases when γ_s or γ_b increases.

5.3.3 Price Discrimination by a Platform

We now return to cases in which the interactions generating network effects take place within a single group of users.[24] Think of the network goods, such as a communication network, that we studied in Chapter 3: As each user of the good generates network effects for any other user of this good, all users can be seen as belonging to the same group. That is, all users care about total participation (i.e., total adoption of the network good). The difference with the setting of Chapter 3, however, is that the monopoly platform is aware that users differ according to the value they attach either to stand-alone benefits or to network benefits. Recall that stand-alone benefits may stem from vertically integrated content or functionalities on a platform that accrue even absent other users participating; as for network effects, they may arise because of direct interaction benefits or because more users give rise to a better match of content to users. As illustrated in Case 5.5, there are clear instances in which different segments of users value differently these two types of benefits.

CASE 5.5 DIFFERENT VALUATIONS OF STAND-ALONE AND NETWORK BENEFITS

Cloud storage services (like Dropbox, Google Drive or Sync.com) offer two primary functions: They allow users to store their own files (a stand-alone benefit), as well as to share files with other users (a network benefit, as it increases with the number of users of the same service). Because companies generate much larger libraries of files than individuals, they value much more the stand-alone benefits than individuals do. This segmentation between companies (or professionals) and individuals also applies to much software: Both segments may value equally the network benefits (e.g., the ability to exchange files with other users) but professionals will be more willing than individuals to take full advantage of the stand-alone benefits (e.g., a set of advanced functionalities). In the case of *gaming consoles*, gamers who spend most of their time using a simple-player mode value the network benefits much less than gamers who often use the multi-player mode. Another example comes from *crowdfunding platforms*. Several studies (see, e.g., Zhang and Liu, 2012) provide evidence that investors in crowdfunding campaigns herd; typically, they tend to invest more in campaigns that have already attracted a larger number of investors, a form of within-group network effect. Kim and Viwanathan (2019) show, however, that experienced investors are less likely to be influenced by other investors' past choices; in other words, experienced investors value less the network benefits than other, less sophisticated, investors. This segmentation between "experts" and "amateurs" is also relevant, for instance, on *do-it-yourself platforms* (such as

---

[24] This subsection draws on Belleflamme and Peitz (2020); some material is taken verbatim from this article.

Instructables, Craftser, or Etsy): Amateur craftspeople typically rely more than experts on the recommendations and reviews provided by other members of the community (a network benefit).

If the platform can observe and verify these differences (while preventing arbitrage), it can set different fees to users of different segments; this is known as *group pricing* (or third-degree price discrimination). Alternatively, the platform may not observe the users' characteristics but it may nevertheless succeed in bringing users to self-select across different versions of the network good; this is known as *versioning* (or second-degree price discrimination). In both cases, the platform has a price instrument for each segment (instead of a unique price, as we assumed in Chapter 3). This allows the platform to account for the fact that the fee it charges to one segment of users affects not only the participation decision of these users but also the participation decision of users in the other segment (as the participation of one segment affects the attractiveness of the platform for the other segment).[25]

This setting could alternatively be viewed as the reduced form of a dynamic model: One group would be the "early adopters" and the other group the "late adopters." We saw in Chapter 4 the difficulties that platforms face at the launch stage because of the coordination problems among users; in particular, if the platform sets a unique positive fee, there exist an equilibrium with no participation (if all users expect that no user will participate, it is indeed a best response for each of them not to participate). However, the problem becomes less acute if the platform can price discriminate. Typically, it could set a negative fee for early users (so as to subsidize their participation) and recoup its initial losses by charging a positive fee to later users (which they would accept paying because they would be certain to enjoy the network benefits generated by the early users). This is the dynamic version of the divide-and-conquer strategy that we described in Chapter 4.

In what follows, we compare group pricing and versioning when the segments of users have either different stand-alone or different network benefits. We illustrate how the platform uses differential pricing to internalize network effects. We also show that under certain conditions, a freemium strategy (which is a form of versioning) allows the platform to achieve the same profit as if it were practicing group pricing (which would require a better knowledge of the users' characteristics).

Segment-Specific Stand-Alone Benefits

Suppose that users belong to either of two segments. They have some basic taste and belong to segment b, or they have a strong interest in the network good and belong

---

[25] This is reminiscent of what happens on two-sided platforms, with the major difference, though, that cross-group network effects do not result from matching consumers of different types but from the platform's ability to practice differential pricing. In the model with group pricing, the current model is a special case of the model in Section 5.3.2: In each consumer segment, the strength of the within-group network effect is equal to the strength of the cross-group network effect.

to group s. They obtain the following utilities on the platform:

$$\begin{cases} v_s = r_s + \beta\,(n_s + n_b) - A_s, \\ v_b = r_b + \beta\,(n_s + n_b) - A_b, \end{cases} \tag{5.6}$$

where n_k is the number of users of segment k on the platform ($k \in \{b,s\}$). We assume that $\beta < 1/2$ and that $r_s > r_b$, meaning that users in segment s place more value on the stand-alone benefits than users in segment b. As far as network benefits are concerned, it is assumed here that all users value them in the same way and care about total participation (i.e., total adoption of the network good, $n_s + n_b$).

Users in both segments have heterogeneous opportunity costs of joining the platform; this opportunity cost is uniformly distributed on a sufficiently large interval; an increase of net utility of $\Delta v_k = 1$ leads to an increase in the number of users of mass 1. As a result, the number of users as a function of prices A_s and A_b are implicitly given by $r_s + \beta\,(n_s + n_b) - A_s = n_s$ and $r_b + \beta\,(n_s + n_b) - A_b = n_b$. We can rewrite this by expressing the number of participating users in one segment as a function of the price charged to that segment and the number of participating users in the other segment: $n_s = (r_s + \beta n_b - A_s)/(1 - \beta)$ and $n_b = (r_b + \beta n_s - A_b)/(1 - \beta)$; we observe thus that network effects make participations in the two segments complementary with one another. Solving this equation system, we obtain user participation as a function of prices A_s and A_b,

$$\begin{cases} n_s\,(A_s, A_b) = \dfrac{(1-\beta)\,(r_s - A_s) + \beta\,(r_b - A_b)}{1 - 2\beta}, \\ n_b\,(A_s, A_b) = \dfrac{(1-\beta)\,(r_b - A_b) + \beta\,(r_s - A_s)}{1 - 2\beta}. \end{cases}$$

As participations are complementary, both n_s and n_b are decreasing functions of the two prices.

Before comparing the platform's choices under group pricing and versioning, let us look at the benchmark case of *uniform pricing* (as was supposed in Chapter 3). If the network good is sold at the same price A to all users (irrespective of the segment they belong to), the platform chooses this price A to maximize:

$$\Pi = A\,[n_s\,(A,A) + n_b\,(A,A)] = A\,\frac{r_s + r_b - 2A}{1 - 2\beta}.$$

The profit-maximizing price is easily found as $A^u = (r_s + r_b)/4$, and the corresponding participation levels are:

$$n_s^u = \frac{(3 - 4\beta)\,r_s - (1 - 4\beta)\,r_b}{4\,(1 - 2\beta)} \quad \text{and} \quad n_b^u = \frac{(3 - 4\beta)\,r_b - (1 - 4\beta)\,r_s}{4\,(1 - 2\beta)}.$$

In what follows, we assume that $(3 - 4\beta)\,r_b > (1 - 4\beta)\,r_s$ to make sure that the monopoly platform chooses to serve both segments of users under uniform pricing. The platform's profit at the optimum is then computed as $\Pi^u = (r_s + r_b)^2/(8\,(1 - 2\beta))$.

Group Pricing

Assume now that the platform has enough information to tell users apart according to the segment they belong to. It thus sells the network good at price A_s to users of segment s and at price A_b to users of segment b. That is, the platform sets A_s and A_b to maximize $\Pi = A_s n_s + A_b n_b$. Solving the system of first-order conditions yields the profit-maximizing prices $A_s^* = r_s/2$ and $A_b^* = r_b/2$. In this specific linear setting, while the platform accounts for the fact that the price charged to one segment affects the net utility of the good in the other segment, the profit-maximizing prices do not respond. Yet, the participation levels do. Evaluated at the profit-maximizing prices, we observe that the participation levels both increase in β:

$$n_s^* = \frac{(1-\beta)\, r_s + \beta r_b}{2\,(1-2\beta)} \quad \text{and} \quad n_b^* = \frac{(1-\beta)\, r_b + \beta r_s}{2\,(1-2\beta)}.$$

Maximal profit is equal to:

$$\Pi^* = \frac{(1-\beta)\left(r_s^2 + r_b^2\right) + 2\beta r_s r_b}{4\,(1-2\beta)},$$

which cannot be lower than Π^u (as the platform has optimally chosen $A_s^* \neq A_b^*$).

Comparing prices and participation levels across segments and with the case of uniform pricing, we can establish the following results:

$$r_s > r_b \Rightarrow A_s^* > A^u > A_b^* \text{ and } n_s^u > n_s^* > n_b^* > n_b^u.$$

That is, when the platform practices group pricing, it charges a higher price to the segment that values the stand-alone benefits the most (segment A); despite the price difference, participation is larger in segment s than in segment b, but smaller than the participation that would prevail under uniform pricing. As for total participation, we find that it is exactly the same under uniform and group pricing: $n_s^* + n_b^* = n_s^u + n_b^u = (r_s + r_b) / (2\,(1-2\beta))$.

The platform internalizes network effects by lowering prices A_s and A_b relative to what would happen if it were to ignore the interaction between the two consumers segments. We can see this by supposing that the platform maximizes its profit for each group with characteristic i separately, taking as given the participation level of the other group. Less mathematically oriented readers may prefer to skip the formal analysis of this situation.

The platform sees participation of group s as $n_s = r_s + \beta(n_s + n_b^e) - A_s$, where n_b^e is the (fixed) expectation it forms for participation in the other group. The profit maximization problem for group s is then $\max_{A_s} A_s \frac{1}{1-\beta}(r_s + \beta n_b^e - A_s)$. The first-order condition yields $A_s = (r_s + \beta n_b^e)/2$. Similarly, on group b, the platform's maximization problem is $\max_{A_b} A_b \frac{1}{1-\beta}(r_b + \beta n_s^e - A_b)$, yielding $A_b = (r_b + \beta n_s^e)/2$. Since $n_s^e > 0$ and $n_s^e > 0$, we must have that both prices are higher than the prices the monopolist chooses under group pricing. Plugging the optimal prices into the participation levels, we find $n_s = (r_s + \beta n_b^e) / (2\,(1-\beta))$ and $n_b = (r_b + \beta n_s^e) / (2\,(1-\beta))$. Imposing fulfilled expectations (i.e., $n_s^e = n_s$ and

$n_b^e = n_b$) and solving, we can obtain explicit solution for prices and participation levels. We obtain the solution for participation levels (denoted by superscript m):

$$n_s^m = \frac{2(1-\beta)r_s + \beta r_b}{4 - 8\beta + 3\beta^2} \text{ and } n_b^m = \frac{2(1-\beta)r_b + \beta r_s}{4 - 8\beta + 3\beta^2}.$$

To find the platform's privately optimal prices, we still need to substitute these values into $A_s = (r_s + \beta n_b)/2$ and $A_b = (r_b + \beta n_s)/2$. Doing so, we find:

$$A_s^m = (1-\beta)\frac{2(1-\beta)r_s + \beta r_b}{4 - 8\beta + 3\beta^2} \text{ and } A_b^m = (1-\beta)\frac{2(1-\beta)r_b + \beta r_s}{4 - 8\beta + 3\beta^2}.$$

Versioning

In contrast with the previous case, we assume here that the platform does not observe (or is not able to verify) the segment characteristics. The platform therefore offers a menu of options with the aim of making users self-select among the options and, thereby, reveal the segment they belong to. Suppose that the platform offers a premium and basic version and that users from the two segments value the two versions differently. In particular, segment s and segment b users have a value of r for the basic version, segment b users are not willing to pay a higher price for the premium version, whereas segment s users are willing to pay $r + \Delta$ (with $\Delta > 0$). If the contract menu is such that segment s users choose the premium version and segment b users the basic version, we have:

$$\begin{cases} v_s = r_s + \beta(n_s + n_b) - A_s, \\ v_b = r_b + \beta(n_s + n_b) - A_b, \end{cases}$$

with $r_s = r + \Delta > r_b = r$ and $\beta < 1/2$. These are the exact same utilities as in expression (5.6), but with a different interpretation. Hence, if the incentive constraint of segment s users is not binding (i.e., if segment s users are strictly better off when they buy the premium version instead of the basic version), then the analysis carried out under group pricing still holds. In particular, the profit-maximizing prices are $A_s^* = r_s/2 = (r + \Delta)/2$ and $A_b^* = r_b/2 = r/2$. As the price for the premium version is $\Delta/2$ above the price of the basic version, users in segment s do indeed strictly prefer the premium version over the basic version (the gain in stand-alone benefits, Δ, outweighs the price increase, $\Delta/2$). In conclusion, in these particular circumstances, the platform achieves the same profit under versioning than under group pricing (it does not need to forego any profit to induce users to reveal their private information about their willingness to pay).

In the special case that $r = 0$, the basic version is sold at a price of zero and, thus, segment b users obtain the good for free. The equilibrium numbers of users in the two segments are then computed as:

$$n_s^* = \frac{1 - \beta}{2(1 - 2\beta)}\Delta \text{ and } n_b^* = \frac{\beta}{2(1 - 2\beta)}\Delta.$$

As for the platform's profit, it is equal to:

$$\Pi^* = n_s^* A_s^* = \frac{1-\beta}{4\,(1-2\beta)}\Delta^2.$$

Even if segment b does not generate any direct revenue, it does so indirectly by raising the network benefits through its participation and, thereby, the willingness to pay of segment s users. To see this, we compare the results we just derived with a hypothetical situation in which segment b users would not exist. In that case, $n_s = r_s + \beta n_s - A_s$; solving for n_s and replacing v_s by Δ, we have $n_s = (\Delta - A_s)/(1-\beta)$. As the platform maximizes $n_s A_s$, we find the optimal price as $\tilde{A}_s = \Delta/2$. It follows that $\tilde{n}_s = \frac{1}{2(1-\beta)}\Delta$ and $\tilde{n}_s\tilde{A}_s = \frac{1}{4(1-\beta)}\Delta^2$. We check that:

$$\Pi^* - \tilde{n}_s\tilde{A}p_s = \frac{1-\beta}{4\,(1-2\beta)}\Delta^2 - \frac{1}{4(1-\beta)}\Delta^2 = \frac{\beta^2}{4\,(1-2\beta)\,(1-\beta)}\Delta^2 > 0,$$

meaning that the platform does indeed achieve a larger profit when offering a menu in which users can obtain the basic version for free. The reason is that giving away the basic version for free leads some segment b users to join; this makes participation more attractive for segment s users, and leads to higher platform profits.

Segment-Specific Network Benefits
We now repeat thee analysis under the alternative assumption that users value the strength of the network effects differently across segments. In particular, segment s and segment b users obtain the following net utilities on the platform:

$$\begin{cases} v_s = r + \beta_s(n_s + n_b) - A_s, \\ v_b = r + \beta_b(n_s + n_b) - A_b, \end{cases} \tag{5.7}$$

with $\beta_b < \beta_s < 1/2$. That is, users no longer differ in terms of stand-alone benefits (they share the same valuation r) but in terms of network benefits: For a given network size ($n_s + n_b$), segment s users have a larger utility than segment b users ($\beta_s > \beta_b$). As before, users have heterogeneous outside options. As a result, participation levels as a function of prices A_s and A_b are implicitly given by $r + \beta_s(n_s + n_b) - A_s = n_s$ and $r + \beta_b(n_s + n_b) - A_b = n_b$. Solving this equation system, we obtain user participation as a function of the two prices:

$$\begin{cases} n_s\,(A_s, A_b) = \dfrac{(1-\beta_b)\,(r - A_s) + \beta_s\,(r - A_b)}{1 - \beta_s - \beta_b}, \\ n_b\,(A_s, A_b) = \dfrac{\beta_b\,(r - A_s) + (1 - \beta_s)\,(r - A_b)}{1 - \beta_s - \beta_b}. \end{cases}$$

If the platform were constrained to set a *uniform price A*, is would choose this price to maximize:

$$\Pi = A\,[n_s\,(A, A) + A_b n_b\,(A, A)] = A\frac{2\,(r - A)}{1 - \beta_s - \beta_b}.$$

It is clear that the optimal price is $A^u = r/2$, with resulting participation levels and profits:

$$n_s^u = \frac{1 + \beta_s - \beta_b}{1 - \beta_s - \beta_b} \frac{r}{2}, \; n_b^u = \frac{1 - \beta_s + \beta_b}{1 - \beta_s - \beta_b} \frac{r}{2}, \text{ and } \Pi^u = \frac{1}{1 - \beta_s - \beta_b} \frac{r^2}{2}.$$

We note that $\beta_s > \beta_b$ implies that $n_s^u > n_b^u$.

Group Pricing

If the platform can tell users from the two segments apart, it chooses A_s and A_b to maximize $\Pi = A_s n_s (A_s, A_b) + A_b n_b (A_s, A_b)$. Solving the system of first-order conditions yields the following profit-maximizing prices:

$$A_s^* = \frac{(2 - \beta_s - 3\beta_b) - (\beta_s - \beta_b)^2}{4(1 - \beta_s - \beta_b) - (\beta_s - \beta_b)^2} r \text{ and } A_b^* = \frac{(2 - 3\beta_s - \beta_b) - (\beta_s - \beta_b)^2}{4(1 - \beta_s - \beta_b) - (\beta_s - \beta_b)^2} r$$

The corresponding participation levels are computed as:

$$n_s^* = \frac{2 + (\beta_s - \beta_b)}{4(1 - \beta_s - \beta_b) - (\beta_s - \beta_b)^2} r \text{ and } n_b^* = \frac{2 - (\beta_s - \beta_b)}{4(1 - \beta_s - \beta_b) - (\beta_s - \beta_b)^2} r.$$

As for the platform's profit, it is equal to:

$$\Pi^* = \frac{2}{4(1 - \beta_s - \beta_b) - (\beta_s - \beta_b)^2} r^2.$$

Comparing prices and participation levels, we find similar results as in the previous case:

$$\beta_s > \beta_b \Rightarrow A_s^* > A^u > A_b^* \text{ and } n_s^u > n_s^* > n_b^* > n_b^u.$$

That is, the segment that enjoys the largest network benefits is charged a higher price and yet participates more than the other segment; participation levels are less different across segments under group pricing than under uniform pricing. In contrast with the previous case, total participation is now larger under group pricing than under uniform pricing:

$$\left(n_s^* + n_b^*\right) - \left(n_s^u + n_b^u\right) = \frac{(\beta_s - \beta_b)^2}{(1 - \beta_s - \beta_b)\left(4(1 - \beta_s - \beta_b) - (\beta_s - \beta_b)^2\right)} r > 0.$$

We note that in this setting, the platform adjusts its prices by internalizing the strength of the network effects in the two segments.[26] To see how this adjustment process affects prices, we solve for the profit-maximizing prices of a platform ignoring this adjustment process. This applies if the platform does not take into consideration that a price change for one segment affects the overall network benefit for the other segment (less mathematically oriented readers may prefer to skip this part).

Suppose that the platform maximizes its profit for each segment separately, taking as given the participation level on the other segment. That is, the platform

---

[26] Recall that in the previous setting with different stand-alone benefits, the optimal group prices were independent of β.

sees participation on segment s as $n_s = r + \beta_s(n_s + n_b^e) - A_s$, where n_b^e is the (fixed) expectation it forms for participation in the other segment. The profit maximization problem for segment s is then $\max_{A_s} A_s \frac{1}{1-\beta_s}(r + \beta_s n_b^e - A_s)$. The first-order condition yields $A_s = (r + \beta_s n_b^e)/2$. Similarly, on segment b, the platform's maximization problem is $\max_{A_b} A_b \frac{1}{1-\beta_b}(r + \beta_b n_s^e - A_b)$, yielding $A_b = (r + \beta_b n_s^e)/2$. Plugging the optimal prices into the participation levels, we find $n_s = \left(r + \beta_s n_b^e\right) / \left(2\left(1 - \beta_s\right)\right)$ and $n_b = \left(r + \beta_b n_s^e\right) / \left(2\left(1 - \beta_b\right)\right)$. Imposing fulfilled expectations (i.e., $n_s^e = n_s$ and $n_b^e = n_b$) and solving, we compute (with the superscript m standing for "myopic"):

$$n_s^m = \frac{2 + \beta_s - 2\beta_b}{4(1 - \beta_s - \beta_b) + 3\beta_s\beta_b}r \text{ and } n_b^m = \frac{2 - 2\beta_s + \beta_b}{4(1 - \beta_s - \beta_b) + 3\beta_s\beta_b}r.$$

To find the platform's optimal prices, we still need to substitute these values into $A_s = (r + \beta_s n_b)/2$ and $A_b = (r + \beta_b n_s)/2$. Doing so, we find:

$$A_s^m = \frac{(1 - \beta_s)(2 + \beta_s - 2\beta_b)}{4(1 - \beta_s - \beta_b) + 3\beta_s\beta_b}r \text{ and } A_b^m = \frac{(1 - \beta_b)(2 - 2\beta_s + \beta_b)}{4(1 - \beta_s - \beta_b) + 3\beta_s\beta_b}r.$$

To get a sense of how prices and participation levels compare according to whether the platform takes network effects across segments into account or not, we focus on the two extreme cases in which $\beta_b = 0$ and $\beta_b = \beta_s$. First, for $\beta_b = 0$, we observe that when the platform internalizes the network effects, it sets a larger price for segment s and a lower price for segment b ($A_s^* > A_s^m$ and $A_b^* < A_b^m$), while raising participation in both segments ($n_s^* > n_s^m$ and $n_b^* > n_b^m$):

$$A_s^* - A_s^m\big|_{\beta_b=0} = \frac{(1-\beta_s)(2+\beta_s)}{4-4\beta_s-\beta_s^2}r - \frac{2+\beta_s}{4}r = \frac{(2+\beta_s)\beta_s^2}{4(4-4\beta_s-\beta_s^2)}r > 0,$$

$$A_b^* - A_b^m\big|_{\beta_b=0} = \frac{2-3\beta_s-\beta_s^2}{4-4\beta_s-\beta_s^2}r - \frac{1}{2}r = -\frac{(2+\beta_s)\beta_s}{2(4-4\beta_s-\beta_s^2)}r < 0,$$

$$n_s^* - n_s^m\big|_{\beta_b=0} = \frac{2+\beta_s}{4-4\beta_s-\beta_s^2}r - \frac{2+\beta_s}{4(1-\beta_s)}r = \frac{(2+\beta_s)\beta_s^2}{4(1-\beta_s)(4-4\beta_s-\beta_s^2)}r > 0,$$

$$n_b^* - n_b^m\big|_{\beta_b=0} = \frac{2-\beta_s}{4-4\beta_s-\beta_s^2}r - \frac{1}{2}r = \frac{(2+\beta_s)\beta_s}{2(4-4\beta_s-\beta_s^2)}r > 0.$$

At the other extreme, when $\beta_b = \beta_s$, we find:

$$A_s^* - A_s^m\big|_{\beta_b=\beta_s} = A_b^* - A_b^m\big|_{\beta_b=\beta_s} = \frac{1}{2}r - \frac{1-\beta_s}{2-3\beta_s}r = -\frac{\beta_s}{2(2-3\beta_s)}r < 0,$$

$$n_s^* - n_s^m\big|_{\beta_b=\beta_s} = n_b^* - n_b^m\big|_{\beta_b=\beta_s} = \frac{1}{2(1-2\beta_s)}r - \frac{r}{2-3\beta_s} = \frac{\beta_s}{2(1-2\beta_s)(2-3\beta_s)}r > 0.$$

Here, the "internalizing" platform sets a lower price for both segments than the "myopic" platform; as with $\beta_b = 0$, optimal participation levels are larger when cross-group network effects are internalized.

Versioning

As we did in the previous case, we construct a versioning scenario that allows the platform to reach the same profit as under group pricing. Suppose that the basic version is valued equally by users in both segment with the strength of the network effect β. As for the premium version, it does not provide segment b users with any stronger network effect but provides segment s users with a stronger network effect $\beta + \delta$. If the contract menu is such that segment s users choose the premium version and segment b users the basic version, we have $v_s = r + (\beta + \delta)(n_s + n_b) - A_s$ and $v_b = r + \beta(n_s + n_b) - A_b$, with $\beta + \delta < 1/2$. Setting $\beta_s = \beta + \delta$ and $\beta_b = \beta$, we have the exact same formulation of utilities as in expression (5.7). We can then use the results we obtained under group pricing, namely:

$$A_s^* = \frac{2 - 4\beta - \delta - \delta^2}{4 - 8\beta - 4\delta - \delta^2} r, \; A_b^* = \frac{2 - 4\beta - 3\delta - \delta^2}{4 - 8\beta - 4\delta - \delta^2} r,$$

$$n_s^* = \frac{2 + \delta}{4 - 8\beta - 4\delta - \delta^2} r, \text{ and } n_b^* = \frac{2 - \delta}{4 - 8\beta - 4\delta - \delta^2} r.$$

We check that for $\delta > 0$, $A_s^* > A_b^*$ and $n_s^* > n_b^*$. Users self-select as postulated if $r + (\beta + \delta)(n_s^* + n_b^*) - A_s^* > r + \beta(n_s^* + n_b^*) - A_b^*$, which is equivalent to $\delta(n_s^* + n_b^*) > A_s^* - A_b^*$. Inserting the equilibrium expressions for participation levels and prices, this inequality becomes $4\delta > 2\delta$, which is clearly satisfied. This shows that segment s consumers self-select into the premium version sold at A_s^* and segment b consumer self-select into the basic version sold at A_b^*. In this specific setting in which segment b consumers do not achieve any extra benefit from the premium version, the platform does not suffer from not being able to observe the segment characteristics; that is, versioning does as well as group pricing.[27]

Lesson 5.7 summarizes the main results that we can draw from our analysis:

LESSON 5.7   *A platform that can identify segments of users that differ according to their valuation of the stand-alone or the network benefits can also use differential pricing to manage network effects more efficiently. Typically, with group pricing, the platform sets a lower price to the low-value segment and a higher price to the high-value segment, compared to the uniform price that it would set absent any discrimination. Under certain circumstances, the platform may also achieve the same profit by inducing users to reveal their characteristics by self-selecting among a menu of versions; in that case, versioning does as well as group pricing, meaning that it is not necessary for the platform to be able to tell users from different segments apart.*

5.3.4   The Freemium Strategy

In many markets, firms offer freemium models combining a premium version and a "free" version, with the particularity that users of the latter must "pay" with their time and their exposure to advertising. For example, the music-streaming platform Spotify offers a free version that contains advertising and, as an alternative, an ad-free

---

[27] In a slightly extended model in which also segment b consumers enjoy a stronger network effect with the premium version, $\beta + \delta_b$, the above versioning strategy remains optimal as long as δ_b is sufficiently small. However, in the extended model, versioning generates lower profits than group pricing.

subscription service.[28] Also, YouTube moved from its pure ad-financed business model to a freemium business model that contains the menu of an ad-based service and a subscription-based service. This allows the platform to better cater to diverse users, some of whom disliking advertising a lot – this is a particular instance of a versioning strategy.

Is this a win-win? Not necessarily as we now show. In the simple model that we will develop here, none of the users is better off when an ad-financed service is replaced by the freemium model and, since the platform fully extracts advertiser surplus, advertisers do not care.[29] Hence, it is only the platform that benefits from menu pricing in our simple model. Here are the main ingredients of the model:

- On the advertiser side, we assume that the advertiser's willingness-to-pay for any exposed user is constant. Thus, the platform will extract the full surplus and the per-user ad price a will be equal to this willingness-to-pay; we can therefore treat a as a parameter.
- On the user side, we assume a unit mass of users. All users of the service attach a value r to the service. If they consume the "free" version (which comes bundled with ads), their utility is reduced by βn_s, where β is the user's nuisance from advertising and n_s is the level of advertising; the ad-nuisance parameter β, which measures the strength of the negative cross-group network effect from advertisers to users, is uniformly distributed on $[1, 2]$. Alternatively, users of the advertising-free version pay a subscription fee A. The value of the outside option is assumed to be nil.

We compare three business models: (i) a *subscription-based* (pipeline) model, (ii) an *ad-financed* platform model, and (iii) a *freemium* platform model (offering a menu consisting of an advertising-free version and a subscription version).

Subscription-Based Model (sub)

Under this model, all users have the same net utility for the advertising-free service, $r - A$, and the firm's profit is given by $n_b A$. The firm therefore sets $A = r$ and all users buy.[30] As we assume a unit mass of users, profit is equal to $\pi^{su} = r$.

Ad-Financed Model (ad)

Under this model, only the version bundled with ads is offered free of charge. The platform sets the ad price at a and decides on the ad volume n_s to maximize its profit

---

[28] The "free" service features some ads that are inserted between songs. If users subscribe to the service by paying a monthly fee, they can listen to the music without being interrupted by advertising. The subscription service offers additional features that improve the experience from the paid-for service for at least some users; in what follows, we abstract away these quality differences.

[29] For simplicity, apart from the number of users increasing the advertisers' gross benefit from participation and the number of advertisers decreasing the users' gross benefit from participation (leading to an attraction/repulsion pendulum), there are no network effects in this model. For instance, positive within-group effects on the consumer side could be added.

[30] Here, no network effects are present and, according to our definition, this firm does not classify as a platform.

$n_s n_b a$. Given an advertising level n_s, a user of type $\beta \in [1, 2]$ has a net utility of $r - \beta n_s$. One option for the platform is to limit the advertising level to make sure that all users participate; this is so if $r - 2n_s = 0$ or $n_s = r/2$. Alternatively, the platform may want to increase the advertising level beyond $n_s = r/2$ and only attract users with $r - \beta n_s \geq 0$, that is, users whose ad-nuisance β is below $\beta_0 \equiv r/n_s$; the number of users is thus $n_b = \beta_0 - 1 = r/n_s - 1$ and the platform's profit is $n_s n_b a = n_s (r/n_s - 1) a = (r - n_s) a$. We clearly see that it is not profitable to set $n_s > r/2$ (as profit decreases in n_s in this range). We can thus conclude that the platform's profit-maximizing conduct in this model is to set $n_s = r/2$, so that $n_b = 1$ and profit is equal to $\pi^{ad} = ar/2$. Comparing π^{ad} and π^{su}, we observe that the ad-financed model dominates the subscription-based model if and only if $a > 2$ – that is, if the revenue from advertising is large enough to compensate the participating user with the largest ad nuisance.

Freemium Model (f)

Under this model, the platform offers a menu with two versions: The service comes either free of charge but with advertising volume n_s (version 1) or free of advertising but at price A (version 2). The platform's profit is then given by $n_s n_b^1 a + n_b^2 A$, where n_b^i denotes the number of users of version $i = 1, 2$. If there is a user $\beta \in (1, 2)$ who is indifferent between the two versions, this user β_1 satisfies $r - \beta_1 n_s = r - A$; all users with $\beta \leq \beta_1$ consume the free version and all users with $\beta \geq \beta_1$ consume the ad-free version. Thus, $\beta_1 = A/n_s$ or, equivalently, $n_s = A/\beta_1$. Clearly, if such a menu is profit-maximizing, it must be that $A = r$. Profit can then be written as $n_s n_b^1 a + n_b^2 A = (r/\beta_1)(\beta_1 - 1)a + (2 - \beta_1)r = r(1 - 1/\beta_1)a + (2 - \beta_1)r$. The first-order condition for profit-maximization yields $ra/\beta_1^2 - r = 0$, which is equivalent to $\beta_1 = \sqrt{a}$. To have $\beta_1 \in (1, 2)$, as initially assumed, we need a to be between 1 and 4. Hence, for $a \in (1, 4)$, the maximal profit is:

$$\pi^f = r(1 - 1/\sqrt{a})a + (2 - \sqrt{a})r = r\left(a - 2\sqrt{a} + 2\right) = r\left(\sqrt{a} - 1\right)^2 + r.$$

Comparison of Business Models

We first check that for $a \in (1, 4)$, *the freemium model is more profitable than the other two models*:

$$\pi^f - \pi^{su} = \left(\sqrt{a} - 1\right)^2 > 0 \text{ and } \pi^f - \pi^{ad} = \tfrac{1}{2}r\left(\sqrt{a} - 2\right)^2 > 0.$$

The platform will thus adopt the freemium model but with what impact for users? Consider the users who adopt the free version. The advertising level they are exposed to is larger under the freemium than under the ad-financed model if $n_s^f = r/\beta_1 > n_s^{ad} = r/2$; this is indeed the case since $\beta_1 < 2$. Hence, *all users who choose the "free offer" are worse off under the freemium than under the ad-financed model*. As for the users who choose the "premium" version, they are as well off under the freemium and the subscription-based models (as $A = r$ in both cases) and cannot be worse off under the ad-financed model, as all their surplus is extracted when buying the premium version. We can thus draw the following lesson from our model:

LESSON 5.8   *If a platform changes its business model from ad-financed to the freemium model, it feels less constrained to limit ad levels because it targets its subscription service to strongly ad-averse users. As a result, it may be that no user is better off and some users are strictly worse off.*

While some of our findings are specific to the particular model, the result that the freemium model features more advertising than the ad-financed business model generalizes to a setting with price-sensitive advertiser demand (see Sato, 2019). A related question is whether, with the introduction of an ad blocker, users who do not adopt the ad blocker will suffer from more advertising. Since the platform will not compete for the very ad-averse users (who will adopt the ad-blocker after incurring some opportunity cost), it will cater to a pool of, on average, less-ad-averse users after the introduction of the ad blocker. This may make it profitable to increase the ad volume compared to the time before the ad blocker was available.[31]

5.4   Pricing and the Formation of Users' Expectations

On two-sided platforms, a user's participation decision depends on the fee they have to pay and the participation level on the other side of the platform. In our analysis above, we assumed that users cannot observe participation levels on the other side (as decisions are taken simultaneously), but they make the equilibrium prediction based on the observation of the fees that the platform charged to both sides. In this section, we relax these assumptions. First, we study what happens when users observe the fee on their side but not on the other side (and are still unable to observe participation levels); we show that the platform is worse off in this situation, and would thus prefer to inform users about the fee that they cannot observe (5.3.1). The second departure from the previous analysis consists in assuming that users do not observe fees but observe participation levels, which are directly chosen by the platform; the main result here is an irrelevance result: Equilibrium profits and surpluses are unchanged in this alternative scenario (5.3.2). Finally, we examine situations in which one group has the possibility of joining the platform before the other group does (users in the second group can thus observe the participation level of the first group when making their decisions); in such situations, a platform that cannot commit to its fees is in general better off than when groups make simultaneous participation decisions (5.3.3).

---

[31]   Our model is too simple to deliver this result since, unlike the setting above, the platform will not make any revenues from users adopting the ad blocker and, in our specification, profits are then linearly decreasing in the ad volume. However, Anderson and Gans (2011) have analyzed a richer model in which ad levels are higher after an ad blocker becomes available.

5.4.1   Observability of Prices

In our previous analysis, we implicitly assumed that each user is able to observe not only the fee they have to pay, but also the fee charged to the other side. However, such a fee may be rather opaque and thus users may not be able to make inferences based on the actual fee. In this case, users may form some expectation on the participation level on the other side that is invariant to the actual fee charged to the other side. As a consistency requirement, expected participation levels have to be the same as realized expectation levels, so that expectations turn out to be correct. In such a situation, a platform may want to disclose the missing fee information, so as to influence the way users form their expectations. Case 5.6 illustrates such price disclosure strategy.[32]

CASE 5.6 SONY REDUCES COST OF PS3 DEVELOPMENT KIT ... AND WANTS IT TO BE KNOWN

In video game markets, game developers know the fees charged by platforms to end users but the reverse is often not the case. To remedy this lack of information, platforms sometimes publicize their decisions to reduce the costs of developing games for them. For instance, Sony announced a cut in the price for developers in 2007 and in 2009. In 2009 it released the statement that it "will deploy various measures to further reinforce game development for PS3 and will continue to expand the platform to offer attractive interactive entertainment experiences only available on PS3," and informed the public that it reduced the price of the development kit from US$10,000 to US$2,000. This announcement was not restricted to the developer community, but spread more widely to users. Thus, Sony's information policy arguably affected the information available to gamers and, therefore, their expectation about the availability of games on the platform.

If the platform is in a monopoly position and if users move simultaneously on both sides, we will see that the platform is better off if fees are fully disclosed. Why is that so? If users do not observe the fee on the other side, the platform has an incentive to raise this fee too much for its own good. A higher fee on the other side decreases the quality of the experience the platform offers. Since this quality deterioration is not observable to users, the platform has a stronger incentive to increase the fee on the other side than if the fee were observable to users. This is similar to the classic opportunism problem (Hart and Tirole, 1990). Starting with the solution in which users observe both fees, a fee increase – for example, on side b – implies that some users on each side stop participating. However, if sellers cannot observe the fee on the buyer side, they expect the same participation level as before and will not adjust participation. Consequently, the platform has a stronger incentive to raise fees. We summarize this finding in the next lesson:

LESSON 5.9   *Consider a platform that charges membership fees so as to maximize profits. If users on each side do not observe the fee on the other side, the monopolist has an incentive to charge higher fees. These fees are too high for its own good and, thus, the platform is better off if fees on both sides are disclosed.*

---
[32] This case is taken from Belleflamme and Peitz (2019c).

The implication for the platform's information disclosure policy is obvious. As a monopolist the platform decides to disclose fees on both sides.[33] We now establish this result by extending the previous model.[34] (Less mathematically oriented readers may want to skip this part.)

To formally analyze the platform's pricing problem, we consider the linear model from above with the modification that buyers expect seller participation level n_s^e and sellers expect buyer participation level n_b^e. Thus the number of active buyers will be $n_b = r_b + \beta_b n_s^e - A_b$ and the number of active sellers $n_s = r_s + \beta_s n_b^e - A_s$. The platform solves $\max_{A_b, A_s}(A_b - f_b)(r_b + \beta_b n_s^e - A_b) + (A_s - f_s)(r_s + \beta_s n_b^e - A_s)$. This gives profit-maximizing fees as a function of the users' expected participation levels, $\tilde{A}_b(n_s^e) = (r_b + c_b + \beta_b n_s^e)/2$ and $\tilde{A}_s(n_b^e) = (r_s + c_s + \beta_s n_b^e)/2$. Using the consistency requirement, $n_k^e = \tilde{n}_k$ ($k = b, s$), we have that $\tilde{n}_b = r_b + \beta_b \tilde{n}_s - (r_b + f_b + \beta_b \tilde{n}_s)/2 = \mu_b/2 + (\beta_b/2)\tilde{n}_s$ and $\tilde{n}_s = r_s + \beta_s \tilde{n}_b - (r_s + f_s + \beta_s \tilde{n}_b)/2 = \mu_s/2 + (\beta_s/2)\tilde{n}_b$, where we recall that μ_k stands for $r_k - f_k$, $k = b, s$. Solving this system of linear equations gives:

$$\tilde{n}_b = \frac{2\mu_b + \beta_b \mu_s}{4 - \beta_b \beta_s}, \text{ and } \tilde{n}_s = \frac{2\mu_s + \beta_s \mu_b}{4 - \beta_b \beta_s}.$$

Thus, price-cost margins will be:

$$\tilde{A}_b - f_b = \frac{2\mu_b + \beta_b \mu_s}{4 - \beta_b \beta_s}, \text{ and } \tilde{A}_s - f_s = \frac{2\mu_s + \beta_s \mu_b}{4 - \beta_s \beta_b}.$$

The monopolist's maximal profit is then equal to:

$$\tilde{\Pi} = \left(\frac{2\mu_b + \beta_b \mu_s}{4 - \beta_b \beta_s}\right)^2 + \left(\frac{2\mu_s + \beta_s \mu_b}{4 - \beta_b \beta_s}\right)^2.$$

Using expression (5.4) to compare the platform's profits when fees on the other side are observable or not, we find:

$$\Pi^* - \tilde{\Pi} = \frac{K_1 \mu_b^2 + K_2 \mu_b \mu_s + K_3 \mu_s^2}{\left(4 - (\beta_s + \beta_b)^2\right)\left(4 - \beta_b \beta_s\right)^2},$$

where:

$$K_1 \equiv 4\beta_b^2 + \beta_s^4 + 2\beta_b^2 \beta_s^2 + 2\beta_b \beta_s^3 > 0,$$

$$K_2 \equiv (\beta_b + \beta_s)\left(4\beta_b^2 + 4\beta_s^2 + \beta_b^2 \beta_s^2\right) > 0,$$

$$K_3 \equiv \left(\beta_b^4 + 4\beta_s^2 + 2\beta_b^2 \beta_s^2 + 2\beta_b^3 \beta_s\right) > 0.$$

It follows that $\Pi^* > \tilde{\Pi}$: *Profits are larger when fees on both sides are known for all users.* Thus, opacity is not in the interest of the monopolist.

---

[33] The disclosure decision can be considered to be a nonprice strategy. In the following chapter, we analyze other nonprice strategies chosen by a platform.

[34] This is a simplified version of Belleflamme and Peitz (2019c). The same point is made by Hagiu and Halaburda (2014) for the case that only one side does not observe the fee on the other, but not vice versa. Both papers also analyze models with competing platforms that we do not cover here.

5.4.2 Committing to Participation Levels

We just argued that buyers or sellers may not observe fees charged on the other side. But even if they do, they face the general problem that they have to form expectations about participation levels on the other side. As discussed before, if all users expect no participation on the other side, it is an equilibrium for none of them to participate. The platform can steer clear of this deleterious situation if it can commit to participation levels or insure users against unexpected drops in participation on the other side.

In this case, we can consider the platform's profit-maximization problem as one of choosing participation levels. We recall that the standard profit-maximization problem in monopoly with profits $P(q)q - C(q) = pQ(p) - C(Q(p))$ has the property that the monopoly outcome is the same regardless of whether the firm sets quantity and the price adjust so as to clear the market or whether the monopolist sets price and serves any demand at this price. We now show that in the platform setting, this equivalence still holds. We record the result in Lesson 5.10 (which some readers may prefer to take away without going through the formal derivation that follows).

LESSON 5.10   *A monopoly platform setting membership fees achieves exactly the same result whether it chooses fees (assuming that users solve the coordination problem) or participation levels (implying that users face no coordination problem).*

Continuing with the previous model, we recall that the numbers of participating sellers and buyers, given fees A_s and A_b, are respectively given by $n_s = r_s + \beta_s n_b - A_s$ and $n_b = r_b + \beta_b n_s - A_b$. This allows us to express fees as a function of participation levels, $A_s = r_s + \beta_s n_b - n_s$ and $A_b = r_b + \beta_b n_s - n_b$, and to rewrite the platform's maximization program as:

$$\max_{n_s,n_b} \Pi = (r_s + \beta_s n_b - n_s - f_s)\, n_s + (r_b + \beta_b n_s - n_b - f_b)\, n_b.$$

The first-order conditions for profit maximization are:

$$\begin{cases} \dfrac{\partial \Pi}{\partial n_s} = r_s - f_s + (\beta_s + \beta_b)\, n_b - n_s = 0, \\[2mm] \dfrac{\partial \Pi}{\partial n_b} = r_b - f_b + (\beta_s + \beta_b)\, n_s - n_b = 0. \end{cases}$$

Solving this system of equations yields the following profit-maximizing participation levels:

$$n_b^{**} = \frac{2\mu_b + (\beta_b + \beta_s)\, \mu_s}{4 - (\beta_b + \beta_s)^2}, \quad n_s^{**} = \frac{2\mu_s + (\beta_b + \beta_s)\, \mu_b}{4 - (\beta_b + \beta_s)^2}.$$

These are exactly the same participation levels as the ones we found when the platform was assumed to choose the fees A_s and A_b – see expression (5.4).

It can easily be shown that the same results are obtained when the platform only commits to one participation level and not to both. For instance, suppose that the platform sets A_s but can commit to n_b. Using $n_s = r_s + \beta_s n_b - A_s$ and $A_b = r_b + \beta_b n_s - n_b$, one can write the platform's profit as a function of its two choice variables, namely A_s and n_b. Solving for the profit-maximizing level of these two variables yields the same results as before.

A question that naturally arises is how the platform can enforce, in practice, the participation levels that it finds optimal. One way is to auction off a certain number of slots on each side. Clearly, when designing the auction on one side, the platform faces a trade-off between rent extraction on this side and participation on the other side. A complication arises if, contrary to what we have assumed so far, some participants have private information about some component that affects their value from participation. Gomes (2014) considers such a problem, taking the example of a platform that operates in the online advertising market and that offers a single sponsored link to one of many sellers.[35]

5.4.3   Sequential Pricing and Participation

In some markets, users on one side observe participation levels on the other side before deciding whether to join a platform. For instance, in the video game industry, it is customary for platforms (i.e., the providers of gaming consoles) to secure the participation of game developers before putting a new console on the market (i.e., attracting the participation of consumers). While many markets are dynamic in nature so that each side has some information on participation level (which, due to entry and exit on the other side may still vary), we take here the extreme stand that all users on one side move first. Suppose, for instance, that sellers move before buyers. Two settings are then conceivable according to whether the platform is able to commit to its fees on both sides before users decide to join the platform. If the platform can commit, then the game has three stages: First, the platform sets A_s and A_b; then sellers decide to join and, finally, upon observing the sellers' participation level, buyers decide to join. Otherwise, if the platform cannot commit to its fees, the game has four stages: First, the platform sets A_s; second, sellers decide to join; third, the platform sets A_b; and, fourth, buyers decide to join. We examine the two settings in turn and compare the equilibrium with the one we obtained previously (when assuming that the platform sets first the two fees and then the two groups of users move simultaneously).

---

[35] The setting used by Gomes (2014) differs from the one we have been using in two important dimensions: Users have heterogeneous network benefits and sellers have private information about β_s. In this model, a seller type is given by (β_s, β_b), where β_s is the seller's profit per click and β_b the buyer's surplus with that seller, which captures how relevant this listing is for the buyer. Since the platform wants to extract profits from the seller, one possibility is to simply auction off the slot to the highest bidder for a click. However, the platform is also concerned about buyer participation and, thus, should have the buyer surplus, β_b, in mind as well. Gomes (2014) shows that the platform's revenue-maximizing mechanism selects the listed seller according to a scoring rule that linearly combines the rent β_s generated by each seller with the seller's relevance β_b.

Commitment

We solve for the subgame-perfect equilibrium of the game by using backward induction. At the third stage of the game, buyers observe A_b and n_s and decide whether or not to join the platform. As we assume a uniform distribution of the outside option, we have that $n_b(n_s) = r_b + \beta_b n_s - A_b$. At the second stage of the game, sellers observe A_b and A_s, and anticipate how, given these fees, their participation will affect the subsequent buyers' participation. As a result, the number of participating sellers is given by:

$$n_s = r_s + \beta_s n_b(n_s) - A_s = r_s + \beta_s(r_b + \beta_b n_s - A_b) - A_s.$$

Solving for n_s, we find:

$$n_s = \frac{r_s - A_s + \beta_s(r_b - A_b)}{1 - \beta_b \beta_s},$$

and consequently,

$$n_b = r_b + \beta_b \frac{r_s - A_s + \beta_s(r_b - A_b)}{1 - \beta_b \beta_s} - A_b = \frac{r_b - A_b + \beta_b(r_s - A_s)}{1 - \beta_b \beta_s}.$$

The values of n_s and n_b are exactly the same as the ones found when sellers and buyers move simultaneously – see expression (5.2). The platform thus faces the same maximization problem in the two settings, which allows us to conclude that *when the platform can commit to its two fees, it is immaterial whether buyers and sellers decide to join the platform simultaneously or one group after the other.*

No Commitment

At the last stage of the game, the number of buyers is given by the same function as in the previous setting: $n_b(n_s) = r_b + \beta_b n_s - A_b$. At the third stage, the platform chooses A_b (given its previous choice of A_s and the participation level of sellers n_s) to maximize $(A_b - f_b) n_b(n_s)$; the profit-maximizing fee is easily found as $A_b(n_s) = (f_b + r_b + \beta_b n_s)/2$. At this price, the participation level of buyers at the fourth stage is computed as $n_b(n_s) = (\mu_b + \beta_b n_s)/2$ (where we recall that $\mu_k = r_k - f_k, k = b, s$). Moving now to stage 2, sellers observe A_s and anticipate how their decisions will affect A_b and n_b; on that basis, the sellers' participation level is determined as the solution to $n_s = r_s + \frac{1}{2}\beta_s(\mu_b + \beta_b n_s) - A_s$, that is,

$$n_s = \frac{2r_s + \beta_s \mu_b - 2A_s}{2 - \beta_b \beta_s}.$$

Plugging this value into $n_b(n_s)$ and $A_b(n_s)$, we find:

$$n_b(n_s) = A_b(n_s) - f_b = \frac{\mu_b + \beta_b(r_s - A_s)}{2 - \beta_b \beta_s}.$$

We can then rewrite the platform's maximization program at stage 1 as follows:

$$\max_{A_s}(A_s - f_s)\frac{2r_s + \beta_s \mu_b - 2A_s}{2 - \beta_b \beta_s} + \left(\frac{\mu_b + \beta_b r_s - \beta_b A_s}{2 - \beta_b \beta_s}\right)^2.$$

From the first-order condition, we find the optimal fee at stage 1 as (with the subscript "nc" for "no commitment"):[36]

$$A_s^{nc} = f_s + \frac{2\left(2 - \beta_b^2 - \beta_b\beta_s\right)\mu_s - \left(2\left(\beta_b - \beta_s\right) + \beta_b\beta_s^2\right)\mu_b}{2\left(4 - \beta_b\left(\beta_b + 2\beta_s\right)\right)}.$$

We can then compute the buyers' fee, the participation levels, and the platform's profits at equilibrium:

$$A_b^{nc} = f_b + \frac{1}{2}\frac{(4 - \beta_b\beta_s)\mu_b + 2\beta_b\mu_s}{4 - \beta_b(\beta_b + 2\beta_s)},$$

$$n_s^{nc} = \frac{2\mu_s + (\beta_b + \beta_s)\mu_b}{4 - \beta_b(\beta_b + 2\beta_s)},$$

$$n_b^{nc} = \frac{1}{2}\frac{(4 - \beta_b\beta_s)\mu_b + 2\beta_b\mu_s}{4 - \beta_b(\beta_b + 2\beta_s)},$$

$$\Pi^{nc} = \frac{4\mu_s^2 + \left(4 + \beta_s^2\right)\mu_b^2 + 4\left(\beta_b + \beta_s\right)\mu_s\mu_b}{4 - \beta_b(\beta_b + 2\beta_s)}.$$

A first question of interest is how this equilibrium compares with the previous case in which the platform can commit to its two fees before users decide to join (either simultaneously or one group after the other), described by expressions (5.3) and (5.4). A few lines of computations reveal that *participation levels are lower on both sides when the two groups of users move in sequence and the platform cannot commit to its fees*: $n_s^{nc} < n_s^*$ and $n_b^{nc} < n_b^*$. As for fees, the comparison is ambiguous. What can be shown is that $\beta_b \leq 1$ is a sufficient condition to have $A_s^{nc} < A_s^*$ and $A_b^{nc} > A_b^*$; that is, *if buyers do not value too strongly the interaction with sellers, then a platform that faces sellers moving before buyers and that cannot commit to its fees sets a lower fee for the first group (sellers) and a higher fee for the second (buyers)* (compared to the simultaneous-move scenario).[37] Finally, it turns out that *the platform achieves larger profits in the sequential move scenario without commitment unless the cross-group network effects are very large* (i.e., $\beta_b + \beta_s$ is close to the admissible upper bound of 2).

A second interesting question is which order of moves does the platform prefer: If it could choose, would the platform allow buyers or sellers to move first? In our analysis, we have assumed that sellers moved first. To obtain the equilibrium in the alternative scenario in which buyers move first, we just need to invert the subscripts b and s in the previous results. Comparing profits in the two scenarios is a cumbersome task, but two specific cases offer sharp results:

- If we assume that net values (i.e., the difference between stand-alone benefits and marginal costs, $\mu_k = r_k - f_k$) are the same on both sides ($\mu_b = \mu_s$), we see that

---

[36] The second-order condition requires $4 > \beta_b(\beta_b + 2\beta_s)$, which is less stringent than the condition imposed in the simultaneous-move game – that is, $2 > \beta_b + \beta_s$.

[37] To be precise, $A_s^{nc} < A_s^*$ if and only if $\beta_s < (2/\beta_b) - \beta_b$ and $A_b^{nc} > A_b^*$ if and only if

$$\beta_s < \left(4 - \beta_b^2\right)/(3\beta_b);$$ both conditions are implied by $\beta_b + \beta_s < 2$ whenever $\beta_b \leq 1$. Note that given the requirement that $\beta_s < 2 - \beta_b$, $\beta_b \leq 1$ makes it possible to have $\beta_s > \beta_b$; this is in this sense that we say that β_b must not be too large.

the platform prefers to let sellers move first if and only if $\beta_b > \beta_s$ – that is, if sellers exert a stronger cross-group network effect on buyers than buyers do on sellers. This finding echoes what was prescribed for solving the chicken-and-egg problem that plagues the launch of two-sided platforms (see Chapter 4): It pays to attract first the group that has the strongest "attraction power."

- If we assume that cross-group network effects are the same on both sides ($\beta_b = \beta_s$), we see that the platform prefers to let sellers move first if and only if $\mu_b > \mu_s$. That is, the platform is better off when the group that moves second is the one whose members create the largest value when they join the platform (because they have the largest stand-alone benefits and/or they are less costly to accommodate).

We can then conclude the following:

LESSON 5.11   *Consider a platform that must decide which group it asks to join first and, at that point, cannot commit to the price it charges to the other group. The platform prefers to invite first the group that exerts a stronger network effect on the other side and that obtains the lower net benefit from the interaction when ignoring network effects.*

The intuition behind this lesson is that the platform uses the first group as a bait to attract users of the second group and extract value from them. The platform is thus better off when the first group is the best possible bait, while the second group is the one that generates the largest value.[38]

---

[38] Of course, a trade-off occurs if, for example, $\beta_b > \beta_s$ and $\mu_s > \mu_b$.

Key Insights from Chapter 5

- Two-sided platforms set two types of fees: Membership fees (which are paid once or renewed on a regular basis) serve to regulate access to the platform; transaction fees (which are paid per effective transaction) serve to regulate the activity on the platform.
- A for-profit two-sided platform sets a relatively low price (possibly below cost) for the group of users that is more sensitive to price changes and/or exerts a stronger cross-group network effect.
- Platforms may be restricted to set fees on one side only or to charge the same fee on both sides. Such constraints are detrimental for the profits of a monopoly platform, and for the welfare of at least one group of participants (the other group may benefit from the constraint if it leads to lower fees for this group).
- If users on a two-sided platform do not observe the fee that is charged to users on the other side, a monopoly platform sets fees that are too high for its own good. If possible, a platform would thus choose to disclose price information on both sides.
- A monopoly platform setting membership fees achieves exactly the same result whether it chooses fees (assuming that users solve the coordination problem) or participation levels (implying that users face no coordination problem).

6   Platform Design

In this chapter, we take a closer look at how the strategies of a profit-maximizing two-sided platform affect user participation and usage in a buyer-seller context. What buyers and sellers can gain by interacting on the platform crucially depends on the platform's price and nonprice strategies. These strategies can therefore be seen as "design decisions," as they shape the popularity of the platform, the ways it operates, and its capacity to monetize its role of bringing buyers and sellers together. In more technical terms, the design decisions allow the platform to determine, endogenously, the network benefits that users will get from their interaction.[1]

As network benefits depend on the strength of the various network effects and on the actual participation levels on the platform, we divide the analysis into two parts. First, we focus on price strategies and take the strength of the network effects as given; we therefore keep the same basic two-stage setting as in the previous chapter (the platform sets prices before buyers and sellers decide to participate), but we enrich this setting with a number of elements that make the platforms' pricing decisions more intricate. Second, we analyze how the platform can further shape network benefits by choosing nonprice strategies that modify the strength of the cross-group network effects: Network benefits change even if participation levels remain fixed.

More precisely, in Section 6.1, we first introduce competition between sellers on the platform and analyze how this affects platform design when all consumers can go to the platform and all trade occurs on the platform. When sellers compete, they exert negative within-group network effects on one another. Yet, at the same time, seller competition also affects buyers' network benefits. One way for the platform to internalize these effects is to increase fees for sellers, so as to limit their number and, thereby, reduce the competition among them. However, with fewer registered sellers, the platform becomes less attractive for buyers (because variety tends to decrease and product prices, to increase). How does this trade-off affect platform pricing? With what impact on product variety? These are questions that we address. Doing so, we also give a more general formulation of the network benefits, which we base on specific models of buyer-seller relationships. If the platform design decision is about the number of admitted sellers, one may wonder if this number is socially

---

[1] Of course, the platform may also take actions that affect the stand-alone benefits it provides – for example, by improving the quality of its stand-alone offerings.

excessive or insufficient. As we show, the answer depends on whether the platform can directly charge buyers.

In a second extension of the setting of Chapter 5, we consider situations in which joining the platform allows buyers to obtain information about more products sold on the market. This is typically so when the platform's main service is a price comparison engine: Buyers who register have access to all prices posted on the platform, whereas buyers who stay out are only informed about local offers. In such situations, when sellers have to set the same price to all buyers, it is common to observe price dispersion (with a homogeneous product or service being, on average, cheaper for informed buyers than for uninformed ones). The question of interest here is how the price strategies of the platform affect the market outcome and, in particular, the strength of competition among sellers and the degree of price dispersion.

As for the nonprice strategies that affect cross-group network effects, recall that we already considered an example of such design decision in the previous chapter when analyzing the effect of the observability of price information.[2] Yet, for the most part, we treated the strength of cross-group network effects, β_b and β_s, as exogenous parameters that are not under the control of the platform. In contrast, we consider here design decisions that endogenously determine the parameters β_b and β_s in the linear specification of network effects or, more generally, the network benefit functions in case they are not linear in participation levels.

In Section 6.2, we examine two specific design decisions that affect cross-group network effects. First, we revisit the issue of product variety, which a platform can also manage through its design of rating, reviews, and recommender systems; our objective here is to assess the extent to which the incentives of platforms when designing these systems are aligned with those of the users. Second, we examine the extent to which an intermediary wants to increase price transparency on the platform. One way to do so is to prevent sellers from engaging in deceiving strategies (such as obfuscating some part of the overall price or luring buyers into purchasing expensive add-ons).

Finally, in Section 6.3, we turn to design decisions that a platform can use to govern the sellers' pricing strategies. The question here is whether platforms can increase their profit by letting sellers choose from a richer set of pricing strategies – for instance, by providing sellers with buyers' personal data so as to facilitate differential pricing. As the nonprice design decisions often affect the cross-group network effects in contrasted ways for the different groups of users, there is a common issue that we explore in all these cases – namely, the tension between extracting higher interaction surplus from one group and preserving the participation of the other group.

---

[2] We showed that a monopoly platform finds it profitable to fully inform users on one side about the prices that it sets on the other side; this is because the disclosure of this information enhances the cross-group network effects; the platform can then capture part of the additional value that this generates.

6.1 Another Look at Price Strategies and Network Benefits

We focus here on a monopoly platform that controls participation of *competing* sellers. We do not give additional nonprice strategies in the hands of the platform. Instead, we ask how a platform uses its prices to manage the level of competition on the platform. As we will see, seller competition introduces additional within-group and cross-group network effects. We first develop a baseline model with two-sided pricing (6.1.1) before looking at a model in which the platform cannot directly charge buyers. We then provide a modified model in which the platform directly controls the number of participating sellers. Subsequently, we extend the analysis to allow for differentially informed buyers leading to price dispersion on the platform; we restrict the pricing instruments available to the platform to fees charged only on the seller side, and we address how a platform controls quality in the presence of seller competition (6.1.2).

6.1.1 Product Variety and Price Levels

In our analysis so far, we have focused on cross-group network effects, abstracting away within-group network effects. This simplification provides a fair representation of many settings but seems a bit restrictive when it comes to analyzing platforms that link buyers and sellers. In particular, as soon as sellers compete in some dimension for the custom of buyers, negative within-group network effects exist among them. That is, for a given set of buyers, an extra seller joining the platform exerts a negative impact on the sellers that are already on board, as it may steal a share of their business. It is thus important to take these negative within-group network effects explicitly into account and, in particular, to examine how they affect the platform's pricing strategies. To this end, we analyze a simple framework (grounded in oligopoly models of sellers' competition) and extend this framework in three directions: first, by restricting the platform to one-sided pricing; second, by allowing the platform to directly control the number of sellers; and, third, by allowing the platform to select certain sellers.

A Simple Framework

Let us define the seller and buyer net surplus of visiting the platform (gross of any opportunity cost) respectively as $v_s = r_s + \pi\,(n_b, n_s) - A_s$ and $v_b = r_b + u\,(n_b, n_s) - A_b$. Here, r_k is the stand-alone utility on side $k \in \{b, s\}$ and A_k is the fixed membership or subscription fee charged by the platform to side k. The general functions $\pi\,(n_b, n_s)$ and $u\,(n_b, n_s)$ represent the net gains from trade for any seller and any buyer on the platform. They both potentially depend on the number of buyers and on the number of sellers who are present on the platform, meaning that any form of cross-group and within-group network effects are permitted. We assume that both functions are twice continuously differentiable in their two arguments.[3] We consider a model with three

---

[3] We focus on fixed fees per participant and do not allow the platform to charge usage fees. As discussed in Chapter 5, this is reasonable in situations in which monitoring transactions is

stages: First, the monopoly platform sets the fixed fees; second, buyers and sellers simultaneously decide to enter (alternatively, the platform admits a certain number of buyers and sellers on the platform and fees then clear the market); and, third, participating sellers play an oligopoly game. We analyze properties of the subgame-perfect Nash equilibrium.

In this monopoly model, we assume that a mass of Z buyers and of Z sellers have an outside option that is uniformly distributed on $[0, Z]$, with Z large.[4] Hence, for given A_s and A_b, the equilibrium number of buyers and sellers is implicitly characterized by $n_s = r_s + \pi (n_b, n_s) - A_s$ and $n_b = r_b + u (n_b, n_s) - A_b$. We postulate that there is a unique solution to this system of equations, $n_s(A_s, A_b)$ and $n_b(A_s, A_b)$, which imposes further restrictions on the functions u and π. From the system of equations, we have $A_s = r_s + \pi (n_b, n_s) - n_s$ and $A_b = r_b + u (n_b, n_s) - n_b$. The platform's profit is $\Pi = n_b(A_b - f_b) + n_s(A_s - f_s)$. In light of the buyers' and sellers' participation decisions, the platform's profit maximization problem can be written as $\max_{n_b, n_s} n_b[r_b + u (n_b, n_s) - n_b - f_b] + n_s[r_s + \pi (n_b, n_s) - n_s - f_s]$. The profit-maximizing number of sellers and buyers on a platform satisfies the system of first-order conditions:[5]

$$
\begin{cases}
\dfrac{\partial \Pi}{\partial n_b} = [r_b + u (n_b, n_s) - 2n_b - f_b] + \dfrac{\partial u (n_b, n_s)}{\partial n_b} n_b + \dfrac{\partial \pi (n_b, n_s)}{\partial n_b} n_s = 0, \\[4mm]
\dfrac{\partial \Pi}{\partial n_s} = [r_s + \pi (n_b, n_s) - 2n_s - f_s] + \dfrac{\partial u (n_b, n_s)}{\partial n_s} n_b + \dfrac{\partial \pi (n_b, n_s)}{\partial n_s} n_s = 0.
\end{cases}
$$

We now focus on situations in which within-group network effects are negative for sellers (reflecting seller competition) and absent for buyers. As for cross-group network effects, they are positive in both directions. We simplify the surplus functions as follows: $\pi (n_b, n_s) \equiv n_b \tilde{\pi} (n_s)$ and $u (n_b, n_s) \equiv n_s \tilde{u}(n_s)$; we will add a parameter as an argument to both functions that captures the intensity of competition among sellers. We provide two examples with these properties (which less mathematically oriented readers may prefer to skip).[6]

prohibitively costly or in which consumers can bypass the platform at negligible cost. Otherwise, a platform may want to impose usage fees if participants are heterogeneous with respect to the benefit they derive from usage. As discussed by Rochet and Tirole (2006), for the case in which sellers' products are independent (neither substitutes nor complements), membership fees are the "right" instrument to use if platforms only face heterogeneity in opportunity costs from participating. Seller competition does not affect this insight.

[4] Due to seller heterogeneity, inframarginal sellers will make a positive net surplus. If sellers were homogeneous, the platform would extract all rents on the seller side. For monopoly pricing with more general distributions, see Hagiu (2009). In models with a discrete number of sellers, we assume that the opportunity cost of the nth seller is n. For expositional convenience, with a finite number of sellers, we treat the number of sellers at stage 1 as a real number.

[5] The second-order conditions require:

$$
\frac{\partial^2 \Pi}{\partial n_b^2} < 0, \quad \frac{\partial^2 \Pi}{\partial n_s^2} < 0 \quad \text{and} \quad \frac{\partial^2 \Pi}{\partial n_b^2} \frac{\partial^2 \Pi}{\partial n_s^2} - \left(\frac{\partial^2 \Pi}{\partial n_b \partial n_s} \right)^2 > 0.
$$

[6] Another example, in which sellers compete on a Salop circle, can be found in Lin, Wu, and Zhou (2016). For further examples, see Teh (2019).

EXAMPLE 6.1   *Cournot competition with horizontally differentiated products*

Suppose that sellers are Cournot competitors with horizontally differentiated products and constant marginal costs c; the demand for variety k, produced by seller k (with $k = 1 \ldots n_s$) is given by $p_k = a - q_k - \gamma q_{-k}$ (with $q_{-k} = \sum_{g \neq k} q_g$) for strictly positive prices and zero otherwise. We suppose here that there is a finite number of discrete sellers and then ignore the integer constraints. (For the corresponding version of this model with a continuum of sellers, see, e.g., Ottaviano and Thisse, 2011.) Solving for the Cournot equilibrium and setting, without loss of generality, $a - c = 1$, we can compute the equilibrium profit for each seller and the consumer surplus as (for details, see Belleflamme and Peitz, 2019a):

$$\pi\,(n_b, n_s) = n_b \tilde{\pi}(n_s) = n_b \frac{1}{(2 + \gamma\,(n_s - 1))^2} \text{ and}$$

$$u\,(n_b, n_s) = n_s \tilde{u}(n_s) = n_s \frac{(1 + \gamma\,(n_s - 1))}{2\,(2 + \gamma\,(n_s - 1))^2}.$$

EXAMPLE 6.2   *Monopolistic competition with CES demand*

As done in Nocke, Peitz, and Stahl (2007), suppose that products are differentiated and a continuum of single-product sellers simultaneously set prices. Conditional on visiting the platform, consumers have CES preferences over the differentiated products. Demand for product j is:

$$q(j) = \frac{p(j)^{-\frac{1}{1-\rho}} E}{\int_0^{n_s} p(i)^{-\frac{\rho}{1-\rho}}\, di},$$

where $p(j)$ is the price of variant j, E is income spent on the differentiated goods industry, and $\rho \in (0, 1)$ is inversely related to the degree of product differentiation. Seller j maximizes their gross profit (per unit mass of buyers) $\tilde{\pi} = (p - c) p^{-\frac{1}{1-\rho}} M$, where c is the constant marginal cost of production and $M \equiv E / \int_0^{n_s} p(j)^{-\frac{\rho}{1-\rho}}\, dj$. Using symmetry, the first-order conditions of profit maximization yield the equilibrium price $p = c/\rho$. In this example, an increase in product variety has no price effect, so $\partial p / \partial n_s = 0$. In equilibrium, the profit per unit mass of buyers and the utility per unit mass of sellers are respectively given by:

$$\tilde{\pi}(n_s) = (1 - \rho) \frac{E}{n_s} \text{ and } \tilde{u}(n_s) = \frac{\rho E}{c} n_s^{\frac{1-2\rho}{\rho}}.$$

A special case is $\rho = 1/2$, as in this case $\tilde{u}(n_s)$ is constant in n_s; this describes a situation in which seller competition generates a negative within-group network effect, whereas seller competition has no effect on a consumer's per-seller gross benefit.

We now study how a change in the degree of competition among sellers may affect the platform's pricing strategy and, with it, the well-being of the various players (platform, sellers, and buyers). The equilibrium numbers of buyers and sellers is determined by the solution to $n_b = r_b + n_s \tilde{u}(n_s) - A_b$ and $n_s = r_s + n_b \tilde{\pi}(n_s) - A_s$. Substituting the first equation into the second, we obtain $n_s = r_s + [r_b + n_s \tilde{u}(n_s) - A_b]\tilde{\pi}(n_s) - A_s$, which implicitly defines the number of sellers as a function of the platform fees A_b and A_s. The positive cross-group network effect is captured by the square bracket – we note that $\tilde{u}(n_s)$ is always increasing in n_s, as more buyers are attracted by a platform hosting more sellers. However, this interacts with a negative within-group network effect stemming from the fact that $\tilde{\pi}(n_s)$ is decreasing in n_s.[7] The platform's profit maximization problem and first-order conditions can be rewritten, respectively, as:

$$\max_{n_b, n_s} n_b[r_b - n_b - f_b] + n_s[r_s - n_s - f_s] + [\tilde{u}(n_s) + \tilde{\pi}(n_s)]n_s n_b,$$

$$
\begin{cases}
\dfrac{\partial \Pi}{\partial n_b} = r_b - 2n_b - f_b + \left[\tilde{u}(n_s) + \tilde{\pi}(n_s)\right] n_s = 0, \\[2mm]
\dfrac{\partial \Pi}{\partial n_s} = r_s - 2n_s - f_s + \left[\tilde{u}(n_s) + \tilde{\pi}(n_s)\right] n_b + \left[\tilde{u}'(n_s) + \tilde{\pi}'(n_s)\right] n_b n_s = 0.
\end{cases}
\tag{6.1}
$$

The system (6.1) implicitly defines the optimal number of buyers and sellers that the monopoly platform attracts, n_b^M and n_s^M and the associated fees that can implement this allocation.

We now perform two exercises to evaluate how seller competition affects the platform's equilibrium decisions and profits. First, we observe that the term $\left[\tilde{u}'(n_s) + \tilde{\pi}'(n_s)\right] n_b n_s$ on the bottom line of expression (6.1) only appears when seller competition is present. The first exercise consists then in the following thought experiment: Upon observing n_b^M, n_s^M and the resulting $\tilde{u}(n_s^M)$ and $\tilde{\pi}(n_s^M)$, let us determine what happens if one wrongly believes that the platform maximized its profit while ignoring seller competition, and thus the term $\left[\tilde{u}'(n_s) + \tilde{\pi}'(n_s)\right] n_b n_s$. This hypothetical platform would solve the following system of equations:

$$
\begin{cases}
r_b - 2n_b - f_b + \left[\tilde{u}(n_s^M) + \tilde{\pi}(n_s^M)\right] n_s = 0, \\
r_s - 2n_s - f_s + \left[\tilde{u}(n_s^M) + \tilde{\pi}(n_s^M)\right] n_b = 0.
\end{cases}
$$

Graphically, the solution to this system is the intersection of the two linear functions depicting the profit-maximizing n_b for given n_s and the profit-maximizing n_s for given n_b. Let us now account for the dependence of $\tilde{u}(n_s)$ and $\tilde{\pi}(n_s)$ on n_s. This implies that the profit-maximizing n_s as a function of n_b is shifted inward if and only if $\tilde{u}'(n_s) + \tilde{\pi}'(n_s) < 0$. In this case, the platform's solution must feature fewer sellers and fewer buyers. If the number of buyers is rather insensitive to the number of sellers, the effect on the number of buyers is weak; otherwise, the effect is strong. The message that emerges from this simple comparison is that seller competition tends to have a negative effect on product variety on a monopoly platform if $\tilde{u}'(n_s) + \tilde{\pi}'(n_s) < 0$. We note that this comparison is artificial, since the absence

---

[7] This has also been pointed out by Hagiu (2009).

of seller competition will have an impact on the level of $\tilde{u}$ and $\tilde{\pi}$ (as we note in our second exercise next).

It is of interest to see on which side a platform makes most or even all of its profits. Denote profit on the buyer side by $\Pi_b = n_b(A_b - f_b) = n_b[r_b + n_s\tilde{u}(n_s) - n_b - f_b]$ and on the seller side by $\Pi_s = n_s(A_s - f_s) = n_s[r_s + n_b\tilde{\pi}(n_s) - n_s - f_s]$. Using the first-order conditions of profit maximization, we obtain:

$$\Pi_b = n_b[n_b - \tilde{\pi}(n_s)n_s],$$

$$\Pi_s = n_s[n_s - \tilde{u}(n_s)n_b] - (\tilde{u}'(n_s) + \tilde{\pi}'(n_s))n_b n_s^2.$$

Thus, it is less likely that sellers are subsidized if $\tilde{u}'(n_s) + \tilde{\pi}'(n_s) < 0$ compared to a model in which cross-group network effects are constant and fixed at the equilibrium value of the present model.[8]

Returning to our two examples, we observe the following:

$$\tilde{u}'(n_s) + \tilde{\pi}'(n_s) = \begin{cases} -\gamma \dfrac{4+\gamma(n_s-1)}{2(2+\gamma(n_s-1))^3} & \text{in Example 6.1,} \\[2mm] E\dfrac{(1-2\rho)n_s^{1/\rho}-cn_s(1-\rho)}{cn_s^3} & \text{in Example 6.2.} \end{cases}$$

It is obvious that $\tilde{u}'(n_s)+\tilde{\pi}'(n_s) < 0$ in Example 6.1. In Example 6.2, we have that $\tilde{u}'(n_s) + \tilde{\pi}'(n_s)$ is locally positive or negative depending on the parameter values; it is necessarily negative if $\rho \geq 1/2$.

Our second exercise consists in assessing directly how the monopoly platform is affected when seller competition becomes stronger – that is, in our examples, when products are closer substitutes: when γ (Example 6.1) or ρ (Example 6.2) increases. As noted in the introduction, a change in these parameters also affects directly the consumer surplus. Letting $\mu \in \{\gamma, \rho\}$, we use implicit differentiation to evaluate how a change in μ affects the platform's optimal number of buyers and sellers, and profit. Using the envelope theorem, we compute the effect of a change in μ on the platform's maximal interior's profit as:

$$\frac{d\Pi}{d\mu} = \left(\frac{\partial \tilde{u}(n_s; \mu)}{\partial \mu} + \frac{\partial \tilde{\pi}(n_s; \mu)}{\partial \mu} \right) n_s n_b.$$

In Examples 6.1 and 6.2, where the degree of product substitutability measures the intensity of competition, both $\tilde{u}$ and $\tilde{\pi}$ decrease when sellers compete more fiercely. That more competition hurts sellers is obvious. To understand that more competition also reduces the surplus that buyers obtain from each seller, we note that in these two models, an increase in γ or ρ has two opposite effects: It decreases prices (because of more seller competition), but it also decreases utility (because buyers have an intrinsic preference for variety); it turns out that the latter effect dominates the former. As a result, in product markets in which competition is more intense, the benefits that

---

[8] For an analysis with general distribution functions, see Hagiu (2009). See also Goos, Van Cayseele, and Willekens (2013) for a related analysis of a monopoly platform matching two groups in the presence of positive cross-group and negative within-group network effects.

both sellers and buyers obtain per transaction are reduced. This leads to a lower profit of the platform.

The main lesson is as follows:

LESSON 6.1   *If the total value generated in a buyer-seller transaction decreases with the intensity of seller competition, then so does the platform's maximal profit.*

As is shown in Belleflamme and Peitz (2019a) for both examples, the platform chooses to attract fewer sellers and fewer buyers in product markets in which competition is more intense.

Extension 1: One-Sided Pricing

In many markets, platforms only charge sellers, but not buyers. Such a situation arises if a platform cannot monitor participation decision by buyers or if it would optimally pay buyers for participation but that such negative fees are not feasible or prohibited. Thus, the platform has a single instrument – the seller fee – to steer the degree of competition on the platform.

One extreme strategy for the platform could then be to set a sufficiently high listing fee, so as to guarantee a monopoly position in each product category (equivalently, the platform could also auction a single slot per product category). However, if the platform suffers from the commitment problem that after selling off one slot it may change its mind and sell a second slot, one possibility is to guarantee the seller exclusivity in a product category.

CASE 6.1 SELECTED DEALS ON GROUPON

The two leading intermediaries in the daily deals market are Groupon and LivingSocial (both owned by Groupon after a merger in October 2016). On these platforms, sellers offer special deals in a metropolitan area to subscribers. In particular, such deals are offered by restaurants and beauty or fitness services. Sellers who want to list a deal submit a proposal specifying the product or service they offer together with price, duration, and discount rate. Consumers who buy into a deal receive a voucher that they can redeem later from the seller. The platforms take a cut from sellers; usually revenues from a deal are shared evenly between platform and seller, with few exceptions tilting the revenue share in favor of one or the other. The importance of seller competition in this market is reflected by the fact that Groupon lists only a fraction of the deals proposed by sellers and, thus, rejects many proposals. Written in a period prior to the merger, Bari Weiss states that Groupon accepted only one out of every eight proposed deals.[9] This suggests that Groupon actively manages seller participation. As Li, Shen, and Bart (2018, p. 1861) observed, "[w]hile more variety may often attract more consumers . . ., it can also create competition between deals in the same category, which then may decrease sales of a deal."

With differentiated products, the fewer sellers are listed on the platform, the lower the product variety. Since buyers can access the platform for free, their participation increases with the number of sellers hosted by the platform. As for sellers, their profits are the ones derived in Example 2. As we showed above, the per-buyer profit is decreasing in the number of sellers. Yet, a countervailing effect is the

---

[9] See Bari Weiss, "Groupon's $6 billion gambler," *Wall Street Journal*, December 18, 2010.

market-expansion effect that arises since more sellers attract more buyers. As formally explored by Nocke, Peitz, and Stahl (2007), when deciding about how much to charge sellers, a platform has to take both effects into account – it maximizes $n_s A_s - C(n_s)$, where n_s depends on A_s and $C(n_s)$ is the platform's weakly convex cost.[10]

As is well-known from the literature on product variety, the fact that sellers engage in business-stealing tends to lead to socially excessive product variety. However, a monopoly platform takes this effect into account. A profit-maximizing platform sets a high fee such that there is always a socially insufficient number of sellers n_s. Thus, product variety is less than in the second best, in which a social planner can pick the number of sellers hosted by the platform.

LESSON 6.2 *A monopoly platform that can only charge sellers restricts entry of sellers in such a way that there is less product variety than what is provided by a social planner who regulates variety but not price.*

By contrast, if a marketplace is not managed and, thus, does not restrict access by charging fees above marginal costs, product variety tends to be socially excessive. The lack of a pricing instrument on the buyer side suggests that the platform is overly concerned with the gross surplus generated on the seller side. To take an extreme example, suppose that sellers are ex ante homogeneous. A monopoly platform will then extract the full seller surplus.[11] This often means that the platform will set a high listing fee and effectively limit competition on its platform. If sellers offer sufficiently close substitutes, this implies that only a single seller will be active and the platform will extract the monopoly rent of this single seller. A platform can create such a commitment by offering a contract that grants exclusivity to the seller on the platform – this has been documented in the case of shopping malls in Ater (2015). By contrast, if the platform can also charge buyers, a lower membership fee on the seller side leads to a larger number of participating sellers. This generates a larger gross surplus on the buyer side, which can be extracted by the platform through the membership fee on the buyer side. Thus, with the additional price instruments, the platform allows for more product variety and generates a larger total surplus.

Extension 2: Direct Control of the Number of Participating Sellers

We revisit here the issue of product variety when a platform taxes seller profits at a constant, exogenous rate. We compare the profit-maximizing design to the solution of a social planner or regulator that can impose a platform design – that is,

---

[10] For follow-up work that allows for richer price instruments, see Teh (2019).

[11] The number of sellers is determined by $A_s = r_s + \tilde{\pi}(n_s) n_b$. With two-sided pricing, the platform maximizes $\max_{n_b, n_s} n_b[r_b - n_b - f_b] + n_s[r_s - n_s - f_s] + [\tilde{u}(n_s) + \tilde{\pi}(n_s)]n_s n_b$. If the platform can only charge sellers the platform's problem is $\max_{n_s} -n_b f_b + n_s[r_s - n_s - f_s + \tilde{\pi}(n_s)n_b]$ subject to $n_b = r_b + n_s \tilde{u}(n_s)$. With two-sided pricing, the platform has an additional price instrument that allows it to obtain higher profits. It may do so by paying buyers for participation or by charging them a positive price, depending on the parameters and functions.

the number of sellers on the platform – but does not control the price that the platform may charge buyers.[12] More specifically, we make the following assumptions: (i) The platform obtains an exogenous fraction α of the seller profit; (ii) the intermediary or the regulator decides how many sellers n_s to admit to the platform; and (iii) sellers do not face any opportunity cost from participating.[13] In contrast to the previous setting, the number of sellers is not determined by the sellers' entry decision; that is, the number of sellers is not a function of the prices set by the platform, but it results from a separate platform design decision.

If the intermediary chooses the same platform design as a welfare-maximizing regulator, platform design can be considered neutral. If more sellers are admitted on the platform than in the second best, the intermediary biases its design in favor of buyers, as they benefit from more sellers on the platform. If fewer sellers are admitted, the bias goes against buyers.

Which type of bias will be observed in such a market environment and how does it depend on the price instruments available to the platform? If the platform cannot set a fee on the buyer side, its profit stems from the gross surplus generated on the seller side and one may therefore suspect that platform design responds to this by introducing a bias against consumers. If the platform can set a price on the buyer side (which may actually be negative), it appears less clear which, if any, bias to expect. The following formal analysis provides a clear answer.

In this modified setting, platform profit is $\Pi(A_b, n_s) = n_b(A_b + \alpha n_s \pi(n_s))$. The number of participating buyers, $n_b(v_b)$ is increasing in the per-buyer net value $v_b \equiv u(n_s) - A_b$ (gross of the opportunity cost from joining) and thus increasing in n_s. Buyer surplus is $CS(v_b)$ with $CS' = n_b$. Per-buyer gross industry profit is $PS(n_s) = n_s \pi(n_s)$, which is decreasing in n_s; the overall net surplus on the seller side is $(1-\alpha)n_b n_s \pi(n_s) = (1-\alpha)n_b PS(n_s)$. We compare the solution of the profit-maximizing platform to the second-best solution in which a welfare-maximizing regulator can fix the number of participating sellers, while the platform continues to control A_b. Welfare is $\Pi(A_b, n_s) + CS(u(n_s) - A_b) + (1 - \alpha)n_b PS(n_s)$.

The platform sets the profit-maximizing price on the buyer side $A_b^*(n_s) = \arg\max_{A_b} n_b(A_b + \alpha PS(n_s))$, which is the solution to:

$$n_b - (A_b + \alpha PS(n_s))n_b' = 0, \qquad (6.2)$$

where n_b' stands for dn_b/dv_b.

Denote the maximal platform profit for given n_s by $\tilde{\Pi}(n_s) = \max_{A_b} n_b(A_b + \alpha PS(n_s))$. The platform design problem of the profit-maximizing platform then is $\max_{n_s} \tilde{\Pi}(n_s)$. Using the envelope theorem, the profit-maximizing number of

---

[12] This means that we are considering a second best, as the regulator controls a design feature, but not the prices.

[13] Our formal exposition is inspired by Choi and Jeon (2020) and Teh (2019). Choi and Jeon (2020) address the more general platform design problem of choosing combinations of the per-buyer net value and gross industry profit.

sellers n_s^* satisfies:

$$n_b' u'(n_s)(A_b^*(n_s) + \alpha PS(n_s)) + n_b \alpha PS'(n_s) = 0. \tag{6.3}$$

We note that, for $\alpha = 1$, (6.2) and (6.3) imply the property that $u'(n_s) = -PS'(n_s)$.

Welfare can be written as $n_b(A_b^*(n_s) + PS(n_s)) + CS$. Evaluated at n_s^*, using the envelope theorem, marginal welfare with respect to n_s is:

$$n_b' u'(n_s^*)(A_b^*(n_s^*) + PS(n_s^*)) + n_b PS'(n_s^*) - n_b'(1 - \alpha)PS(n_s^*)A_b^{*'}(n_s)$$
$$+ n_b(u'(n_s^*) - A_b^{*'}(n_s^*)). \tag{6.4}$$

From expression (6.3), we have:

$$n_b' u'(n_s^*)(A_b^*(n_s^*) + PS(n_s^*)) + n_b PS'(n_s^*) = (1 - \alpha)\left[n_b' u'(n_s)PS(n_s^*) + n_b PS(n_s^*)\right].$$

Substituting into (6.4), we find that the marginal welfare evaluated at n_s^* is:

$$(1 - \alpha)\left[n_b' u'(n_s^*)PS(n_s^*) + n_b PS(n_s^*)\right] - (1 - \alpha)n_b' PS(n_s^*) + n_b(u'(n_s^*) - A_b^{*'}(n_s)).$$

Since $n_b'(A_b + \alpha PS(n_s)) - n_b = 0$, the price on the buyer side increases in the number of sellers according to:

$$\frac{dA_b^*}{dn_s} = -\frac{[n_b''(A_b + \alpha PS(n_s)) - n_b']u'(n_s) + n_b'(\alpha PS'(n_s))}{-[n_b''(A_b + \alpha PS(n_s)) - n_b'] + n_b'}.$$

For $\alpha = 1$, we have:

$$\frac{dA_b^*}{dn_s} = \frac{[n_b''(A_b + PS(n_s)) - n_b']u'(n_s) + n_b' PS'(n_s)}{[n_b''(A_b + PS(n_s)) - n_b'] - n_b'}.$$

Evaluated at n_s^*, the pass-through rate dA_b^*/dn_s is equal to $u'(n_s^*)$ if and only if $u'(n_s^*) = -PS'(n_s^*) = -(n_s^* \pi'(n_s^*) + \pi(n_s^*))$, which always holds, as observed above. Thus, the profit-maximizing solution implements the planner's solution n_s^W. Whenever $n_s^W \neq n_s^*$, platform design is biased. If $\alpha < 1$, the platform admits a socially excessive number of sellers $n_s^* > n_s^W$ and, thus, platform design is biased in favor of buyers because the platform does not fully internalize the reduction of industry profits from more intense competition.

Consider now the case that the platform cannot charge buyers (e.g., because this is technically not feasible or because it is not possible to charge a negative price and the zero-price constraint is binding).

Platform profit is $\Pi(0, n_s) = \alpha n_b n_s \pi(n_s) = \alpha n_b PS(n_s)$; buyer surplus is $CS(u(n_s))$ with $CS' = n_b$; and producer net surplus is $(1 - \alpha)n_b PS(n_s)$. Again we compare the profit-maximizing solution of the platform to the second-best solution in which a welfare-maximizing regulator can fix the number of participating sellers. Welfare is $CS(u(n_s)) + n_b PS(n_s)$.

The profit maximization problem is $\max_{n_s} \Pi(0, n_s)$. The profit-maximizing number of sellers n_s^* satisfies $n_b' u'(n_s)(PS(n_s)) + n_b PS'(n_s) = 0$, while the welfare-maximizing number of seller n_s^W satisfies $n_b' u'(n_s)(PS(n_s)) + n_b PS'(n_s) + n_b u'(n_s) = 0$. Since $u' > 0$, it is always the case that $n_s^W > n_s^*$; that is, the design of the profit-maximizing platform features a socially insufficient number of sellers and, therefore, platform design is biased against buyers.

The takeaway from the analysis is that platform design crucially depends on the price instruments available to the platform. In the special case that the platform can charge buyers and it extracts the full surplus from sellers, platform design is neutral and implements the welfare-maximizing outcome. In all other cases, platform design is biased, as summarized in the following lesson:

LESSON 6.3   *Suppose that the platform taxes seller profits at a constant, exogenous rate. If the platform offers its service for free to buyers, platform design is biased against buyers, whereas if the platform sets its profit-maximizing price on the buyer side and the platform does not extract the full surplus from sellers, platform design is biased in favor of buyers.*[14]

Extension 3: Targeted Offers to Sellers

More generally, a platform may not only decide on how many sellers to host but, taking into account that markets are often not symmetric and products differ by the degree of substitutability, may also actively pick sellers with particular characteristics by making discriminatory offers. For instance, in the case of shopping malls, the empirical literature has established that a shopping mall manages its portfolio of shops to internalize externalities – see Pashigian and Gould (1998). In particular, a shopping mall provides better terms to those shops which serve as magnets and generate business for other stores (such as, traditionally, anchor stores). Thus, a shopping mall manager becomes a private regulator of the ecosystem it controls.

CASE 6.2 PLATFORM DESIGN OF ROPPONGI HILLS

Roppongi Hills is a mini-city in Tokyo privately developed and managed by the Japanese real-estate developer Mori Buildings.[15] Roppongi Hills features retail space, residential and office buildings, entertainment and cultural facilities. Mori Buildings actively manages this mini-city – for example, by selecting retailers not simply by renting a place out to the highest bidder but by providing a diverse and unique mix of stores. Beyond retail, it aimed at the overall success and attractiveness of the mini-city it created. For instance, it gave the most prominent place in the mini-city to an art museum.

Translated into the digital world, this means that a digital platform may internalize externalities by setting discriminatory membership or access fees on the seller side. Similarly, to internalize externalities, advertising-financed platforms may offer better terms to advertisers who post ads that are less annoying or more attractive to buyers.

In other environments, a platform may make additional design decisions that affect the degree of competition among sellers. This means that the platform also makes some nonprice decisions. An offline example is the perceived product

---

[14] This is shown more generally by Choi and Jeon (2020).

[15] We draw on material presented in Boudreau and Hagiu (2009) and Elberse, Hagiu, and Egawa (2007).

differentiation between different brands in a department store that uses the shop-in-the-shop business model. The design decision of the department store is to choose which services to centralize and which decisions to delegate to individual shops. Providing more centralized uniform services arguably reduces perceived product differentiation between shops. This intensifies competition between shops, leading to a lower per-consumer profit. On the other side, buyers experience lower prices and may be more attracted to visit the department store.[16] Another instance is the ease with which consumers can search among products that are likely to be a good match to their tastes. We return to this issue in the context of the design of search engines later in this chapter.

6.1.2   Seller Competition and Differentially Informed Buyers

As a natural extension of our simple setting, we continue to focus on price strategies and consider an environment in which some consumers are informed about local offers and others are informed of all offers because they buy via a platform such as a price comparison website. One motivation for looking at this more specific setting is the observation of price dispersion on the Internet, even for arguably homogeneous products and services.

CASE 6.3 PRICE DISPERSION ON SHOPPER.COM

Baye, Morgan, and Scholten (2004) examine seller pricing on the price comparison site Shopper.com.[17] They assembled a data set containing 4 million daily price observations for more than 1,000 consumer electronics products for some period in 2000–2001. They find a price difference between the seller with the lowest price and the seller with the next lowest price. This price difference is larger the smaller the total number of listed sellers for this product: The difference between the two lowest prices is 3.5 percent when seventeen sellers are listed on the price comparison site; it increases to 22 percent when only two sellers are listed.

    Why would a firm engage in the effort of listing a product if it is offered at a higher price and therefore will not generate any sales? An obvious answer is that the product may turn out to be more expensive but that, at the point of listing the product, the firm did not know yet whether it would generate any sales.[18] Alternatively, a higher-priced product may simply not attract consumers who know about lower-priced offers, but some consumers may not have this information and, therefore, take the offer as a take-it-or-leave it offer.

    Formalizing the latter, Baye and Morgan (2001) consider an environment in which buyers are present on a local market with a single seller, unless they acquire access

---

[16] This is not the whole story as the expected utility of a consumer is also affected by the perceived product differentiation between firms.

[17] Further studies documenting price dispersion include Baye et al. (2009) and Gorodnichenko, Sheremirov, and Talavera (2018).

[18] This happens if firms have heterogeneous opportunity costs of selling that are private information. Hansen (1988) and Spulber (1995) construct the pure-strategy equilibrium in which firms set price as a function of the their privately observed cost. Firms almost always set price above marginal costs. For a textbook treatment, see Belleflamme and Peitz (2015, pp. 47–49).

to a platform by paying a fee. Such access provides information on other sellers who post their offers on the platform. Sellers can advertise on the platform by paying a listing fee. Products offered by sellers are homogeneous, and, for given fees set by the intermediary, the model is closely connected to Varian (1980), as some buyers are informed only about the local offer and others are informed also about competing advertised offers.

Since sellers cannot price discriminate, buyers not active on the platform also benefit from more intense competition on the platform. Thus, the intermediary faces a difficulty in making profits on the buyer side and does not have an incentive to implement the perfectly competitive outcome, as this destroys seller profits (and, hence, revenues on the seller side) as well as revenues on the buyer side (buyers can buy at marginal cost from the local offer in any case). To extract rents on the seller side, the intermediary has to ensure that sellers do not always advertise, as this would drive price down to marginal costs. As Baye and Morgan (2001) show, the intermediary sets fees so as to ensure full consumer participation but limited seller participation, and the product market always features price dispersion. Many online price-comparison search engines fit this description.

Formal Model

The model goes as follows.[19] Suppose that there are two local markets. On each market, there is a single seller and a unit mass of consumers. The two sellers sell identical products at constant marginal cost which, for simplicity, is supposed to equal zero (the cost of delivering goods to consumers is also zero). Each consumer has demand $2-p$. Consumers in local market i only have access to seller i. Therefore, the expected profits of seller i when it charges a price p to consumers in its local market is $\pi(p) = p(2-p)$; the monopoly price is easily computed as $p^m = 1$. It costs a consumer $0 < z < 1/2$ to visit a local store.[20]

The intermediary opens a digital platform and, thereby, eliminates geographic boundaries between the two local markets. In the absence of such a virtual market-place, each seller simply charges the monopoly price to all of its local consumers to earn profits of $\pi(1) = 1$. In contrast, with the creation of a digital platform, sellers and consumers can globally transmit and access price information. The intermediary runs the flows of information by charging an access fee, $A_s \geq 0$, to sellers posting their price on the website and a subscription fee, $A_b \geq 0$, to consumers accessing price information from the website.

We analyze the following game: In the first stage, the intermediary announces the fees A_s and A_b; in the second stage, given the fees, consumers decide whether or not to subscribe to the website; sellers choose their price for the product and decide

---

[19] We present here a simplified version of Baye and Morgan (2001), which is a condensed (but partly identical) version of the one in Belleflamme and Peitz (2015).

[20] The assumption that $z < 1/2$ ensures that a consumer who is charged the monopoly price p^m obtains sufficient surplus to make a visit worthwhile. The consumer surplus at some price p is indeed computed as $v(p) = \frac{1}{2}(2-p)^2$; hence, $v(p^m) - z = 1/2 - z > 0$.

whether or not to post it on the website; finally, consumers shop. We solve the game for its symmetric subgame-perfect equilibria.

Solving the Model

We solve the model by proceeding backwards: We first characterize the consumers' optimal shopping; we then turn to the sellers' posting and pricing decisions; this allows us to move to the consumers' subscription decisions and, finally, to the intermediary's fee-setting decision. As the analysis becomes quite technical, some readers may choose to go directly to the next section, in which we draw the main insights from the model.

We start by characterizing *optimal shopping by consumers*. We will establish the following results: *(1) Non-subscribing consumers visit and purchase from their local seller. Subscribing consumers (2a) first visit the website and (2b) purchase at the lowest price available there. (2c) If no price is listed, they visit and purchase from their local seller.* Part (1) is obvious because non-subscribing consumers earn sufficient surplus to cover the cost of their physical visit: for all $p \leq p^m$, $v(p) \geq v(p^m) > z$. Part (2a) is obvious as well because visiting the platform costs nothing (once the subscription fee is paid). What subscribing consumers do next depends on whether at least one price is listed on the platform. If no price is listed, the previous reasoning applies and subscribing consumers visit and purchase from their local seller. On the other hand, if at least one price is listed, part (2b) applies: The optimal conduct is to purchase at the lowest available price on the platform. This conduct is clearly optimal when the subscriber observes the advert of their local seller (say i) on the platform, for it saves them the cost z of physically visiting the seller. In contrast, if only seller j has posted its price on the platform, the subscriber needs to decide whether it is worth paying z to obtain an additional price quote from their local seller i. Letting $G(p)$ denote the equilibrium consumer beliefs about seller i's price when it does not post its price, we can express the condition as $\int_0^{p_j}(v(t) - v(p_j))dG(t) \geq z$. Define $\bar{p}$ as the value of p_j for which the previous equation holds with equality. Then, given the consumers' decision rule, seller i will not charge prices below $\bar{p}$ when it does not post its price. This implies that for any $G(\cdot)$ consistent with equilibrium pricing, $\int_0^{\bar{p}}(v(t) - v(\bar{p}))dG(t) = 0$, which cannot be true given the way we defined $\bar{p}$. We therefore have a contradiction, which establishes part (2b).

We turn now to *sellers' pricing and posting decisions*. Suppose that in each local market, a fraction $\lambda^I > 0$ of consumers subscribe to the website (in total, there are thus $2\lambda^I$ subscribers). Suppose, also, that each seller posts its price with probability α, and the posted price has an atomless cumulative distribution function $F(p)$. Let us first derive the expected profits of a *non-posting seller*. Such a seller will only attract customers residing in its locale. It will attract all local customers if no price is listed on the website (which occurs with probability $1 - \alpha$) or only the share $(1 - \lambda^I)$ of local consumers who do not subscribe (which occurs with probability α). In any case, the seller will optimally set the monopoly price $p^m = 1$. The expected profits are thus computed as (where the superscript N stands for 'nonposting'):

$$E\pi_i^N = (1 - \alpha) + \alpha(1 - \lambda^I) = 1 - \alpha\lambda^I. \tag{6.5}$$

Consider now a *posting seller i*. Whatever the decision of seller j, seller i pays the access fee A_s and makes a profit $\pi(p_i)$ on its $\lambda^U \equiv 1 - \lambda^I$ nonsubscribing local consumers. The profits seller i collects from the $2\lambda^I$ subscribing consumers depend on the other seller's decision. With probability $(1 - \alpha)$, seller j does not post its price and seller i makes a profit $\pi(p_i)$ on all subscribers. However, with probability α, seller j also posts its price p_j and seller i only sells if it has posted the lowest price: that is, if $p_j \geq p_i$, which occurs with probability $1 - F(p_i)$. Collecting these results and considering a price $p_i = p$, we compute the expected profits of a posting seller as:

$$E\pi_i^P = \lambda^U \pi(p) + 2\lambda^I \left[(1 - \alpha) + \alpha(1 - F(p))\right] \pi(p) - A_s$$
$$= (1 + \lambda^I)\pi(p) - 2\alpha\lambda^I F(p) \pi(p) - A_s. \tag{6.6}$$

For F in the previous equation to be part of a symmetric Nash equilibrium, seller i's expected profit must be the same for all prices in the support of F. For sellers to randomize between posting price or not at equilibrium, we must have that the expected profits from posting price p must equal the expected profits from not posting and charging the monopoly price. Equating (6.5) and (6.6) and solving for F yields a candidate for the distribution of posted prices in a symmetric equilibrium (recalling that $\pi(p) = p(2 - p)$):

$$F(p) = \frac{(1 + \lambda^I)p(2 - p) + \alpha\lambda^I - 1 - A_s}{2\alpha\lambda^I p(2 - p)}. \tag{6.7}$$

As $\pi(p) = p(2 - p)$ is continuous and increasing up to $p^m = 1$, $F(p)$ is increasing and is thus an atomless distribution with support $[p_0, 1]$. To find the lower bound of the support of F, set $F(p_0) = 0$ in equation (6.7) and solve to get:

$$p_0 = \frac{1}{1 + \lambda^I} \left(1 + \lambda^I - \sqrt{(1 + \lambda^I)(\lambda^I - A_s + \alpha\lambda^I)}\right),$$

with $0 < p_0 < 1$. At the monopoly price, we must have that $F(1) = 1$. Imposing this and recalling that $\pi(p^m) = 1$, we can rewrite equation (6.6) as $E\pi_i^P = (1 + \lambda^I) - 2\alpha\lambda^I - A_s$. Equating the latter expected profits to expression (6.5) yields a seller's propensity to post its price:

$$\alpha^* = \max\{0, 1 - (A_s/\lambda^I)\}.$$

Therefore, sellers' posting decisions can be summarized as follows. When access fees are not too high $(A_s < \lambda^I)$, sellers are indifferent between posting and not posting their price, and earn expected profits of $E\pi_i^N = E\pi_i^P = 1 - \lambda^I + A_s$.

In contrast, when $A_s > \lambda^I$, sellers do not find it profitable to post their price and equilibrium expected profits are $E\pi_i^N = 1 > E\pi_i^P$.

Posted prices (which are in the interval between p_0 and 1) are always lower than non-posted prices (which are equal to $p^m = 1$). Because the virtual marketplace eliminates geographical distance, each seller can use it to steal business from its distant rival. However, to do so, the seller must randomly select both the timing of posting prices (i.e., $\alpha^* \in (0, 1)$) and the level of "discount" (i.e., $1 - F(p)$) to "confuse" the rival seller and prevent it from undercutting systematically the posted price. As a result, there is equilibrium price dispersion.

We are now in a position to analyze *consumers' subscription decisions*. Given the subscription fee A_b, the proportion of other subscribing consumers $2\lambda^I$ and the posting strategy of sellers (α, F), each consumer decides optimally whether or not to subscribe. A *subscribing consumer* obtains surplus V^I. They face the following potential prices and costs: (i) With probability α^2, both sellers post their price and the price is the lower of two draws from the price distribution F; (ii) with probability $(1 - \alpha)^2$, neither seller posts a price and the consumer has to pay the monopoly price, plus the physical visit cost z; (iii) with the remaining probability, only one seller posts its price, which is a draw from F. In any case, the subscription fee A_b is incurred. Denote $h_2(p)$ the density of the lowest price in two draws from F; it can be shown that $h_2(p) = 2(1 - F(p))f(p)$. Collecting terms the expected surplus of a subscriber can be written as $V^I = \alpha^2 \int_{p_0}^1 v(p) h_2(p) dp + 2\alpha(1 - \alpha) \int_{p_0}^1 v(p) dF(p) + (1 - \alpha)^2 \left(\frac{1}{2} - z\right) - A_b$. A *nonsubscribing consumer* saves the subscription fee but incurs the physical visit cost z and does not benefit from comparison shopping on the website. With probability α, their local seller posts its price and the price distribution is thus F; with probability $(1 - \alpha)$, the local seller does not post its price and charges $p^m = 1$. Hence, the expected surplus of a nonsubscriber is computed as $V^U = \alpha \int_{p_0}^1 v(p) dF(p) + (1 - \alpha)\frac{1}{2} - z$.

Let us denote by $\beta(A_s, \lambda^I)$ the value of A_b that solves the equation $V^I = V^U$. That is, $\beta(A_s, \lambda^I)$ corresponds to the maximum amount a consumer would be willing to pay for a subscription when the seller's access fee is A_s and a fraction λ^I of consumers in each locale subscribe. In the case where all consumers subscribe ($\lambda^I = 1$), each consumer is willing to pay up to $A_b^*(A_s) \equiv \beta(A_s, 1)$ for a subscription.

At the second stage of the game, when the intermediary sets an access fee $A_s \in [0, 1]$ and a subscription fee $A_b \in [0, A_b^*(A_s)]$, three equilibria are possible. (i) *Inactive market for information*: No consumer subscribes ($\lambda^I = 0$) and no seller posts its price ($\alpha^* = 0$). (ii) *Active market for information with partial consumer participation*: In each locale, a fraction $\lambda^I \in (A_s, 1)$ of consumers subscribe, where λ^I solves $\beta(A_s, \lambda^I) = A_b$ and each seller posts its price with probability $\alpha^* = (\lambda^I - A_s)/\lambda^I$. (iii) *Active market for information with full consumer participation*: All consumers subscribe ($\lambda^I = 1$) and each seller posts its price with probability $\alpha^* = 1 - A_s$. Note that the latter two equilibria exhibit price dispersion, but prices are more competitive with full consumer participation. The creation of a virtual marketplace results in lower average prices for consumers, larger consumer surplus and lower profits. This is all the more true if consumer participation is large.

We finally examine the *intermediary's fee-setting decision*. We assume that the only cost to the intermediary of establishing a virtual marketplace is a fixed set-up cost, K. The intermediary's problem is to maximize expected revenues from fees less the fixed set-up cost, $\max_{A_s,A_b} E\Pi = 2\alpha A_s + 2\lambda^I A_b - K$. The intermediary faces the following chicken-and-egg problem: To increase the willingness to pay of one group, the intermediary needs to raise the participation of the other group, but it can only do so by lowering the fee that it charges to this other group. Here, a larger consumer participation forces sellers to post prices more intensively. It turns out that for a given access fee, the increased revenues stemming from sellers (due to their larger posting intensity) more than offset the loss in revenues stemming from consumers (due to the initial reduction of the subscription fee). Therefore, the intermediary finds it profitable to reduce the subscription fee so as to induce full consumer participation.

Main Insights

According to the previous analysis, sellers make higher profits when the services of the intermediary are not available. Yet, when the platform exists and consumers visit it, competing sellers are willing to pay to post their price because they would suffer if only the price of the rival was posted on the website. The creation of the platform results in lower average prices, greater buyer surplus, and lower seller surplus.

In particular, without the platform, each consumer is served by a single local firm, which sells at the monopoly price. Consumers than benefit from the presence of the intermediary. As Ronayne (2019) observed, in contrast to the early days of electronic commerce, many sellers have their own websites, in which case buyers often have little difficulty in engaging in search across different websites and making comparisons even in the absence of a dedicated intermediary offering price comparisons. Ronayne (2019) shows that if consumers are likely to find out about competing offers even in the absence of the dedicated intermediary, buyers will be worse off with the introduction of a dedicated intermediary because expected retail prices go up.[21]

Collecting the previous insights, we can draw the following lesson:

---

[21] Ronayne and Taylor (2020) add another dimension of loyalty. Not only firms on the direct sales channel may have loyal consumers, also the intermediary may have loyal consumers who stick to it and do not look for lower prices on the direct channel. If the intermediary charges a per-unit fee to sellers, it faces a trade-off: It may set a high fee and only cater to its loyal consumers or it may set a lower fee to prevent shoppers from bypassing the platform, since then sellers do not have an incentive to set low prices on the direct sales channel. As Ronayne and Taylor (2020) show in a model with unit demand, if there are sufficiently few consumers loyal to the intermediary compared to those loyal to one of the direct sales channel, the intermediary sets a low fee; otherwise, it sets a high fee to extract all the surplus from its loyal consumers. Therefore, an exogenous conversion of consumers being loyal to a seller's direct channel to become, instead, loyal to the platform may lead some shoppers to buy via the direct channel. Overall, consumers may be worse off. In particular, consumer surplus drops discontinuously when switching from the low-fee to the high-fee environment. Thus,

LESSON 6.4   *Equilibrium price dispersion arises when a monopoly intermediary organizes a digital platform, because it is costly for sellers to advertise prices on the platform. Although consumers visit the platform and buy from the cheapest seller on the digital platform, sellers earn positive profits. Whether or not the presence of an intermediary offering price comparison services leads to lower or higher retail prices depends on the degree of seller competition in the intermediary's absence.*

Galeotti and Moraga-González (2009) provide yet another perspective on the issue. They consider a monopoly platform catering to a fixed discrete number of horizontally differentiated sellers and a continuum of buyers; the platform can charge sellers and buyers for its service. Their microfoundation of the buyer-seller interaction goes as follows: Sellers choose the probability of participation (this is interpreted as their decision to inform consumers about their product) and a price. Unlike Baye and Morgan (2001), Galeotti and Moraga-González conclude that buyers on the platform draw product-specific match values (this gives rise to horizontal differentiation), while they obtain zero utility if they do not join the platform. They buy the product that maximizes the difference between match value and price. Thus, a seller who increases the participation probability intensifies competition. The authors assume that, in the second stage, sellers set price and make participation decisions, and buyers make participation decisions. Their decisions are guided by the membership fees set by the platform in the first stage.

At the participation stage, buyers and sellers are homogeneous. Therefore, the platform can extract the full surplus generated by intermediation. Galeotti and Moraga show that in such a case, platform pricing is second-best efficient – that is, a planner with the same instruments would implement the same allocation: The platform sets prices on both sides so as to ensure full participation by buyers and sellers, and this implements the social planner's second-best allocation.

6.2   Nonprice Strategies and Network Effects

In this section, we shed some light on how platforms use nonprice strategies – or "platform design decisions" – to manage network effects. We can see these strategies as chosen by the platforms before the games that we have been analyzing so far unfold. That is, platforms commit first to some design decision; then they set fees (or participation levels); finally, users make their participation decisions – which platform(s) to join, what to do on a platform. The main impact of the first-stage

even though consumers loyal to the intermediary choose the lower price among competing offers in contrast to consumers who are loyal to a particular direct channel, a market with more consumers loyal to the intermediary at the expense of consumers who are loyal to a particular direct sales channel may make consumers worse off overall because seller fees set by the intermediary feed into retail prices. Another observation is that consumers are even worse off under price-parity clauses, which inhibit sellers from attracting shoppers to the direct sales channel by setting lower direct-channel prices.

design decisions is to determine the strength of the cross-group network effects. That is, these decisions endogenously determine the parameters β_b and β_s in the linear specification of network effects or, more generally, the functional form of network effects in case they are not linear in participation levels.

We presented a number of such strategies in Chapter 4 when discussing how platforms can build trust among users. Many platform design decisions aim indeed at alleviating asymmetric information problems; think, for example, of cancellation and return policies, dispute settlement mechanisms, certification systems and minimum quality standards, insurance mechanisms, secure payment systems, or liability rules. In our discussion, we indicated how some of these strategies are likely to increase cross-group network effects on both sides, while other strategies may have contrasted impacts across buyers and sellers (or across heterogeneous users within a given group).

In this section, we take a closer look at two other design decisions. First, we analyze when and how a platform may twist the design of its rating and recommendation systems to increase its profits (6.2.1). A platform may indeed find it profitable to sacrifice informativeness if that increases its revenues – for instance, by modifying the aggregate rankings of products or sellers or by varying the ordering and display of individual reviews. Second, we discuss the incentives for platforms to impose price transparency. This is most obvious in the case of price search engines, as their raison d'être is to facilitate price comparison for consumers. However, sellers may then engage in obfuscation strategies, hiding part of the overall price or attracting consumers with offers that turn out to be unattractive and then convince them to buy a higher-priced product. As a seller has strong incentives to do so under seller competition, platforms have to take a stand regarding such obfuscation strategies (6.2.2).

Before analyzing these two strategies, let us note that, in general, a platform incurs some costs to modify its design. It must then balance marginal benefits and costs, taking into account the following chain of events: Changing the design affects the cross-group network effects, which brings the platform to adjust its price strategy and the users to adjust their participation decisions. Moreover, in a competitive context, the reactions of the other platforms must also be factored in. We record these elements in the following lesson; we will keep them in mind in our analysis.

LESSON 6.5   *An intermediary that uses price and nonprice strategies on its two-sided platform has to take the interplay between price and nonprice strategies into account when deciding on the profit-maximizing price structure. Several types of platform design decisions have a conflicting impact on the network benefits derived by the two sides.*

For instance, a platform may impose a minimum quality standard, which is costly for sellers to implement. For a given number of sellers, consumers may benefit from this standard, whereas for a given number of consumers, sellers will suffer. As Hermalin (2016) shows, when a platform taxes trade and sellers are heterogeneous in their cost to provide quality (a convex cost which is incurred irrespective of the number of units sold), a profit-maximizing platform wants to impose a minimum quality standard even if seller quality is observable to buyers (once they are on the platform).[22]

6.2.1   Designing Rating and Recommender Systems

As discussed in Chapter 2, the design of rating and recommender systems affects the surpluses obtained by buyers and sellers from their interactions. Take, as an extreme example, a dating platform that randomly matches men and women and, thereby, makes it quite costly for men and women to find the "perfect" match. If, by contrast, the dating site has developed an algorithm that makes a perfect prediction as to which match is "perfect," the expected utility for men and women to participate on the platform grows larger.

We also argued in Chapter 2 that reviews, ratings, and recommendations are an important source of network effects, and we saw how a platform can increase the values of β_b and β_s by improving on its rating and recommendation system. In particular, we showed that the platform's profits tend to increase in $\beta_b + \beta_s$. However, while it is true that better services increase usage, a profit-maximizing platform may be willing to reduce usage if this increases its profits. In this section, we consider situations in which the platform can affect β_b and β_s, and analyze when and how a platform may want to "manipulate" or somewhat degrade rating and recommendation systems to increase its profits.

Design of Rating Systems

In Chapter 2, we identified reasons that rankings and reviews lose informativeness because of the actions taken by the transaction partners. The assumption was that the platform aims to maximize the informativeness, possibly battling against errors and gaming. While more informative rankings and reviews tend to make the platform more attractive (and are a source of positive network effects), a for-profit platform is ultimately interested in maximizing profit. It may, then, have an incentive to sacrifice informativeness if that increases its revenues. In addition to measures taken by the platform that affect the aggregate rankings of products or sellers, the platform may vary the ordering and display of individual reviews. The findings by Vana and Lambrecht (2019) provide some indications as to how a different design of the listing of reviews can affect purchase probability.

The literature on certifying intermediaries provides some insights into the design of rating systems by a profit-maximizing platform. In particular, platforms may deliberately design their system so as to avoid the worst offending behavior – that is, it features a minimum quality threshold – but to offer few clues about product quality otherwise. In such a case, rating inflation and presumed design flaws that

---

[22] If quality is unobservable to consumers, all active sellers will set quality equal to minimum quality and earn the same revenue. In this case, it is obvious that the platform has an incentive to introduce a minimum quality standard to avoid a race to the bottom. The minimum quality standard serves to exclude sellers that are less efficient in providing quality; see Hermalin (2016).

limit the informativeness of a rating system would actually indicate that a profit-maximizing intermediary with market power sacrifices buyer participation in favor of higher margins. This is the lesson one can draw from the work on certifying intermediaries by Lizzeri's (1999), who shows that in an adverse selection environment, a platform discloses only whether a product satisfies a minimum quality threshold.[23] In his setting, a monopoly intermediary charges a fee to sellers for providing its certification service.[24] As a result, the intermediary certifies minimum quality for products that are traded via the intermediary. Translated into the context of rating systems, the platform commits to its rating system and charges sellers for being listed. Thus, Lizzeri's result says that the rating system is designed in such a way that only the worst offenders disappear from the platform.

LESSON 6.6   *A profit-maximizing platform may deliberately design its rating system so as to limit its informativeness. As a result, sellers of rather low quality may do better on such a platform than on a platform that maximizes the quality of its rating system, while high-quality sellers do worse.*

Bouvard and Levy's (2018) further investigate the potential tension between informativeness and rent extraction. In their setting, the platform cannot commit to a certification technology and establishes a reputation for accuracy; for its service, it charges a fixed fee to participating sellers upfront. Applied to ratings systems, this means that the platform can redesign features that reflect the rating system's accuracy, and the fixed fee corresponds to a listing fee charged to sellers (as is observed, for example, on some price search engines).

Sellers have different opportunity costs of providing high quality. While higher accuracy attracts high-quality sellers, it repels low-quality sellers. As a result, the profit of a platform is first increasing and then decreasing in the level of accuracy it provides to sellers seeking certification. Thus, a profit-maximizing platform provides an intermediate level of accuracy. Applied to rating systems, instead of offering certification, a platform may make use of buyer reviews and ratings to (noisily) reveal quality. The design decisions regarding the rating system then affect its accuracy.

Platform competition improves the information available to buyers when sellers have to make a discrete choice between platforms: It enables full disclosure in Lizzeri's (1999) setting and increases accuracy in Bouvard and Levy's (2018) setting. By contrast, under seller multihoming, Bouvard and Levy's (2018) show that platforms have weaker incentives for accuracy under competition.

There is a close link between certification and rating systems. In particular, a platform may award badges if a seller meets a certain quality threshold that is (at least partly) based on buyer feedback. New sellers who have a hard time meeting this threshold may decide not to exert much effort and settle for a life without the

---

[23] Similarly, Albano and Lizzeri (2001) analyze a moral hazard problem.

[24] The timing is as follows: First, the intermediary sets its fee and commits to an information disclosure policy. Second, after observing the intermediary's decision, sellers decide whether to pay the fee, offer their products through the intermediary, and submit their product for testing. Third, consumers observe all previous decisions, and the seller makes a take-it-or-leave-it offer.

badge or not to enter the market. More capable new sellers strive hard to meet the threshold. We would expect that replacing an old badge with a more demanding new badge would have the following effects: Sellers who do not find it too difficult to meet the more stringent requirements of the new badge may exert a lot of effort, while sellers who would have tried to achieve the old badge, but have a harder time to meet the more stringent requirement, may reduce their effort (compared to the one with the old badge in place) and resign themselves to a life without the badge (or decide altogether to stay out). This suggests that, after replacing the old by the new badge, sellers strive less for an intermediate quality that would have qualified them to receive the old badge. As a result, the more demanding badge leads to fatter tails of the sellers' quality distribution. Hui et al. (2018) provide supporting evidence using proprietary eBay data for the period 2008–2010 when eBay replaced the "power seller" badge with the more stringent "eBay Top Rated Seller" badge in September 2009.

Search Engine Bias and Quality Degradation

As is the case for review and rating systems, platforms may have incentives that are not aligned with those of buyers when it comes to design recommender systems. In particular, a profit-maximizing platform may have an incentive to distort the recommender system or make it less informative. Already in 1998, Sergey Brin and Lawrence Page (the founders of Google) were worried about biases introduced by commercial search engines. As they wrote, "we expect that advertising funded search engines will be inherently biased towards the advertisers and away from the needs of the consumers" (Brin and Page, 2012, p. 3832). More precisely, they foresaw a number of biases of commercial search engines (which may survive in the market), as reported in Case 6.4.

CASE 6.4 BIASES OF COMMERCIAL SEARCH ENGINES

"[A] search engine could add a small factor to search results from 'friendly' companies, and subtract a factor from results from competitors. This type of bias is very difficult to detect but could still have a significant effect on the market. Furthermore, advertising income often provides an incentive to provide poor quality search results. For example, we noticed a major search engine would not return a large airline's homepage when the airline's name was given as a query. It so happened that the airline had placed an expensive ad, linked to the query that was its name. A better search engine would not have required this ad, and possibly resulted in the loss of the revenue from the airline to the search engine. In general, it could be argued from the consumer point of view that the better the search engine is, the fewer advertisements will be needed for the consumer to find what they want. This of course erodes the advertising supported business model of the existing search engines. However, there will always be money from advertisers who want a customer to switch products, or have something that is genuinely new. But we believe the issue of advertising causes enough mixed incentives that it is crucial to have a competitive search engine that is transparent and in the academic realm." (Brin and Page, 2012, p. 3832)

Time has moved on, and with it the reality of search engines. As far as the theoretical literature is concerned, recent work has uncovered several reasons for which platforms operating as search engines may have an incentive to bias their search results. First, a platform may favor search results from which it can extract larger profits. Second, partial integration of the platform with some sellers or content providers may reinforce the previous motivation. Finally, a platform may discourage search so as to reduce competition among sellers. We examine these three motivations in turn and comment on empirical results when available.

Search Engine Bias to Favor More Profitable Sellers

A platform may bias the order of recommendations if different offers lead to different commissions or to different purchase probabilities. Regarding the former, such higher margins occur if the platform has a specific partner program for which it charges higher commissions. Regarding the latter, if an offer is available on different distribution channels and some buyers multihome, these multihoming buyers are likely to purchase elsewhere if offers on alternative distribution channels are available at a lower price. Therefore, a profit-maximizing platform would place offers that were cheaper elsewhere in a lower position than if such lower-priced alternatives were not available.[25] As reported in Case 6.5, major hotel booking platforms seem to distort their rankings.

CASE 6.5 RANKING DISTORTIONS ON BOOKING AND EXPEDIA

Hotel booking platforms such as Booking and Expedia provide rankings based on different characteristics. Booking and Expedia use a default to place their recommendations – Expedia calls this list "Recommended" and Booking, "Top Picks." These platforms do not provide clear information on how they construct the lists; this is in contrast to other listings that a user can obtain and that are based on price or reviewer ratings. Thus, platforms maintain discretion over how they order the available offers in the list.

Hunold, Kesler, and Laitenberger's (2020) use data from July 2016 to January 2017 from Booking, Expedia, and the meta-search site Kayak for hotels in 250 cities (most of them within Europe), featuring more than 18,000 hotels. They find that for a given price on a hotel booking platform, a lower price on the other platform or on the hotel's website leads to a worse position on the list. This suggests that hotel booking platforms adjust their recommendations.

A platform has an incentive to make the ranking position dependent on the profitability of establishing a match between user and hotel. The platform's expected revenue is the price of the hotel times the commission times the probability that a successful match leads to a transaction. This probability is likely to be heterogeneous across hotels: Some hotels run their own websites, others do not. Those with a website may charge different prices on their own website than on the platform; prices may also differ across platforms. The probability that a consumer does not book on the platform should then be higher if a better offer exists elsewhere and the larger this price difference is. This would be the outcome in a consumer choice model with the following two groups of consumers. Consumers in the first group look for their preferred hotel on the platform and book. Consumers in the second group have a two-step decision process: In the first step, they look for their preferred hotel on the platform; in the second step, they book through a different channel if a sufficiently lower price is available. Given such consumer behavior, such properties may be reflected by the platform's ranking and the ranking

---

[25] If the platform is allowed to impose a price-parity clause that prevents sellers from offering lower prices elsewhere, it no longer has the incentive to bias search results in that way. However, several jurisdictions have declared such price-parity clauses illegal on competition grounds; we will address this issue in our second book.

algorithm may place hotels that have better outside offers further down in the ranking. Hunold, Kesler, and Laitenberger's (2020) finding is compatible with Booking deliberately designing the ranking for its own purposes. Consumers steered by this ranking make mistakes, as they overlook offers that are better for them.

While the algorithm may use information on lower prices elsewhere as an input of the ranking outcome, an observed ranking bias may be obtained even without the use of such external information. The ranking algorithm may simply track purchase probabilities from the past and use them to predict the likelihood that a particular hotel in a particular ranking position makes a sale. Clearly, if some consumers multihome and the hotel is available at a lower price through a different distribution channel, this leads to a lower probability that consumers purchase on the platform under consideration. Hence, standard profit maximization using information on past sales, but not on prices outside the platform, leads to a ranking in which hotels with lower prices elsewhere are punished by putting them further down the list.

In the case of ad-based search engines, the interaction between organic and sponsored links can provide a reason that search engines opt to bias their search results – this insight is relevant not only for general search engines, but also for platforms such as Booking, which offers advertising opportunities in addition to providing organic search results.[26] As Xu, Chen, and Winston (2012), Taylor (2013), and White (2013) point out, organic links give producers a free substitute to sponsored links on the search engine. Hence, if the search engine provides high quality in its organic links, it cannibalizes its revenue from sponsored links (if it is not able to fully recoup them through higher charges on its sponsored links). At the same time, providing better (i.e., more reliable) organic search results makes the search engine more attractive. If consumers have search costs, a more attractive search engine obtains a larger demand. However, if the latter effect is (partially) dominated by self-cannibalization, a search engine optimally distorts its organic search results.

To sum up this discussion, we record the following lesson:

LESSON 6.7 *A profit-maximizing platform may degrade the quality of its recommender systems or provide biased recommendations. This tends to reduce the size of within-group network effects among buyers.*

Search Bias Due to Partial Integration

A misalignment of buyer and platform incentives may also be the result of partial vertical integration. In particular, this may be alleged to give rise to or exacerbate *search engine bias* – an issue that received prominence in the Google Shopping case in the European Union. Does partial vertical integration lead to additional worries about search engine bias, or can integration possibly reduce search engine bias? The issue had appeared already in the 1980 leading to regulatory interventions with the aim to ensure "search neutrality," as the following case illustrates.

---

[26] Our discussion of search engine bias closely follows the exposition in Peitz and Reisinger (2016).

CASE 6.6 AIRLINE RESERVATION SYSTEMS

In the 1980s, the US Department of Transport was concerned about biased listings on computerized reservation systems (CRS) offered by several US airlines. "Each CRS consists of a central computer database that is connected to terminals in participating travel agencies. These databases contain complete information about all scheduled airline flights."[27] Among the five existing CRS, SABRE (owned by American Airlines) with a revenue share of 43 percent and Apollo (owned by a consortium, in particular United Airlines) with a revenue share of 32 percent were the largest.[28] A CRS is a two-sided platform with airlines as the sellers and travel agents as the buyers. A travel agent enters a request into the system and receives a list of offers in return. The CRS obtains a commission on each flight booked through the system that is charged to the airline providing the flight. In addition, the travel agent pays a subscription fee to the CRS it uses. For the period before 1984, it is reported that CRS biased listings in favor of the airline that owns the CRS, placing its offers on top of the list and thus leading to more bookings for this airline. More specifically, the Civil Aeronautics Board found "that certain system owners had written the computer program algorithms in such a manner that their CRS screens would display all of their own flights before listing those of competitors, even though other flights might more closely match the agents' specifications. Because travel agents work under heavy time pressures, they tend to recommend the flights listed first."[29] In November 1984, the Civil Aeronautics Board introduced a rule that prohibited such a search bias (however, that rule apparently was not fully effective, as the airline controlling the CRS continued to enjoy more bookings).

In what follows, we present the models of de Cornière and Taylor (2014) and Burguet, Caminal, and Ellman (2016) to systematically analyze the costs and benefits of search engine integration.

Search engine bias may arise (with and without partial vertical integration) when search engine and websites are advertising-financed and users view advertising as a nuisance. To show this, de Cornière and Taylor (2014) analyze a market with a monopoly search engine, two websites, sellers-cum-advertisers and users. The websites offer horizontally differentiated content. This is formalized by the Hotelling line, with platform 1 located at point 0 and platform 2 at point 1, and users uniformly distributed on the unit interval. Prior to search, users are not aware of their preferred content. This implies that without searching, a user cannot identify which website has the content that interests them the most. A user incurs a user-specific search cost when engaging in search on the search engine (specifically, the search cost is drawn from some cumulative distribution function). The search engine decides on how to allocate users to the two websites. The search engine is said to be biased if its chosen user allocation differs from the one that maximizes the expected user utility (and, thus, the user participation rate).

Websites and the search engine obtain revenues exclusively from advertising posted by sellers, which users are assumed to dislike. The search engine works as

---

[27] Quote taken from Competitive Enterprise Inst. v. U.S. D.O.T 856 F.2d 1563 (D.C. Cir. 1988).

[28] The following information is extracted from Airline Computer Reservation Systems: Hearing Before the Subcommittee on Aviation of the Committee on Public Works and Transportation, House of Representatives, One Hundredth Congress, Second Session, September 14, 1988, pp. 45–49.

[29] Quote taken from Competitive Enterprise Inst. v. U.S. D.O.T 856 F.2d 1563 (D.C. Cir. 1988). Also quoted in Ezrachi and Stucke (2016, p. 137).

follows: If a user decides to use the search engine, they enter a query. The search engine then directs the user to one of the websites. The search engine's decision rule is a threshold rule such that all users to the left of the threshold are directed to platform 1 and those to the right are directed to platform 2. A key assumption is that ads on the search engine and those on the media platforms are imperfect substitutes.

The search engine faces the following trade-off. On the one hand, it is interested in high user participation. Other things being equal, a larger number of search engine users leads to higher profits because advertisers are willing to pay more to the search engine. Therefore, the search engine cares about relevance to users. In addition, since users dislike advertising, they prefer to be directed to a site that shows few ads. These considerations align the incentives of the search engine with those of users. On the other hand, the search engine obtains profits from advertisers and, thus, aims to maintain a high price for its own links. Therefore, if ads on a specific website are particularly good substitutes for ads on the search engine, the search engine prefers to bias results against this website.

Here we explain the model ingredients more formally. Users obtain a utility $r(d) - \beta_b^i(n_s^i) - z$ where $r(d)$ is the stand-alone utility that depends on the user's location and is decreasing in distance from the website, $\beta_b^i(n_s^i)$ reflects the nuisance of advertising on website i, and z is a user's search cost. The expected per-user revenue of the representative advertiser who posts n_s^0 ads on the search engine and n_s^i ads on website i is given by $R(n_s^0, n_s^1, n_s^2) = r_0(n_s^0) + \hat{x} r_1(n_s^1, n_s^0) + (1-\hat{x}) r_2(n_s^2, n_s^0)$ when $\hat{x}$ users are on website 1. The assumption that ads on the search engine and those on the media platforms are imperfect substitutes means that the marginal value of an ad on one outlet decreases as the number of advertisements on the other outlet increases,

$$\frac{\partial^2 r_i(n_s^i, n_s^0)}{\partial n_s^0 \partial n_s^i} \leq 0.$$

This implies that the advertising revenue generated by a website falls if the amount of advertising on the search engine rises (which is treated as exogenous). The advertiser pays a per-impression price a_i giving rise to the advertiser's expected per-user profit of:

$$\pi_s = R(n_s^0, n_s^1, n_s^2) - a_0 n_s^0 - \hat{x} a_1 n_s^1 - (1-\hat{x}) a_2 n_s^2.$$

The per-user profit of the search engine is $a_0 n_s^0$ and of the two websites $\hat{x} a_1 n_s^1$ and $(1-\hat{x}) a_2 n_s^2$, respectively.

The timing of the game is as follows. First, websites choose their advertising levels and the search engine chooses the threshold $\hat{x}$ such that users to the left of x will receive website 1 as a recommendation and users to the right of $\hat{x}$ website 2. Second, the advertising market clears. Third, users decide whether or not to rely on the search engine. Finally, those users who rely on the search engine type in a query and visit the website suggested by the search engine. When deciding whether or not to rely on the search engine, a user knows the threshold and has an expectation about the websites' advertising levels.

When deciding whether or not to use the search engine, a consumer knows that an expectation about the advertising levels on the media platforms, denoted by $E[n_s^i]$. Then, the expected utility of a consumer from using the search engine with a threshold $\hat{x}$ is:

$$\int_0^{\hat{x}} r(x)dx + \int_{\hat{x}}^1 r(1-x)dx - \hat{x}\beta_b^1(E[n_s^1]) - (1-\hat{x})\beta_b^2(E[n_s^2]) - z.$$

Maximizing expected utility with respect to $\hat{x}$ gives the consumer-preferred recommendation policy x^* which leads to maximal user participation. If the search engine chooses a different threshold, it introduces a bias in favor of one of the websites.

Market clearing in the advertising market means that per-user price of the ad is equal to the advertiser's marginal willingness to pay for an ad and:

$$a_0 = \frac{\partial r_0}{\partial n_s^0} + \hat{x}\frac{\partial r_1}{\partial n_s^0} + (1-\hat{x})\frac{\partial r_2}{\partial n_s^0}.$$

Thus, the per-user ad price the search engine receives is nonincreasing in the ad levels on the two websites, n_s^1 and n_s^2. The search engine bias then goes against website 1 if $\frac{\partial r_1}{\partial n_s^0} > \frac{\partial r_2}{\partial n_s^0}$ and too many consumers receive the recommendation to go to website 2; that is, the search engine chooses a threshold to the left of x^*.

De Cornière and Taylor (2014) then analyze the effects of vertical integration of the search engine with one of the websites – say, website 1. Suppose that there is partial integration without control of ad levels – that is, website 1 shares a fraction ρ_1 of its profit with the search engine but retains full control with respect to its ad level (this corresponds to partial ownership, but no control rights for the search engine). Then, the search engine has an incentive to bias its result in favor of website 1 because it benefits directly from this website's revenues. However, it also benefits more from higher user participation, implying that the search engine wants to implement higher-quality (i.e., less-biased) results. Because of these two potentially countervailing forces, partial integration can increase or decrease the level of bias. In particular, if the search engine were biased to the detriment of website 1 without integration, partial integration might mitigate this bias. Even if the search engine is biased in favor of website 1 without integration, partial integration can lead to a reduction in the bias. If the websites are symmetric, partial (or full) integration always leads to an increase in bias. However, users may be better off because of lower ad levels.

Burguet, Caminal, and Ellman (2016) propose a different setup to analyze the effect of vertical integration on search engine bias, which is not based on ad nuisance. They explicitly model consumer search for sellers' products. User i is interested in the content of one of the N websites only – this website is denoted by $n(i)$ – while any other content generates a net utility of zero. Each website's content interests the same fraction of users, $1/N$.

Users do not know which website matches their interests and need the help of a search engine. Suppose that the search engine can perfectly identify the relevant website $n(i)$ once a user i has typed in the search query. When using the search engine, a user incurs a search cost.[30] The search engine displays a link to a website after a user has typed in the query. The search engine chooses the probability that the link leads to the content matching the user's interest. Since the links to websites are nonpaid, this corresponds to organic search.

The search engine also features sponsored search in which it advertises the sellers' products. This is the source of profits for the search engine and websites. Sellers belong to one of J different product categories, indexed by j. User i values only one category $j(i)$. Each category of products interests the same fraction of users, $1/J$. There are two sellers in each category. Seller 1 provides the best match to a user, leading to a net utility of v_1. Producer 2 provides a worse match such that $0 < v_2 < v_1$. The sellers' margins are m_1 and m_2. Users' and sellers' interests are assumed to be misaligned, and, thus, $m_2 > m_1$. In addition, it is assumed that buyer preferences dominate for the welfare ranking – that is, $v_1 + m_1 > v_2 + m_2$. The monopoly search engine provides a single link after a user has typed in a query for product search in a particular category.[31] Then, the search engine sets a pay-per-click price. The search engine chooses to display the link of producer 1 with some probability and the link of producer 2 with the remaining probability.[32]

Absent vertical integration, search results are distorted because websites compete for advertisers. As Burguet, Caminal, and Ellman (2016) show, generically, the search engine will distort, at most, one type of search – product search or content search – setting the other at the optimal value. If the search engine was integrated with all websites, it would internalize the externality exerted by one website on others and, as a result, improve its reliability. This is an unambiguously positive effect. However, in case the search engine is integrated only with a fraction of the websites, it has an incentive to divert search from nonaffiliated websites to affiliated ones. Here, partial integration may lead to a lower consumer surplus compared to no integration.

The findings from the theoretical literature suggest that search engine bias may arise due to (partial) integration. However, partial integration sometimes is a remedy for search engine bias prior to integration, and, in any case, its consumer-welfare

---

[30] The search cost is heterogeneous across consumers and drawn from some cumulative distribution function.

[31] Both models described here (Burguet, Caminal, and Ellman, 2016, and de Cornière and Taylor, 2014) assume that users visit only a single website after typing in a query. However, in reality users may click on multiple search results (in sequential order). They can be expected to broadly follow the respective ranking of the results. In such a situation, advertisers exert negative externalities on each other when bidding for more prominent placement. Athey and Ellison (2011) and Kempe and Mahdian (2008) study the question of how the optimal selling mechanism of the search engine takes these externalities into account.

[32] This is a simplified version of the model of Burguet, Caminal, and Ellman (2016), which is developed in Peitz and Reisinger (2016).

implications are ambiguous.[33] So, to ascertain whether recommender systems work better or worse under (partial) integration, a detailed understanding of the specific case is needed. What is clear is that when (partial) integration reduces bias and increases buyer participation, integration tends to improve the recommender system.

LESSON 6.8   *Partial integration of a platform with sellers or content providers may increase or decrease the bias of its recommender system. Even if partial integration increases bias, it may increase buyer participation and buyer surplus.*

Search Discouragement to Reduce Sellers' Competition

Finally, a platform may want to make its recommender system less informative so as to discourage search. Chen and He (2011) and Eliaz and Spiegler (2011) provide a reason for which a search engine may bias its recommendations or search results if it takes a cut from the transaction between buyer and seller – this is so with sponsored links. In this case, it is in the search engine's best interest that sellers' revenues from sponsored links be high. Because revenues increase if product market competition between sellers becomes softer, the search engine may distort search results so as to relax product market competition. As formalized in Chen and He (2011) and Eliaz and Spiegler (2011), a monopoly search engine has an incentive to decrease the relevance of its search results, thereby discouraging users from searching extensively. This quality degradation leads to less competition between sellers and, thus, to higher seller revenues, which can be partly extracted by the search engine.

A search engine tends to have an interest in guiding consumers to products they like.[34] If the rents that accrue to buyers and sellers are correlated, a platform operating as a search engine is interested in establishing such a match, as it may extract part of the rent on the seller and, possibly, also on the buyer side.

However, the search engine's incentives to provide the best search results may be compromised if the search engine charges only sellers. Then, as Chen and He (2011) and Eliaz and Spiegler (2011) show,[35] a monopoly search engine may bias its search results when sellers compete. This is then an instance of a platform that makes its recommender system less informative so as to discourage search. We note that it is in its best interest that the seller with the highest value be ranked first. A seller's value increases, as product market competition with other sellers is relaxed. Therefore, the search engine may distort search results to relax product market competition between sellers so as to afford a higher gross profit to the highest-value seller(s).

---

[33] More generally, a bias affects the use of price and nonprice instruments available to sellers. In the model of de Cornière and Taylor (2019), consumers have access to one integrated offer and one nonintegrated competing offer through an intermediary. Sellers can adjust price and quality of their product to the bias. The intermediary introduces a recommendation bias because of vertical integration. It is then possible that in response to the bias, quality and price increase and that the net effect for consumers is that they are better off.

[34] The following discussion is similar to the one in Peitz and Reisinger (2016).

[35] Xu, Chen, and Winston (2010, 2011), Hagiu and Jullien (2011), Casner (2020) analyze related models.

In Chen and He (2011) and Eliaz and Spiegler (2011), the search engine has an incentive to decrease the relevance of its search results and, thus, discourages buyers from searching extensively. This degrades the quality of the platform. The platform faces a trade-off between fewer buyers using the search engine and higher profits on a per-buyer base, which it obtains from fees charged to sellers. The monopoly distortion introduced by the platform consists in fewer buyers on the platform who have to pay higher product prices than absent the distortion of the search results.

More generally, a platform such as eBay increases the value to buyers if it guides buyers to more attractive products and, at the same time, provides incentives to sellers to set lower prices. This raises design questions about which subset of offers to present in which way to buyers (see Dinerstein et al., 2018).

LESSON 6.9 *In the presence of seller competition, a platform may decide to recommend products to consumers in a way that discourages consumer search and effectively relaxes seller competition.*

6.2.2 Behavioral Biases and Obfuscation

Behavioral "biases" and limited cognition often lead to suboptimal consumer decisions. For example, a consumer who is not aware of some extra charges after paying the subscription fee for a service may regret their subscription decision, as they may end up paying more than what they were willing to pay. Consumers who suffer from a misperception are highly valuable to sellers; indeed, sellers do not have to provide attractive deals to attract these consumers to join – what looks attractive at first sight may turn out to be less attractive after all. This issue arises in particular with seller competition, as sellers have an incentive to attract buyers with an eye-catching deal and later exploit them – for example, through hidden fees or highly profitable add-ons.

Suppose, in particular, that consumers have limited attention and sellers' offers contain some basic features and some auxiliary features that are more difficult to identify for consumers. Because of limited attention, consumers face a trade-off between understanding the basic features of a lot of offers (browsing behavior) and fully understanding few offers (inspection behavior). Interventions that regulate auxiliary features (e.g., strict liability regime or an unfair contract terms principle) remove the consumers' worries about these auxiliary features and encourage them to browse rather than inspect. This intensifies competition between sellers who compete for these consumers. Thus, regulating auxiliary features of complex offers can intensify competition and increase consumer welfare; for a formal analysis, see Heidhues, Johnen, and Köszegi (2021).

Suppose that consumers buy a single item and not a basket, so that it does not matter whether a seller carries many products. Then, fully rational consumers without any search costs should evaluate purchase options based on the effective price, which includes the retail price, together with shipping and handling fees for the item (and differences in service quality). This implies that from a consumer's point of view, it would not matter how large the delivery fee is as long as the effective price remains the same. In such a case, there would be full pass on. However, sellers are concerned about not being able to pass on to consumers a delivery cost that they have to bear with free delivery. For this to happen, there must be frictions in consumer behavior, stemming from behavioral biases, limited cognition, or search costs.[36] If the final price is clearly shown upfront, price may be seen as salient and consumers will react to changes in the shipping and handling fee.[37] If there are hidden fees, consumers will respond more strongly to the initially observable part of the final price than to the hidden fees. This has been confirmed by Hossain and Morgan (2006), who document that buyers on eBay respond more strongly to list prices than to shipping and handling fees. Case 6.7 provides some other evidence along these lines.

CASE 6.7 PRICE OBFUSCATION ON STUBHUB

Blake et al. (2018) analyze the outcome of a large-scale field experiment conducted by Stub-Hub, a leading online secondary ticket marketplace in the USA. Before the experiment was launched in August 2015, the platform used a "upfront fee" strategy; under this strategy, the website reports the final price that include any extra fees when a consumer first views the ticket inventory. When the experiment started, the platform used a "back-end fee" strategy for half of the consumers; under this alternative strategy, the consumer sees added fees (such as shipping and handling) only after they have selected a particular ticket and gone to the checkout page.

Blake et al. (2018) observe that users exposed to the upfront fee strategy are more likely to exit before exploring any ticket than consumers exposed to the back-end fee strategy. Furthermore, users exposed to the back-end fee strategy return to the ticket inventory more often after having selected a particular ticket. This suggests that the back-end fee strategy makes price comparisons more difficult and, thus, can be seen as a price obfuscation strategy.

The platform may want to restrict the way sellers can charge buyers in response to behavioral biases by buyers. If left unregulated by the platform, sellers may exploit buyers' behavioral biases. For a given number of buyers, such exploitation is in the interest of the platform if it can extract part of this extra surplus on the seller side. However, such exploitation also affects the participation decision of buyers: Consumers may become dissatisfied with the overall experience on the platform. Thus, it is unclear whether a platform benefits or not from imposing the transparency of the seller offers, thereby making it harder or impossible for sellers to exploit the buyers' behavioral biases.

Consumers may suffer from a platform's action if they have a behavioral bias and the platform has market power. Johnen and Somogyi (2019) consider a monopoly platform that brings sellers' additional fees to the attention of consumers. In their model, there are many different sellers, with always two sellers offering a service in a specific category. The platform is assumed to charge participation fees to both groups. Sellers post a transaction fee and can also charge an add-on for additional services.

---

[36] Next we will use the term "behavioral bias" broadly to include behaviors such as rational inattention.

[37] For a theory of how salience affects consumer behavior, see Bordalo, Gennaioli, and Shleifer (2013).

There are two groups of buyers, naive and sophisticated buyers. Naive buyers presume that there is a zero add-on fee, while sophisticate buyers foresee the add-on fee. If they foresee a high add-on fee, sophisticated buyers can make a costly investment to avoid paying this add-on fee.

The decision whether to force sellers to make this add-on fee transparent is part of the platform's information policy. Under transparency, a fraction of naive consumers becomes sophisticated. Johnen and Somogyi (2019) show that in their setting, a monopoly intermediary has weak incentives to enforce transparency on its platform. These incentives are weaker than in the case of nonintermediated trade between buyers and sellers.

LESSON 6.10 *A platform may have only weak incentives to make sellers' add-on fees transparent and, thus, to protect buyers from being exploited by sellers.*

This suggests that the private incentives of a platform regarding transparency (for instance, of terms and conditions) may be in conflict with those of consumers. Consumer protection regulations that force the platform to ensure transparency of its terms and conditions may then be asked for: It can be welfare-improving because shrouding fees induce inefficient avoidance behavior in sophisticated buyers. But on the other hand, shrouding makes sellers' products look cheaper for naifs and encourages them to join the platform. In this way, shrouding can lead to more participation on a monopoly platform and possibly increase welfare. However, platforms may well impose (or attempt to impose) price transparency, as Cases 6.8 and 6.9 illustrate.

CASE 6.8 RAKUTEN'S FREE DELIVERY POLICY[38]

Rakuten Ichiba is the largest e-commerce site in Japan. Sellers on this platform (about 50,000 of them) used to be free to set retail prices and delivery fees. In 2019, Rakuten announced that its participating sellers would have to adhere to a free delivery policy for shippings above Yen 3,980 (around US$36 at the beginning of 2020).[39] Rakuten argued that this was meant to increase transparency for consumers. Many sellers complained. A group of 450 sellers filed a complaint with the Japanese competition watchdog, the Japan Fair Trade Commission, alleging an abuse of a dominant position by Rakuten. In particular, they complained that with a free delivery policy in place, they would be forced to bear part of the delivery costs if they could not fully pass them on to consumers through a higher retail price. In February 2020, the Japan Fair Trade Commission took the rarely used possibility of asking the Tokyo District Court to intervene and disallow this practice.

CASE 6.9 SELLERS' OBFUSCATION STRATEGIES ON PRICEWATCH

PriceWatch is a US-based price search engine for electronics products such as tablets, monitors, central processing units (CPUs), and other computer parts. According to Ellison and

---

[38] Material for this case has been collected from a number of newspaper articles: In particular, *Japan Times*, "Rakuten faces backlash from cybermall tenants over free delivery plan," January 19, 2020; *Competition Policy International*, "Japan: JFTC to open antitrust probe into Rakuten," January 23, 2020; *Japan Today*, March 1, 2020.

[39] "In December, the company said purchases worth Yen 3,980 or more, including tax, will be free of delivery fees, excluding those for frozen goods and some other items, starting March 18. For Okinawa Prefecture and remote islands, the threshold will be Yen 9,800." *Japan Times*, "Rakuten faces backlash from cybermall tenants over free delivery plan," January 19, 2020.

Ellison (2009), the platform hosted at the turn of the millennium many small and almost identical sellers, who attracted most of their customers through PriceWatch. "PriceWatch presents a menu that contains a set of predefined categories. Clicking on one returns a list of websites sorted from cheapest to most expensive in a twelve listings per page format. The categories invariably contain heterogeneous offerings: Some include products made by higher and lower quality manufacturers, and all include offers with varying return policies, warranties, and other terms of trade" (Ellison and Ellison, 2009, p. 432). Ellison and Ellison document a number of price obfuscation strategies chosen by sellers, as well as attempts by PriceWatch to combat these practices. Reminiscent of the case of Rakuten, shipping and handling fees are one such dimension. "In its early days PriceWatch did not collect information on shipping costs and sorted its lists purely on the basis of the item price. Shipping charges grew to the point that it was not uncommon for firms to list a price of $1 for a memory module and inform consumers of a $40 'shipping and handling' fee at check out. PriceWatch fought this with a two-pronged approach: It mandated that all firms offer United Parcel Service (UPS) ground shipping for a fee no greater than a PriceWatch-set amount ($11 for memory modules); and it added a column that displayed the shipping charge or a warning that customers should be wary of stores that do not report their shipping charges. Many retailers adopted an $11 shipping fee in response, but uncertainty about the cost of UPS ground shipping was not completely eliminated ... The meaning of 'UPS ground shipping' was also subject to manipulation: One company explicitly stated on its website that items ordered with the standard UPS ground shipping were given lower priority for packing and might take two weeks to arrive. More recently, PriceWatch mandated that retailers provide it with shipping charges and switched to sorting low-price lists based on shipping-inclusive prices. This appears to be working, but is only fully satisfactory for customers who prefer ground shipping: Those who wish to upgrade to third-, second-, or next-day air must search manually through retailers' websites." (Ellison and Ellison, 2009, pp. 434–435)

6.3   Platform Governance Regarding Sellers' Selling Strategies

On many platforms, sellers (or service providers) have some freedom to decide how they sell their product or service to buyers (or consumers): at which price or prices, under which terms and conditions, and so on. The platform can do two things: It can limit the instruments available to the seller and it can limit the information it makes available to sellers.[40] These decisions determine how the value of transactions is divided between the two sides – that is, the intensity of the cross-group network

---

[40] The information the platform gives to a seller may also affect a capacity-constrained seller's willingness to close a deal rather than to wait for more valuable deals. This issue arises for instance on ride-hailing platforms when a driver (as the seller of a service) has to decide whether to accept a request. An important piece of information for the driver is the revenue they obtain when accepting to provide a ride. As Romanyuk and Smolin (2019) show, a platform's full information disclosure leads to socially excessive rejections by the sellers. The reason that rejection is socially excessive is that each seller rejects low-value deals, as this increases its chances of getting high-value deals. Such a rejection harms consumers and the other sellers. The former are directly harmed because the seller does not internalize the consumer surplus. Since the seller remains available after rejecting the deal, it continues to compete with other sellers for newly arriving consumers. Romanyuk and Smolin (2019) discuss when a profit-maximizing platform implements socially optimal, coarse information structures that prevent sellers from excessively rejecting proposed deals. In other words, the platform chooses an obfuscation strategy to prevent inefficient cream-skimming by sellers.

effects. Hence, another channel through which platforms can affect network effects is by interfering with the sellers' selling strategies. For instance, a platform may give sellers access to a richer set of pricing strategies. In particular, sellers may want to make targeted offers to certain groups of buyers; to be able to do so, they may need access to some of the platform's user data or be offered platform services (e.g., keyword bidding) that allow for targeted pricing. Case 6.10 describes that major platforms propose such advanced pricing services to their sellers.[41]

CASE 6.10 PRICING TOOLS FOR SELLERS ON DIGITAL PLATFORMS

Many platforms exploit the vast amounts of data that they collect to provide data analytics and advanced pricing tools to the sellers who operate on their marketplace. The goal is to allow sellers to practice various forms of price discrimination. For instance, Airbnb proposes its Smart Pricing tool, which it describes as follows on its blog (emphasis added):[42] "Deciding on the right price to charge for your listing can be a challenging task for anyone. You search your area to see what other hosts are charging, compare your listing to theirs, and wonder how you measure up. But what you don't know is the price those listings actually get booked for (and how often they, in fact, get booked). *You can't tell how much interest your own listing is generating, or if travelers are willing to pay the price you're asking. This is where Smart Pricing comes in*, by keeping your nightly prices competitive as demand in your area changes." Similarly, Harrison (2020) reports that "Amazon does provide tools that help sellers use dynamic pricing on the Amazon Marketplace. Sellers can set pricing rules based on the Buy Box or on the lowest price for that item, and they can change those rules based on the fulfillment channels of their competitors."[43] Etsy provides yet another example by helping sellers to practice geographical price discrimination, as Steiner (2019) reports (emphasis added): "Etsy wants to help UK sellers compete in the US and will launch a new pricing tool this week, according to the company's Chief Financial Officer Rachel Glaser. It's more expensive for international sellers to ship cross-border than it is domestically. But because of Etsy's new free-shipping initiative where it penalizes sellers who don't offer some form of free shipping in the US, that put international sellers at a disadvantage. *What international sellers need is a tool where they can present a price that's different in the US than in their domestic markets*, she said."[44]

In this section, we explore how a monopoly platform governs the seller ability to price discriminate and/or to target offerings. Depending on how network effects are affected on the two sides, the platform may choose to curb this ability (e.g., by imposing strict privacy rules) or to foster it (e.g., by providing sellers with data about buyers). We first develop a number of simple numerical examples to draw useful

---

[41] A different instance in which a platform restricts the sellers' price instruments is relevant in a setting in which the seller uses the platform as only one of multiple distribution channels. In particular, a platform may ask sellers not to sell a lower price on alternative distribution channels. So-called price-parity clauses have been investigated by competition authorities as potentially anti competitive. We will analyze the effect of such clauses in our second book on platforms. Such a pricing restriction is different in nature from the one analyzed here because it also constrains the seller pricing off the platform.

[42] See https://blog.atairbnb.com/smart-pricing/ (last accessed August 25, 2020).

[43] See Susan Harrison, "Why Am I Paying $ 60 for That Bag of Rice on Amazon.com?" The Markup, April 28, 2020, https://tinyurl.com/ybxxzgf4 (last accessed August 25, 2020).

[44] See Ina Steiner, "Etsy Helps UK Sellers Compete in US with New Pricing Tool," eCommerceBytes, August 14, 2019, www.ecommercebytes.com/C/abblog/blog.pl?/pl/2019/8/1565819902.html (last accessed August 25, 2020).

insights about the effects of two forms of differential pricing: behavior-based pricing (6.3.1) and targeted offers (6.3.2). In the process, we observe how buyers' and sellers' cross-group network effects are affected, which allows us to conjecture which policy a platform would want to apply. We then analyze this issue more formally by using the model of platform pricing that we developed in Chapter 5 (6.3.3).

6.3.1   Behavior-Based Pricing

One way a platform may affect buyer and seller benefits that are realized is by allowing sellers to condition price on consumer behavior. In this subsection, we discuss the effect of tracking with the help of a few numerical examples that illustrate the non-trivial way in which the availability of personal data affects the strength of network effects on the two sides of the platform.

The tracking of previous purchases or search behavior on a platform, may enable participating sellers to make personalized offers.[45] Thanks to the platform, a seller may be able to advertise a product to a particular group of consumers, or to advertise the product among the seller's portfolio, which is most likely to match consumer preferences depending on the information available to the seller or the platform.[46] Of course, targeting may allow the seller to adjust its price. In particular, we may expect that if a seller is monopolist in a particular product category and is better able to match consumer preferences, it will optimally charge a higher price. In the extreme, the seller may not even provide a better match and simply personalize prices to consumer groups. Such personalized prices may be achieved through a uniform list price and targeted discounts. Then, "knowing your customer" may allow for higher profits when the advertised product is the same for all consumers, as the seller can personalize its price according to the willingness to pay of specific consumers. This is a well-known result from the economics of price discrimination, which can be illustrated by a simple numerical example.[47]

Numerical Example on Group Pricing and Targeting

Suppose that there is a "large" number of consumers (say 100) who are interested in a particular good produced by one seller at zero cost per unit (there may be fixed costs). Consumers are assumed to have different valuations (willingness to pay), which are randomly drawn between 0 and 100. To keep things simple, each real number between 0 and 100 is equally likely. What does the seller optimally do to maximize its profits? Without further information about consumers, it has to offer the same price to all consumers. The profit-maximizing price is 50, at which 50 consumers buy and, thus, the seller's profit is 2,500.

---

[45] This subsection is taken mostly verbatim from Larouche, Peitz, and Purtova (2016). The corresponding material was written by Martin Peitz. We do not use quotation marks.

[46] A consumer may make inferences on the likelihood that a product will fit their tastes based on the context (an environment in which targeted advertising is practiced or where it is not), and possibly also on the content of an ad. Anand and Shachar (2009) show that a seller may want to use targeted ads combined with advertising content.

[47] For an elaborate textbook treatment of the economics of price discrimination, see Belleflamme and Peitz (2015).

Table 6.1 Numerical example: Effects of group pricing

	Price	Number of buyers	Profit	Total profit
1 group	50	50	2,500	2,500
2 groups				
Group 1 (50–100)	50	50	2,500	
Group 2 (0–50)	25	25	625	3,125

Can the seller do better if it has additional information about consumers? Suppose that the seller does not perfectly know how much consumers value the product, but that it can distinguish two groups of consumers based on consumer data: It identifies those who are willing to pay more than 50 and those who are willing to pay less.[48] In this case the seller optimally charges 50 to those consumers belonging to the group with valuations over 50, and charges 25 to those belonging to the group with valuation less than 50. From the first group it makes a profit of 50 times 50 (= 2,500) and from the latter of 25 times 25 (= 625) leading to an overall profit of 3,125. Table 6.1 summarizes all these numbers.

What this simple example shows is that by segmenting the market, a seller can increase its profits. In the example, consumers benefit as well, since some consumers obtain the product at 25, who would not have bought at a uniform price of 50, absent that market segmentation. If (perhaps thanks to the information service provided by a platform) the seller is able to segment the market even better (e.g., distinguishing four instead of two consumer groups), it can further increase its profits.[49] However, if the seller obtains an increasingly better estimate of a consumer's valuation, consumers eventually do worse overall, since a larger fraction of the potential gains from trade are extracted by the seller. One may, therefore, be tempted to conclude that a seller necessarily benefits from the use of consumer data, while it is unclear whether consumers benefit, at least when a seller is on its own in a particular product category.

This conclusion, however, is premature. It ignores the dynamic dimension: With the help of a platform, a seller learns from the behavior of consumers about their valuations and consumer behavior may be sensitive to such dynamic considerations. It is therefore useful to take another look at the numerical example above.[50]

---

[48] Here, we reconsider the formal analysis given at the beginning of this chapter. The argument holds more generally if the seller can identify consumers as belonging to a particular group and groups differ in their distribution of valuations. Network effects are present, if a larger number of consumers improves the precision by which the seller can predict a consumer's type. For simplicity, we take the number of users as given.

[49] See Belleflamme and Peitz (2015, chapter 8) for a short exposition. We also considered other information disclosure policies of the platform at the beginning of this chapter.

[50] See also the exposition in Belleflamme and Peitz (2015, chapter 10). A more elaborate exposition is provided by Fudenberg and Villas-Boas (2006).

Numerical Example on Behavior-Based Pricing and Personal Data

We introduce dynamics in the simplest form into the above numerical example. Suppose that consumers consider buying the product in each of two periods (the product is short-lived and provides a value only for the concurrent period; such a situation also applies to subscriptions to a particular service for a particular period of time). The seller maximizes profits as the sum of first-period and second-period profits and is able to track consumer behavior, but lacks any other information on consumers. Thus, the seller will not have any information about consumers in the first period, but in the second period, the seller knows which consumers bought in the first period. If consumers make myopic decisions – that is, they ignore in period 1 that they will again be active in period 2 – the seller can charge (i) 50 to all consumers in the first period and (ii) in the second period, the same price to those who bought in the first period and 25 to those who did not. The reason is that by buying the product in period 1, a consumer reveals that they have a valuation of at least 50. Thus, in the second period, we replicate the result from the numerical example above. The seller makes a profit of 3,125 in the second period and a total profit of 5,625. Here, being able to track consumers increases the seller's profits because otherwise the seller could only make a profit of 2,500 in each period.[51]

However, this result may be questioned on the grounds that consumers may be forward-looking and understand the implications of their first-period behavior. We take another look at the pricing of the seller presuming that the seller sets the prices for period 2 in period 2 (previously we did not need to specify whether those prices are set in period 1 or 2). As we will see next, this has drastic consequences on the outcome. First, we see that with the pricing strategy that was optimal under consumer myopia, forward-looking consumers will behave differently. A consumer who decides whether to buy in the first period takes into account that this affects the second-period price they will face. Clearly, a consumer with a valuation slightly above 50 will not buy in the first period, since this will imply that they have to pay 50 in the second period, while they know that they will face a price of 25 if they decline the offer in the first period. Hence, at a price of 50, fewer consumers will buy in the first period. This in turn implies that the seller will set different prices in the second period from the ones under consumer myopia. It will also lead to an adjustment of the first-period price.

Let us first consider the pricing period 2, when all consumers above some value V (greater than or equal to 50) have bought in period 1. Then the seller will charge V to consumers who bought in period 1 and half of V to those who did not. Thus, a consumer obtains their valuation minus the first-period price plus the difference between their valuation and value V, if they buy in the first period, while they obtain

---

[51] The seller can actually do better than this. It maximises its profit by setting a price slightly above 57 in the first period and the same price to consumers who bought in the first period and half this price to those who did not. Maximal profits are approximately 5,714, with approximately 2,449 in the first period and 3,265 in the second.

the difference between their valuation and half of V, if they do not buy in the first period. There is a critical consumer such that all consumers with higher valuation buy in the first period and all consumers with a lower valuation do not buy in the first period. When setting its first-period price, the seller takes into account how this critical consumer behaves, and the subsequent second-period prices depend on the first-period price. Maximizing its overall profits, the seller charges 30 in the first period. In the second period, the seller charges 60 to consumers who bought in period 1 and 30 to those who did not buy in period 1. With these prices, a consumer with valuation of 60 is indifferent about whether or not to buy in the first period. This is seen as follows: If this consumer buys in the first period their net surplus is 30 in the first period and 0 in the second. If they buy in the second period their net surplus is 0 in the first period and 30 in the second. All consumers with higher valuations buy in the first period. Thus, in period 1 the seller sells its product at price 30 to forty consumers and makes a first-period profit of 1,200. In period 2, it sells its product at price 60 to forty consumers and makes a profit of 2,400 from those consumers; it sells at price 30 to the remaining thirty consumers with valuation above 30 and makes an additional profit of 900. Hence, the seller makes a second-period profit of 3,300, which is more than if it faced myopic consumers (3,125), and also more than if it did not track consumers (2,500). However, the seller's first-period profit of 1,200 is much lower than what it would have been in the case where it did not track consumers and in the case of myopic consumers. Overall, the seller is worse off with consumer tracking (a profit of 4,500) than if it did not track (a profit of 5,000). To facilitate the comparison between the two scenarios, we report all these numbers in Table 6.2.

The general lesson that emerges from these examples is the following:

LESSON 6.11 *Even if a seller is a monopolist in its product category, with the ability to track consumers and make targeted price offers, it does not necessarily obtain higher profits once consumers rationally anticipate that they are tracked (and infer future prices).*

Table 6.2 Numerical example: Behavior-based pricing

	PERIOD 1			PERIOD 2				TOTAL profit
	Price	Number of buyers	Profit		Price	Number of buyers	Profit	
Myopic consumers				Buyers	50	50	2,500	
				Non-buyers	25	25	625	
	50	50	2,500				3,125	5,625
Forward-looking consumers				Buyers	60	40	2,400	
				Nonbuyers	30	30	900	
	30	40	1,200				3,300	4,500

As illustrated, the seller would be better off if it could credibly convey to consumers that it did not seek to learn about consumer behavior. Here, committing to a privacy policy may help the seller to commit not to track consumer behavior and, thus, may avoid a situation where the seller engages in price discrimination which runs counter to its own interests when it cannot commit to future prices.

This insight directly translates into a platform context. An individual seller may lack the means and commitment power regarding the ability to exclude consumer tracking. However, a platform concerned about its attractiveness for consumers to join may have an incentive to ensure that sellers do not have the ability to make targeted offers. It may therefore want to restrict the flow of information about consumer characteristics to sellers.

6.3.2   Targeting

So far we have focused on the use of personal data when each independent seller sells a single (totally differentiated) product. Arguably of more practical relevance is an analysis that allows for multiple differentiated products. As alluded to at the beginning of this section, targeting may increase the fit between product and consumer tastes (and, thus, the match quality); it may also reduce the search cost a consumer incurs to find a product which provides a sufficiently good fit. Before addressing these two issues we explore some pricing implications when two sellers on a platform compete with differentiated products.[52]

Suppose that there are two sellers in the market, which we call RED and BLUE, each offering a single product. Products are differentiated: At equal prices, some consumers prefer RED and others BLUE. If sellers lack information about consumer tastes, they post a uniform price applicable to all consumers. As a result, each seller will set a price that allows for a positive profit margin, such that none of the sellers gains from charging a different price. Consider now a situation where sellers can learn whether consumers are RED or BLUE lovers. They can then make targeted offers to these two consumer groups. The BLUE seller is willing to sacrifice almost all its profit margin when making a targeted offer to RED lovers since it knows that it is at a disadvantage when competing for those consumers. The same applies for the RED seller with respect to BLUE lovers. The implication is that if both sellers have access to this information, they will compete more fiercely than in the absence of information. In addition, each seller has an incentive to acquire this information. Hence, sellers will acquire personal data at some cost and obtain lower profits even when abstracting from those costs. Again, we are in a situation in which sellers would benefit from a stringent privacy policy, which does not allow them to extract information on consumer tastes. Here, it is of no help if one seller implements such a privacy policy on its own initiative. Rather, it benefits from the competitor

---

[52] This short exposition also connects to the exposition in Section 6.1.1 in which we analyzed seller competition on a platform.

doing so. Therefore, sellers may benefit from a privacy policy implemented by the platform.

While our example suggests that competition tends to be more intense when sellers have access to personal data of consumers, we should not conclude that all consumers necessarily benefit, because consumers who are very attached to a particular product configuration may end up paying more than under uniform pricing. Also, we should not conclude that more intense competition necessarily improves the allocation. Indeed, it is not in the interest of society if some BLUE lovers buy from RED and vice versa. If sellers do have some, but not very precise, information about consumer tastes, we must expect such a situation to arise. Therefore, starting in a situation in which sellers do not possess any information about consumer tastes, obtaining more information may actually lead to an inefficient allocation.

Similar to our two-period example with a single seller and a single product, we may ask what happens if sellers have to track consumer behavior to make inferences about consumer tastes in a subsequent period. If we consider a two-period setting in which the sellers lack any information about consumer tastes in the first period, each seller initially sets one price for all consumers. A consumer who buys from BLUE and not from RED (at similar prices) reveals to the sellers that they are a BLUE lover because otherwise they would have bought RED. In this way, sellers learn from consumer behavior in period 1 which group a consumer belongs to. However, as suggested before, we need to be a bit more careful here. Some consumers are strong BLUE lovers; others may have only a slight preference at equal prices. If, in line with numerical example 2, seller BLUE decides to offer a lower price than RED in the first period, it then not only attracts BLUE lovers, but also those RED lovers with only a weak preference for RED. By attracting more consumers in the first period, a seller invites tougher competition in the second period. Effectively, sellers are inclined to compete fiercely on price in the second period with consumer tracking. However, this renders consumers less valuable for sellers in the first period. Consequently, sellers compete less fiercely in the first period. This leads to initially higher prices and may actually harm consumers overall.[53] A platform managing the interaction between sellers and buyers would then take the effects on seller and buyers surplus into account when deciding about its privacy policy.

We return to the situation of a monopoly seller, but now postulate that a seller has the option of offering personalized products. Personalized products increase the match quality, yet we may wonder if it is indeed in the interest of a seller to increase a match quality. The following simple numerical example sheds some light on the issue.

---

[53] This is the key insight from Fudenberg and Tirole (2000). For a textbook treatment, we again refer to Belleflamme and Peitz (2015, chapter 10).

Table 6.3 Numerical example: Consumers' valuations

		Blue	Bland	Red
Scenario 1	*Blue lovers (50)*	80	50	0
	Red lovers (50)	0	50	80
Scenario 2	*"Strong" blue lovers (25)*	85	50	0
	"Weak" blue lovers (25)	75	50	0
	"Strong" red lovers (25)	0	50	85
	"Weak" red lovers (25)	0	50	75

Numerical Example on Targeted Advertising, Match Quality, and Versioning

Suppose that there is a single seller in a particular product category. Using the same terminology as in the previous example, we postulate that there are BLUE lovers and RED lovers in the population. For the moment, we do not consider lovers of varying degrees and it is sufficient to have identical consumers in each of the two groups. There are 50 BLUE lovers and 50 RED lovers. The seller can offer a single noncustomized product, which we call BLAND. All consumers have valuation 50 for BLAND. The seller also has the option to offer customized products BLUE or RED (it may choose any combination of products). BLUE lovers are assumed to have valuation 80 for BLUE and 0 for RED and vice versa for RED lovers. Thus, if the seller lacks any information about consumer tastes and consumers randomly select a single product among those on offer (they lack the time or resources to consider more than one product; alternatively, the seller can only send a single ad to each consumer), it is best for the seller to offer only BLAND and charge a price of 50. All consumers will buy and the seller obtains a profit of 5,000. We report the consumers' valuations in Table 6.3.

Suppose now that the seller has access to consumer data that makes it possible to tell RED lovers from BLUE lovers. It can target an ad announcing a different product depending on the consumer type. Even though this opens up new possibilities, the seller can replicate the strategy of an uninformed seller and sell the BLAND product to all consumers at price 50. However, it can do better and offer BLUE to BLUE lovers and RED to RED lovers and charge a price of 80. All consumers will buy and the seller makes a profit of 8,000. This shows that the seller benefits from offering customized versions to respective customer groups through the use of targeted advertising.

The example does not provide any meaningful guidance on how to view customization and tailored advertising from a consumer perspective, since the seller is able to extract all expected surplus. Whether consumers gain or lose from targeting and customization depends on the dispersion of consumer tastes, with and without the availability of consumer data. Consumers are better off from targeted advertising if consumers in the target group have more heterogeneous tastes about the targeted product than the whole consumer population about the BLAND product. To see this, we slightly modify the example and introduce "weak" and "strong" lovers of the two customized products. Suppose that, of the 50 BLUE lovers, 25 have valuation 85 and 25 have valuation 75 for BLUE; all these consumers continue to have valuation 0 for RED and 50 for BLAND. This holds vice versa for RED lovers. Now the seller sets a price of 75 after customization and targeting and obtains a profit of 7,500. Half of BLUE lovers and half of RED lovers (those with the highest valuation, at 85) are strictly better off when the seller sells customized products with targeted advertising. Thus, in this example, both consumers and the seller benefit from customization and targeting.

The following lesson summarizes this insight:

LESSON 6.12   *Sellers tend to be interested in improving match quality and offering customized products, if they can make use of personal data. Whether consumers benefit from such actions cannot be unambiguously determined.*

However, since customization increases total surplus, consumers will benefit as long as the fraction of the surplus that goes to consumers does not decrease with targeting and customization (in the numerical example, it increases from zero to some positive fraction). Mandatory privacy rules may have the consequence that targeting and customization will be hampered to the detriment of sellers, society, and also, depending on the situation, consumers.

In the above examples, consumers hold personal data. If this information is not disclosed, a seller faces an asymmetric information problem, as it cannot assess which products are of interest to the consumer in question. So far, we ignored the possibility that a seller's profit is directly affected by the consumer type, conditional on the consumer buying a product. However, this is not always the case. For instance, a bank providing a loan is interested in the default risk of a particular client, which is likely to be correlated with certain personal data. Here, privacy protection that makes it impossible for a bank to gather the relevant data may lead the bank to be more restrictive in its lending, as it faces the problem that it collects bad risks. A similar issue occurs for an online retailer who has some customers who are very likely to return products which then have to be sold at a loss. A related point can be made when monitoring the activity of a consumer provides incentives for the consumer not to take actions which go against the interest of the seller; for instance, in the case of an insurance contract, engaging in activities which are likely to lead to a loss. This is an instance of moral hazard. Monitoring in repeated interactions with moral hazard provides incentives to avoid socially inefficient activities. This monitoring relies on information disclosure (in particular, tracking of past behavior) and, possibly, information sharing among sellers.

6.3.3   Should a Platform Authorize Sellers to Price Discriminate?

The previous examples gave us clear indications as to how equipping sellers with more advanced pricing instruments affects the surplus of sellers and buyers and, thereby, the strength of cross-group network effects on the platform. We now want to analyze, in a more systematic way, the policy that a platform may choose with respect to these pricing instruments. To do so, we use the specific model of monopoly platform pricing (with linear cross-group network effects and membership fees) that we introduced in Chapter 5. We extend this model in two directions. First, we provide some microfoundations for the buyer/seller interactions on the platform; in particular, we derive the surpluses for buyers and sellers (which determine the values of β_b and β_s) when sellers are able to practice different levels of price discrimination. Second, we examine the level of price discrimination that the platform should allow, at the start of the game, in order to maximize its profit.[54]

A Specific Model of Platform Pricing: A Reminder

We briefly recap here the pricing problem of the previous chapter in which the platform sets membership fees A_b and A_s for, respectively, buyers and sellers. Recall that buyers and sellers interacting on the platform obtain the following net surpluses: $v_b = r_b + \beta_b n_s - A_b$ and $v_s = r_s + \beta_s n_b - A_s$ (where, in each group $k = b, s$, r_k is the valuation of the stand-alone services and β_k, the valuation of the interaction with one more member of the other group). Assuming that the opportunity cost of joining the platform is uniformly distributed so that an increase in net surplus by Δ increases participation by Δ, the numbers of buyers and sellers joining the platform are given by: $n_b = r_b + \beta_b n_s - A_b$ and $n_s = r_s + \beta_s n_b - A_s$. Solving these equation in n_b and n_s, we have that:

$$n_b = \frac{r_b - A_b + \beta_b(r_s - A_s)}{1 - \beta_b \beta_s} \text{ and } n_s = \frac{r_s - A_s + \beta_s(r_b - A_b)}{1 - \beta_b \beta_s}.$$

The platform chooses A_b and A_s to maximize its profit $\Pi = (A_b - f_b) n_b + (A_s - f_s) n_s$. Solving the system of first-order conditions and assuming that $\beta_s + \beta_b < 2$, we find the following profit-maximizing fees (see the details in Chapter 5):

$$\begin{cases} A_s^* - f_s = \frac{1}{2}\mu_s + \frac{1}{2}\frac{\beta_s - \beta_b}{4 - (\beta_s + \beta_b)^2} \left(2\mu_b + (\beta_s + \beta_b)\mu_s\right), \\ A_b^* - f_b = \frac{1}{2}\mu_b + \frac{1}{2}\frac{\beta_b - \beta_s}{4 - (\beta_s + \beta_b)^2} \left(2\mu_s + (\beta_s + \beta_b)\mu_b\right), \end{cases}$$

where μ_k ($k = s, b$) stands for the difference $r_k - f_k$ between the stand-alone benefit (r_k) and the marginal cost (f_k). From there, we derive the platform's profit at its maximum as:

---

[54] Yang (2020) considers the related problem of a platform operating as a data broker and providing some information on consumer valuations to a seller that is privately informed about its marginal cost of production. As he shows, the revenue-maximizing mechanism leads to perfect price discrimination for all consumers with a valuation above some cutoff, while consumers below the cutoff do not buy.

$$\Pi^* = \frac{\mu_s^2 + \mu_b^2 + \mu_s\mu_b\left(\beta_s + \beta_b\right)}{4 - (\beta_s + \beta_b)^2}.$$

We see clearly in the latter expression that the platform's profit increases with the intensity of the cross-group network effects (i.e., β_b and β_s). The intuition for this result is that a larger β_k increases the surplus created by transactions between the two sides, and the monopoly platform can extract part of that increase. Importantly, changes in β_b or in β_s have exactly the same impact on the platform's maximum profit. Actually, in this specific linear model, it is the sum of the two cross-group network effects ($\beta_b + \beta_s$) that matters for the platform: *The platform's profit increases if transactions on the platforms generate more value, regardless of how the increased value is split between buyers and sellers.*

Microfoundations of Transactions on the Platform

We now provide two specific models of transactions between buyers and sellers on the platform, allowing for varying levels of price discrimination by sellers. The objective is to make β_b and β_s (which measure the per transaction gains of buyers and sellers) depend on the level of price discrimination, which we denote by λ.

EXAMPLE 6.3   *Imperfect personalized pricing*

Suppose that the platform invests in data gathering and data analytics to enable sellers hosted on the platform to practice personalized pricing (i.e., first-degree price discrimination) with probability λ and, thereby, to obtain higher profits per buyer. There are many monopolistic single-product sellers; each buyer has a willingness to pay for one unit from each seller. For concreteness, suppose that for each product, aggregated buyer demand is given by the demand function $Q(p)$. Each buyer has unit demand but, when joining the platform, they neither know their distribution of willingness to pay nor which sellers will be able to learn their willingness to pay. If sellers can charge a personalized price, a buyer's benefit will be zero, but if sellers can only set the uniform price p, a buyer's expected benefit will be $CS(p)$, the buyer surplus at price p. On the other side, sellers set a price equal to the buyer's willingness to pay if informed about it (and if it is larger than their marginal cost c); otherwise, they set the uniform monopoly price p_m.[55] In the former case, their expected profit is $CS(c)$ and in the latter case, profit is $\pi_m \equiv (p^m - c) Q(p_m)$, where c is the seller's constant marginal cost.

In sum, given the platform's information policy λ, the expected benefits from transactions for buyers and sellers are:

$$\beta_b(\lambda) = (1 - \lambda)CS(p_m) \text{ and } \beta_s(\lambda) = \lambda CS(c) + (1 - \lambda)\pi_m. \qquad (6.8)$$

Thus, $\beta_b(\lambda)$ is a linearly decreasing function of λ and $\beta_s(\lambda)$ a linearly increasing function of λ.

---

[55] In this simple setting, the seller's uniform price is independent of the platform's data sharing policy.

EXAMPLE 6.4   *Segmentation of buyers*

A related formal illustration is to assume that the platform can design its information policy so as to only partially reveal a buyer's valuation. For concreteness, we make the following assumptions: (i) a buyer's valuation is uniformly distributed on the $[0, 1]$-interval, (ii) marginal costs of production are zero, and (iii) the platform has an information policy according to which it collects purchase-relevant buyer information. When deciding whether to join the platform, buyers do not yet know their valuation. Thus, they are ex ante homogeneous and value each seller interaction with the expected net surplus derived from this interaction.

Before making a purchase on the platform, buyers learn their type; depending on the platform's information policy, sellers may have no, some, or full information about a buyer's valuation when making a take-it-or-leave-it offer. At one extreme, sellers are able to perfectly infer a buyer's valuation; at the other extreme, they do not have any information other than knowing the distribution buyer valuations are drawn from. In the former case, passing this information on to monopoly sellers allows them to set personalized prices and fully extract all gains from trade, namely $1/2$; we have thus $\beta_s = 1/2$, while $\beta_b = 0$. In the latter case, each seller maximizes its profit by setting a uniform price equal to $1/2$ in which case the per-buyer seller profit is $1/4$ and the per-seller buyer net surplus is $1/8$; it follows that $\beta_s = 1/4$, while $\beta_b = 1/8$.

However, in the latter case, there is a deadweight loss and the platform can implement information policies that make sellers and buyers better off. Clearly, the information policy that allows for personalized prices is the best outcome for sellers ($\lambda = 1$). What is the best information policy for buyers ($\lambda = 0$) when sellers have the price setting power? Consider a deterministic policy that partitions the set of possible valuations into possibly infinitely many disjoint subsets s_i; that is, if $v \in s_i$, $v \notin s_j$ for all $j \neq i$ and $\cup_i s_i = [0, 1]$. The best such policy is to partially reveal the valuation to sellers according to the information partition with $s_i = [1/(2^i), 1/(2^{i-1}))$ with $i \in \mathbb{N}$. Thus, the smaller the buyer valuation, the more precise is the information the firm receives. With this platform information policy in place, the monopoly seller sets the price equal to $1/(2^i)$ to buyers belonging to s_i. The expected per-buyer seller profit is $\beta_s = 1/3$ and the expected per-seller buyer surplus is $\beta_b = 1/6$ and all gains from trade are realized. The information policy can be modified to as to implement any (β_b, β_s) with $\beta_b + \beta_s = 1/2$ and $\beta_b \leq 1/6$.[56] In sum, the information policy is such that:

$$\beta_b(\lambda) = (1 - \lambda)/6 \text{ and } \beta_s(\lambda) = (2 + \lambda)/6, \text{ with } \lambda \in [0, 1]. \qquad (6.9)$$

Here again, $\beta_b(\lambda)$ decreases in λ while $\beta_s(\lambda)$ increases in λ.

---

[56] See Ali, Lewis, and Vasserman (2019).

Platform's Profit-Maximizing Information Design

In choosing to what extent it facilitates price discrimination by sellers, the platform has to balance the negative effect on the cross-group network effect enjoyed by buyers with the positive effect on the cross-group network effect enjoyed by sellers.[57] In the specific model that we consider here, we know that, once the platform has set its profit-maximizing subscription fees, it is the sum of the two effects that matters: Abstracting any other constraint, the platform would thus choose the value of λ that maximizes the total value from transactions – that is, $\beta_b(\lambda) + \beta_s(\lambda)$.

In Example 6.3, we see from expression (6.8) that:

$$\beta_b(\lambda) + \beta_s(\lambda) = CS(p_m) + \pi_m + \lambda \left[CS(c) - (CS(p_m) + \pi_m) \right].$$

As $p_m > c$, we know that $CS(c) > CS(p_m) + \pi_m$: Total surplus at the marginal cost ($CS(c)$) is larger than total surplus at the monopoly price ($CS(p_m) + \pi_m$). This implies that $\beta_b(\lambda) + \beta_s(\lambda)$ is an increasing function of λ. The platform would thus prefer to set $\lambda = 1$, thereby allowing sellers to practice personalized pricing. Indeed, at $\lambda = 1$, the deadweight loss vanishes and the total value from transactions is maximized. Of course, the platform must take into account the cost of collecting and processing buyer data that enable sellers to price discriminate. If this cost increases in λ, then the cost of reaching $\lambda = 1$ may outweigh the benefits.

Interestingly, perfect price discrimination ($\lambda = 1$) is also the situation that maximizes the net surplus for both buyers and sellers. We recall indeed from Chapter 5 that the equilibrium participation levels–and thus net surpluses–are equal to:

$$n_b^* = v_b^* = \frac{2\mu_b + (\beta_b + \beta_s)\,\mu_s}{4 - (\beta_b + \beta_s)^2} \text{ and } n_s^* = v_s^* = \frac{2\mu_s + (\beta_b + \beta_s)\,\mu_b}{4 - (\beta_b + \beta_s)^2}.$$

We see that they both increase in $(\beta_b + \beta_s)$, meaning that they reach a maximum at $\lambda = 1$. This result may look surprising for buyers. Indeed, buyers are stripped of any surplus from transactions if price discrimination is perfect: $\beta(1) = 0$. Yet, the platform compensates this loss by decreasing the membership fee that it charges to buyers, resulting in a larger net surplus for them. The platform has indeed an incentive to encourage the participation of buyers because they become very valuable for sellers (as $\beta_s(\lambda)$ reaches its maximum at $\lambda = 1$).

Expression (6.9) in Example 6.4 reveals that $\beta_b(\lambda) + \beta_s(\lambda) = 1/2$ for $\lambda \in [0, 1]$. As the maximum value for transactions is equal to $1/2$ in this example, the platform can choose any value of λ in the range $[0, 1]$. If the cost of data collection and processing is increasing in λ, where a higher λ corresponds to richer information, then $\lambda = 0$ is the profit-maximizing choice.

The following lesson summarizes the main insights from our analysis:

LESSON 6.13 *A monopoly platform has an incentive to collect and process buyers' data so as to improve sellers' ability to price discriminate and increase the*

The optimal information design may well depend on the pricing instruments available to the *platform*; see Lefez (2020). For a reduced-form approach that can be applied to the platform's information design, see Choi and Jeon (2020).

total value from buyer-seller transactions. As the value of transactions is also redistributed from buyers to sellers, the platform may have to adjust its fee structure (typically by charging buyers less and sellers more).

Key Insights from Chapter 6

- A profit-maximizing intermediary that uses price and nonprice strategies on its two-sided platform takes the interplay between these two types of strategies into account.
- A profit-maximizing intermediary that directly controls the number of participating competing sellers on its two-sided platform typically biases this number in favor of consumers when, in addition to taxing sellers, it can also charge consumers, but always against consumers if it lacks this pricing instrument.
- Price dispersion for a homogeneous product arises when a monopoly intermediary organizes a digital platform, because it is costly for sellers to advertise prices on the platform. Sellers earn positive profits even though consumers visit the platform and buy from the cheapest seller on the digital platform. The presence of an intermediary offering price comparison services on the level of retail prices is ambiguous; it depends on the degree of seller competition that results in the absence of the intermediary.
- When consumers need the help of an intermediary to make more-informed choices, a platform may have an incentives to make sellers' add-on fees transparent, and thus, to protect buyers from being exploited by sellers. However, incentives may be too weak from a welfare perspective leading to less transparency than what would be socially optimal.
- A profit-maximizing platform may degrade the quality of their recommender systems or provide biased recommendations. This tends to reduce the size of within-group network effects among buyers.
- A profit-maximizing platform has an incentive to collect and process buyers' data so as to improve sellers' ability to price discriminate because this increases the total value from buyer-seller transactions.

The Road Ahead

In this epilogue, we give a preview of the topics that we will develop in our next book on platform competition and platform regulation; we also summarize what this book has already taught us about these topics.

Platform Competition

This book has taken a particular view on platforms as managers of network effects. A platform's success depends on at least some users enjoying network benefits. A monopoly platform will then make money from those users who do best and, as we have seen, may even sacrifice some of those network benefits if this gives rise to higher profits. On top of considering the incentives of its potential users, a platform must often also take into account the behavior of other firms offering substitutes to its services. Such substitutes may be relevant for just a group of its users or for all of them. An instance of the former situation is the case of platform businesses catering to two groups of users that compete against vertically integrated offers; these vertically integrated offers may stem from a firm with a similar type of service or from economic actors trying to bypass the platform. Competing platforms offering substitute services to all groups of users are an example of the latter situation. We briefly review here a number of issues pertaining to platform competition that we will study in our second book.

Tipping

Network effects may be sufficiently strong such that, in the long term, only a single platform is viable; that is, the market tips at some point. To illustrate this possibility, we examined in Chapter 4 the (static) competition between two two-sided platforms that offer homogeneous services for two groups of users (based on Caillaud and Jullien, 2003). We showed that in this setting, the market tips at equilibrium. More generally, market tipping is a likely outcome if there are strong mutual positive cross-group network effects, strong positive within-group network effects, scale economies, and highly substitutable services offered by the two platforms. Such a situation can be called "competition for the market."

Otherwise, multiple platforms may survive in the market and make both positive profits. Outcomes under platform competition depend on a number of market characteristics, including the differentiation between platforms and the ability of users to use multiple platforms to interact with other users. In this book, we did not take a look at models of platform competition; simple workhorse models are presented, for example, in Rochet and Tirole (2003), Anderson and Coate (2005), and Armstrong (2006).

Pricing

In one version of platform competition, in Armstrong (2006), users on two sides have to decide which of two horizontally differentiated platforms to join; this means that all users singlehome; platforms set participation fees on both sides of the market. In equilibrium, platforms' equilibrium profits are increasing in the degree of product differentiation on both sides of the market (as in standard models of price competition with differentiated products). Furthermore, equilibrium profits are decreasing in the strength of the cross-group network effects: The larger the cross-group network effects, the more fiercely platforms compete to attract additional users on each side. Users of the group which exerts stronger network effects on the other group tend to face lower prices. This is in line with the result we have derived in Chapter 5 with a single platform. However, if cross-group network effects become too strong, only one platform will attract users in equilibrium. These results are derived under the assumption that users observe participation fees on both sides and make the correct inferences about user participation on the other side. If users do not observe fees on the other side, the platform may decide to disclose this information. As we have seen in Chapter 5, a platform that faces no competition has an incentive to disclose to users the price that they do not observe. However, this is, in general, not the case under platform competition (see Hagiu and Halaburda, 2014, and Belleflamme and Peitz, 2019c). This suggests that a platform oligopoly may feature more opaqueness than a platform monopoly and the assumption that prices are observable on both sides appears to be more problematic from a theory perspective.

Homing

An important determinant of the emerging price structure in oligopoly are the homing decisions by users. If only one side can multihome (for technological or contractual reason), the emerging market structure features a competitive bottleneck (Armstrong, 2006): Users on the multihoming side have to obtain access to platform A to reach this platform's singlehoming users on the other side. Thus, under some assumptions, a multihoming user does not need to take into consideration whether it joins platform B when making its participation decision regarding platform A. In other words, each platform behaves as a monopolist on the multihoming side. This affects the price structure on the singlehoming side; under some conditions it leads to lower prices under singlehoming (for details, see Belleflamme and Peitz, 2019b). Whether users can multihome also affects the conditions under which platform competition is viable. Thus, important market outcomes are affected by the ability of one side of the market to multihome. Clearly, as analyzed by Armstrong and Wright (2007), if both sides can multihome, multihoming on one side affects the attractiveness of multihoming on the other. If all users on one side multihome, users on the other side do not have much of an incentive to multihome since they have access to all users on the other side when joining only one platform. This suggests that absent contractual or technological restrictions, there is an interplay between homing decisions on the two sides. Public policy interventions with regard to homing should take implications on the other side into account.[1]

Constrained Pricing

In many market environments, platforms would choose to subsidize users on one side in equilibrium, if this were possible. If unit costs are low, they may even set negative prices. However, prices below marginal cost or negative prices may not be feasible. In this case, platforms are constrained to use price instruments on one side only. Alternatively, instead of setting prices they may fix participation levels directly (or fix the price that is to be paid by users on the other side). In particular, if the cross-group network effect is negative in one direction, the market environment may feature a zero price on one side. Users enjoy a free offer but suffer from the externality to bear with the presence of users on the other side. This is a feature of many advertising-financed media markets: namely, when users experience advertising as a nuisance. There is then an attraction/repulsion pendulum and multiple platforms are likely to be active in equilibrium. Yet, as the nuisance becomes less pronounced and there appear strong positive within-group network effects (for instance, because users enjoy a joint user experience), the ensuing attraction loop reduces the chances that more than one platform can profitably operate in the market. This appears to be more likely in digital markets with better targeted ads and benefits that increase in the number of users on the same side (i.e., positive within-group network effects like the ones generated on social networks). This helps explain why monopolization has become a concern in digital media markets, including social networks, while it may be less of an issue in traditional media markets.

Competition "for" or "in" the Market

To focus on the question whether more than one platform is viable in the market, we restrict attention to platforms catering only to one user group (i.e., we abstract from the second side linked through cross-group network effects in case they exist). In this setting, we analyze how the shape of the network benefit function relative to the potential size of the market determines whether platforms compete in the market or for the market.[2] For simplicity, let us focus on the extreme case such that all contestable users will join the platform generating the highest gains from participation. Competition concerns arise if the incumbent platform becomes eventually difficult to displace because of unsurmountable network benefits (or scale economies) and, as a result, the firm relaxes its effort in providing a high net benefit to users. Such

---

[1] It is also possible that only some users on each side multihome. Such partial equilibrium multihoming has implications on the platforms' strategic price-setting incentives; see Bakos and Halaburda (2020).

[2] The following argument has also been developed in Motta and Peitz (2020, pp. 13–15). Parts are taken verbatim from this document without quotation marks.

a platform's protected position may manifest itself through high prices, low service quality, intrusive advertising, or little innovation.

Suppose that platforms offer utility $U(N)$ to each consumer who buys; this function is increasing in N if there are positive direct network effects. For simplicity, all users are assumed to have the same intensity of use and firms set the same usage price to all their users. A firm that provides this utility incurs fixed costs and constant per-user costs. Denoting the average per-unit cost by $AC(N)$, the per-unit gains from participation for each user are $U(N) - AC(N)$. These gains are increasing in the number of users if (i) $AC(N)$ is decreasing in N or (ii) $U(N)$ is increasing in N.[3]

To highlight the importance of the shape of the benefit functions for competition, we consider a numerical example. Suppose that there are two platforms which offer incompatible network goods at zero cost. There are two groups of consumers of equal size who coordinate their actions within the group but not necessarily across groups. Therefore, consumers of both groups may join the same platform or it could be that one group joins one platform while the other group joins the competing platform. We set $U(0) = 0$ and $U(2) = B$, where the number in brackets stands for how many groups join the platform in question. We then look at two polar cases: $U(1) = B$ and $U(1) = 0$.

In the case with $U(1) = 0$, there are social costs when the two consumer groups do not coordinate on the same platform: Such a market outcome is inefficient since no network benefits are realized; prices will be equal to zero and consumers will obtain a net benefit of zero. In contrast, consumer welfare is larger if both consumer groups join the same platform. In such a market, a successful newcomer has to quickly make sure that consumers coordinate their decisions. Otherwise, market entry is impossible; this is particularly so if one consumer group is already locked in. We understand thus that from a competition perspective, it is essential in such a situation to keep "competition for the market" open. Any successful attempt by a firm to lock in a group of consumers is lethal. Maintaining competition *in* the market would, however, be highly inefficient. The situation in which only one network is active cannot be detrimental to consumers.

In the other case, with $U(1) = B$, all network benefits already materialize with the participation of only one group (the participation of both groups is no longer necessary). This case looks less worrisome from the point of view of competition since the market is large enough for both firms to attract sufficient consumers by generating the benefit B. Put differently, network effects are such that a fraction of consumers is sufficient for network benefits to materialize. If any upfront investment is lower than the profits that are realized in this situation (gross of these investment costs), then both firms can survive in the market and there is "competition in the market." However, if one of the two platforms operates as the incumbent and has been able to attract both consumer groups, the potential entrant has to convince at least one group to switch to make entry viable. Thus, even though the incumbent's offer

---

[3] A large part of the literature on network effects and two-sided platforms (including most models in this book) assumes that network benefits are proportional to network size, that is, $U(N) = r + \beta N$.

does not improve if it serves two instead of one group of consumers (since $U(2) = U(1) = B$), this firm has a strong incentive to attract more than one group so as to reduce the ability of the rival to become a viable competitor. This shows that despite the incumbent's claim that it is actually not subject to positive network effects when maintaining a large, compared to a moderate, consumer base, it may have strong incentives to strategically deter entry. The claim that serving all consumers is a proof of superior quality of its product is not necessarily correct. By depriving the rival of a sufficiently large user base (here, one group of users), the incumbent can make the rival's offer unattractive. In effect, the market tips (if it is not straightforward that all consumers switch to the entrant almost simultaneously). While, in such a market, it is possible (and desirable) to have competition in the market, some features may lead to market tipping; importantly, while some of these features may be given, other features can be affected by the action of the firm that has become dominant. In such markets, interventions that enable consumers to switch easily from one product to another create an environment in which potential entrants can try their luck.

In sum, in the example in which $U(1) = 0$, a large critical base is required for network effects to materialize; this leads to competition for the market. In contrast, in the example in which $U(1) = B$, only a smaller critical base is required for network effects to materialize; here, the market may sustain competition in the market. In both instances, an incumbent platform has a strong incentive to lock in consumers. In the first example, it is sufficient to lock in a small number of them, while in the second example an incumbent platform has to lock in a large number to remove a competitive threat. In general, it is not obvious whether consumers actually benefit from lower prices or better products when a platform attempts to attract them in the first place. Particular concerns are coordination failures among consumers and delayed monetization by a platform. In these cases, an established platform with an inferior offering may continue to dominate the market, even though a competing platform could make other offers available that would be more attractive for at least one group of consumers.

We observe that characteristics of the market, which are often at least to some extent exogenous but sometimes in parts determined by the platforms' actions, may affect the strength of network effects. This is well recognized at least since Katz and Shapiro (1985): The degree of interoperability determines to what extent network effects are firm-specific or apply to the whole industry. A lack of interoperability may lead to a less efficient outcome, but this is not necessarily the case. Mandated interoperability may lead to lower quality and overall a less efficient outcome (see also Chapter 3).

In a market in which competition in the market is viable it may even be desirable to intervene and keep competition in the market alive because it may be difficult to revert to actual competition once one firm has become dominant – for instance, because rivals could not benefit from learning-by-doing, could not upgrade the offerings to consumers, and thus have fallen behind. Of course, it is not easy to negotiate the trade-off between, on the one hand, potential distortive effects of an early intervention and, on the other hand, the benefits of keeping competition open; this would, in any case, require a more careful analysis. However, these considerations illustrate that dynamic considerations are important.

Consider next an intermediate case to the ones presented so far, with $U(1)$ a bit smaller than $U(2)$. In this case, if the same firm serves the second group of consumers, then each consumer enjoys a benefit increment of $U(2) - U(1)$. Yet, even if the platform that attracts both groups is able to extract more surplus per consumer than platforms competing in the market, it may still be desirable from a consumer welfare perspective that competition is sustained in the market (as this leads to lower prices). The intermediate case also points to an inherent difficulty in such markets, namely, that efficiencies and anticompetitive effects often come together: One platform achieved dominance through a superior offer in the past and thanks to network effects, it is able to sustain this position. In one example, this requires that the dominant firm makes switching difficult for at least one consumer group; in the other example, for both consumer groups. While public interventions that lead to competition for the market would be undesirable when $U(1)$ is very small relative to $U(2)$, such remedies may be desirable when $U(1)$ is close enough to $U(2)$.

Contestability

The contestability of a network industry depends on the ability of a firm with a superior stand-alone quality or larger marginal network effects to attract users. As mentioned, users often face a coordination problem in the presence of network effects. All users may agree that a particular product or service is superior, but if they are currently using a different product or service, it may be difficult to convince some of them to go first. Coordinating user expectations is a key concern for new entrants to succeed against established entrants. The lack of entrants may hint at a "kill zone"; potential entrants may have given up challenging certain incumbents protected by network effects and a lack of willingness (or ability) of users to coordinate on alternative products or services.

Of course, the market environment may be such that entrant platforms can devise counterstrategies. If an entrant can address specific subgroups and network effects mostly materialize for such special audiences, then the entrant may overcome its initial disadvantage. Also, if the entrant has rich price instruments and can convince a key group of users to adopt (by lowering the price for this key group), it is in a better position to succeed. Furthermore, if using the entrant's offer does not require users to drop the incumbent's offer (thus, multihoming is feasible), it becomes easier for an entrant to overcome the incumbency advantage. As illustrated, the shape of the network benefit function determines the fraction of users that need to be convinced to adopt the new product or service.

Competition Policy and Regulation

Competition policy concerns and regulatory initiatives regarding large digital platforms have been on the agenda for a few years. The European Commission and a number of national competition authorities have run a number of abuse cases involving large digital platforms including GAFA. There is an intense debate about under-enforcement in merger control (e.g., Facebook/Instagram, Facebook/WhatsApp, Google/DoubleClick). The European Commission and the CMA in the UK commissioned two influential reports addressing perceived competition enforcement gaps and how to close them (Crémer et al., 2019; Furman et al., 2019). Against this backdrop, economists are asked for insights regarding, for instance, the performance of platform markets, theories of harm and efficiencies, and the incentive effects of regulatory interventions.

Competition law and regulation often require the definition of the relevant market. While this exercise has been criticized by some competition economists, the under-lying idea is to limit the scope of the investigation to a small part of the economy. In the context of platforms, a frequent mistake has been to define the market too narrowly: First, markets have been defined ignoring significant cross-group effects with the risk of wrongly assessing the market power of a firm; second, markets have sometimes been defined on the basis of business models rather than product or services, which also leads to too narrow a definition of the market. While not specific to certain platform contexts, there is also the risk of defining the market too broadly, as the actual substitution possibilities of a service need to be considered and not just the substitutability that is perceived by a bystander. For example, users may become used or addicted to a certain platform (which limits their set of perceived substitutes); alternatively, some users may not consider platforms that offer similar services as substitutes but as providing independent services (for instance, advertisers may not see two platforms as substitutes because the "eyeballs" they can reach on each platform form distinct groups). In markets with two-sided platforms, applying the SSNIP test is in general challenging; in particular, if one group does not make any monetary payment. However, the concept of demand substitution continues to be applicable in principle.[4]

Well-known and broad competition concerns also apply to platforms. However, there are novel theories of harm that apply only to platforms and, in particular, two-sided ones. Also, traditional wisdom may lead to false positives and false negatives; for instance, prices below marginal cost do not indicate predatory intent of a two-sided platform (see Chapter 5).[5] Competition concerns include (i) cartelization between platforms; (ii) platform design decisions that facilitate collusion among some participants on a platform; (iii) facilitating practices; and (iv) abuses of a dominant position. One example of facilitating strategy is the imposition of price-parity clauses of oligopolistic two-sided platforms on the seller side according to which sellers are not allowed to offer better deals off the platform (see, e.g., Edelman and

---

[4] See Franck and Peitz (2019).

[5] In a series of contributions (several of them together with Schmalensee), Evans elaborates on a number of competition policy implications derived from the theory of two-sided platforms (e.g., Evans, 2003). For another early account of common mistakes when analyzing two-sided platforms using perceived wisdom from traditional markets, see Wright (2004). For a recent survey, see Jullien and Sand-Zantman (2021).

Wright, 2015). As for abuses of a dominant position, one may think of decisions that foreclose competitors; for instance, a platform may integrate vertically or engage in long-term contracting with selected parties and, thereby, foreclose competitors in this vertically related market (see Chapter 6); another possibility is to leverage market power in adjacent markets and foreclose competitors on these markets (e.g., through virtual bundling and tying strategies as, for example, in Choi and Jeon, 2021). Theories of harm in platform markets have to take into account the specificities of network effects, complementarities between different groups if applicable, scale economies, and constraints such as zero-pricing constraints on one side which may limit the possibility of entrants to successfully enter a market.

Merger control should also account for specificities of platforms.[6] One issue that is not restricted to mergers involving platforms, but has been raised in particular in the context of digital platforms, is the removal of potential competitors (see Motta and Peitz, 2021). Scale economies or network effects may give strong incentives to incumbent firms to merge with firms that pose a competitive threat; consumers may suffer from such mergers (Katz, 2021). Mergers are also a means to advance platform envelopment (see Chapter 4); such mergers may lead to important efficiencies, but they may also raise competition concerns as they may protect a strong position of a platform in one market by reducing the competitive threat from adjacent markets.

In addition to competition policy, platforms are subject to liability rules, IP laws (in particular, regarding copyright and trademarks), laws against unfair trade practices, and consumer protection laws. While privacy protection as part of consumer protection applies to firms in general, they are of particular relevance in the context of digital platforms, as consumers may be rather impatient and thus not pay much attention to giving up their privacy, providing personal data, and not restricting the use of that data.

Finally, digital platforms (if they have certain characteristics) may be subjected to specific regulation. Also, depending on the services they offer, they may be included under existing sector regulation. Beyond short-term effects of regulation, the impacts of such regulation on entry and innovation need to be considered.

A Follow-Up on Competition and Regulation

The issues just described lead to a number of important considerations that partly require formal investigation. Also, a number of recent antitrust and merger cases have shown that competition economics may need some rethinking relative to traditional analysis – partly because platforms may use novel practices to increase their market power and partly because there are important trade-offs between short-term efficiencies and long-term contestability (understood here as the ability of a competitor with a superior product or service to successfully enter the market).

---

[6] Motta and Peitz (2021) collect some specific theories of harm from the literature.

As already announced, we have started writing a second book on platforms in which we elaborate on platform competition and regulation, with a focus on competition policy. This book will complement the present book: It will dig into strategic interaction among platforms and how this competition affects price and nonprice variables. From a competition perspective, we will address market definition and market power; we will develop theories of harm arising from unilateral or multilateral conduct addressing horizontal and vertical concerns. We will also draw on the policy debate on platform regulation and on the interaction between "private regulation" (by a platform) and public regulation that limits private regulation of the platform. Doing so, we will keep in mind that possible market failures are not only due to network effects but also to market power, asymmetric information, behavioral biases and limited cognition (often with complex interaction between these different sources).

With the start of the commercial Internet, we have experienced a world of largely unchecked digital platforms entering with innovative services, many of them failing but some of them succeeding. By now, we are experiencing a more "stable" environment in which a few large platforms dominate large ecosystems, but in which also some specialized platforms enjoy consistently high margins. In this new world, entry and exit still happen, but some large players exert strong influence on large parts of the economy and our daily lives. Competition policy and regulation will be key in shaping this new world.

Bibliography

ACCC (2019). Digital platforms inquiry. Final Report.

Albano, G. and A. Lizzeri (2001). Strategic certification and the provision of quality. *International Economic Review 42*, 267–283.

Ali, S. N., G. Lewis, and S. Vasserman (2019). Voluntary disclosure and personalized pricing. *NBER Working Paper No. 26592.*

Anand, B. N. and R. Shachar (2009). Targeted advertising as a signal. *Quantitative Marketing and Economics 7*(3), 237–266.

Anderson, C. (2006). *The Long Tail: Why the Future of Business is Selling Less of More.* New York: Hyperion Press.

Anderson, S. and S. Coate (2005). Market provision of broadcasting: A welfare analysis. *Review of Economic Studies 72*, 947–972.

Anderson, S. and J. Gans (2011). Platform siphoning: Ad-avoidance and media content. *American Economic Journal: Microeconomics 3*, 1–34.

Aral, S. (2001). The problem with online ratings. *MIT Sloan Management Review 55*, 45–52.

Armstrong, M. (1998). Network interconnection in telecommunications. *Economic Journal 108*(448), 545–564.

Armstrong, M. (2006). Competition in two-sided markets. *Rand Journal of Economics 37*, 668–691.

Armstrong, M. and J. Wright (2007). Two-sided markets, competitive bottlenecks and exclusive contracts. *Economic Theory 32*, 353–380.

Arthur, W. B. (1989). Competing technologies, increasing returns, and lock-in by historical events. *Economic Journal 99*, 116–131.

Artle, R. and C. Averous (1973). The telephone system as a public good: Static and dynamic aspects. *Bell Journal of Economics and Management Science 4*, 89–100.

Ater, I. (2015). Vertical foreclosure using exclusivity clauses: Evidence from shopping malls. *Journal of Economics and Management Strategy 24*, 620–642.

Athey, S. and G. Ellison (2011). Position auctions with consumer search. *Quarterly Journal of Economics 126*, 1213–1270.

Augereau, A., S. Greenstein, and M. Rysman (2006). Coordination versus differentiation in a standards war: 56K modems. *Rand Journal of Economics 37*, 887–909.

Bajari, P. and A. Hortacsu (2004). Economic insights from internet auctions. *Journal of Economic Literature 42*, 457–486.

Bakos, Y. and H. Halaburda (2020). Platform competition with multihoming on both sides: Subsidize or not? *Management Science 66*, 5599–5607.

Banerjee, A. V. (1992). A simple model of herd behavior. *Quarterly Journal of Economics 107*, 797–817.

Baye, M. R., J. R. J. Gatti, P. A. Kattuman, and J. Morgan (2009). Clicks, discontinuities, and firm demand online. *Journal of Economics and Management Strategy 18*, 935–975.

Baye, M. R. and J. Morgan (2001). Information gatekeepers on the internet and the competitiveness of homogeneous product markets. *American Economic Review 91*(3), 454–474.

Baye, M. R., J. Morgan, and P. Scholten (2004). Information gatekeepers on the internet and the competitiveness of homogeneous product markets. *Journal of Industrial Economics 52*, 463–496.

Belleflamme, P., N. Omrani, and M. Peitz (2015). The economics of crowdfunding platforms. *Information Economics and Policy 33*, 11–28.

Belleflamme, P. and M. Peitz (2015). *Industrial Organization: Markets and Strategies* (2nd ed.). Cambridge, UK: Cambridge University Press.

Belleflamme, P. and M. Peitz (2018a). Inside the engine room of platforms: Reviews, ratings, and recommendations. *Economic Analysis of the Digital Revolution*, Volume 5 of *Funcas Social and Economic Studies*. Madrid: Funcas.

Belleflamme, P. and M. Peitz (2018b). Platforms and network effects. Volume 2 of *Handbook of Game Theory and Industrial Organization*. London: Edward Elgar Publisher.

Belleflamme, P. and M. Peitz (2019a). Managing competition on a platform. *Journal of Economics and Management Strategy 28*, 5–22.

Belleflamme, P. and M. Peitz (2019b). Platform competition: Who benefits from multihoming? *International Journal of Industrial Organization 64*, 1–26.

Belleflamme, P. and M. Peitz (2019c). Price disclosure by two-sided platforms. *International Journal of Industrial Organization 67*, 102529.

Belleflamme, P. and M. Peitz (2020). Network goods, price discrimination, and two-sided platforms. CRC TR 224 Discussion Paper 188.

Belleflamme, P. and E. Toulemonde (2009). Negative intra-group externalities in two-sided markets. *International Economic Review 50*, 245–272.

Bergemann, D., A. Bonatti, and T. Gan (2019). The economics of social data. Cowles Foundation Discussion Paper No. 2203.

Blake, T., S. Moshary, K. Sweeney, and S. Tadelis (2018). Price salience and product choice. Unpublished manuscript.

Bolton, G., B. Greiner, and A. Ockenfels (2013). Engineering trust: Reciprocity in the production of reputation information. *Management Science 59*, 265–285.

Bordalo, P., N. Gennaioli, and A. Shleifer (2013). Salience and consumer choice. *Journal of Political Economy 121*, 803–843.

Boudreau, K. and A. Hagiu (2009). Platforms rules: Multi-sided platforms as regulators. *Platforms, Markets and Innovation*. London: Edward Elgar Publisher.

Bouvard, M. and R. Levy (2018). Engineering trust: Reciprocity in the production of reputation information. *Management Science 64*, 4755–4774.

Brandes, L. and Y. Dover (2018). Post-consumption susceptibility of online reviewers to random weather-related events. Unpublished manuscript.

Brin, S. and L. Page (1998). The anatomy of a large-scale hypertextual web search engine. *Computer Networks and ISDN Systems 30*, 107–117.

Brin, S. and L. Page (2012). Reprint of: The anatomy of a large-scale hypertextual web search engine. *Computer Networks 56*, 3825–3833.

Brynjolfsson, E., Y. Hu, and D. Simester (2011). Goodbye Pareto principle, hello long tail: The effect of search cost on the concentration of product sales. *Management Science 57*, 1373–1386.

Burguet, R., R. Caminal, and M. Ellman (2016). In Google we trust? *International Journal of Industrial Organization 39*, 44–55.

Cabral, L. (2000). Stretching firm and brand reputation. *Rand Journal of Economics 31*, 658–673.

Cabral, L. (2011). Dynamic price competition with network effects. *Review of Economic Studies 78*, 83–111.

Cabral, L. and A. Hortacsu (2010). The dynamics of seller reputation: Evidence from eBay. *Journal of Industrial Economics 58*, 54–78.

Cai, H., G. Z. Jin, C. Liu, and L.-A. Zhou (2014). Seller reputation: From word-of-mouth to centralized feedback. *International Journal of Industrial Organization 34*, 51–65.

Caillaud, B. and B. Jullien (2003). Chicken and egg: Competition among intermediation service providers. *Rand Journal of Economics 34*, 309–328.

Cairns, J. (1962). Suppliers, retailers, and shelf space. *Journal of Marketing 26*, 34–36.

Casner, B. (2020). Seller curation in platforms. *International Journal of Industrial Organization 72*, 102659.

Chakraborty, I., J. Deb, and A. Öry (2019). Managing word-of-mouth content. Unpublished manuscript.

Che, Y.-K. and J. Hörner (2018). Recommender systems as mechanisms for social learning. *Quarterly Journal of Economics 133*, 871–925.

Chen, Y. and C. He (2011). Paid placement: Advertising and search on the internet. *Economic Journal 121*(556), 309–328.

Chen, Z., C. Choe, J. Cong, and N. Matsushima (2020). Data-driven mergers and personalization. Monash Business School, Centre for Global Business Discussion Paper 2020-01.

Chevalier, J. A. and D. Mayzlin (2006). The effect of word of mouth on sales: Online book reviews. *Journal of Marketing Research 43*, 345–354.

Chintagunta, P. K., S. Gopinath, and S. Vekataraman (2010). The effects of online user reviews on movie box office performance: Accounting for sequential rollout and aggregation across local markets. *Marketing Science 29*, 944–957.

Chiou, L. and C. Tucker (2017). Search engines and data retention: Implications for privacy and antitrust. *NBER Working Paper 23815*.

Choi, J. and D.-S. Jeon (2020). Two-sided platforms and biases in technology adoption. CESifo Working Paper No. 8559.

Choi, J. and D.-S. Jeon (2021). A leverage theory of tying in two-sided markets with non-negative price constraints. *American Economic Journal: Microeconomics 13*, 283–337.

Choi, J., D.-S. Jeon, and B. Kim (2019). Privacy and personal data collection with information externalities. *Journal of Public Economics 173*, 113–124.

Condorelli, D., A. Galeotti, and V. Skreta (2018). Selling through referrals. *Journal of Economics and Management Strategy 27*, 669–685.

Condorelli, D. and J. Padilla (2020a). Data-driven envelopment with privacy-policy tying. Unpublished manuscript, University of Warwick.

Condorelli, D. and J. Padilla (2020b). Harnessing platform envelopment in the digital world. *Journal of Competition Law and Economics 16*, 143–187.

Crémer, J., Y.-A. de Montjoye, and H. Schweitzer. (2019). Competition policy for the digital era. Final report presented to the European Commission.

Cusumano, M. A., A. Gawer, and D. Yoffie (2019). *The Business of Platforms Strategy in the Age of Digital Competition, Innovation, and Power*. New York: Harper Business.

de Bijl, P. and M. Peitz (2002). *Regulation and Entry into Telecommunications Markets.* Cambridge, UK: Cambridge University Press.

de Cornière, A. and G. Taylor (2014). Integration and search engine bias. *Rand Journal of Economics 45*, 576–597.

de Cornière, A. and G. Taylor (2019). A model of biased intermediation. *Rand Journal of Economics 50*, 854–882.

de Cornière, A. and G. Taylor (2020). Data and competition: A general framework with applications to mergers, market structure, and privacy policy. TSE Working Paper 20-1076.

de Ruyt, C. (1983). *Macellum : Marché alimentaire des romains.* Louvain-la-Neuve, Belgium: Institut Supérieur d'Archéologie et d'Histoire de l'Art.

Dinerstein, M., L. Einav, J. Levin, and N. Sundaresan (2018). Consumer price search and platform design in internet commerce. *American Economic Review 108*, 1820–59.

Doganoglu, T. and J. Wright (2006). Multihoming and compatibility. *International Journal of Industrial Organization 24*, 45–67.

Dranove, D. and N. Gandal (2003). The DVD vs. DIVX standard war: Empirical evidence of network effects and preannouncement effects. *Journal of Economics and Management Strategy 12*, 363–386.

Dzieza, J. (2018). Prime and punishment – dirty dealing in the $ 175 billion Amazon Marketplace. *The Verge, December 19.*

Easley, D. and J. Kleinberg (2010). *Networks, Crowds, and Markets: Reasoning About a Highly Connected World.* Cambridge, UK: Cambridge University Press.

Economides, N. (1996). The economics of networks. *International Journal of Industrial Organization 16*, 673–699.

Edelman, B., M. Luca, and D. Svirsky (2017). Racial discrimination in the sharing economy: Evidence from a field experiment. *American Economic Journal: Applied Economics 9*, 1–22.

Edelman, B. and J. Wright (2015). Price coherence and excessive intermediation. *Quarterly Journal of Economics 130*, 1283–1328.

Elberse, A., A. Hagiu, and M. Egawa (2007). Roppongi Hills: City within a city. Harvard Business School Case No. 707-431.

Elberse, A. and F. Oberholzer-Gee (2007). Superstars and underdogs: An examination of the long tail phenomenon in video sales. *MSI Reports: Working Paper Series 07/004*, 49–72.

Eliaz, K. and R. Spiegler (2011). A simple model of search engine pricing. *Economic Journal 121*(556), F329–F339.

Elliott, T. (1998). Advertising. *New York Times*, 17 April, C7.

Ellison, G. and S. F. Ellison (2009). Search, obfuscation, and price elasticities. *Econometrica 77*, 427–452.

Ennis, S. and A. Fletcher (2020). Developing international perspectives on digital competition policy. Unpublished manuscript, CCP and Norwich Business School, University of East Anglia.

Evans, D. (2003). The antitrust economics of multi-sided platform markets. *Yale Journal on Regulation 20*, 325–381.

Evans, D., A. Hagiu, and R. Schmalensee (2006). *Invisible Engines: How Software Platforms Drive Innovation and Transform Industries.* Cambridge, Mass.: MIT Press.

Evans, P. and A. Gawer (2016). The rise of the platform enterprise: A global survey. *The Emerging Platform Economy Series*, 1–29.

Ezrachi, A. and M. Stucke (2016). *Virtual Competition: The Promise and Perils of the Algorithm-Driven Economy*. Cambridge, Mass.: Harvard University Press.

Farrell, J. and G. Saloner (1985). Standardization, compatibility and innovation. *Rand Journal of Economics 16*, 70–83.

Farrell, J. and G. Saloner (1986). Installed base and compatibility: Innovation, product preannouncements and predation. *American Economic Review 76*, 940–955.

Filistrucchi, L., D. Geradin, E. van Damme, and P. Affeldt (2014). Market definition in two-sided markets: Theory and practice. *Journal of Competition Law and Economics 10*, 293–339.

Fisman, R. and T. Sullivan (2016). Everything we know about platforms we learned from medieval France. *Harvard Business Review*, March 24.

Fleder, D. and K. Hosanagar (2009). Blockbuster culture's next rise or fall: The impact of recommender systems on sales diversity. *Management Science 55*, 697–712.

Fradkin, A., E. Grewal, and D. Holtz (2017). The determinants of online review informativeness: Evidence from field experiments on Airbnb. Unpublished manuscript.

Franck, J.-U. and M. Peitz (2019). Market definition and market power in the platform economy. *CERRE Report*.

Fudenberg, D. and J. Tirole (2000). Customer poaching and brand switching. *Rand Journal of Economics 31*, 634–657.

Fudenberg, D. and M. Villas-Boas (2006). Behavior-based price discrimination and customer recognition. *Handbooks in Information Systems: Economics and Information Systems*. Amsterdam: Elsevier.

Fujita, M. and J. Thisse (2013). *Economics of Agglomeration: Cities, Industrial Location, and Globalization* (2nd ed.). Cambridge, UK: Cambridge University Press.

Furman, J., D. Coyle, A. Fletcher, D. McAuley, and P. Marsden (2019). Unlocking digital competition. Report of the Digital Competition Expert Panel.

Galeotti, A. and J. L. Moraga-González (2009). Platform intermediation in a market for differentiated products. *European Economic Review 53*, 417–428.

Gandal, N., M. Kende, and R. Rob (2000). The dynamics of technological adoption in hardware/software systems: The case of compact disc players. *Rand Journal of Economics 31*, 43–61.

Gans, J. S. and S. P. King (2003). The neutrality of interchange fees in payment systems. *Topics in Economic Analysis and Policy 3*, Art. 1.

Gao, M. (2018). Multi-seller membership pricing. Unpublished manuscript.

Garone, E. (2016). The man behind the million dollar homepage. *BBC.com*, September 14.

Goel, V. (2017). Customers waiting on new iPhones crimp Apple's profits. *New York Times*, May 2.

Gomes, R. (2014). Optimal auction design in two-sided markets. *Rand Journal of Economics 45*, 248–272.

Goos, M., P. Van Cayseele, and B. Willekens (2013). Platform pricing in matching markets. *Review of Network Economics 12*, 437–457.

Gorodnichenko, Y., V. Sheremirov, and O. Talavera (2018). Price setting in online markets: Does IT click? *Journal of the European Economic Association 16*, 1764–1811.

Goyal, S. (2012). Social networks on the web. *Oxford Handbook of the Digital Economy*. Oxford: Oxford University Press.

Grilo, I., O. Shy, and J.-F. Thisse (2001). Price competition when consumer behavior is characterized by conformity or vanity. *Journal of Public Economics 80*, 385–408.

Griva, K. and N. Vettas (2011). Price competition in a differentiated products duopoly under network effects. *Information Economics and Policy 23*, 85–97.

Hagiu, A. (2009). Two-sided platforms: Product variety and pricing structures. *Journal of Economics and Management Strategy 18*, 1011–1043.

Hagiu, A. and E. Altman (2017). Finding the platform in your product. *Harvard Business Review 95*, 94–100.

Hagiu, A. and H. Halaburda (2014). Information and two-sided platform profits. *International Journal Industrial Organization 34*, 25–35.

Hagiu, A. and B. Jullien (2011). Why do intermediaries divert search? *Rand Journal of Economics 42*, 337–362.

Hagiu, A., B. Jullien, and J. Wright (2020). Creating platforms by hosting rivals. *Management Science 66*, 3234–3248.

Hagiu, A. and S. Rothman (2016). Network effects aren't enough. *Harvard Business Review 94*, 65–71.

Hagiu, A. and D. Spulber (2013). First-party content and coordination in two-sided markets. *Management Science 59*, 933–949.

Hagiu, A. and J. Wright (2015a). Marketplace or reseller? *Management Science 61*, 184–203.

Hagiu, A. and J. Wright (2015b). Multi-sided platforms. *International Journal of Industrial Organization 43*, 162–174.

Hagiu, A. and J. Wright (2019). Controlling vs. enabling. *Management Science 65*, 577–595.

Hagiu, A. and J. Wright (2020a). Data-enabled learning, network effects and competitive advantage. Unpublished manuscript.

Hagiu, A. and J. Wright (2020b). When data creates competitive advantage. *Harvard Business Review* January-February.

Hagiu, A. and J. Wright (2021). Platform leakage. Unpublished manuscript.

Hansen, R. G. (1988). Auctions with endogenous quantity. *Rand Journal of Economics 19*, 44–58.

Hart, O. and J. Tirole (1990). Vertical integration and market foreclosure. *Brookings Papers on Economic Activity: Microeconomics 21*, 205–286.

He, S., B. Hollenbeck, and D. Proserpio (2021). The market for fake reviews. MPRA Paper 105507.

Heidhues, P., J. Johnen, and B. Köszegi (2021). Browsing versus studying: A pro-market case for regulation. *Review of Economic Studies 88*, 708–729.

Hermalin, B. (2016). Platform-intermediated trade with uncertain quality. *Journal of Institutional and Theoretical Economics 172*, 5–29.

Hervas-Drane, A. (2015). Recommended for you: The effect of word of mouth on sales concentration. *International Journal of Research in Marketing 32*, 207–218.

Hoernig, S., R. Inderst, and T. Valletti (2014). Calling circles: Network competition with nonuniform calling patterns. *Rand Journal of Economics 45*, 155–175.

Holland, M. (2007). Two-sided markets: A challenge to competition policy? Unpublished manuscript.

Hollenbeck, B., S. Moorthy, and D. Proserpio (2019). Advertising strategy in the presence of reviews: An empirical analysis. *Marketing Science 38*, 793–811.

Hossain, T. and J. Morgan (2006). ... Plus shipping and handling: Revenue (non) equivalence in field experiments on eBay. *Advances in Economic Analysis and Policy 6*, 1–30.

Hui, X., M. Saeedi, G. Spagnolo, and S. Tadelis (2018). Certification, reputation and entry: An empirical analysis. Unpublished manuscript.

Hui, X., M. Saeedi, and N. Sundaresan (2019). Adverse selection or moral hazard: An empirical study. *Journal of Industrial Economics 66*, 610–649.

Hui, X., M. Saeedi, N. Sundaresan, and Z. Shen (2016). Reputation and regulations: Evidence from eBay. *Management Science 62*, 3604–3616.

Hunold, M., R. Kesler, and U. Laitenberger (2020). Rankings of online travel agents, channel pricing, and consumer protection. *Marketing Science 39*, 92–116.

Hurkens, S. and A. Lopez (2014). Mobile termination, network externalities, and consumer expectations. *Economic Journal 124*, 1005–1039.

Jackson, M. O. (2008). *Social and Economic Networks*. Princeton: Princeton University Press.

Jeon, D.-S. and N. Nasr (2016). News aggregators and competition among newspapers on the internet. *American Economic Journal: Microeconomics 8*, 91–114.

Jin, G. Z. and A. Kato (2006). Price, quality, and reputation: Evidence from an online field experiment. *Rand Journal of Economics 37*, 983–1005.

Johnen, J. and R. Somogyi (2019). Deceptive products on platforms. NET Institute Working Paper 19-13.

Johnson, C. (2009). Project 'Gaydar'. *Boston Globe*, September 20.

Jullien, B. and I.-U. Park (2019). Communication, feedbacks and repeated moral hazard with short-lived buyers. *Toulouse School of Economics Working Paper 1027*.

Jullien, B. and A. Pavan (2019). Information management and pricing in platform markets. *Review of Economic Studies 86*, 1666–1703.

Jullien, B. and W. Sand-Zantman (2021). The economics of platforms: A theory guide for competition policy. *Information Economics and Policy 54*, 100880.

Karaca-Mandic, P. (2011). Role of complementarities in technology adoption: The case of DVD players. *Quantitative Marketing and Economics 9*, 179–210.

Katz, M. (2021). Big tech mergers: Innovation, competition for the market, and the acquisition of emerging competitors. *Information Economics and Policy 54*, 100883.

Katz, M. and C. Shapiro (1985). Network externalities, competition and compatibility. *American Economic Review 75*, 424–440.

Katz, M. and C. Shapiro (1986). Technology adoption in the presence of network externalities. *Journal of Political Economy 95*, 822–841.

Kempe, D. and M. Mahdian (2008). A cascade model for advertising in sponsored search. *Proceedings of the 4th International Workshop on Internet and Network Economics (WINE)*.

Kihlstrom, R. E. and M. H. Riordan (1984). Advertising as a signal. *Journal of Political Economy 92*, 427–450.

Kim, K. and S. Viwanathan (2019). The experts in the crowd: The role of experienced investors in a crowdfunding market. *MIS Quarterly 43*, 347–372.

Klein, T., C. Lambertz, and K. Stahl (2016). Adverse selection and moral hazard in anonymous markets. *Journal of Political Economy 124*, 1677–1713.

Kottasová, I. (2017). Apple: Yes, we're slowing down older iPhones. *CNN Tech*. December 21.

Laffont, J.-J., P. Rey, and J. Tirole (1998a). Network competition: I. overview and nondiscriminatory pricing. *Rand Journal of Economics 29*, 1–37.

Laffont, J.-J., P. Rey, and J. Tirole (1998b). Network competition: II. price discrimination. *Rand Journal of Economics 29*, 38–56.

Lambin, X. and E. Palikot (2018). The impact of online reputation on ethnic discrimination. Unpublished manuscript, Toulouse School of Economics.

Larouche, P., M. Peitz, and N. Purtova (2016). Consumer privacy in network industries. *CERRE Report*.

Lefez, W. (2020). Price recommendations and the value of data: A mechanism design approach. Unpublished manuscript.

Leyden, B. (2020). Platform design and innovation incentives: Evidence from the product ratings system on Apple's app store. Unpublished manuscript.

Li, H., Q. Shen, and Y. Bart (2018). Local market characteristics and online-to-offline commerce: An empirical analysis of Groupon. *Management Science 64*, 1860–1878.

Li, L. I. (2010). Reputation, trust, and rebates: How online auction markets can improve their feedback mechanisms. *Journal of Economics and Management Strategy 19*, 303–331.

Li, L. I., S. Tadelis, and X. Zhou (2016). Buying reputation as a signal: Evidence from online marketplace. NBER Working Paper No. 22584.

Li, L. I. and E. Xiao (2014). Money talks: Rebate mechanisms in reputation system design. *Management Science 60*, 2054–2072.

Lin, M., R. Wu, and W. Zhou (2016). Two-sided pricing and endogenous network effects. Unpublished manuscript.

Livingston, J. A. (2005). How valuable is a good reputation? A sample selection model of internet auctions. *Review of Economics and Statistics 87*, 453–465.

Lizzeri, A. (1999). Information revelation and certification intermediaries. *Rand Journal of Economics 30*, 214–231.

Luca, M. and O. Reshef (2020). The impact of prices on firm reputation. Harvard Business School Working Paper 20-128.

Luca, M. and G. Zervas (2016). Fake it till you make it: Reputation, competition, and Yelp review fraud. *Management Science 62*, 3412–3427.

Marshall, A. (1890). *Principles of Economics*. London: Macmillan.

Mayzlin, D., Y. Dover, and J. Chevalier (2014). Promotional reviews: An empirical investigation of online review manipulation. *American Economic Review 104*, 2421–2455.

McAfee, P. (1992). A dominant strategy double auction. *Journal of Economic Theory 56*, 434–450.

McCabe, M. J. and C. M. Snyder (2005). Open access and academic journal quality. *American Economic Review: Papers and Proceedings 95*, 453–459.

McDonald, C. G. and V. C. Slawson (2002). Reputation in an Internet auction market. *Economic Inquiry 40*, 633–650.

Melnik, M. I. and J. Alm (2002). Does a seller's ecommerce reputation matter? Evidence from eBay auctions. *Journal of Industrial Economics 50*, 337–349.

Milgrom, P. and J. Roberts (1986). Price and advertising signals of product quality. *Journal of Political Economy 94*, 796–821.

Mody, M., J. Wirtz, K. So, H. Chun, and S. Liu (2020). Two directional convergence of platform and pipeline business models. *Journal of Service Management 31*, 693–721.

Motta, M. and M. Peitz (2020). Intervention triggers and underlying theories of harm. Expert report to the European Commission.

Motta, M. and M. Peitz (2021). Big tech mergers. *Information Economics and Policy 54*, 100868.

Muchnik, L., S. Aral, and S. J. Taylor (2013). Social influence bias: A randomized experiment. *Science 341*, 647–651.

Nair, H., P. Chintagunta, and J.-P. Dubé (2004). Empirical analysis of indirect network effects in the market for personal digital assistants. *Quantitative Marketing and Economics 2*, 23–58.

Nelson, P. (1974). Advertising as information. *Journal of Political Economy 82*, 729–754.

Nocke, V., M. Peitz, and K. Stahl (2007). Platform ownership. *Journal of the European Economic Association 5*, 1130–1160.

Nosko, C. and S. Tadelis (2015). The limits of reputation in platform markets: An empirical analysis and field experiment. NBER Working Paper No. 20830.

Oestreicher-Singer, G. and A. Sundararajan (2012a). Recommendation networks and the long tail of electronic commerce. *MIS Quarterly 36*, 65–83.

Oestreicher-Singer, G. and A. Sundararajan (2012b). The visible hand? Demand effects of recommendation networks in electronic markets. *Management Science 58*, 1963–1981.

Ohashi, H. (2003). The role of network effects in the US VCR market, 1978-1986. *Journal of Economics and Management Strategy 12*, 447–494.

Ott, M., C. Cardie, and J. Hancock (2012). Estimating the prevalence of deception in online review communities. *Proceedings of the 21st international conference on World Wide Web*, 201–210.

Ottaviano, G. and J.-F. Thisse (2011). Monopolistic competition, multiproduct firms and product diversity. *Manchester School 79*, 938–951.

Pagano, M. (1989). Trading volume and asset liquidity. *Quarterly Journal of Economics 104*, 255–274.

Pagano, M. and J. Padilla (2005). The economics of cash trading: An overview. Report for Euronext.

Park, S. (2004). Quantitative analysis of network externalities in competing technologies: The VCR case. *Review of Economics and Statistics 86*, 937–945.

Parker, G. G. and M. W. van Alstyne (2005). Two-sided network effects: A theory of information product design. *Management Science 51*, 1494–1504.

Parker, G. G., M. W. Van Alstyne, and S. P. Choudary (2016). *Platform Revolution: How Networked Markets Are Transforming the Economy and How to Make Them Work for You.* New York: W. W. Norton and Company.

Pashigian, P. and E. Gould (1998). Internalizing externalities: The pricing of space in shopping malls. *Journal of Law and Economics 41*, 115–142.

Peitz, M. (2006). Marktplätze und indirekte Netzwerkeffekte. *Perspektiven der Wirtschaftspolitik 7*, 317–333.

Peitz, M. and M. Reisinger (2016). Media economics of the Internet. Volume 1A of *Handbook of Media Economics*, 445–530. Amsterdam: Elsevier.

Puffert, D. (2002). Path dependence in spatial networks: The standardization of railway track gauge. *Explorations in Economic History 39*, 282–314.

Resnick, P., R. Zeckhauser, J. Swanson, and K. Lockwood (2006). The value of reputation on eBay: A controlled experiment. *Experimental Economics 9*, 79–101.

Rochet, J.-C. and J. Tirole (2002). Cooperation among competitors: Some economics of credit card associations. *Rand Journal of Economics 33*, 549–570.

Rochet, J.-C. and J. Tirole (2003). Platform competition in two-sided markets. *Journal of the European Economic Association 1*, 990–1029.

Rochet, J.-C. and J. Tirole (2006). Two-sided markets: A progress report. *Rand Journal of Economics 37*, 645–667.

Rohlfs, J. (1974). A theory of interdependent demand for a communications service. *Bell Journal of Economics 5*, 16–37.

Romanyuk, G. and A. Smolin (2019). Cream skimming and information design in matching markets. *American Economic Journal: Microeconomics 11*, 250–76.

Ronayne, D. (2019). Comparison websites. Warwick Economics Research Paper Series 1056.

Ronayne, D. and G. Taylor (2020). Competing sales channels. University of Oxford, Department of Economics Discussion Paper 843.

Rysman, M. (2004). Competition between networks: A study of the market for yellow pages. *Review of Economic Studies 71*, 483–512.

Rysman, M. (2019). The reflection problem in network effect estimation. *Journal of Economics and Management Strategy 28*, 153–158.

Sato, S. (2019). Freemium as optimal menu pricing. *International Journal of Industrial Organization 63*, 480–510.

Satterthwaite, M. and S. Williams (1989). The rate of convergence to efficiency in the buyer's bid double auction as the market becomes large. *Review of Economic Studies 56*, 477–498.

Scott Morton, F., P. Bouvier, A. Ezrachi, B. Jullien, R. Katz, G. Kimmelman, D. Melamed, and J. Morgenstern (2019). Report of the committee for the study of digital platforms, market structure and antitrust subcommittee. Stigler Center for the Study of the Economy and the State.

Simcoe, T. and J. Watson (2019). Forking, fragmentation, and splintering. *Strategy Science 4*, 283–297.

Spence, A. M. (1975). Monopoly, quality, and regulation. *Bell Journal of Economics 6*, 417–429.

Spulber, D. (1995). Bertrand competition when rivals' costs are unknown. *Journal of Industrial Economics 41*, 1–11.

Spulber, D. (1999). *Market Microstructure: Intermediaries and the Theory of the Firm.* Cambridge: Cambridge University Press.

Tadelis, S. (2016). Reputation and feedback systems in online platform markets. *Annual Review of Economics 8*, 321–340.

Tan, H. and J. Wright (2018a). A price theory of multi-sided platforms: Comment. *American Economic Review 108*, 2761–2762.

Tan, H. and J. Wright (2018b). Pricing distortions in multi-sided platforms. Unpublished manuscript.

Taylor, G. (2013). Search quality and revenue cannibalisation by competing search engines. *Journal of Economics and Management Strategy 22*, 445–467.

Teh, T. H. (2019). Platform governance. Unpublished manuscript.

Trégouët, T. (2015). Gender-based price discrimination in matching markets. *International Journal of Industrial Organization 42*, 34–45.

Tucker, C. and J. Zhang (2011). How does popularity information affect choices? Theory and a field experiment. *Management Science 57*, 828–842.

Vana, P. and A. Lambrecht (2019). The effect of individual online reviews on purchase likelihood. Unpublished manuscript.

Varian, H. (1980). A model of sales. *American Economic Review 70*, 651–659.

Vellodi, N. (2019). Rating design and barriers to entry. Unpublished manuscript.

Wen, W. and F. Zhu (2019). Threat of platform-owner entry and complementor responses: Evidence from the mobile app market. *Strategic Management Journal 40*, 1336–1367.

Wernerfelt, B. (1988). Umbrella branding as a signal of new product quality. *Rand Journal of Economics 19*, 458–466.

Weyl, E. G. (2010). A price theory of multi-sided platforms. *American Economic Review 100*, 1642–1672.

White, A. (2013). Search engines: Left side quality versus right side profits. *International Journal of Industrial Organization 31*, 690–701.

Wilson, R. (1985). Incentive efficiency of double auctions. *Econometrica 53*, 1101–1115.

Wimmer, B. S., K. S. Philander, and M. Redona (2018). The effects network externalities on platform value and management: Evidence from Internet poker users. Unpublished manuscript.

Wright, J. (2004). One-sided logic in two-sided markets. *Review of Network Economics 3*, 42–63.

Xu, H., D. Liu, H. Wang, and A. Stavrou (2015). E-commerce reputation manipulation: The emergence of reputation-escalation-as-a-service. *Proceedings of 24th World Wide Web Conference (WWW 2015)*, 1296–1306.

Xu, L., J. Chen, and A. Winston (2010). Oligopolistic pricing with online search. *Journal of Management Information Systems 27*, 111–141.

Xu, L., J. Chen, and A. Winston (2011). Price competition and endogenous valuation in search advertising. *Journal of Marketing Research 48*, 566–586.

Xu, L., J. Chen, and A. Winston (2012). Effects of the presence of organic listing in search advertising. *Information System Research 23*, 1284–1302.

Yang, K. H. (2020). Selling consumer data for profit: Optimal market-segmentation design and its consequences. Unpublished manuscript.

Zervas, G., D. Proserpio, and J. W. Byers (2015). A first look at online reputation on Airbnb, where every stay is above average. Unpublished manuscript.

Zhang, J. and P. Liu (2012). Rational herding in microloan markets. *Management Science 58*, 892–912.

Zhang, X. and F. Zhu (2011). Group size and incentives to contribute: A natural experiment at Chinese Wikipedia. *American Economic Review 101*, 1601–1615.

Zhu, F. (2019). Friends or foes? Examining platform owners' entry into complementors' spaces. *Journal of Economic and Management Strategy 28*, 23–28.

Index

Printed in the United States
by Baker & Taylor Publisher Services